D1571812

VERSE BY VERSE

THE OLD TESTAMENT

VOLUME ONE

VERSE BY VERSE

THE OLD TESTAMENT

VOLUME ONE
GENESIS THROUGH 2 SAMUEL, PSALMS

D. KELLY OGDEN
ANDREW C. SKINNER

DESERET
BOOK

SALT LAKE CITY, UTAH

Library of Congress Cataloging-in-Publication Data
Ogden, D. Kelly (Daniel Kelly), 1947– author.
  Verse by verse : the Old Testament / D. Kelly Ogden, Ellis T. Rasmussen, Andrew C. Skinner.
      volumes   cm
  Includes bibliographical references and index.
    ISBN 978-1-60907-591-0 (hardbound : alk. paper)
    1. Bible. Old Testament—Commentaries. I. Rasmussen, Ellis T., 1915–2011, author. II. Skinner, Andrew C., 1951– author. III. Title.
    BS1151.52.O33 2013
    221.7—dc23   2013022790

Printed in the United States of America
R.R. Donnelley, Crawfordsville, IN

10   9   8   7   6   5   4   3

Ellis T. Rasmussen
Old Testament scholar, mentor, and friend
1915–2011

Ellis T. Rasmussen was one of the great Old Testament scholars of The Church of Jesus Christ of Latter-day Saints. For thirty years Dr. Rasmussen taught Old Testament and other scripture at Brigham Young University, where he also served as chairman of the department of Ancient Scripture and as dean of Religious Instruction. He wrote numerous books and articles, guided study tours to the Holy Land and other lands of the Near East, and served with his wife, Oda Fonnesbeck Rasmussen, as special representatives of the Church and Brigham Young University in the Holy Land. Perhaps his greatest contribution to the Church, however, came through his role from 1972 to 1981 in supervising, under the direction of apostles Thomas S. Monson, Boyd K. Packer, and Bruce R. McConkie, the preparation of the Latter-day Saint edition of the Bible published in 1979 and the 1981 editions of the three other standard works of the Church.

We pay tribute to Dr. Ellis T. Rasmussen and express our gratitude for his life's work.

CONTENTS

PREFACE

The series Verse by Verse, which began with *The Four Gospels, Acts through Revelation,* and *The Book of Mormon,* continues here with *The Old Testament,* a commentary that is one book in two volumes.

The division between our volumes reflects the way in which courses on the Old Testament are structured in the institutes of religion of The Church of Jesus Christ of Latter-day Saints and on the campuses of Brigham Young University: Genesis through 2 Samuel, together with Psalms; and 1 Kings through Malachi. Each volume has its own table of contents, preface, list of sources, and index. The introduction to both volumes appears in this one. Occasionally, cross-references between the volumes appear in the text.

The central and unique aspect of our commentary is its focus on seeing Jesus Christ in the verses of the Old Testament. Special feature sections describe the lives of Joseph, Moses, Joshua, Ruth, Job, Elijah, Elisha, Jeremiah, and Esther as types and foreshadowings of Jesus Christ.

Because the Old Testament is as long as all the other standard works combined, we have been selective in treating the subjects addressed in the thousand-year span of sacred scripture. We have provided a clear, concise explanation of significant events and doctrines recorded by the ancient patriarchs, prophets, historians, and poets, and we have attempted to clarify and resolve significant textual problems and inconsistencies—passages that appear to have been transmitted to us incorrectly. This commentary is thus at the same time both comprehensive and easily understood. We are certain that students of the Old Testament will find much in it to nurture their passion for intellectual and spiritual growth, learning, and understanding.

Several features of this commentary are especially helpful to Latter-day Saints. Passages of scripture from the Pearl of Great Price, the Book of Mormon, and the Doctrine and Covenants that directly correlate with Old Testament passages are included in the text. Photos, paintings, drawings, maps, and charts illustrate scriptural content, and important archaeological discoveries are discussed. Certain topics, such as the names of God, the concept of perfection, prophecies of the Messiah, how to understand Isaiah, the two prophets in Jerusalem in the last days, and others, are treated in more depth.

We have used the following terms in precise ways in this commentary:

- Except in quotations from other works, *Temple* is capitalized when referring to a sanctuary of God, as approved by God and his prophets (which occasionally requires a judgment on our part); *temple* is not capitalized when it refers to pagan structures and shrines. Similarly, *Church* is capitalized when identifying the Church of Jesus Christ, which he established; the apostate church, contrariwise, is indicated by lowercase *church*.
- The designation *Near East* is preferred to *Middle East*.
- The name *Palestine* is used for that time in history when it designated the former land of Canaan, or Israel, beginning in the second century after Christ, in the days of the Roman emperor Hadrian, and continuing into the twenty-first century. In Old Testament times, the country was at first called Canaan, then Israel, and then—when divided into two kingdoms—Israel and Judah. Following the

return of the Jews from exile during the period of Persian rule, the land was called Yehud (Judah), or, in the later Greek form, Judea.

- The abbreviations B.C. ("before Christ") and A.D. (*anno domini,* "the year of our Lord," meaning "after the birth of Christ") are used instead of terms that avoid the name of Christ: B.C.E. ("before the common era") and C.E. ("of the common era").
- The abbreviation *ca.,* for the Latin *circa* ("about"), indicates an approximate date.
- The abbreviation *ff* means "and following," referring to the verse or page cited plus the following verses or pages.
- Bible Dictionary refers to the dictionary at the end of the Latter-day Saint edition of the King James Version of the Bible.
- Bible Map refers to the maps at the end of the Latter-day Saint edition of the King James Bible. The maps in printings beginning in 2013 are particularly helpful; they are also available online at lds.org.
- Topical Guide refers to the topical guide at the end of the Latter-day Saint edition of the King James Bible.

We extend appreciation to a number of individuals who have made this commentary possible. Foremost is Dr. Ellis T. Rasmussen, whose work on the Old Testament commentary he wrote in the early 1990s for use in Brigham Young University Independent Study courses was essential to our writing this commentary. Approximately one-third of the material in our volumes is drawn from those original writings of Dr. Rasmussen and is used by permission of BYU, Division of Continuing Education.

We also acknowledge with appreciation other colleagues and students at Brigham Young University for their helpful suggestions during the many years we have been preparing this commentary. We thank Connie Lankford Brace for her assistance in typing and proofreading and for her patience with innumerable corrections and additions; Jillian Mather for meticulously checking for accuracy every scripture reference throughout these volumes; and professors Jeffrey R. Chadwick, David B. Galbraith, Shon D. Hopkin, and our legal scholar and friend, Jay Deverich, for reading the entire manuscript and giving us valuable feedback. We thank Anne Bills for her colloquial rephrasing of Joshua 7:10–11, Debbie Gardner for her insights into Ruth 1:14–22, Cynthia Litchko for her perspective on 1 Samuel 13:2–18, and Bill Moss for his thoughts on 2 Samuel 6:12–23. We also extend heartfelt appreciation to Deseret Book Company, particularly Cory Maxwell, director of publishing; Lisa Roper, product manager; Suzanne Brady, managing editor; Shauna Gibby, designer; and Malina Grigg, typographer.

INTRODUCTION

The Old Testament, as it is called by Christians, or the Hebrew Bible, as it is known to the Jewish people, is a collection of thirty-nine books that present the history of God's dealings with his covenant children from the creation of the world to the time of the prophet Malachi (around 400 B.C.). It contains the prophecies of ancient prophets, seers, and revelators that extend far into the future, including the Millennium and beyond. Thus, it may justly be said that our origin and destiny are the purview of the Old Testament.

The earliest copies of Old Testament records we know of were written in Hebrew, one of the Semitic languages of the ancient Near East used by the family of Israel and related peoples. Those earliest records may date to the twelfth century B.C., in addition to the records of Moses' prophetic predecessors, which go back to the beginning of time. Given what we know about Moses, the author of the first five books, it may be that his original writings (*autographs*), which have long since disappeared, were composed in Egyptian. Moses was raised in Pharaoh's court, and Hebrew may not have been his primary language for writing (see Exodus 2:10; 4:10; Acts 7:21–22).

WHY MAKE THE EFFORT?

At the beginning of our study of the Old Testament, we might appropriately ask why we should spend time with something so lengthy and, at times, difficult to understand or appreciate, especially since Latter-day Saints are blessed to have

1

both living prophets and volumes of modern scripture that might make the Old Testament seem outdated or superfluous in our day. Sadly, as well as ironically, it has been our experience as teachers of the Old Testament that it has sometimes been treated as the stepchild of the standard works. Reasons for studying, appreciating, embracing, pondering, and cherishing the Old Testament are profound. We will mention a few.

First, the Old Testament is the human family's first testament of Jesus Christ. The Savior himself commanded the Jewish people to study the Old Testament in order to gain a witness that he was the Messiah-Redeemer. "Search the scriptures," he said, "for in them ye think ye have eternal life: and they are they which testify of me" (John 5:39). In this passage Jesus was correcting a theological error among his people, which is easier for us to see if the word "and" (Greek, *kai*) is translated as "but." Jesus is saying, in essence, "You study the scriptures because you think that activity brings eternal life, *but* the scriptures testify of *me,* and *I* give eternal life." In Jesus' day, the scriptures were the canonical books of the Old Testament or Hebrew Bible, often called the Torah, which included the Law, the Prophets, and the Writings. The Jewish sages of Jesus' day believed that the act of studying the Torah alone brought eternal life. This belief is confirmed in a statement by the great rabbi and contemporary of Jesus, Hillel, preserved in the Mishnah: "He who has acquired words of Torah has acquired for himself the life of the world to come" (*Pirke Aboth* 2:8).

But Jesus pointedly taught that mere study of the scriptures, which in his day *was* the Old Testament, did not bring salvation. Sacred writ was given to testify of him, and he, God, was *the* vehicle of salvation. It never was and never would be the case that written words on a page atoned for sins: only the blood of the holy Messiah does that. The Old Testament does, however, bring earnest truth-seekers to Jesus Christ and his doctrine. In our day, Elder Bruce R. McConkie of the Quorum of the Twelve Apostles wrote, "The Old Testament is designed and prepared to teach the truths of salvation and to bear witness of the one who should come to redeem mankind and put into full operation all of the terms and conditions of the Father's great and eternal plan of salvation" (*New Witness*, 392).

A second reason for studying the Old Testament is that Jesus quoted from it extensively, and if we want to understand Jesus, *really* understand him and what he taught, we must know what he studied. He used three books as principal sources for his instruction: Deuteronomy to deal with hard questions and difficult situations, such as when others tried to tempt or entrap him; Isaiah to teach of himself and to teach his disciples; Psalms to teach the people, and they were some of the scriptures from which he quoted most often. If our discipleship is to run deep, we must not ignore that which mattered to the Master.

A third reason for studying the Old Testament follows from the first two. The Old Testament contains a description of the doctrines, ordinances, principles, and history of the plan of salvation. Elder McConkie said: "The Old Testament contains a revealed and abbreviated account of the creation of this earth, of man, and of all forms of life. It tells of the fall of man and of the Lord's dealings with Adam and the ancient patriarchs before the flood. It speaks of the Abrahamic and Israelitish covenants. A major portion tells how Israel became a nation, possessed their promised land, and, as the sheep of the Lord's pasture, were fed the prophetic word down through the ages. Included are poetical, prophetic, legalistic, doctrinal, didactical, and historical books. And, above all, interwoven through the whole account, from Adam to Malachi, is the promise of a Savior, a Redeemer, a Deliverer, a Messiah, a Suffering Servant, a Son of God, who would be born of woman" (*New Witness*, 391–92). The gospel of Jesus Christ is manifest in considerable detail throughout the Old Testament.

A fourth reason for studying the Old Testament is that the Old Testament testifies of Jehovah, the premortal Jesus Christ, and his unmatched power. It proclaims forcefully as well as subtly that the Lord's "mighty acts of deliverance anciently were types of . . . his ultimate act of deliverance, the Atonement" (Jackson, in *Studies in Scripture,* 4:1). The very concept of a redeemer is first and best exemplified for us in the Old Testament law of redemption, initially set forth in Leviticus 25. As first used in sacred writ, *redemption* "is a purely Hebrew word, belonging to the realm of family law, which denotes primarily the action of the next of kin to recover the forfeited property of a kinsman or to purchase his freedom if he has fallen into slavery" (Buttrick, *Interpreter's Dictionary of the Bible,* 4:21). Such is the essence of the Savior's work spiritually—paying the price and liberating us from our sins, through our repentance—and such is the way the Old Testament uses temporal matters to teach about spiritual, eternal matters. That he was the coming Deliverer and Redeemer was known from the beginning and all through the Old Testament period by at least some faithful disciples.

Fifth, the Old Testament is the foundation of all other scripture that has followed. The scriptures are as a tree of life, and we are invited to come and partake of the fruit and be enlightened and live. The Old Testament may also be said to be the father of all other scripture, and to know the father helps to better understand the children. The greater our knowledge of the Old Testament, the better we will understand the succeeding standard works. The New Testament, the Book of Mormon, the Doctrine and Covenants, and the Pearl of Great Price all become more understandable and meaningful the more we know about the people, places, and doctrines first presented in the Old Testament.

Probably obvious, but important to state, is the fact that the Old Testament is the foundation of the New Testament. The Old Testament is really the Old *Covenant.* The words which translators rendered as "testament" primarily mean "covenant." Thus the New Testament is also really the New Covenant. The Old and New Testaments, or Covenants, derive their names in relation to each other. The Old Covenant contains the pre-Meridian laws, ordinances, sacrifices, symbols, and promises related to the coming of the Messiah. The New Covenant records are the fulfillment of the same. No one understood this better than the prophet Jeremiah, who spoke of both the old and the new covenants:

"Behold, the days come, saith the Lord, that I will make a new covenant with the house of Israel, and with the house of Judah:

"Not according to the covenant that I made with their fathers in the day that I took them by the hand to bring them out of the land of Egypt; which my covenant they brake, although I was an husband unto them, saith the Lord:

"But this shall be the covenant that I will make with the house of Israel; After those days, saith the Lord, I will put my law in their inward parts, and write it in their hearts; and will be their God, and they shall be my people" (Jeremiah 31:31–33).

The Old Testament is the foundation for both the New Testament and the Book of Mormon. The doctrine presented in the Book of Mormon is built upon the teachings of the brass plates, which may have been a version of the Old Testament originating in the northern kingdom, just as our current Old Testament (the King James Version) is a reflection of the southern kingdom, or Judahite, version of the Old Testament record. The great Book of Mormon scholar Sidney B. Sperry said, "The Brass Plates may well have been the official scripture of the Ten Tribes" (Nyman and Tate, *Second Nephi*, 209).

After the death of King Solomon, the house of Israel, with its united twelve tribes, split into two kingdoms: the northern kingdom, also known as the kingdom of Israel, or Ephraim, was headquartered in Samaria; and the southern kingdom, or the kingdom of Judah, was headquartered in Jerusalem. Both kingdoms kept scriptural records that contained the same core teachings and prophetic books, including the five books of Moses, a history of God's dealings with ancient Israel, and the prophecies of many Old Testament prophets (1 Nephi 3:3, 20; 4:15–16; 5:11–14).

Lehi was of the lineage of the tribe of Joseph through

Manasseh from the northern kingdom. He became custodian of the brass plates, which included information about his fore-fathers (1 Nephi 3:3). The profundity of the Book of Mormon witness of Jesus as Messiah and Son of God may well be di-rectly tied to the profundity of the northern kingdom version of the Old Testament in which it is grounded. The Book of Mormon is another testament of Jesus Christ (Title Page), and from it we infer that the northern kingdom brass plates contained many more of the testimonies, prophecies, and pro-found witnesses of the Messiah than did the southern king-dom version of the Old Testament with which the rest of the Christian world is familiar. The teachings of Zenock, Neum, and Zenos—prophets of the Old Testament era whose words are not preserved in our southern kingdom version of the Old Testament—are truly magnificent in their messianic expressions (1 Nephi 19:10–21; Alma 33:14–17; 34:7; Helaman 8:18–20).

A sixth reason to immerse ourselves in the study of the Old Testament is to understand and appreciate the influence it has had on language and culture. For example, many idioms in the English language derive directly from the Old Testament, par-ticularly the King James Version. Consider the following: land of milk and honey (Joshua 5:6); a mother in Israel (Judges 5:7); God save the king (1 Samuel 10:24); still small voice (1 Kings 19:12); mantle of the prophet (2 Kings 2:14); steady the ark (1 Chronicles 13:9–10); hair stood on end (Job 4:15); at their wits' end (Psalm 107:27); skin of my teeth (Job 19:20); apple of his eye (Psalm 17:8); lily of the valley (Song of Solomon 2:1); a time for every purpose under heaven (Ecclesiastes 3:1); line upon line (Isaiah 28:10); a marvelous work and a wonder (Isaiah 29:14); set thine house in order (Isaiah 38:1); hollow of his hand (Isaiah 40:12); drop in a bucket (Isaiah 40:15); can a leopard change its spots? (Jeremiah 13:23); handwriting on the wall (Daniel 5); windows of heaven (Malachi 3:10); and book of remembrance (Malachi 3:16).

The Old Testament exerted monumental influence on the life and culture of the United States of America from the earliest periods of the nation's history. The first book printed in the colonies was the Bay Psalm Book (1640). Historians have continually asserted that the early colonial mind, especially in New England, "was saturated with the Old Testament rather than the New. All children were raised on the Bible from the cradle, and writers could assume, as we can no longer do, that the stories of Moses in the bulrushes, or Lot's wife, or Ruth amid the alien corn, or Abraham's sacrifice, were known to them as our children know the complex lore of missiles and moon-conquest" (Baker, "Place of the Bible," 56). The Old Testament mind-set created and promoted by colonial leaders became so well entrenched in American life that New England itself was also seen as a "holy land."

Old Testament influence on colonial education, both formal and informal, was tremendous. George Washington, for example, received tutoring that contained liberal doses of Old Testament literature and lore. The young future president was taught to look for life's answers in the Old Testament. On one of the pages of Washington's schoolboy notebooks, penned in his own distinctive handwriting, is the instruction: "If you can't find it in the Book of Ezekiel, look in Israel" (Wilbur, *Making of George Washington*, 126). "Israel" was the name generally applied in the eighteenth century to the first five books of the Old Testament.

We might ask why the interest in the Old Testament? Early on, the Puritans thought of themselves as the children of Israel. The Old Testament was so important to the colonists not because they liked the Jews but because several of the colonial founders believed the colonists were a continuation of Israel, that they were Israel restored. The Puritans adopted an Exodus motif with regard to themselves. King James I was their Pharaoh, America their Canaan, and the Atlantic Ocean their Red Sea. The Old Testament, suffice it to say, was a most powerful influence in shaping American culture and character (see Skinner, "Influence of the Hebrew Scriptures").

Perhaps the best reason for studying the Old Testament

is that we have been commanded to do so. In February 1831 the Lord declared that the "elders, priests and teachers of this church shall teach the principles of my gospel, which are in the Bible and the Book of Mormon, in the which is the fulness of the gospel" (D&C 42:12). The Old Testament is a significant part of that injunction.

Every Latter-day Saint has been commanded "to warn his neighbor" by declaring the gospel and testifying of its truth. In a revelation given in May 1829 to Hyrum Smith, the Lord commanded, "Seek not to declare my word, but first seek to obtain my word, and then shall your tongue be loosed; then, if you desire, you shall have my Spirit and my word, yea, the power of God unto the convincing of men" (D&C 11:21). We cannot obtain the Lord's word and thus cannot have his convincing power to testify of its truth without a knowledge of the Old Testament. Years ago, President Marion G. Romney confirmed this truth: "People who walk in darkness may not be able to discern the fundamental meaning and the basic principles contained in the Old Testament. But as Latter-day Saints, we have no excuse. Therefore, it is very important that we do not hide the true teachings in the Old Testament from our children or from those we are called to teach by getting lost in things of lesser importance. . . . The Old Testament provides many examples of the importance of heeding and following the Lord's warnings concerning impending distress or disaster. . . . We today have been given the responsibility to warn the inhabitants of the earth. We must remember this solemn responsibility and ponder it in our minds and hearts" (*Ensign,* Sept. 1980, 6–7).

Life is not long enough for us to directly experience all we need to know. There is economy in learning from others who have come before us. Some of our greatest insights into life come to us from the experiences, joys, trials, pains, and heartaches of personalities introduced to us in the Old Testament. It is one of the world's best sources for stories that teach us great principles to live by.

Elder Richard G. Scott of the Quorum of the Twelve has given us an inkling of the power that could come to each of us if we make the study of the Old Testament a serious undertaking in our lives. He said: "Scriptures are like packets of light that illuminate our minds and give place to guidance and inspiration from on high. . . . Do you use all of the standard works, including the Old Testament? I have found precious truths in the pages of the Old Testament that are key ingredients to the platform of truth that guides my life and acts as a resource when I try to share a gospel message with others. For that reason, I love the Old Testament. I find precious jewels of truth spread throughout its pages" (*Ensign*, Nov. 2011, 6–7).

For all of these reasons and many more as well, we know that a serious study of the Old Testament will bless our lives immeasurably.

Having established the value of studying the Old Testament, we might also ask why we should study the King James rendering of it, or the King James Version of the Bible as a whole, for that matter. There are some practical reasons. The King James Version of the Bible has been for centuries the best-known version of the Bible in English. It was the most commonly used Bible at the time the Restoration began, all our latter-day prophets have concurred with its use, and it has been used throughout our dispensation in all Church publications. The language of the other standard works is similar to the language of the King James Version of the Bible. In fact, the best commentaries on the Old Testament are the other standard works of the Church. Joseph Smith's revisions of the Old Testament are also in harmony with the tone and expression of the King James Version (see Joseph Smith Translation). In addition, the King James Version has superior literary quality to other translations of the Bible in English. Many authorities consider it to be the masterpiece of the English language.

A more important reason for studying the King James Version of the Old Testament is that its translators believed in the divine Sonship and divine mission of Jesus Christ. Their renderings strengthen rather than destroy faith; some other versions have subtle changes that could raise doubts.

In 1992, the First Presidency of the Church (Ezra Taft Benson, Gordon B. Hinckley, and Thomas S. Monson) issued a statement regarding the King James Version of the Bible:

"The Lord has revealed clearly the doctrines of the gospel in these latter days. The most reliable way to measure the accuracy of any biblical passage is not by comparing different texts, but by comparison with the Book of Mormon and modern-day revelations.

"While other Bible versions may be easier to read than the King James Version, in doctrinal matters latter-day revelation supports the King James Version in preference to other English translations. All of the Presidents of the Church, beginning with the Prophet Joseph Smith, have supported the King James Version by encouraging its continued use in the Church. In light of all the above, it is the English language Bible used by The Church of Jesus Christ of Latter-day Saints.

"The LDS edition of the Bible (1979) contains the King James Version supplemented and clarified by footnotes, study aids, and cross-references to the Book of Mormon, the Doctrine and Covenants, and the Pearl of Great Price. These four books are the standard works of the Church. We encourage all members to have their own copies of the complete standard works and to use them prayerfully in regular personal and family study, and in Church meetings and assignments" (*Ensign*, Aug. 1992, 80).

STUDY HELPS

The Latter-day Saint edition of the King James Bible, including the Old Testament, is the best English-language Bible in the world. Not one word of the currently used King James text has been changed in the Latter-day Saint edition, but numerous study helps have been added. The purpose of the creation of a Latter-day Saint edition of the King James Bible in the 1970s was, according to President Spencer W. Kimball, "to assist in improving doctrinal scholarship throughout the Church." The basic charge, as noted by then-Elder Thomas S. Monson, who chaired the publication committee, was to "help people understand the Bible" (in Anderson, *Ensign,* Oct. 1979, 9, 12). President Boyd K. Packer, in the October 1982 general conference, pointed out that this new and unusual edition of the Bible was additional fulfillment of Ezekiel's prophecy of two sticks (records) testifying of each other in the latter days. President Packer predicted that succeeding generations would be able to develop gospel scholarship far beyond that which their forefathers had been able to achieve (*Ensign,* Nov. 1982, 51).

Numerous prestigious awards have been presented to the Church in the United States and in Great Britain to recognize the unique contribution of the LDS edition of the Bible. One citation came in October 1982 from the Laymen's National Bible Committee: "Presented to The Church of Jesus Christ of Latter-day Saints in appreciation of outstanding service to the Bible cause through the publication of its own new edition of the King James version, which features interpretive chapter headings, a simplified footnote system, and the linking of references to all other LDS scriptures, thereby greatly enhancing the study of the Bible by its membership" (in Monson, *Ensign,* Dec. 1985, 48).

All that we have said about the LDS edition of the Bible published in 1979 is true of the current edition, released in 2013. Except for some refinements to the content of footnotes, organization of the Bible Dictionary, and updating of maps, the latest edition of the Bible remains the same.

Unique features of the Latter-day Saint edition of the King James Bible essential to our study of the Old Testament include the following:

Pagination is standard in all editions, regardless of the size of the print.

Chapter headnotes, prepared by Elder Bruce R. McConkie, often contain valuable interpretive commentary.

Footnotes provide specific kinds of additional information, and each verse is independently footnoted.

Cross-references, approximately 28,000 of them, involve all the standard works of the Church and use easily recognizable abbreviations as follows:

TG—the Topical Guide is an alphabetical index and concordance of topics for all of the standard works. Nearly 600 pages long with 750 major subheadings and a total of nearly 3,500 topics, it cites some 50,000 verses. Fifty-eight categories of information about Jesus Christ in eighteen pages of single-spaced small print list thousands of references. That listing is, as President Boyd K. Packer said, "the most comprehensive compilation of scriptural information on the name Jesus Christ that has ever been assembled in the history of the world" (*Ensign,* Nov. 2005, 72).

JST—excerpts from the Joseph Smith Translation provide more than six hundred important changes Joseph Smith made in his inspired revision. Short passages changed by the Prophet (usually those fewer than eight words) are at the foot of the page; longer ones are in the Appendix at the end of the Bible. Verse numbers sometimes differ between the Joseph Smith Translation and the King James Version. Words Joseph Smith added are in italics in the Joseph Smith Translation, and those italics have been retained in our commentary in quotations from the Joseph Smith Translation.

HEB and GR—alternate translations or explanations are given to clarify the English translation of the original Hebrew or Greek term.

OR—alternate renderings explain archaic or difficult passages.

IE—this abbreviation (for Latin *id est,* "that is") explains idioms and difficult constructions.

BD—the Bible Dictionary contains 1,285 entries, internally cross-referenced, including a glossary of some King James Version vocabulary; for example, *by and by* and *anon* mean "immediately"; *corn* means "grain"; *prevent* means "come before, precede"; see also *bottles, lawyer, meet,* and others. Latter-day Saint topics such as "Aaronic Priesthood"; "Dispensations"; "Ephraim, Stick of"; "Family"; "Joseph Smith

Translation"; "Melchizedek Priesthood"; and "War in Heaven" are included.

Maps and Gazetteer help readers visualize historical events in their geographical context. Fourteen maps and thirty-two photographs, all in color, with descriptions, references, and index of place-names show the physical setting and location of Bible stories and teachings. References to Bible maps in our commentary are to the 2013 printing of the LDS edition of the King James Bible (also available online at lds.org). If you desire more detailed maps, consult a good Bible atlas, such as the *Macmillan Bible Atlas*.

Italicized words in the text of the King James Bible are not in the Hebrew or Greek texts; in most cases they were supplied by the translators to help the passage make more sense in English. That stylistic device has been retained in the Latter-day Saint edition of the King James Bible.

THE ORGANIZATION OF THIS COMMENTARY

A glance at the Contents of each volume of our commentary shows that we have not followed exactly the order of the books in the Old Testament as found either in the King James Bible or in the ancient Hebrew Bible. Rather, we have discussed the individual books chronologically, according to our understanding of the historical period to which they belong, and we have correlated the books of Samuel and of Kings with parallel accounts in Chronicles. Thus, this first volume of our commentary addresses the Pentateuch, or the five books of Moses, and then the historical and prophetic books in chronological order through 2 Samuel (and 1 Chronicles); the literary work Psalms is inserted between the books of Samuel according to its place in the chronology. The second volume of our commentary begins with 1 Kings (including corresponding accounts in 1 and 2 Chronicles) and treats the historical and prophetic books in chronological order; literary works such as

Proverbs, Ecclesiastes, Song of Solomon, and Lamentations are placed within that chronology; and Job, a literary work that has no apparent time frame, is grouped with the others.

The accompanying chart shows the arrangement of books in the Old Testament in English editions of the Bible, including the King James Version. This arrangement is different from that of the Hebrew Bible, the version with which Jesus was familiar, because the arrangement of the books in the English Old Testament was based on theological significance to the translators, not on the date of composition or authorship.

THE BOOKS OF THE ENGLISH OLD TESTAMENT

The Prologue	Histories	The Writings	The Prophets
Genesis	Exodus	Job	**Major Prophets**
	Leviticus	Psalms	Isaiah
	Numbers	Proverbs	Jeremiah
	Deuteronomy	Ecclesiastes	Ezekiel
	Joshua	Song of Solomon	Daniel
	Judges	Lamentations	
	Ruth		**Minor Prophets**
	1–2 Samuel		Hosea
	1–2 Kings		Joel
	1–2 Chronicles		Amos
	Esther		Obadiah
	Ezra		Jonah
	Nehemiah		Micah
			Nahum
			Habakkuk
			Zephaniah
			Haggai
			Zechariah
			Malachi

The three divisions of the Hebrew Bible—the Law, the Prophets, and the Writings—are well-known from several passages in the New Testament, including Matthew 5:17; 7:12; 11:13; 22:40; Luke 24:44; and Acts 13:15. The category known as the Writings is not mentioned by name in the New Testament, but the first book of that category is the Psalms, from which Jesus quoted extensively. He also quoted from other books in that category.

THE ANCIENT DIVISIONS OF THE HEBREW BIBLE

The Law	The Prophets	The Writings
Genesis	**Former Prophets**	Psalms
Exodus	Joshua	Proverbs
Leviticus	1–2 Samuel	Job
Numbers	1–2 Kings	Song of Songs
Deuteronomy		Ruth
	Later Prophets	Lamentations
	Isaiah	Ecclesiastes
	Jeremiah	Esther
	Ezekiel	Daniel
	Hosea	Ezra
	Joel	Nehemiah
	Amos	1–2 Chronicles
	Obadiah	
	Jonah	
	Micah	
	Nahum	
	Habakkuk	
	Zephaniah	
	Haggai	
	Zechariah	
	Malachi	

THE SEQUENCE OF BOOKS IN THE KING JAMES VERSION OF THE BIBLE

Prologue. Moses received revelation from the Lord about the Creation and the populating of the world. He wrote a brief record of his ancestors from Adam and Eve and the great patriarchs through the days of Joseph, as presented in the book of Genesis.

Histories. The books of Exodus, Leviticus, Numbers, and Deuteronomy preserve a record of Moses' own life and ministry and a sketch of Israelite history and the laws given to Israel by which they were expected to live. The books of Joshua through Nehemiah present the historical record of the children of Israel as a united kingdom, then divided into two kingdoms (the northern kingdom of Israel and the southern kingdom of Judah), their destruction and deportation, the great exile, and the return from exile to inhabit their promised land once again (including short histories of Israelites in the lands of their exile). The historical books, therefore, span the centuries between Moses and the end of the Old Testament record, approximately a thousand years.

Writings, or Literary Books. Job, Psalms, Proverbs, Ecclesiastes, the Song of Solomon, and Lamentations constitute the literary and didactic (instructional) works that have been preserved and canonized to help us learn from the philosophical reflections of ancient Israelites about the lessons they themselves had learned from life. In our commentary, these books are discussed in their logical and chronological position; for example, Psalms during David's time, and Proverbs during Solomon's time.

Prophets. The books of Isaiah through Malachi contain the writings of prophets of God during the first millennium before Christ. They are presented in the King James Version of the Bible according to their length, and since Isaiah, Jeremiah, Ezekiel, and Daniel are the longest, the translators placed them first. The books of the rest of the prophets descend to the close of the biblical record according to chronological order. In our commentary, however, we have presented all the prophets in their approximate chronological order without regard to the length of the books.

Understanding the basic order of the Old Testament books as they appear in the King James Bible (in the categories Prologue, Histories, Writings, and Prophets) helps the reader see that some prophetic books fit the time period of corresponding historical books. For example, the experiences recorded in the book of Jonah correspond to the time period of 2 Kings, and the prophetic book of Malachi fits in the same century as the historical books of Esther, Ezra, and Nehemiah.

THE RELIABILITY AND HISTORICITY OF THE OLD TESTAMENT

Some scholars of the ancient Near East have found it fashionable to label the Bible as a collection of myths, legends, and fairy tales. Nonetheless, literary and archaeological discoveries from ancient Israel and neighboring lands continue to shed light on the biblical record and help to authenticate it.

It is important to remember that archaeology doesn't actually *prove* anything, but numerous material evidences do help to correct some notions that cast doubt on the reliability of biblical scripture. Throughout these two volumes of commentary, we use the word *corroborate* to illustrate the value of many tangible finds in helping establish the credibility of our oldest scriptural record. The word *corroborate* derives from Latin *roboro,* which means "to strengthen, to confirm, to make more certain." The serious student of the Bible who seeks, in addition to the witness of the Spirit, some physical evidence to corroborate the true words of God in the Old Testament will find that a number of archaeological discoveries confirm that the writers of the Bible really did know what they were talking about. Following are a few of those discoveries and the scripture passage in our commentary where they are discussed:

- Stele of Merneptah mentioning "Israel" (introduction to Exodus)
- Silver amulets in Jerusalem with the priestly benediction (Numbers 6:22–27)
- The burning of Hazor by Joshua (Joshua 11:1–23)
- Solomonic gates at Hazor, Megiddo, and Gezer (1 Kings 9:10–28)
- The high place at Dan (1 Kings 12:25–33)
- Ivories at the palace of Ahab in Samaria (1 Kings 22:1–40)
- The Moabite Stone or Mesha Stele (2 Kings 3:1–5)
- The Black Obelisk of Shalmaneser (2 Kings 10:29–31)
- Tiglath-pileser's Inscription (2 Kings 15:16–26)
- Hezekiah's Broad Wall, Water Tunnel, and Inscription (2 Kings 18:1–8)
- The Lachish siege panels and Sennacherib Prism (2 Kings 18:13–37; 19:35–37)
- Lachish Letters (2 Kings 25:1–7)
- The Chronicle of Nebuchadnezzar, or Babylonian Chronicle (2 Kings 25:1–7)
- Clay seals in City of David; biblical personalities mentioned (2 Kings 25:1–7)
- The tomb plaque of King Uzziah on the Mount of Olives (Isaiah 6:1)
- The Royal Steward Inscription in Jerusalem (Isaiah 22:15–19)
- The Cyrus Cylinder (Daniel 12:1–3)

GENESIS

The first word of the book of Genesis in Hebrew is *bereshith* (literally, "in the beginning"), from which the book takes its name. In ancient times books were often named after the first word or phrase of their texts. The English term *Genesis* derives from the Greek *geneseos,* which appears in the Greek translation of the Old Testament called the Septuagint, dating from around 250 B.C. The Greek word *geneseos* can mean "birth," "genealogy," or "history of origin." The book of Genesis tells Israel who they are and who they belong to—the Lord Omnipotent. Genesis starts with an account of the Creation in order to give Israel an understanding of their place in God's plan.

Thus, Genesis not only provides a scriptural account of the Creation but also records the covenants that God entered into with the forebears of the house of Israel. This is of immense value to Latter-day Saints who are the heirs of those covenants.

There is much in Genesis that reflects the general picture of life and culture in the ancient Near East as known from other ancient sources. Genesis bears the stamp of an authentic ancient text. Yet there is also much that presents the fingerprint of prophetic authorship. Joseph Smith's inspired revision of the first few chapters of Genesis, what we know as Moses 2–8 and call the writings of Moses, is a more correct version of the text (D&C 35:20). And even more significantly, Moses 1, known as the visions of Moses, is a totally new revelation in modern times. It provides us with the missing introduction to the book of Genesis, just as Genesis provides the introduction to the rest of the Bible. The visions of Moses were revealed to the Prophet Joseph Smith in June 1830; the writings were revealed from June to December 1830.

The missing introduction to Genesis, Moses 1, provides the sweeping, cosmic foundation for the narrower, specific discussion of this earth found in the rest of Genesis. Moses 1 centers on six themes:

- the greatness of God, and the nothingness of man without God
- Jesus Christ as the Only Begotten Son and Creator of worlds without number
- the reality and intentions of Satan
- God's purposes and intentions
- the calling and education of Moses as a great writer-prophet
- the nature of transfiguration

Moses 1 is unparalleled in its scope and is an indispensable way to begin a study of our "beginnings" as recorded in the book of beginnings.

Another valuable resource for information and insight into Genesis is the Bible Dictionary in the LDS edition of the Bible. The following are particularly relevant: "Canon," "Cherubim," "Joseph Smith Translation," "Genesis," "God," "Devil," "Adam," "Eve," "Michael," "Fall of Adam," and "Dispensations." Similarly, the following entries in the *Encyclopedia of Mormonism* will be helpful: "Old Testament"; "Book of Abraham"; "Creation, Creation Accounts"; "God the Father"; "Origin of Man"; "Adam"; "Eve"; "Earth," especially the sections on the age of the earth, the origin and destiny of the earth, and the Great Flood; "Garden of Eden"; "Fall of Adam"; "Adamic Language"; and "Adam-ondi-Ahman."

The Book of Mormon, the world's best commentary on the Bible, also offers fascinating and vital commentary on Adam and Eve, the Fall, and the Atonement; see Alma 12:21–36; 22:12–14; 42:2–10; and Helaman 14:15–18.

Genesis 1:1 (Moses 2:1; Abraham 4:1)

The account starts with "In the beginning God," and those four words constitute a profound message to all the world—to the religious world, to the scholarly world, and to the scientific world. Right from the beginning God is the foremost and preeminent focus. Here we begin to learn about the Creator, and by learning more about his Creation we can exercise more faith and trust in him.

The Hebrew text of verses 1–2 can literally be read in a single sentence: "In the beginning of God's creating of [this] heaven and earth, the earth was empty and desolate."

The Lord has not revealed to humankind the detailed process by which this earth and the universe in which it is positioned were created. Scientific theories come and go, and refinements to natural laws continue to be proposed. Probably our present finite intellectual and spiritual capacities will not allow us to fully comprehend the divine powers and divine actions that brought these things about. We are increasingly drawn to the wisdom of Moroni: "Behold, are not the things that God hath wrought marvelous in our eyes? Yea, and who can comprehend the marvelous works of God? Who shall say that it was not a miracle that by his word the heaven and the earth should be; and by the power of his word man was created" (Mormon 9:16–17). The Lord has promised that the time will come, during the Millennium, when all things will be revealed, "hidden things which no man knew, things of the earth, by which it was made, and the purpose and the end thereof" (D&C 101:33).

The Hebrew word used here for God, *'elohim,* is literally a plural noun, though it is always translated in the singular when referring to the true and living God, owing to a principle grammarians and theologians call the plural of majesty. But Joseph Smith taught that the head of the Gods called the Gods together (*History of the Church,* 6:308), and "they, that is the Gods, organized and formed the heavens and the earth" (Abraham 4:1). The term *created* is used to translate the Hebrew *bara'* or *baurau,* which means to "organize," to "shape, form, or fashion." There is no suggestion in the word that matter was created out of nothing. Quite the contrary, the word suggests an ordering of preexisting realities, as ancient rabbis taught.

Joseph Smith explained: "You ask the learned doctors why they say the world was made out of nothing, and they will answer, 'Doesn't the Bible say He *created* the world?' And they infer, from the word create, that it must have been made out of nothing. Now, the word create came from the word *baurau,* which does not mean to create out of nothing; it means to organize; the same as a man would organize materials and build a ship. Hence we infer that God had materials to organize the world out of chaos. . . . The pure principles of element are principles which can never be destroyed; they may be organized and re-organized, but not destroyed. They had no beginning and can have no end" (*History of the Church,* 6:308–9; see also D&C 93:33). On another occasion the Prophet Joseph Smith taught that "this earth was organized or formed out of other planets which were broke up and remodelled and made into the one on which we live" (Ehat and Cook, *Words of Joseph Smith,* 60).

Creation of other parts of the universe, including other earths, is mentioned in Moses 1:35 and 7:29–36 and alluded to in Genesis 1:16.

Genesis 1:2 (Moses 2:2; Abraham 4:2)

The earth after it was organized and formed was, of course, not "without form and void," but rather, as understood from the Hebrew and as read in the Abraham account, was "empty and desolate"—that is, it was unpopulated and unplanted. At this point, when the earth was being prepared as a habitable abode for man, it was enveloped in waters upon which the "Spirit of God" moved or brooded or hovered over.

The creative force, here called the "Spirit of God," which acted upon the elements to shape and prepare them to sustain life on earth, is also the Light of Christ, as referred to in parts of the Doctrine and Covenants (D&C 88:7–13). Regarding how the Holy Ghost directs the powers of nature, Elder James E. Talmage, himself a scientist, stated:

"Through the power of the Spirit, the Father and the Son operate in their creative acts and in their general dealings with the human family. The Holy Ghost may be regarded as the minister of the Godhead, carrying into effect the decision of the Supreme Council.

"In the execution of these great purposes, the Holy Ghost directs and controls the varied forces of nature. . . . Gravitation, sound, heat, light, and the still more mysterious and seemingly supernatural power of electricity, are but the common servants of the Holy Ghost in His operations. No earnest thinker, no sincere investigator supposes that he has yet learned of all the forces existing in and operating upon matter; indeed, the observed phenomena of nature, yet wholly inexplicable to him, far outnumber those for which he has devised even a partial explanation. There are powers and forces at the command of God, compared with which electricity is as the pack-horse to the locomotive, the foot messenger to the telegraph, the raft of logs to the ocean steamer. With all his scientific knowledge man knows but little respecting the enginery of creation; and yet the few forces known to him have brought about miracles and wonders, which but for their actual realization would be beyond belief. These mighty agencies . . . do not constitute the Holy Ghost, but are the agencies ordained to serve His purposes" (*Articles of Faith*, 160–61).

Scriptures such as John 1:1–4 and Hebrews 1:1–2 also show that that power was exerted by the Son, under the command of the Father (see also Helaman 12:8–14; Jacob 4:6–9).

Genesis 1:3–4 (Moses 2:3–4; Abraham 4:3–4)

This light which was brought to bear upon the primeval planet earth was apparently from sources other than the sun, into whose rays the earth was later brought (v. 14). The light which enlightened all creation before our current luminary was God himself (D&C 88:7–13). So shall it be again when the earth achieves its ultimate celestial destiny; God will be the light of this sphere (Revelation 21:23; 22:5).

In verse 4 we begin to see how God called the successive phases of creation "good." Indeed, his creations are good—glorious and beautiful (vv. 4, 10, 12, 18, 21, 25, 31).

Genesis 1:5 (Moses 2:5; Abraham 4:5)

While the condition of light was called by God's word for "day" and the condition of absence of light was called by his term for "night," there is no reason to assume that his day and night were of the same length as ours, which are measured for us by our planet's revolutions in the sunlight. Other periods are indicated for others of God's realms (Psalm 90:4; 2 Peter 3:8; Abraham 3:4; 5:13; and facsimile 2, figures 1–5). Indeed, even after Adam was placed in the garden, "the Gods had not appointed unto Adam his reckoning" (Abraham 5:13).

Genesis 1:6–8 (Moses 2:6–8; Abraham 4:6–8)

The English word *firmament* is derived from the Latin word used to translate the Hebrew word *raqiya,* meaning "expanse." "Expanse" is the word used in Abraham 4:6. This expanse is all or any part of space. From the surface of the earth outward, this expanse includes the atmosphere in which the birds fly and in which the clouds float as "waters . . . above" the earth, as well as all the space of the astral universe beyond (vv. 7, 14–18, 20).

Our atmosphere includes water vapor and clouds floating a short distance above the earth, but on parts of the surface of the earth is the fluid water of the oceans, seas, lakes, and rivers. Thus the atmosphere permits a division of waters "above" (in the air) from waters "below" (on the surface).

The evaporation-condensation cycle of water brings rain and dew to the land, making life possible on what would otherwise be a desolate planet.

"Heaven" (v. 8) is understood from the context to connote the same thing as the English word *sky*. English, Hebrew, German, and several other languages use the same word to refer to the sky, heaven, the abode of God, and paradise, the place of the (good) departed dead.

Genesis 1:9–10 (Moses 2:9–10; Abraham 4:9–10)

The first activity of the third "day" evidently entailed a wrinkling of the earth's solid crust to let some matter appear above the enveloping waters and become dry land. Evidence is given later (Genesis 10:25) that there was only one land mass at first. This was in preparation for the earth to support living things which had been "spiritually" created before they were "naturally upon the face of the earth" (compare Moses 3:4–7). Later the waters also were made a suitable medium for sustaining life (Abraham 4:20–21). The grand object of the Creation was life—to support mortal life in order to test and prepare earth's inhabitants for eternal life.

Genesis 1:11–13 (Moses 2:11–13; Abraham 4:11–13)

A second project of the third "day" was the creation of varieties of plant life, each with power to reproduce itself according to its species or kind.

Genesis 1:14–19 (Moses 2:14–19; Abraham 4:14–19)

The work of the fourth "day" describes the establishment of the earth in its orbital relationship to the other astronomical bodies of our system so that its rotation upon its axis and its revolutions about its orbit, with its axis not quite perpendicular to the orbital plane, would provide day and night and the year's seasons, while its satellite moon could provide light at night and another means of marking time. The technical balance of the earth's placement as to heat, light, radiation, motion, and gravity are marvelous today as we learn more and more about the hazards of trying to take living beings into space beyond the compatible milieu of this earth.

Genesis 1:20–23 (Moses 2:20–23; Abraham 4:20–23)

Varieties of fowl, fish, and other creatures were created as the project of the fifth "day." Note that these, like the plants, were provided with the power to reproduce themselves—each according to its specific kind.

The word in verse 21 translated "great whales" (Hebrew, *tanninim*) does not refer specifically to whales; it is rendered in other passages of the Old Testament as "serpents," "dragons," and "sea-monsters," and can even mean "crocodile." The footnote's "great sea-monsters" is adequate for our purposes.

The Hebrew word *'umilu* ("and fill") is correctly translated here in the command to "fill the waters in the seas." Later the same word is rendered, in verse 28, with the English words "and replenish." *Replenish* means "fill," as may be seen in any dictionary, but some have thought it means "re-fill," which is an error.

Genesis 1:24–28 (Moses 2:24–28; Abraham 4:24–28)

The sixth "day" or creative period witnessed the crowning event of creation—the establishment of humankind on the earth. The first part of the sixth day was used in bringing forth the wild beasts, the animals for man's use (generically called "cattle" in King James English), and the insects, or "creeping things." Note again that the Creators found that all things functioned properly, or were "good," among these families of creatures.

Verse 26 does not indicate who said to whom, "Let us make man in our image," but Moses 2:26 says it was God the Father speaking to him who was eventually to be his Only Begotten Son. This is in harmony with passages already considered that indicate that the work of creation was done by the Son under the direction of the Father (John 1:1–4, 14; Hebrews 1:1–3; Moses 1:32–33). The use of the plural "us" and "our" clearly indicates the involvement of more than one God in the creative process (see also Genesis 3:22).

Regarding the participation of many individuals in the Creation, Elder Bruce R. McConkie taught that in addition to God the Father, his Son (Jehovah), and Michael, Joseph Smith also was involved in some aspect of the Creation, though not the Creation of mortal bodies for Adam and Eve.

"As to this man, Joseph Smith, let us say—Here is a man who was chosen before he was born, who was numbered with the noble and great in the councils of eternity before the foundations of this world were laid. Along with Adam and Enoch and Noah and Abraham, he sat in council with the Gods when the plans were made to create an earth whereon the hosts of our Father's children might dwell. Under the direction of the Holy One and of Michael, who became the first man, he participated in the creative enterprises of the Father" (*Ensign,* May 1976, 94).

President Joseph Fielding Smith professed the same belief: "It is true that Adam helped to form this earth. He labored with our Savior Jesus Christ. I have a strong view or conviction that there were others also who assisted them. Perhaps Noah and Enoch; and *why not Joseph Smith,* and those who were appointed to be rulers before the earth was formed? We know that Jesus our Savior was a Spirit when this great work was done" (*Doctrines of Salvation,* 1:74–75).

The phrase, making man "in our image, after our likeness" certainly suggests that God has a body. The Prophet Joseph Smith taught that "God Himself was once as we are now, and is an exalted man, and sits enthroned in yonder heavens! That is the great secret. . . . if you were to see Him today, you would see Him like a man in form—like yourselves in all the person, image, and very form as a man; for Adam was created in the very fashion, image and likeness of God, and received instruction from, and walked, talked and conversed with Him, as one man talks and communes with another" (*Joseph Smith* [manual], 40).

It is important to point out that the terms "man" and "mankind" as they appear throughout the King James translation of the Hebrew Old Testament text simply represent the generic concept "human" or "humankind." "Man" usually means "male and female," as indicated in verse 27 (see also D&C 20:18). A father cannot create children without a mother, so the male and female were created in the image of a Father and a Mother, their Heavenly Parents. Abraham's account of the Creation clearly implies that the Gods are male and female: "So the Gods went down to organize man [humankind] in their own image, in the image of the Gods to form they him, male and female to form they them" (Abraham 4:27).

The First Presidency (Joseph F. Smith, John R. Winder, and Anthon H. Lund) declared, "All men and women are in the similitude of the universal Father and Mother, and are literally the sons and daughters of Deity" (*Messages of the First Presidency,* 4:203). And President Spencer W. Kimball confirmed the origins of humankind in this way: "The Creators breathed into their nostrils the breath of life and man and woman became living souls. We don't know exactly how their coming into this world happened, and when we're able to understand it the Lord will tell us" (*Ensign,* Mar. 1976, 72).

In verse 28 God is speaking to the man and the woman. If God spoke to them, then both God and his offspring used a common language. We sometimes refer to this pure language of God as the Adamic language.

Genesis 1:28–31 (Moses 2:28–31; Abraham 4:28–31)

Note the important responsibilities, privileges, and powers given to mankind, in order that they might fulfill the purposes of creation as sons and daughters of God.

1. To reproduce: procreate children and care for them—an exercise in potential godliness;
2. To fill (replenish) the earth and subdue it, using all of its resources and facilities;

3. To have dominion, or rulership, among all other creatures—another exercise in godliness. God is definitely concerned about the environment—he spent a lot of effort creating this earth, and now that we've been given dominion he expects us to take good care of it. We are to exercise dominion over other living things, but not unrighteous dominion. Moses 5:1 replaces "subdue" (Genesis 1:28) with "till," which implies Adam's obligation to manage the earth and enhance its lifegiving ability.

In verse 29 we see that the produce of plants and trees was given to man for "meat." This is simply the King James English term for food. What we call meat, the King James Bible refers to as "flesh." But more than just for food, "all things which come of the earth, in the season thereof, are made for the benefit and the use of man, both to please the eye and to gladden the heart" (D&C 59:18). The Lord of creation cares about beauty and aesthetic value.

At the conclusion of the creation of all nature with its interrelationships and balances, the Creator saw that everything functioned properly and was "very good." Doctrinally, the Creation is one of the three pillars of eternity (three key elements of the plan of salvation), along with the Fall and the Atonement.

Looking back over Genesis 1, we can see that the account of the creative periods is very brief. But it is dignified brevity, which is how ancient Hebrew writers sometimes wrote. Much more is meant than is actually written. What we have is presented with monumental diction, stately cadence, and reverent grandeur.

It should be remembered, too, that there was no intention of answering all the questions: who, what, where, when, how, and why. "Who," "what," and especially "why" are adequately answered for us in Genesis and in the elaborations on Genesis found in the other standard works. The opening chapter of Genesis was never intended as a textbook of geology, archaeology, anthropology, or astronomy, though the details of "where," "when," and "how" can come later (see Article of Faith 9; D&C 101:32–33; 121:26–32).

There is so much about the creative process and the early history of our earth that remains in the realm of the unknown. Nevertheless, we should never lose faith in the things we know because of the things we don't know.

Genesis 2:1–5 (Moses 3:1–5; Abraham 5:1–5)

Observe that the break between chapters 1 and 2 disrupts the continuity of the narrative. This division into chapters and verses was not part of the original text but is the result of relatively recent editing and is sometimes more bothersome than beneficial.

Verse 1 sums up the divine accomplishments—the completion of the creation of both the heavens and the earth and all the host of animate and inanimate things. A more detailed summary in verses 4 and 5 specifies that there had been a dual creation process, entailing the creation of everything "before it was in the earth, and . . . before it grew." The corresponding verses in Moses 3:4–5 (compare D&C 77:2) make it clear that all things were created spiritually in heaven before they were formed in their earthly material counterparts. But note again that verse 1 asserts that both phases of creation of "the heaven and the earth were finished, and all the host of them." The narrative then continues with a more topical, less chronological statement of the way in which man was presented with his status and his facilities, his resources, and his responsibilities on earth.

Before that narrative is considered, however, note that the last of the divine edicts in the seven creative periods was the one in which God blessed and consecrated the seventh day as the day in which he had concluded and rested "from all his work which he had made."

We are taught in modern revelation, unique in Judeo-Christian theology, about the definition of the word *rest*.

While it can mean to cease all activity, it obviously means something else when speaking about God and Creation and the seventh day. God has never completely ceased activity. Such an idea is unthinkable. According to modern revelation, "rest" refers to the fulness of God's glory (D&C 84:24). Thus, on the seventh day, after God had placed life on earth, he rested—he entered into or enjoyed or basked in the glory that only a perfect Creator-God can experience by seeing the earth come to life with human beings, plants, and animals.

No further mention of the Sabbath is found in the Bible until the Ten Commandments in Exodus 20, but it is assumed that the practice of sanctification of the Sabbath was kept by the patriarchs of Genesis and their societies. The Hebrew word *shabbat* ("sabbath") which now means "cessation, rest, stop," obviously carried a different connotation anciently. Over the centuries before the Restoration, theology influenced meaning—and not for the better. The Septuagint (the Greek translation of the Old Testament), the Samaritan, and other manuscripts indicate that God ended his work on the *sixth* day and then rested on the seventh.

During the seventh one-thousand-year period of this world's temporal existence there will be another divine Sabbath, according to Revelation 8 and 20; see also Doctrine and Covenants 77:6, 7, 12, 13. Compare Isaiah 11:6–9; 65:17–25, word pictures of what we call the Millennium.

Remember that when scripture speaks of a "day" (as in v. 4), the term is often used in the same sense that we sometimes mean when we say, for example, "back in my grandfather's day . . ."—referring not to a twenty-four-hour period but to a general time frame. President Brigham Young tersely stated: "It is said in this book (the Bible) that God made the earth in six days. This is a mere term, but it matters not whether it took six days, six months, six years, or six thousand years. The creation occupied certain periods of time. We are not authorized to say what the duration of these days was" (*Discourses of Brigham Young,* 100).

The title "Lord God" is used frequently in chapters 2 and 3, but seldom anywhere else. The usual title for Deity in the Old Testament—appearing more than 6,800 times—is LORD, written in small capital letters in our King James Version, and referring to Jehovah, the same Being who later entered this world as a baby in Bethlehem, that is, Jesus Christ. The Son of God, the great Jehovah, created this world (Moses 1 and 2:4–25); (see also "The Name of God" in this chapter, page 40; "Names and Titles for God," Ogden and Skinner, *Book of Mormon*, 1:43.)

Genesis 2:6 (Moses 3:6; Abraham 5:6)

A reminder that the evaporation-condensation cycle was a phenomenon necessary to establish life on earth.

Genesis 2:7 (Moses 3:7; Abraham 5:7)

A statement concerning the creation of man's physical body with added detail about its earthly and spiritual components is in order. From other sources, it is evident that the term "breath of life" refers to the spirit, for it is the spirit combined with the body that constitutes "a living soul" (D&C 88:15). For other allusions to this dual nature of man, see Numbers 16:22; Job 32:8; 1 Kings 17:17–23; Luke 23:46; Doctrine and Covenants 93:33–35; see also Doctrine and Covenants 77:2 for a reference to the spirits of other living things.

The Lord God "formed" man—the Hebrew verb *yatzar* is the same word used for the work of the potter in Jeremiah 18:2–3. God shaped "the dust of the ground," that is, the elements of the earth, into a physical body for the first human being. There are word plays involved in the account of the creation of man. The name Adam derives from *adamah*, which generally means "ground," and Adam means "man." However, Adam's beginning as a mortal being was not from physical materials just scraped together from the ground and shaped into a body; he was born as all others are born (Moses 6:59). The bodies of Adam and Eve were patterned after the image and likeness of our Father and Mother in Heaven.

President Brigham Young taught, "When you tell me that father Adam was made as we make adobes from the earth, you tell me what I deem an idle tale. When you tell me that the beasts of the field were produced in that manner, you are speaking idle words devoid of meaning. There is no such thing in all the eternities where the Gods dwell. Mankind are here because they are the offspring of parents . . . and power was given them to propagate their species, and they were commanded to multiply and replenish the earth" (*Journal of Discourses*, 7:285; *Discourses of Brigham Young*, 104–5).

President Joseph Fielding Smith was of the same mind. He said, "Life did not commence upon this earth spontaneously. Its origin was not here. Life existed long before our solar system was called into being. . . . The Lord has given us the information regarding his creations, and how he has made many earths . . . and when the time came for this earth to be peopled, the Lord, our God, transplanted upon it from some other earth, the life which is found here" (*Doctrines of Salvation* 1:139–40).

The account in Moses 3:7 mentions Adam's status as "the first flesh upon the earth, the first man also." If the orderly accounts of the creation of all things prior to and in preparation for man given in Genesis 1 and Moses 2 and given also in the Temple in an account that President Joseph Fielding Smith called "the clearest of all these" accounts (*Doctrines of Salvation*, 1:75)—if all these are accounts of the physical or material creation, a question arises as to how Adam could be termed "the first flesh upon the earth." Several explanations are possible; for example, "also" in the next phrase, "the first man also," can be understood in the sense of the Hebrew word *gam,* which is not only a connective like "also" but is frequently used as a parallel phrase meaning "even"—the second phrase being an explanation of the preceding phrase. "First" may sometimes refer to status rather than priority of occurrence; for example, "the First Lady," or "the First Presidency."

President Joseph Fielding Smith explained what was meant by the term "flesh":

"Adam was the first man upon the earth, according to the Lord's statement, and the first flesh also. That needs a little explanation.

"Adam did not come to this earth until it was prepared for him. The animals were here. Plants were here. The Lord did not bring him here to a desolate world, and then bring other creatures. It was all prepared for him, just according to the order that is written in our scriptures, and when it was all ready for Adam he was placed upon the earth.

"Then what is meant by the 'first flesh'? It is simple when you understand it. Adam was the first of all creatures to fall and become flesh, and flesh in this sense means mortality, and all through our scriptures the Lord speaks of this life as flesh, while we are here in the flesh, so Adam became the first flesh. There was no other mortal creature before him, and there was no mortal death until he brought it, and the scriptures tell you that. It is here written, and that is the gospel of Jesus Christ" (*Seek Ye Earnestly*, 280–81).

The First Presidency of the Church has clarified: "It is held by some that Adam was not the first man upon this earth, and that the original human being was a development from lower orders of the animal creation. These, however, are the theories of men. The word of the Lord declares that Adam was 'the first man of all men' (Moses 1:34), and we are therefore in duty bound to regard him as the primal parent of our race" (Joseph F. Smith, John R. Winder, and Anthon H. Lund, *Improvement Era,* Nov. 1909, 80).

President Marion G. Romney further commented: "For many years I had an assignment from the First Presidency to serve on what was then known as the Church Publications Committee. We were expected to read and pass upon material submitted for use in the study courses of our auxiliary organizations. In reading these materials my spirit was sometimes offended by the use of language which expressed the views of those who did not believe in the mission of Adam. I have reference to words and phrases such as 'primitive man,' 'prehistoric man,' 'before men learned to write,' and the like. Sometimes these terms are used in ways which evidence a misunderstanding of the mission of Adam. The connotation of these terms, as used by unbelievers, is out of harmony with our understanding of the mission of Adam as taught by such teachers as Enoch, Moses, and Nephi. . . .

"I am not a scientist. I do not profess to know much about what they know. My emphasis is on Jesus Christ, and him crucified, and the revealed principles of his gospel. If, however, there are some things in the strata of the earth indicating there were men before Adam, they were not the ancestors of Adam. And we should avoid using language and ideas that would cause confusion on this matter" (*Symposium on the Old Testament*, 4).

As to Adam's status, it is noteworthy that he is also identified as the premortal archangel Michael in Doctrine and Covenants 107:41–56 and 78:15–16. He was the leader of the forces of the Lord against the forces of Satan in the war in heaven before the world was (Revelation 12:7–12). He is and ever shall be our patriarch and leader, even in the final battle against the forces of evil at the end of the Millennium, according to Doctrine and Covenants 29:26; 78:15–16; 88:111–14; compare also Daniel 10:13, 21; 12:1. Joseph Smith said that Adam is "the father of the human family, and presides over the spirits of all men" (*Joseph Smith* [manual], 104). President Joseph Fielding Smith stated that "Adam was not a 'cave man' but perhaps the most nearly perfect man in form and feature to our Father and Creator" (*Doctrines of Salvation* 1:140). He is the first as to priesthood and shall continue so in the end of the world also (Moses 6:7; D&C 84:16; 27:11).

The Prophet Joseph Smith further taught: "The Priesthood was first given to Adam; he obtained the First Presidency, and held the keys of it from generation to generation. He obtained it in the Creation, before the world was formed, as in Gen. 1:26, 27, 28. He had dominion given him over every living creature. He is Michael the Archangel, spoken of in the Scriptures. Then to Noah, who is Gabriel; he stands next in authority to Adam in the Priesthood; he was called of God to this office, and was the father of all living in his day, and to him was given the dominion. These men held keys first on earth, and then in heaven.

"The Priesthood is an everlasting principle, and existed with God from eternity, and will to eternity, without beginning of days or end of years. The keys have to be brought from heaven whenever the Gospel is sent. . . . The Priesthood is everlasting" (*History of the Church*, 3:385–87).

Genesis 2:8, 15 (Moses 3:8, 15; Abraham 5:8, 11)

These verses review the introduction of plant life into the earth and the preparation of a garden eastward in a land called "Pleasantness," or Eden, from which Adam could eat, and in which he could occupy himself "to dress it and to keep it." As to the location of the Garden of Eden in the earth as we know it, see Doctrine and Covenants 107:53; 116; 117:8; and read the following quotations:

Brigham Young: "In the beginning, after this earth was prepared for man, the Lord commenced his work upon what is now called the American continent, where the Garden of Eden was made. In the days of Noah, in the days of the floating of the ark, he took the people to another part of the earth: the earth was divided, and there he set up his kingdom" (*Journal of Discourses*, 8:195; *Discourses of Brigham Young*, 102).

Brigham Young: "It is a pleasant thing to think of and to know where the Garden of Eden was. Did you ever think of it? I do not think many do, for in Jackson County was the Garden of Eden. Joseph has declared this, and I am as much bound to believe that as to believe that Joseph was a prophet of God (*Journal History*, March 15, 1857)" (in Widtsoe, *Evidences and Reconciliations*, 396).

Wilford Woodruff: "Joseph, the Prophet, told me that

the Garden of Eden was in Jackson County, Missouri. When Adam was driven out he went to the place we now call Adam-ondi-Ahman, Daviess County, Missouri. There he built an altar and offered sacrifices" (Cowley, *Wilford Woodruff,* 481).

Genesis 2:10–14 (Moses 3:10–14; Abraham 5:10)

Beyond the land called "Eden," four tributaries, or heads of a river, converged toward the garden to water it and bring mineral resources. The names of these rivers and lands of man's primeval home were later applied to other rivers and places where man lived, such as those of the valleys of Mesopotamia and the Nile—but those rivers by no means converge into one garden area (see Widtsoe, *Evidences and Reconciliations,* 394–95).

Genesis 2:9, 16–17 (Moses 3:9, 16–17; Abraham 5:9, 12–13)

In the midst of the garden were placed, among the other trees, the "tree of life" and the "tree of knowledge of good and evil." Of the fruit of all trees, including the tree of life, man could freely eat, so long as he did not partake of the tree of knowledge of good and evil. If no such permission or prohibition—alternate choices with their consequences—had been given, and no warning had been voiced about the phenomenon of death, could there have been any development of the power to decide and to do what man's intelligence and sense of judgment directed, according to his own agency? There could have been no opportunity to learn good from evil, helpful from harmful, virtue from vice, sweet from bitter, joy from sorrow, constructive from destructive, harmonious from discordant. "If only one course of action is open to us, we are not free agents. Freedom presupposes a law which can be broken as well as kept" (Smith and Sjodahl, *Doctrine and Covenants Commentary,* 158).

The scriptural answer to the question, "Why did there have to be a choice between seemingly contradictory commandments?" is explained by Lehi: "It must needs be that there was an opposition [or opposites]; . . . Wherefore, man could not act for himself save it should be that he was enticed by the one or the other" (2 Nephi 2:15–16).

Genesis 2:18 (Moses 3:18; Abraham 5:14)

Evidence that this chapter is in topical but not chronological sequence comes from the fact that the account of the creation of a companion for Adam is found *before* the account of the naming of the animals in Abraham and *after* that event in Genesis and Moses.

Instead of "I will make . . ." the Septuagint and Vulgate versions of Genesis have "*we* will make . . ."—again pointing to a plurality of Gods involved in the creative enterprises.

"It is not good that the man should be alone." The modern Hebrew term for a bachelor is *ravak,* from the adjective *reyk,* meaning "empty," "incomplete." There are numerous situations in modern society that show the wisdom of these timeless words of God. To keep a man safe from the temptations and evils of an increasingly immoral world (for example, the vile seductions of pornography), it is indeed good to have and cherish a loving companion and not spend too much time alone, away from that companion.

Genesis 2:19–20 (Moses 3:19–20; Abraham 5:20–21)

The beginnings of man's earthly language are hinted at in the story of the naming of the animals. More about Adam's means of communication will be found in Moses 6:5–6. Of paramount importance is the fact that he possessed "a language which was pure and undefiled" (Moses 6:6).

The reasons for the insertion of this story at this point in Genesis and Moses, and in a slightly different sequence in Abraham's account, are not readily evident.

Genesis 2:21–25 (Moses 3:21–25; Abraham 5:15–19)

Though there existed male and female members of other species, there was, as yet, no companion for Adam (v. 20). The phrase "help meet for him" is translated from the Hebrew *'ezer kanegdo,* which is more properly translated as "a help (or support) suitable (or appropriate, complementary) to him." "Suitable" or "appropriate" is the intent of the King James English "meet." The Hebrew *'ezer* (help, support) also carries the connotation of coming to the aid of someone. The Hebrew does not evince a meaning of second class status. The indication is that they as companions would be at once mutually beneficial, complementary, and appropriate to each other's nature (see First Presidency, "The Family: A Proclamation to the World").

In addition to the "help meet" designation, further indications of the ideal compatibility of the married couple are shown in the fact that they were made of the same material; therefore, it is pointed out that every bridal pair should also become "one flesh" by being united in their life-goals, and unselfishly concerned with their common needs.

The miracles of the formation of our own bodies, entailing the assimilation of materials, the organization of the intricate life-process systems, the preparation for independent existence at the proper moment of separation, the marvels of biological inheritance, etc., are still amazing in spite of all we understand about them. Certainly the creation of the first bodies of this earth was no less miraculous. Various opinions have been published by Latter-day Saint writers about the manner whereby the bodies of Adam and Eve were brought to the earth, but there is little profit in speculating (note the promises of future revelation on things presently unknown: D&C 101:32–34; 121:26–32).

In connection with the creation of Eve's body, President Spencer W. Kimball commented succinctly, "The story of the rib, of course, is figurative" (*Ensign,* Mar. 1976, 71).

About the eternal union of Adam and Eve in the Garden of Eden, President Joseph Fielding Smith taught: "When Eve was given to Adam, it was not 'until death doth you part,' but it was a perpetual union. . . . The Prophet Joseph Smith taught that 'marriage is an institution of heaven, instituted in the garden of Eden, and that it should be solemnized by the authority of the everlasting priesthood.' Except a man and his wife enter into an everlasting covenant and be married for eternity, while in this probation, by the power and authority of the Holy Priesthood, 'they will cease to increase when they die; that is, they will not have any children after the resurrection. But those who are married by the power and authority of the priesthood in this life, and continue without committing the sin against the Holy Ghost, will continue to increase and have children in the celestial glory'" (*Restoration of All Things*, 242, 243). President Smith also clearly stated that "God the Father married Adam and Eve. . . . The ceremony on that occasion was performed by the Eternal Father himself whose work endures forever" (*Doctrines of Salvation*, 2:71).

The first man and woman ever married on this planet received clear instruction that they were to remain together. Their marriage was to be eternal. As the lyrics of a modern song ask: "Doesn't anybody stay together any more? If love doesn't last forever, then what's forever for?"

Verse 25 actually belongs at the beginning of Genesis 3 in the Bible. Note that the record says Adam and Eve were not ashamed, though naked, which is understandable. After all, what engenders shame? Is it not consciousness of wrongdoing or guilt? Obviously they had no cause for shame yet.

THE NAME OF GOD

Whereas the name of Deity used in Genesis 1 and 2:1–3 was "God," the names "Lord God" are used together in the remainder of chapter 2 and chapter 3. "God" is the English substitute in the Bible for the Hebrew word *Elohim,* while "LORD" (in small capital letters) is the English substitute for the Hebrew word *YHWH* (usually pronounced Jehovah or Jahweh/Yahweh.) *Elohim* is used throughout the Bible, either as a plural common noun to speak of the gods of the heathen nations, or as a proper noun, treated as a singular though it is plural in form, to designate the Supreme

Being. Latter-day Saints use it specifically for the Father. *Jehovah* is always a proper noun, the name of "the one God" as understood by Judaism. Latter-day Saints now understand *Jehovah* to refer specifically to the Son, though it was also used at times to refer to the Father in the early years of this dispensation. Neither name is easily translated, but it is apparent that *Elohim* is the plural of *El* or *Eloah*, the root of which can be understood to mean "strength" or "might." As a plural, therefore, it could mean "the Almighty" or "Omnipotence." *Jehovah* is related to the verb "to be" and may mean "He who is" or even "He who causes to be"; this is in keeping with his reference to himself as "I AM" (Exodus 3:14–16). The two names used together may perhaps mean "Jehovah of the Gods"; a more attractive hypothesis would be that they are the same expressions as rendered "the Lord Omnipotent" in the Book of Mormon (Mosiah 3:5, 17, 18; 5:2, 15).

It is appropriate that the details of the earthly facets of creation considered in this chapter, and the details of the interaction of Deity and man in the next, should be attributed to the Lord Jesus Christ, by whom God the Father made the worlds (recall references to their respective roles in Moses 1:32–33; 2:1; John 1:1–3; Hebrews 1:1–2).

Genesis 3:1–3 (Moses 4:1–9)

Into this setting of the Garden of Eden came one called "the serpent," who said, "Yea, hath God said, Ye shall not eat of every tree of the garden?" Satan thus invited a reexamination of God's admonition. This continues to be one of his tactics. The book of Moses (4:7) says Satan, or Lucifer, "spake by the mouth of the serpent" (*Satan* is a Hebrew word meaning "adversary.") His motivation is clear from Moses' account. He had already "drawn away many after him," and "he sought also to beguile Eve, for he knew not the mind of God, wherefore he sought to destroy the world" (Moses 4:6). After having ruined the progression of a third part of the hosts of heaven, he tried to ruin the entire plan of salvation by drawing away our first parents, especially the mother of the human family, one of God's choicest daughters. Perhaps he understood that if you can ruin the mother, you can destroy the family. But ultimately Satan did not know what God knew; he did not comprehend the plan.

The reason Satan was so interested in the adversarial role was, as Lehi taught, "because he had fallen from heaven, and had become miserable forever, he sought also the misery of all mankind. . . . he seeketh that all men might be miserable like unto himself" (2 Nephi 2:18, 27).

The question of why Satan chose the serpent as his representative and symbolic image is not entirely clear in this text. Certainly, the serpent was regarded as "more *subtil* than any beast of the field" (v. 1; emphasis added). But this is also a play on words. The term "subtil" or "cunning" in Hebrew is *'arum;* the word for "naked" (v. 7), Hebrew *'erum,* is the same root, with only one vowel different. In addition, *'arum* also means "wise" or "prudent," and this points us to something else about the serpent. As we shall see in Exodus, the serpent was a powerful symbol of Jehovah and hence of Jesus Christ (see commentary at Exodus 4:1–9 and at Numbers 21:1–9).

When Moses tried to remind Jehovah, after the prophet's call to be the deliverer of Israel, that the people would look upon him as one without authority or credentials, Jehovah invoked the symbol of the serpent, "that they may believe that the Lord God of their fathers, the God of Abraham, the God of Isaac, and the God of Jacob, hath appeared unto thee" (Exodus 4:5; see also vv. 1–4). Later on, the serpent of Moses and Aaron consumed the serpents of Pharaoh's magicians, symbolic of the overwhelming power of the true and living God as opposed to the false gods of the Egyptians (Exodus 7:10–13). Pharaoh was believed to be a living god on earth, and the symbol of his divinity that he wore as part of his crown was the cobra.

Moses raised the brazen serpent in the wilderness, which was an instrument of physical healing for the people, but which also pointed to the physical *and* spiritual healing provided by the future Messiah. Hence, Jesus referred the Jews to the raised serpent as a potent symbol of his Messiahship (John 3:14–15). By usurping and manipulating the symbol of the serpent in Eden, Satan tried to validate his false identity and his lies, insisting that following his ways would elevate our first parents to the status of the very God represented by the true image of the serpent (Moses 4:10–11). Satan came to Eve clothed, as it were, in the garb of the Messiah, using the signs, symbols, and even the language of the Messiah, promising things that only the Messiah could rightfully promise. "(And [Satan] spake by the mouth of the serpent.) . . . And the serpent said unto the woman: Ye shall not surely die; . . . ye shall be as the gods" (Moses 4:7, 10–11). In reality only the One who would work out an infinite atonement could legitimately make these kinds of promises. Perhaps that is one of the reasons why Satan is justly called a liar from the beginning (Moses 4:4; D&C 93:25). For more on this subject, see Skinner, "Serpent Symbols and Salvation," 42–55. For more in the scriptures about this adversary to God's ways, his origins, and purposes, see 2 Nephi 2:17–18; Doctrine and Covenants 29:36–45; 76:28; 88:110; Moses 4:1–4; Abraham 3:27–28; Isaiah 14:12–15; Luke 10:18; 2 Thessalonians 2:3–4; Jude 1:6; and Revelation 12.

The woman rehearsed to the serpent the commandment of God not to eat of the fruit, "lest ye die." A *choice* is implied: "Don't eat of it, unless you are willing to die."

Genesis 3:4–6 (Moses 4:10–12)

By what persuasive means did Satan entice Eve to partake of the fruit? Is it not typical of the ways in which he still tries to stimulate us to satisfy our curiosity, our appetites and urges, while allaying our fears of the consequences?

For his own purposes, Satan sought to persuade our first

parents to do a deed that would separate them from the presence of God in spiritual death and later separate their spirits from their bodies in physical death; then they would be like his unembodied spirit followers and subject to him (2 Nephi 9:8).

Satan's combining a falsehood (that they would not die) with a half truth (that by simply partaking they would "be as gods") was persuasive. Satan's statement was intended for his own gain; but ironically, by their response Eve and Adam launched into the desirable process of learning good from evil by experience through the use of their own agency. Thanks to the Father and his Beloved Son, their choice did not relegate them and their descendants to a hopeless predicament. Instead, it initiated a program, already planned, whereby humankind could work toward eternal life.

It is true that, in a sense, Adam and Eve would also become as gods, knowing good and evil (v. 22). The fruit of the tree became pleasant to Eve's eyes, and she saw that it was desirable to make her wise (Moses 4:12). She partook of the forbidden fruit partly because of that perception and partly because she was deceived (v. 13; 1 Timothy 2:14–15). As Paul wrote, "The serpent beguiled [deceived or tricked] Eve through his subtilty" (2 Corinthians 11:3). The devil specializes in subtle half-truths, such as "partake of the forbidden fruit, and ye shall not die [which was a lie], but ye shall be as God, knowing good and evil [which would become the truth]" (2 Nephi 2:18). Later, when she fully understood the potential of her choice, made available through the plan of redemption, she rejoiced in it (Moses 5:4–11).

The actions of our first parents, which constitute the Fall, are greatly misunderstood among those who have not had the benefit of modern prophets or modern scripture. Sometimes great blame has been placed on Eve for the Fall, and her actions branded as a great sin, so much so that she has been regarded as evil, unworthy of, or of lesser value than Adam. All these notions are false. The Fall did have physical consequences, but it was a step forward in the great plan of God.

Elder James E. Talmage explained: "Here let me say that therein consisted the fall—the eating of things unfit, the taking into the body of the things that made of that body a thing of earth: and I take this occasion to raise my voice against the false interpretation of scripture, which has been adopted by certain people, and is current in their minds, and is referred to in a hushed and half-secret way, that the fall of man consisted in some offense against the laws of chastity and of virtue. Such a doctrine is an abomination. . . . The fall was a natural process, resulting through the incorporation into the bodies of our first parents of the things that came from food unfit, through the violation of the command of God regarding what they should eat. Don't go around whispering that the fall consisted in the mother of the race losing her chastity and her virtue. It is not true. . . . Let it not be said that the patriarch of the race, who stood with the gods before he came here upon the earth, and his equally royal consort, were guilty of any such foul offense. . . .

"Our first parents were pure and noble, and when we pass behind the veil we shall perhaps learn something of their high estate, more than we know now. But be it known that they were pure; they were noble. It is true that they disobeyed the law of God, in eating things they were told not to eat; but who amongst you can rise up and condemn?" (*Jesus the Christ*, 30–31).

President Joseph Fielding Smith offered this significant insight: "Adam did only what he had to do. He partook of that fruit for one good reason, and that was to open the door to bring you and me and everyone else into this world, for Adam and Eve could have remained in the Garden of Eden; they could have been there to this day, if Eve hadn't done something.

"One of these days, if I ever get to where I can speak to Mother Eve, I want to thank her for tempting Adam to partake of the fruit. He accepted the temptation, with the result that children came into this world. And when I kneel in prayer, I feel to thank Mother Eve, for if she hadn't had that influence over Adam, and if Adam had done according to the commandment first given to him, they would still be in the Garden of Eden and we would not be here at all. We wouldn't have come into this world. . . .

"Brethren and sisters, let's thank the Lord, when we pray, for Adam. If it hadn't been for Adam, I wouldn't be here; you wouldn't be here; we would be waiting in the heavens as spirits pleading for somebody to do what the scriptures say . . . to pass through a certain condition that brought upon us mortality" (Conference Report, Oct. 1967, 121–22).

As to whether Adam and Eve transgressed, the Prophet Joseph Smith taught that "Adam did not commit sin in eating the fruits, for God had decreed that he should eat and fall" (*Words of Joseph Smith,* 63; spelling modernized).

Elder Dallin H. Oaks has taught that Adam and Eve did not sin in partaking of the forbidden fruit: "It was Eve who first transgressed the limits of Eden in order to initiate the conditions of mortality. Her act, whatever its nature, was formally a transgression but eternally a glorious necessity to open the doorway toward eternal life. Adam showed his wisdom by doing the same. And thus Eve and 'Adam fell that men might be' (2 Ne. 2:25; [see also Moses 6:48])."

"Some Christians condemn Eve for her act, concluding that she and her daughters are somehow flawed by it. Not the Latter-day Saints! Informed by revelation, we celebrate Eve's act and honor her wisdom and courage in the great episode called the Fall (see Bruce R. McConkie, 'Eve and the Fall,' *Woman,* Salt Lake City: Deseret Book Co., 1979, pp. 67–68). Joseph Smith taught that it was not a 'sin,' because God had decreed it (see *The Words of Joseph Smith,* ed. Andrew F. Ehat and Lyndon W. Cook, Provo, Utah: Religious Studies Center, Brigham Young University, 1980, p. 63). Brigham Young declared, 'We should never blame Mother Eve, not the least' (in *Journal of Discourses,* 13:145). Elder Joseph Fielding Smith said: 'I never speak of the part Eve took in this fall as a sin, nor do I accuse Adam of a sin. . . . This was a transgression of the law, but not a sin . . . for it was something that Adam and Eve had to do!' (Joseph Fielding Smith, *Doctrines of Salvation,* comp. Bruce R. McConkie, 3 vols., Salt Lake City: Bookcraft, 1954–56, 1:114–15).

"This suggested contrast between a *sin* and a *transgression* reminds us of the careful wording in the second article of faith: 'We believe that men will be punished for their own *sins,* and not for Adam's *transgression*' (emphasis added). It also echoes a familiar distinction in the law. Some acts, like murder, are crimes because they are inherently wrong. Other acts, like operating without a license, are crimes only because they are legally prohibited. Under these distinctions, the act that produced the Fall was not a sin—inherently wrong—but a transgression—wrong because it was formally prohibited. These words are not always used to denote something different, but this distinction seems meaningful in the circumstances of the Fall" (*Ensign,* Nov. 1993, 73. For use of the term *transgression* in the case of the fall of Adam and Eve, see 2 Nephi 2:21–22; 9:6; Mosiah 3:11; D&C 29:40–41; Moses 6:53.

To be sure, there were monumental consequences of the Fall, as the following statements attest. Elder Bruce R. McConkie explained: "Death entered the world by means of Adam's fall—death of two kinds, temporal and spiritual. Temporal death passes upon all men when they depart this mortal life. It is then that the eternal spirit steps out of its earthly tenement, to take up an abode in a realm where spirits are assigned, to await the day of their resurrection. Spiritual death passes upon all men when they become accountable for their sins. Being thus subject to sin they die spiritually; they die as pertaining to the things of the Spirit; they die as pertaining to the things of righteousness; they are cast out of the presence of God. It is of such men that the scriptures speak when they say that the natural man is an enemy to God and has become carnal, sensual, and devilish by nature.

"If a man 'yields to the enticings of the Holy Spirit, and

THE OLD TESTAMENT

putteth off the natural man and becometh a saint through the atonement of Christ the Lord' (Mosiah 3:19), then he is born again. His spiritual death ceases" (*Promised Messiah,* 349–50).

Perhaps as dramatic as the effects of the Fall on Adam, Eve, and their posterity were the effects on the physical universe. President Brigham Young stated: "When the earth was framed and brought into existence and man was placed upon it, it was near the throne of our Father in heaven. . . . but when man fell, the earth fell into space, and took up its abode in this planetary system, and the sun became our light. When the Lord said—'Let there be light,' there was light, for the earth was brought near the sun that it might reflect upon it so as to give us light by day, and the moon to give us light by night. This is the glory the earth came from, and when it is glorified it will return again into the presence of the Father, and it will dwell there, and these intelligent beings that I am looking at, if they live worthy of it, will dwell upon this earth" (*Journal of Discourses,* 17:143). Also, "this earthly ball, this little [opaque] substance thrown off into space, is only a speck in the great universe; and when it is celestialized it will go back into the presence of God, where it was first framed" (*Journal of Discourses,* 9:317).

And, finally, an article in the official Church newspaper in Nauvoo said in 1842: "The earth no longer [at the transgression of Adam] retained its standing in the presence of Jehovah: *but was hurled into the immensity of space;* and there to remain until it has filled up the time of its bondage to sin and Satan. It was immediately cursed, and Adam and Eve were obliged to procure their food and raiment by the sweat of the brow" (*Times and Seasons* 3, no. 7 [Feb. 1, 1842]: 672; emphasis added).

Genesis 3:7–10 (Moses 4:13–16)

Just exactly what Eve ate and then gave to her husband so that he ate also is probably not as important as understanding what it did to them. They had known the good of

48

having all things provided that were needed to sustain life, but perhaps they had not learned of such things as joy or gratitude. Through their act they learned shame and even fear of death. They experienced remorse, confession, and repentance. Although we may not fully know *why* it is true, there seems to be a need for opposites in all things (2 Nephi 2:10–16). Ultimately an atonement was provided, and they could then know joy and gratitude for redemption, which they never could have known if they had not transgressed (Moses 5:10–11). Adam and Eve made a covering (fig leaves) because of the Fall, and then God made a covering (Atonement) because of the Fall.

Their shame in being naked, when they had felt no shame before, suggests that consciousness of their urges and inclinations and the influences of Satan must somehow have caused embarrassment. In any case, their reluctance to be seen of God is quite understandable.

Genesis 3:11–13 (Moses 4:17–19)

Since God knows all things, why did he question them as to where they were and what they had done? His questions gave them the opportunity to explain and repent of any wrongdoing and plainly link the results of the deed to the deed itself.

Genesis 3:14–15 (Moses 4:20–21)

Beginning with Satan, who had transgressed most, the Lord began to mete out judgment and justice. Satan had contradicted God's warning and had told Eve that death would not result from partaking of the fruit of the tree of knowledge, and he had enticed her with the promise that it would make her wise so she could be as the gods. This mixture of falsehood and truth made Satan deserving of the title, "father of lies."

Satan was left on earth, however, so that humans could learn by contrast the true value of God's ways (D&C 29:39; 2 Nephi 2:10–16). Apparently, however, he was granted less freedom in his methods of appealing to mankind. The words of God spoken to the serpent seem to suggest a limitation of Satan's modes of operation. He was to crawl, to feed on "dirt," and to be able only to bruise the heel of the "seed of the woman" while her seed, especially one Seed, could bruise or even crush his head (see Hebrew footnotes on v. 15; for scriptural comments on this, see Romans 16:20; Hebrews 2:14; D&C 19:2–3). In this single verse (v. 15), we find mention of the plan of salvation and an early prophecy of Christ's atonement. Elder James E. Talmage explained: "Brief mention of the plan of salvation . . . appears in the promise given of God following the fall—that though the devil, represented by the serpent in Eden, should have power to bruise the heel of Adam's posterity, through the seed of the woman should come the power to bruise the adversary's head. It is significant that this assurance of eventual victory over sin and its inevitable effect, death, both of which were introduced to earth through Satan the arch-enemy of mankind, was to be realized through the offspring of woman; the promise was not made specifically to the man, nor to the pair. The only instance of offspring from woman dissociated from mortal fatherhood is the birth of Jesus Christ, who was the earthly Son of a mortal mother, begotten by an immortal Father" (*Jesus the Christ,* 43). In Jesus alone has the prophecy, spoken at the time of the Fall, been fulfilled. Children of God have been given power to resist Satan, and even those who are overcome by him may be aided by others having the power to cast him out in the name of Jesus Christ. Thus we see that his freedom to act and his power to overcome are indeed limited (James 4:7; Matthew 10:1; D&C 24:13).

Genesis 3:16 (Moses 4:22)

Through bringing death into the world, Eve also became able to bring new life to earth (Moses 5:11; 2 Nephi 2:23). But the Lord let her know what humbling and what inconvenience she would suffer in fulfilling her mission of preparing bodies for other spirits to come to earth to live. The Hebrew text is in the form of synonymous parallelism: "I will greatly multiply your pain in child bearing; in pain you shall bring forth children." By suffering the pains and feeling the responsibilities of motherhood, mothers become co-creators with God and develop that most Godlike quality of love. God's pronouncement is not a punishment of womankind for Eve's transgression but an admonition of what women can do in the extraordinary roles of wife and mother.

President Spencer W. Kimball taught that instead of "rule" in the final declaration of the verse, the word "preside" is to be preferred because that is what the honorable husband does (*Ensign*, Mar. 1976, 72). Additionally, in the Hebrew original of that verse, the letter *beth* (pronounced "bait") may be translated as "with." Thus, the Lord was advising Eve that Adam "shall rule *with* thee," which perfectly corresponds to our doctrine and definition of exaltation in the celestial world (see Hafen, *Ensign*, Aug. 2007, 27).

Genesis 3:17–19 (Moses 4:23–25)

The responsibilities of man to labor for a living outside of Eden's provident environs were pointed out to Adam by the Lord. "Sorrow" is again used to translate Hebrew *etzev*, which denotes "hurt, pain, grief," in reference to the toil of man and to the travail of woman.

The necessity of working for a living, using the earth's resources, is related to the challenge in the earlier command to "multiply, and replenish the earth, and subdue it" (Genesis 1:28). But work is also a divine commandment as well as a necessity, one much reiterated in our day (D&C 42:42; 60:13; 68:30–31; 75:3). The Lord feels so strongly about work that he decreed that the idler shall not have place in his Church, "except he repent and mend his ways" (D&C 75:29).

In addition, the opportunity to work is also a great gift. We have had experiences where the necessity of going to work helped ease the pressure of other burdens, allowing us to think about other things long enough to gain fresh perspective on other problems, thus proving to be a tremendous blessing in the end. Heavenly Father's plan involves work. All must work. God has his work (Moses 1:39), and so must we have ours. Elder Neal A. Maxwell of the Quorum of the Twelve offered this powerful observation: "Work is always a spiritual necessity even if, for some, work is not an economic necessity" (*Ensign*, May 1998, 38; Elder Maxwell's entire address is an enlightening discussion of the principle of work). Moreover, Lehi teaches the need for opposition in all things in order for us to achieve our full potential (2 Nephi 2:14–30).

Genesis 3:20 (Moses 4:26)

Note the connection between earlier verses (especially verse 16) and this one, in which the significance of Eve's name is given as the "mother of all living." In its Hebrew form, her name is an ancient common noun for "life." Eve was the first of all the many women who would come to earth and give life; compare Moses 1:34, where Adam is also designated the first of "many" men—the "many" referring to the greatness of their posterity.

Adam and Eve are frequently called in the scriptures "our first parents" (1 Nephi 5:11; also 2 Nephi 2:15; 9:9; Mosiah 16:3; Alma 12:21; 42:2, 7). "Michael, or Adam, [was] the father of all" (D&C 27:11; 138:38). "Eve . . . was the mother of all living . . . the first of all women" (Moses 4:26).

Genesis 3:21 (Moses 4:27)

Teaching about the sanctity of the body and the importance of reserving it to proper uses and avoiding abuses, the Lord made "coats of skins" (or garments; see footnote *a*) and clothed the first man and woman. Certain types of exhibition and exposure are used commonly today in advertisements and entertainments to attract and entice people to actions having little to do with the primary and proper purposes of their beautifully formed and marvelous bodies.

The coats of skin spoken of in this verse have long been recognized as ritual garments of power, and not just by

Latter-day Saints. From Jewish tradition preserved in the Talmud comes this: "And there was a certain coat of skins which God had made for Adam. When Adam died this coat became the possession of Enoch; from him it descended to Methusaleh, his son; Methusaleh gave it to Noah, who took it with him into the ark. And when the people left the ark Ham stole this coat, and hid it from his brothers, giving it secretly thereafter to Cush, his son. Cush kept it hidden for many years, until out of his great love he gave it to Nimrod, the child of his old age. When Nimrod was twenty years of age he put on this coat, and it gave him strength and might" (Polano, *Talmud*, 27).

Genesis 3:22–24 (Moses 4:28–31)

The truth that Satan had enticingly mixed with a falsehood is here confirmed: by their act of eating the forbidden fruit the man and woman had begun to be "as gods, knowing good and evil" (v. 5). But to prevent their choosing to return to the primeval "good" of living in the Garden of Eden, where perfect food was freely available, they were expelled from the garden, and the way to the "tree of life" was closed and guarded. Finding ways to supply needs and avoid discomforts have produced pure and applied sciences and arts ever since.

The meaning of the "cherubim" and the "flaming sword which turned every way" to guard the garden and the tree of life is difficult to find (see Alma 12:21; 42:3; Moses 4:31). The Hebrew word *cherub* derives from an Akkadian word referring to winged land-animals. Many Semitic peoples have placed at the gates of their temples some type of composite beast, in statuary, made up of parts resembling eagles, lions, bulls, serpents, and men and called them in their languages by equivalents of the name *cherubim,* but where they derived the concept or what they meant to symbolize is not fully known.

The tree of life in Lehi's vision represented the love of God made manifest in the Atonement provided through his

Only Begotten Son (1 Nephi 8, 11). This leaves open the possibility that the cherubim and flaming sword represent the restrictions that make it impossible for man to gain atonement and eternal life in any other way than the way the gospel provides.

Again we emphasize the importance of understanding the transgression and Fall of our first parents—seeing it all from a divine perspective. President Joseph Fielding Smith explained the process and purposes of Adam and Eve's transgression in the garden:

"I never speak of the part Eve took in this fall as a sin, nor do I accuse Adam of a sin. One may say, 'Well did they not break a commandment?' Yes. But let us examine the nature of the commandment and the results which came out of it.

"In no other commandment the Lord ever gave to man, did he say: 'But of the tree of the knowledge of good and evil, thou shalt not eat of it, *nevertheless, thou mayest choose for thyself.*' [Moses 3:17]

"It is true, the Lord warned Adam and Eve that to partake of the fruit they would transgress a law, and this happened. But it is not always a sin to transgress a law. . . .

"Before partaking of the fruit Adam could have lived forever; therefore, his status was one of immortality. When he ate, he became subject to death, and therefore he became mortal. This was a transgression of the law, but not a sin in the strict sense, for it was something that Adam and Eve had to do! . . .

"Adam said: ' . . . because of my transgression my eyes are opened, and in this life I shall have joy, and again in the flesh I shall see God.'

"Eve said: 'Were it not for our transgression we never should have had seed, and never should have known good and evil, and the joy of our redemption, and the eternal life which God giveth unto all the obedient.' [Moses 5:10–11]

"We can hardly look upon anything resulting in such

benefits as being a sin, in the sense in which we consider sin" (*Doctrines of Salvation*, 1:114–15).

President Smith also taught: "What did Adam do? The very thing the Lord wanted him to do. I hate to hear anybody call it a sin, for it wasn't a sin. . . . Now this is the way I interpret that: The Lord said to Adam, 'Here is the tree of the knowledge of good and evil. If you want to stay here, then you cannot eat of that fruit. If you want to stay here, I forbid you to eat it. But you may act for yourself and you may eat if you want to. And if you do eat it, you will die'" ("Fall—Atonement—Resurrection—Sacrament," 124).

"Because of Adam's transgression," President Smith wrote elsewhere, "a spiritual death—banishment from the presence of the Lord—as well as the temporal death, were pronounced upon him. The spiritual death came at the time of the fall and banishment; and the seeds of the temporal death were also sown at the same time; that is, a physical change came over Adam and Eve, who became mortal, and were thus subject to the ills of the flesh which resulted in their gradual decline to old age and finally the separation of the spirit from the body.

"Before this temporal death took place the Lord, by his own voice and the visitation and ministration of angels, taught Adam the principles of the gospel and administered unto him the saving ordinances, through which he was again restored to the favor of the Lord and to his presence. Also, through the atonement, not only Adam, but all his posterity were redeemed from the temporal effects of the fall, and shall come forth in the resurrection to receive immortality" (*Doctrines of Salvation*, 1:111–12).

The gospel of Jesus Christ teaches that the consequences of the Fall (physical and spiritual death) are overcome by a prearranged redemption. A Savior, the Son of God himself, would overcome the effects of both physical and spiritual death by providing resurrection, a gift of God to all mankind, and by providing the way back to the presence of God and actually bringing each soul back into the presence of God for a final judgment. Where we go at that point is up to each of us. The Savior of the world has done his part; he overcame all consequences of the Fall.

———

At this point the Joseph Smith Translation of Genesis adds another fifteen verses (Moses 5:1–15) before resuming the Bible's account. These are very significant teachings about the first of many children of Adam and Eve and their teaching them—with the Holy Ghost—the principles of the gospel, their obedience in offering sacrifices, the appearance of an angel explaining the purpose of their sacrifice, and their recognition of the benefits of the Fall and the coming Redemption, and the role of Satan in opposing the plan of salvation.

For additional help in understanding the next chapters, you may also want to consult the following entries in the Bible Dictionary: "Abel," "Enoch," "Noah," "Ark," "Rainbow," "Shem," "Ham," "Japheth," and "Zion"; see also articles on Enoch and Noah in the *Encyclopedia of Mormonism.*

———

Genesis 4:1–2 (Moses 5:16–17)

Our first parents began to have children, and Eve acknowledged that children came from a heavenly home. The entire human family was organized and ordered in that heavenly setting before they began to populate the earth. "The Father called all spirits before Him at the creation of man, and organized them. He (Adam) is the head, and was told to multiply," said Joseph Smith (*History of the Church,* 3:387). That families were organized at this premortal council is evident from other scriptures and from the writings of modern prophets. President Harold B. Lee taught: "You are all the sons and daughters of God. Your spirits were created and lived as organized intelligences before the world was. You have been blessed to have a physical body because of your obedience to certain commandments in that premortal state. You are now born into a family to which you have come, into the nations through which you have come, as a reward for the kind of lives you lived before you came here and at a time in the world's history, as the Apostle Paul taught the men of Athens and as the Lord revealed to Moses, determined by the faithfulness of each of those who lived before this world was created" (*Ensign,* Jan. 1974, 5; see also McKay, *Home Memories,* 226–31). The house of Israel was established (Deuteronomy 32:9); Mary was appointed to be the mother of Christ (1 Nephi 11:14–20; Mosiah 3:8; Alma 7:10); and the family lineage of Joseph Smith was preestablished (2 Nephi 3:14–15). In fact, the "times" and "bounds" of everyone's habitation were determined (Deuteronomy 32:8; Acts 17:26). Thus, Cain and Abel were born at the appointed time, but they were not the first.

Restored scripture (JST Genesis 4:1–13; 5:1–3; Moses 5:1–15) reveals that much time had passed and many events had occurred before the birth of Cain and Abel. Adam and Eve had worked together for years and had had children who had grown up and in turn had children before Cain and Abel were born. They had received commandments and revelations, helping them understand and anticipate the redeeming sacrifice of the Savior—and they had taught these things to their children and grandchildren. The story of Cain and Abel then unfolds, to help teach us essential doctrines.

Moses 5:16 informs us that Adam and Eve did not cease to call upon God, and they didn't give up on their children. The existence of other children of Adam and Eve are implied later in Genesis where mention of Cain's wife occurs. Another son, Seth, and his descendants are reported in detail beginning in Genesis 5.

Genesis 4:3–7 (Moses 5:18–31)

The chosen professions of Abel and of Cain are described, as well as their offerings to the Lord. That Cain's sacrifice had not been proper is evidenced in the Lord's question, "If thou doest well, shalt thou not be accepted?" Cain did not offer a blood sacrifice, which foreshadowed the Atonement of Jesus Christ. The Prophet Joseph Smith explained:

"By faith in this atonement or plan of redemption, Abel offered to God a sacrifice that was accepted, which was the firstlings of the flock. Cain offered of the fruit of the ground, and was not accepted, because he could not do it in faith; he could have no faith, or could not exercise faith contrary to the plan of heaven. It must be shedding the blood of the Only Begotten to atone for man, for this was the plan of redemption; and without the shedding of blood was no remission. And as the sacrifice was instituted for a type by which man was to discern the great Sacrifice which God had prepared, to offer a sacrifice contrary to that, no faith could be exercised, because redemption was not purchased in that way, nor the power of atonement instituted after that order; consequently Cain could have no faith; and whatsoever is not of faith, is sin. But Abel offered an acceptable sacrifice, by which he obtained witness that he was righteous, God Himself testifying of his gifts.

"Certainly, the shedding of the blood of a beast could be beneficial to no man, except it was done in imitation, or as a type, or explanation of what was to be offered through the gift of God Himself—and this performance done with an eye looking forward in faith on the power of that great Sacrifice for a remission of sins" (*Joseph Smith* [manual], 48.)

Cain was mocking God. Satan had commanded Cain to make the offering, and Cain did not do it out of loyalty to God or faith in Jesus Christ (Moses 5:18). When something is done in the kingdom of God *without faith in Christ,* it is sin. Also, it is human nature to get angry when we are caught doing something wrong. It is possible that Satan's suggestion that Cain make an offering to the Lord was made with the intent and expectation that Cain would offer an improper sacrifice and thereby incur disfavor with God. Even after Cain's unacceptable offering the Lord did not immediately reject him. Rather, the Lord warned him and counseled with him.

The Lord is a God of second chances! Note the detailed warning by the Lord given to Cain *after* the sacrifice but *before* the final pact with Satan. It is clear who suggested this first "murder to get gain." This concept is alive and well in the world today—in nations, corporations, and the hearts of individuals. Knowing God and then to willfully love and serve Satan in preference to God and to commit murder, shedding innocent blood, are sufficient to bring one to perdition. It is still so, according to Doctrine and Covenants 76:26, 32, 43, and 132:27; compare John 17:12. The word *perdition* (Latin, *perdere*) means "complete and irreparable loss or ruin."

Genesis 4:8–16 (Moses 5:32–41)

When Abel's murder became known and Cain was confronted with the charges and with the punishment, he showed no regret or remorse. He sarcastically denied knowledge of and responsibility for his brother. It would have been better if he had ceased his evil ways rather than perpetuate them among his descendants, as we shall later see that he did. For his deed, however, Cain could not have gained forgiveness through the vicarious suffering of the Redeemer; murder requires the doer himself to pay the consequences (1 John 5:16; D&C 42:18; Mosiah 15:26–27; 16:1–5). Notice the alternate translation of verse 13, where Cain says to the Lord, "My iniquity [or guilt] is too great to be forgiven."

The Prophet Joseph Smith taught that Cain did *not* act out of ignorance. He held the holy priesthood and knew what he was doing. Therefore, he was cursed, as will others who willfully refuse to do things in the way God has appointed (*Joseph Smith* [manual], 108). The scriptures teach that anyone who is cursed brings the curse upon himself (Alma 3:19; 13:3–7; compare Moses 5:40; 7:8, 22).

The earthly punishment of Cain made him a fugitive and a wanderer shut out from the presence of the Lord and separated from his relatives, except those who were part of his society (Moses 5:12–15, 26–29, 41ff). This was overwhelming at first, and he blamed Satan for tempting him and God for rejecting his offerings (vv. 11–13; Moses 5:37–38). Cain feared that "every one that findeth me shall slay me" (v. 14).

The stated purpose of the "mark" (Hebrew, "sign," or identifier) set upon Cain by the Lord was to prevent others assuming a prerogative to punish him. Many false assumptions have been generated over the centuries about the "mark of Cain." Other scriptures somewhat clarify the purpose of such an identification (v. 15a). There is a question about why the mark would be perpetuated upon the descendants of the one punished. "The sins of the parents cannot be answered upon the heads of the children" in God's justice (Moses 6:54). Nevertheless, parents can and do pass on impairments and disadvantages, blessings and advantages, to their children; and refinements and extensions of Cain's evil "secret" were known and used by his descendants and others (Ether 8:11–19), and they too suffered thereby.

Lessons from this terrible episode in the early history of earth may be applied to us and can be summarized as follows:

- Cain was jealous of Abel, and that emotion often gets us in trouble.
- Cain tried to hide what he had done, and that usually makes matters worse.
- Cain withdrew himself from his family after the deed, and when we find ourselves withdrawing from sources of good, we are moving away from our best sources of help.

Genesis 4:17–24 (Moses 5:42–59)

Cain and his wife had a son whom they named Enoch. As indicated in footnote 17b, we should not confuse the Enoch of Cain's lineage and the city of his name with the Enoch of Seth's lineage and the city of his name (the city of Enoch, or Zion).

Though the Satanic pact of murder-for-gain was perpetuated (Moses 5:49ff), the society of Cain and his brethren and their descendants apparently also had to be economically productive through ordinary work to gain a livelihood because the scriptures speak of their herdsmen, artists, and artisans.

Lamech, who murdered his own great-grandfather for divulging a covenant with Satan, stated that he would be "avenged seventy and seven fold" compared to the mere "seven-fold" vengeance that was specified for anyone who would kill Cain. This seems to be a cynical deduction that if Cain could be "protected" after what he had done, Lamech should receive more protection in view of his more heinous crime.

Lamech admitted to his wives, "I have slain a man to my wounding, and a young man to my hurt"—which sounds as if he had killed two persons. However, this is one of the first of many hundreds of examples throughout biblical literature of a figure of speech called "synonymous parallelism," a familiar form of expression with the second phrase simply repeating the idea of the first phrase. We will discuss more about parallelism later, in the Psalms (see also 1 Samuel 31:3).

Genesis 4:25–26 (Moses 6:1–3)

In another genealogical line, God revealed himself to Seth as the son who replaced Abel (Moses 6:3). This knowledge of God was passed on further to his son, for in the days of Seth and Enos "men began to call upon the name of the Lord." In Genesis, it is clear that this is the sacred name of *YHWH* (Jehovah) that men began to supplicate at that time. Seth's line perpetuated the priesthood of God that was once given to Abel (Moses 6:2; D&C 84:16; 107:42).

It is important to reiterate at this point that the gospel and ordinances of the priesthood of God were on the earth from the beginning. Adam and Eve taught their children the principles of salvation and the plan of redemption. "In the beginning was the gospel preached through the Son. And the gospel was the word" (JST John 1:1). "And thus the Gospel began to be preached, from the beginning, being declared by holy angels sent forth from the presence of God, and by his own voice, and by the gift of the Holy Ghost. And thus all things were confirmed unto Adam, by an holy ordinance, and the Gospel preached" (Moses 5:58–59). The plurality of Gods, the spiritual creation, the importance of moral agency, the role of Satan, the eternal nature of marriage, the priesthood and its blessings, the role of the Holy Ghost, the law of sacrifice, the principles and covenants and ordinances of the gospel, the knowledge of a Redeemer to come, the purpose of Temples, and more, were all known from the beginning. Adam, Enoch, Noah, the brother of Jared, Abraham, and Moses all had the gospel.

Joseph Smith explained: "Perhaps our friends will say that the Gospel and its ordinances were not known till the days of John, the son of Zacharias. . . . But we will here look at this point: For our own part we cannot believe that the ancients in all ages were so ignorant of the system of heaven as many suppose. . . . It will be noticed that, according to Paul, (see Gal. 3:8) the Gospel was preached to Abraham. We would like to be informed in what name the Gospel was then preached, whether it was in the name of Christ or some other name. If in any other name, was it the Gospel? . . . And if it had ordinances what were they? Our friends may say, perhaps, that there were never any ordinances except those of offering sacrifices before the coming of Christ, and that it could not be possible for the Gospel to have been administered while the law of sacrifices of blood was in force. But we will recollect that Abraham offered sacrifice, and notwithstanding this, had the Gospel preached to him . . . So, then, because the ancients offered sacrifice it did not hinder their hearing the Gospel; but served . . . to open their eyes, and enable them to look forward to the time of the coming of the Savior, and rejoice in His redemption.

"We find also, that when the Israelites came out of Egypt they had the Gospel preached to them, according to Paul in his letter to the Hebrews, which says: 'For unto us was the

Gospel preached, as well as unto them: but the word preached did not profit them, not being mixed with faith in them that heard it' (see Heb. 4:2). It is said again, in Gal 3:19, that the law (of Moses, or the Levitical law) was 'added' because of transgression. What, we ask, was this law added to, if it was not added to the Gospel? . . . From these few facts, we conclude that whenever the Lord revealed Himself to men in ancient days, and commanded them to offer sacrifice to Him, that it was done that they might look forward in faith to the time of His coming, and rely upon the power of that atonement for a remission of their sins" (*History of the Church*, 2:16–17).

Genesis 5:1–3 (Moses 6:4–10)

Almost from the beginning a "book of remembrance" (Moses 6:5–10) or "book of the generations of Adam" was kept in the pure and undefiled language of God. (The confusion of tongues and loss of this language will be noted later.) This was the real beginning of the writing of scripture. These earliest records that formed the basis of scripture, particularly the Old Testament, are genealogical or family history records. It is well known among Hebrew scholars that the word *generations* used in the early sections of Genesis and also in the books of Moses and Abraham is translated from the Hebrew *toledoth* meaning "family or genealogical history." The word "generations" is used many times in Genesis, and beginning with Adam in Genesis 2:4, the phrase "These are the generations of [*toledoth*] . . ." is used ten times with each successive patriarch to knit together the human family and demonstrate its close relationship to God. Clearly the intent in Genesis is to point back to divine origins and not to point forward (Harrison, *Introduction to the Old Testament*, 546).

Significantly, the use of *toledoth* also implies that a written record was kept by the patriarch with whom that Hebrew word was associated. "Thus in Genesis 6:9, the phrase 'These are the generations of Noah' does not necessarily mean 'This is the history involving Noah,' . . . Instead, the expression could well be interpreted as meaning 'This is the history written (or possessed) by Noah,' which once more would be in full accord with ancient Near Eastern literary practices" (Harrison, *Introduction to the Old Testament*, 547). The early portion of the book of Genesis, then, provides us with a pattern for how the rest of Genesis, as well as the whole Old Testament, was formed. Each successive patriarch or prophet wrote his own record of activities to be added to previous sections.

Both the pattern for the book of remembrance as well as the pure language in which it was written were revealed by God (Moses 6:5, 46). In the last days, preparatory to the peaceful reign of the Lord on earth, "a pure language" will be restored (Zephaniah 3:9), and that will surely contribute to peace on earth.

Seth is described as being in the "likeness and image" of his father Adam, just as Adam was described as being in the "likeness and image" of God (Genesis 1:26–27). The name Seth in Hebrew comes from the verb meaning "to put or place."

Genesis 5:4–24 (Moses 6:11 through 8:4)

During four generations and some five hundred years, according to Adam's book of remembrance, there were "preachers of righteousness" (Moses 6:23) who declared repentance and prophesied. Then Enoch (of Seth's line) was called to become a great prophet-missionary-reformer. His ministry was needed, for the followers of the cult of Cain had become numerous, and violence was rampant (Moses 5:28–31, 47–57). To those who had become sensual and devilish, Enoch preached repentance. The sons of God, distinguished from the sons of men, were obliged to segregate themselves in a new home called Cainan after their forefather, the son of Enos. Do not confuse this Cainan with the wicked people of Canaan of Moses 7:6–10.

Enoch was successful in combating the evils of the time (Moses 6:27–29) and built up a righteous culture called *Zion*, meaning, "the pure in heart" (Moses 7:18ff). Enoch's name, *Hanokh,* in Hebrew, means "dedicated"—from the same root word as the term *Hanukkah* ("dedication")—which tells something of his commitment to the cause of God.

The teachings of Enoch covered seven major categories and embrace some information found nowhere else in scripture. He taught about—

1. The Fall of man and its results
2. The nature of salvation and the means of achieving it
3. Sin, as seen in the evils of his time, in contrast to the righteousness of the godly who were his followers
4. The cause, purpose, and effects of the anticipated flood of Noah's time
5. The scope of Satan's triumph and the resultant sorrows of God
6. The first advent of the Messiah
7. The second advent of the Messiah and his peaceful, millennial reign

The details of Enoch's gospel teachings deserve careful study and attention. Whereas Genesis contains a total of only four verses about Enoch and his ministry (Genesis 5:21–24), the Joseph Smith Translation adds a span of 116 verses (Moses 6:26–8:4), containing the call of Enoch; his expositions of the doctrines of the gospel; his conversations with the Lord and visions of the future; his service as army general, prophet, and seer; the establishment of the City of Enoch or Zion; their translation to heaven; and their prophesied return, after a five-thousand-year leave of absence from earth, to the New Jerusalem in the Millennium.

This great patriarch and prophet is also spoken of in the New Testament in Jude 1:14–15 and in Hebrews 11:5, where we read about Enoch being translated, and in the Doctrine and Covenants. Not only were Enoch and his city translated and taken from the earth (v. 24) but others also reached that level of righteousness (JST Genesis 14:25–40).

Enoch was a powerful prophet and seer, a similitude of Christ. His life and ministry centered mightily on the Lord Jesus. As do all true prophets, Enoch possessed the testimony of Jesus (Revelation 19:10), and armed with this knowledge, he led the people of the city of Zion. Like the future Messiah, Enoch was a savior to his people, working great righteousness and preaching the gospel of Jesus Christ. The Lord even said to Enoch that the city of Zion would be his abode forever. Enoch will dwell with Christ in the same eternal community, governed by the law of the celestial kingdom (D&C 105:3–5).

As a seer, Enoch "beheld also things which were not visible to the natural eye; and from thenceforth came the saying abroad in the land: A seer hath the Lord raised up" (Moses 6:36). Enoch's calling was certainly a type and a foreshadowing of the work of the Great Seer—Jesus Christ. We note, for example, the seeric powers of Jesus in his calling of Nathanael (John 1:47–51).

Some of the most stunning things Enoch saw pertained to the first and second comings of the Savior (see, for example, Moses 7:47–65). He witnessed in vision "the Son of Man lifted up on the cross, after the manner of men" (Moses 7:55) and saw the creations of God mourn and the earth groan at the death of their God (Moses 7:56). In similitude of Jesus Christ, Enoch knew personally the kind of persecution experienced by the Savior, for "all men were offended because of him" (Moses 6:37). This was precisely Jesus' experience (Matthew 11:6; 26:31) as well as the experience of those who followed him (Matthew 24:10).

Finally, Enoch experienced the same unity with God that the Father and the Son enjoy. The Lord said to his seer: "Behold my Spirit is upon you, . . . *and thou shalt abide in me, and I in you;* therefore walk with me" (Moses 6:34; emphasis added). This promise prefigured the words Jesus prayed on the eve of Gethsemane during his great High Priestly, or Intercessory, Prayer (John 17:21) and also paralleled Jesus' expressions during his teaching sessions and prayers with the

Nephites after his resurrection (3 Nephi 11:27; 19:23, 29). Enoch was an impressive witness, similitude, and foreshadowing of Jesus Christ.

Genesis 5:25–32 (Moses 8:5–12)

After Enoch and his people, Zion, had been taken to heaven and only a branch of his line remained to perpetuate the work of the Lord, sin and evil became the common way of life among the people of the earth. Methuselah and his son Lamech (not to be confused with the Lamech of Cain's line), both prophesied of the coming of a great man of their lineage, Noah (Moses 8:3, 9; Genesis 5:29).

Just as Mormon was a spiritually sober and serious youth at the early age of ten (Mormon 1:2), so Noah was found worthy and responsible at the age of ten to be ordained to the priesthood (D&C 107:52). As a patriarch and a prophet like those before him, Noah taught repentance and tried to bring peace and rest to the earth (Moses 8:16–21). The earth was under a curse (Genesis 3:17–18) and suffered not just thorns and thistles but all manner of moral evils, which were perpetuated more readily and easily than the good way of life. Noah's name means "comfort" or "rest," and he would bring some comfort to his parents and to the Lord for helping save a small remnant of God's children in the earth. His converts who remained righteous apparently were taken up to join the city of Enoch (Moses 7:27).

Like Enoch, Noah was another whose life was a similitude of the Messiah to come. His name immediately points us to him who is the ultimate giver of comfort and rest—Jesus of Nazareth. Like Jesus, Noah was a preacher of righteousness who declared the doctrine of Christ—faith, repentance, baptism, and the gift of the Holy Ghost (compare Moses 8:23–24; 3 Nephi 11:30–40). Like Jesus, Noah was threatened with death at the hands of enemies and unbelievers. And like Jesus, Noah was preserved in dangerous moments to allow him to pursue his divinely appointed mission (compare Moses

8:18, 26; Luke 4:29–30), though ultimately Jesus surrendered his life.

Jesus was sinless and perfect (2 Corinthians 5:21; 1 Peter 2:22; Hebrews 4:15). He walked and talked with God, his Father (JST Matthew 4:1; John 11:41). As a similitude and foreshadowing of Jesus, Noah was called "perfect in his generation; and he walked with God" (Moses 8:27). Though Jesus is the true Lord of heaven and earth (Psalm 24:1), Noah, in the likeness of the Lord, received dominion over the earth and all living things in his time. Noah, like Adam, "was the father of all living in his day" and the giver of life in the likeness of Jesus the Messiah. Noah fulfilled the prophecy of his grandfather Methuselah "that from his loins should spring all the kingdoms of the earth (through Noah)" (Moses 8:3).

Finally, Noah returned to earth as the angel Gabriel, after his mortal mission was completed, to announce the births of both John the Baptist and Jesus the Christ. Eighteen centuries later, Noah—again as Gabriel—visited the Prophet Joseph Smith to restore priesthood keys (D&C 128:21), which constitute the authority to oversee and direct God's power. Noah will return to earth after Christ's second coming to attend the marriage supper of the Lamb (D&C 27:5–7). Noah was a minister of the Lord, and his life and actions demonstrate that he was a similitude and a foreshadowing of Jesus Christ.

Genesis 6:1–2 (Moses 8:13–16)

As the population of the earth began to increase, marriages between women who kept the Lord's covenant and men who did not began to take place.

President Joseph Fielding Smith taught: "Because the daughters of Noah married the sons of men contrary to the teachings of the Lord, his anger was kindled, and this offense was one cause that brought to pass the universal flood. You will see that the condition appears reversed in the Book of Moses [8:13–21]. It was the daughters of the sons of God who were marrying the sons of men, which was displeasing unto the Lord. The fact was, as we see it revealed, that the daughters who had been born, evidently under the covenant, and were the daughters of the sons of God, that is to say of those who held the priesthood, were transgressing the commandment of the Lord and were marrying *out of the Church*. Thus they were cutting themselves off from the blessings of the priesthood contrary to the teachings of Noah and the will of God" (*Answers to Gospel Questions,* 1:136–37).

Regarding the daughters of Noah who had perverted the ways of the Lord, President Smith also said: "Noah was a righteous man, and therefore we must conclude that he followed the admonition of the Lord to multiply. We reach the conclusion then, that Noah had numerous sons and daughters, but only three of his sons and their wives had faith enough to follow Noah into the Ark. What of the others? We get some light from [Moses 8:15]" (*Answers to Gospel Questions,* 2:175).

On the matter of marrying outside the covenant, or outside the Church, the prophets have given clear counsel. President Brigham Young taught:

"One of the first transgressions of the family called Israel, was their going to other families or other nations to select partners. This was one of the great mistakes made by the children of Abraham, Isaac and Jacob, for they would go and marry with other families, although the Lord had forbidden them to do so, and had given them a very strict and stringent law on the subject" (*Discourses of Brigham Young,* 196).

President Young also testified: "Since I was baptized into this Church and kingdom, if all the female beauty had been simmered down into one woman not in this kingdom, she would not have appeared handsome to me; but if a person's heart is open to receive the truth, the excellency of love and beauty is there. How is it with you, sisters? Do you distinguish between a man of God and a man of the world? It is one of the strangest things that happens in my existence, to think that any man or woman can love a being that will not receive the truth of heaven. The love this Gospel produces is far above the love of women: it is the love of God—the love of eternity—of eternal lives" (*Journal of Discourses,* 8:199–200).

President Joseph F. Smith forcefully asserted: "I would rather take one of my children to the grave than I would see him turn away from this Gospel. I would rather take my children to the cemetery, and see them buried in innocence, than I would see them corrupted by the ways of the world. I would rather go myself to the grave than to be associated with a wife outside of the bonds of the new and everlasting covenant. Now, I hold it just so sacred" (*Gospel Doctrine,* 279).

President Spencer W. Kimball also spoke emphatically: "Religious differences imply wider areas of conflict. Church loyalties and family loyalties clash. Children's lives are often frustrated. The nonmember may be equally brilliant, well trained and attractive, and he or she may have the most pleasing personality, but without a common faith, trouble lies ahead for the marriage. There are some exceptions but the rule is a harsh and unhappy one. There is no bias nor prejudice in this doctrine. It is a matter of following a certain program to reach a definite goal. . . . Marrying outside the faith has always been forbidden" (*Miracle of Forgiveness,* 240).

Genesis 6:3 (Moses 8:17)

As hinted here and clarified in the book of Moses, the Lord had granted unto mankind an extended probationary period of one hundred twenty years to be taught a better way and to repent in the days of Noah, "when once the long-suffering of God waited" (1 Peter 3:20), before bringing the cleansing Flood upon them.

Genesis 6:4 (Moses 8:18–21)

"Giants," Hebrew *nephilim,* "fallen ones," were "those who fell" and now caused others to fall. It seems that the apostate sons of God, who took the daughters of men to wife, boasted of their children as men of prowess, mighty men, as good as the men of old, and in their vain satisfaction in physical excellence and security they hearkened no more to spiritual teachings from Noah. Perhaps they were physically large men whose heroic deeds, or boasting of great deeds, made them appear larger than life, as it were.

Genesis 6:5 (Moses 8:22)

Man's opportunity for exercising choice, or moral agency, is impaired when only evil is before him constantly and good is not found in his society. This was the society in which Noah lived, where "every imagination of the thoughts of [man's] heart was only evil continually." The heart in the ancient world was regarded as the seat of one's will, reason, emotion, and desire. Thus, all men were thoroughly corrupt. A merciful God could not continue to send his spirit children to be born into a world such as that, where chances of degradation were much greater than the chances of exaltation. One can see that the few righteous souls of the time needed to be "saved by water" (1 Peter 3:20–21; see also 4:6.) The Lord mercifully provided means so those who would not hear the gospel, because their minds were blinded in the days of Noah, would afterwards have opportunity to hear it, that they might be judged like men who heard it in the flesh, though they could only learn to live according to God's instructions in the spirit world. On God's merciful concern for man, see also Doctrine and Covenants 133:53–54.

President John Taylor further described the reasons behind the Flood:

"I will go back to show you how the Lord operates. He destroyed a whole world at one time save a few, whom he preserved for his own special purpose. And why? He had more than one reason for doing so. This antediluvian [meaning "before the Flood"] people were not only very wicked themselves, but having the power to propagate their species, they transmitted their unrighteous natures and desires to their children, and brought them up to indulge in their own wicked practices. And the spirits that dwelt in the eternal worlds knew this, and they knew very well that to be born of such parentage would entail upon themselves an infinite amount of trouble, misery and sin. And supposing ourselves to be of the number of unborn spirits, would it not be fair to presume that we would appeal to the Lord, crying, 'Father, do you not behold the condition of this people, how corrupt and wicked they are?' Yes. 'Is it then just that we who are now pure should take of such bodies and thus subject ourselves to most bitter experiences before we can be redeemed, according to the plan of salvation?' 'No,' the Father would say, 'it is not in keeping with my justice.' 'Well, what will you do in the matter; man has his free agency and cannot be coerced, and while he lives he has the power of perpetuating his species?' 'I will first send them my word, offering them deliverance from sin, and warning them of my justice, which shall certainly overtake them if they reject it, and I will destroy them from off the face of the earth, thus preventing their increase, and I will raise up another seed.' Well, they did reject the preaching of Noah, the servant of God, who was sent to them, and consequently the Lord caused the rains of heaven to descend incessantly for forty days and nights, which flooded the land, and there being no means of escape, save for the eight souls who were obedient to the message, all the others were drowned. But, says the caviller [one who raises frivolous objections], is it right that a just God should sweep off so many people? Is that in accordance with mercy? Yes, it was just to those spirits that had not received their bodies, and it was just and merciful too to those people guilty of the iniquity. Why? Because by taking away their earthly existence he prevented them from entailing their sins upon their posterity and degenerating them, and also prevented them from committing further acts of wickedness" (*Journal of Discourses,* 19:158–59).

Genesis 6:6–7 (Moses 8:23–26)

Noah was not simply a bad-weather prophet. He knew and taught the gospel of Jesus Christ: faith, repentance, baptism, and receiving the gift of the Holy Ghost (Moses 8:24).

Understandably the wicked conditions caused the Lord to sorrow and to grieve in his heart. This is the meaning expressed awkwardly by the phrase "it repented the Lord," from a Hebrew word (*nikham*) meaning basically "to sigh," and by extension "to be sorry, moved to pity or compassion," also "to suffer grief, or repent." Moses 8:25 indicates that *Noah* felt that way.

A general, complete cleansing of all the earth was imminent, as expressed also in verses 13 and 17.

Genesis 6:8–10 (Moses 8:27)

Noah found grace, being a just man, "perfect" in his generations. "Perfect" is the translation of Hebrew *tamim,* meaning "complete, whole, having integrity"; it does not mean "without sin," as we often interpret "perfect" to mean (on the concept of perfection, see commentary at Genesis 17:1–8).

The first occurrence of the word "generations" in verse 9 is translated from *toledoth,* discussed above (5:1–3). The second occurrence is rendered from *doroto,* meaning the "cycles of his years," implying "his times" or "all through his life."

Genesis 6:11–13 (Moses 8:28–30)

In contrast to Noah, the world around him was "corrupt," meaning both in English and Hebrew "low," "debased," "degraded." Recalling that the work and glory of God is "to bring to pass the immortality and eternal life" (Moses 1:39), or exaltation of man, it is a tragedy that many people responded only to the sensual and devilish, resisted regeneration, and suffered degradation to a state inferior to their starting status in mortality. It is so today.

Of the conditions at his Second Coming, Jesus prophesied: "As it was in the days of Noah, so it shall be also at the coming of the Son of Man" (Joseph Smith–Matthew 1:41). And how was it in the days of Noah? First of all, people did not listen to a prophet's voice, as we know from the book of Moses. They did not repent, were not baptized in the name of the Son of God, and did not have the gift of the Holy Ghost.

The great Flood was a direct consequence of these omissions, something the King James Bible does not make clear but the Joseph Smith Translation does (see Moses 8:24).

Second, without the benefit of spiritual renewal that proceeds from the first principles and ordinances of the gospel, the people of Noah's era degenerated into a horrible condition which was the exact opposite of peace and prosperity. As Joseph Smith's inspired revision of the biblical text states: "And it came to pass that Noah continued his preaching unto the people, saying: Hearken, and give heed unto my words; . . . The earth was corrupt before God, and it was *filled with violence*. And God looked upon the earth, and, behold, it was corrupt, for all flesh had corrupted its way upon the earth. And God said unto Noah: The end of all flesh is come before me, for the earth is *filled with violence,* and behold I will destroy all flesh from off the earth" (Moses 8:23, 28–30; emphasis added).

Apparently, this same condition is developing in the last days, which presents us with an interesting parallel. Noah came before the Flood, a time of destruction of all the earth's inhabitants which served as the earth's baptism by water; Joseph Smith came before the Fire, a second time of destruction of all the wicked which will be the earth's baptism by fire. Conditions are very much the same in the two parallel times—corrupt and filled with violence. Does that mean it will be impossible to live a good, wholesome life during the era before the Second Coming? We do not know how difficult life will be for the Saints during those years, but we do know that it will be possible to remain faithful. Moses 8:27 says, "Noah found grace in the eyes of the Lord; for Noah was a just man, and perfect in his generation; and he walked with God, as did also his three sons," as will all faithful sons and daughters of God in these last days.

With verse 13, Joseph Smith's revision of the text of Genesis as recorded in the book of Moses ends. Genesis 1:1 through 6:13 totals 151 verses; the parallel material in Moses chapters 2–8 totals 314 verses. We gratefully acknowledge the additional light and knowledge, especially about Enoch and his mission, provided by the Lord through the Prophet Joseph Smith. Further changes in the text of the Bible are now noted as Joseph Smith Translation entries at the foot of the page, with longer passages in the Appendix at the end of the Bible.

Genesis 6:14–22

A very large, three-storied barge was needed to preserve pairs of the unclean beasts, which were unsuited for food or for sacrifice, and groups of seven of the clean beasts and birds, as well as food for them and for Noah and his family. The barge, or ark, was made of gopher wood, a water-resistant wood. *Gopher* is a Hebrew word occurring only here in the Bible; it may be related to, or written by mistake for, *kopher,* which means "pitch" (or asphalt, tar, or bitumen), a word which occurs twice in the same verse.

Accepting the standard measure for the "cubit" in Old Testament times as approximately 18 inches, the ark was 450 feet long, 75 feet wide, and 45 feet high. It is estimated that such a giant carrier would have had an interior of about 1,500,000 cubic feet. Its construction was certainly a miraculous feat of engineering, possible only with divine help.

Verse 16 mentions a "window" in the ark, but read the curious footnote for 16*a.* Some translations render the Hebrew *tsohar* as "light." According to one Jewish source, this "window" could refer to "a precious stone which illuminated the whole interior of the Ark" (Hertz, *Pentateuch,* 26–27). Compare Ether 2:23–24 and 3:1, 4. Light and ventilation would of course be requisite in a vessel "tight like unto a dish, . . . tight like unto the ark of Noah" (Ether 6:7), as the Book of Mormon describes both the ark and the Jaredite vessels. Light-bearing stones may have been the sources of light for both Noah's ark and the Jaredite barges.

In verse 18 the Lord promises that he would establish his covenant with Noah, a "second Adam." Though we often call the great covenant relationship we have with the Lord the

Abrahamic covenant, it is good to remember that the same covenant was first established with Adam, Enoch, and Noah (see JST Genesis 8:23).

Genesis 7:1–24

We feel for Noah and his wife: they had to leave children and grandchildren outside the ark. Note the facts concerning the time periods involved. The day, month, and year of Noah's life when they entered the ark are given. The duration of the rains from above and the flow from the deep underground sources are mentioned (v. 11), as are the time of floating, the duration of recession of the waters, and the date of disembarkation (Genesis 8:13–14). For a year and ten days they were confined in the ark.

"Prevailed" in verse 19 is translated from a Hebrew word that means "increased." Verse 20 may mean that the water increased to a depth of fifteen cubits (about twenty-two feet) above the mountaintops. It is apparent from Ether 13:2 that the Flood was not just a local phenomenon but covered all of the earth's lands. The Flood, as the earth's baptism by water, was a complete immersion. Elder Mark E. Petersen, an apostle during the last half of the twentieth century, wrote:

"The flood had a far greater purpose than merely to wipe out Noah's neighbors. God baptized the earth! He would not baptize a portion of it any more than we would be satisfied with a partial immersion if we were baptizing some person.

" . . . He baptized the earth by His own almighty power, for His own purposes, and the destruction of the wicked was only incidental thereto. And He will yet baptize it with fire, according to the baptismal pattern for us all" (*Noah and the Flood*, 61).

President Joseph Fielding Smith explained that "the flood could *not* have been a *local flood* as some wish us to believe. . . . *It was the baptism of the earth, and that had to be by immersion.* . . . [In the beginning] this earth was born in water. Before the land appeared the whole sphere was covered with water. [Then, with the flood of Noah, it was *born again*]" (*Doctrines of Salvation*, 2:319–20, 324).

Many commentators have cited substantial evidence that there was a flood such as here described, but they have also frankly admitted that all the facts known are not yet sufficient to give a complete and understandable picture of the cataclysm. The problems are not such as to impugn the credibility of the account of the event, however. Both the Savior and latter-day revelation treat the Flood as a real occurrence (Matthew 24:39; Luke 17:26; Moses 7:34, 43, 50; 8:17). In the mouth of two or three witnesses will every word be established: the Book of Mormon also attests the Flood with another three witnesses: Alma 10:22; 3 Nephi 22:9; and Ether 6:7; 13:2. Latter-day prophets and apostles have described the great Flood theologically as the baptism of the earth. President Joseph Fielding Smith was one (see *Doctrines of Salvation* 2:321–22); Elder Bruce R. McConkie was another (see *Mormon Doctrine*, 289). The Prophet Joseph Smith himself stated: "Noah was born to save seed of everything, when the earth was washed of its wickedness by the flood" (*History of the Church*, 1:283). The earth is a living entity, and Enoch had heard Mother Earth yearn for a cleansing of "the filthiness which is gone forth out of me" (Moses 7:48). The Flood removed that filthiness or wickedness, just as baptism removes sin from human beings.

Genesis 8:1–19

God remembered Noah and everything with him in the ark (v. 1), implying that the patriarch's condition was never removed from the thoughts of Deity and that Noah was never left solely responsible for caring for the life in the ark.

Verse 4 mentions the "mountains [plural] of Ararat," or possibly the Ararat range as the ark's resting place. Today's Mount Ararat on the border of Turkey and Armenia is an extinct volcano which rises to about 17,000 feet. This may or may not be the same place that Noah's ark came to rest, since at the time of the Flood, the earth's land mass had not yet been completely divided (see Genesis 10:25) and antediluvian (pre-Flood) sites were in a different geographical configuration.

Genesis 8:20–22

Noah was quick to build an altar, in Hebrew *mizbeakh*, which means "place of sacrifice." By means of a sacrifice, Noah expressed his gratitude for salvation, and the Lord made a promise that the ground would not again be cursed, and the seasons would not cease while earth existed. This is an ancient example of the principle reiterated in modern times that the Lord accepts or honors those who are willing to observe their covenants by sacrifice (D&C 97:8). In verse 22 we see the first reference to seasons of the year occurring after the Flood.

Genesis 9:1–4

The first commandment given to Adam is repeated: be fruitful, multiply, and fill the earth. Like Adam, Noah was given "dominion" over all things. He was told that man may eat meat as well as vegetable foods—though the blood is forbidden (compare our provisions and restrictions; D&C 49:19; 59:18–19). In the Joseph Smith Translation, Genesis 9:11 gives pointed instruction to avoid wanton killing of animals: "Blood shall not be shed, only for meat, to save your lives; and the blood of every beast will I require at your hands."

Genesis 9:5–7

Possibly because of rampant violence and bloodshed before the Flood, special warnings were issued to Noah's descendants against murder, and the principle of capital punishment for murder was established. The Church of Jesus Christ of Latter-day Saints accepts capital punishment when it is administered in accordance with established laws of the land. In 1890 the First Presidency made the following statement:

"We solemnly make the following declarations, viz:

"That this Church views the shedding of human blood with the utmost abhorrence. That we regard the killing of human beings, except in conformity with the civil law, as a capital crime which should be punished by shedding the blood of the criminal, after a public trial before a legally constituted court of the land . . .

"The revelations of God to this Church make death the penalty for capital crime, and require that offenders against life and property shall be delivered up to and tried by the laws of the land" (First Presidency [Wilford Woodruff, George Q. Cannon, and Joseph F. Smith] in *Millennial Star* (Jan. 1890): 33–34; emphasis added; see also *Encyclopedia of Mormonism,* "Capital Punishment," 1:255). In recent years, as the Church has expanded across many countries in the world, it has reiterated its support of civil authorities to determine their stance on the issue of capital punishment: The Church regards the question of whether and in what circumstances the state should impose capital punishment as a matter to be decided solely by the prescribed processes of civil law.

It is possible that Noah was commanded not to eat blood to emphasize the seriousness of taking life. Such a principle is emphasized in another way in our dispensation (D&C 49:18, 21).

There is something about blood that is symbolic of mortality, as we shall see later in the Mosaic laws about sacrifice involving blood offerings. Ultimately, blood symbolizes and points to Him whose blood was shed to atone for all sin, sorrow, and suffering (Hebrews 9:12–15, 22–28; 10:1–20).

Genesis 9:8–17

Lest men should later seek only to avoid punishment rather than to attain righteousness, God gave reassurances that floods would never again be his instrument of cleansing the earth (see also Moses 7:50–52). The rainbow, whether then created or simply adopted as the sign of the covenant at that time, was made the sign of God's promise. Regarding the involvement of the rainbow at the second coming of Jesus Christ, the Prophet Joseph Smith revealed: "I have asked of the Lord concerning His coming; and while asking the Lord, He gave a sign and said, 'In the days of Noah I set a bow in the heavens as a sign and token that in any year that the bow should be seen the Lord would not come; but there should be seed time and harvest during that year: but whenever you see the bow withdrawn, it shall be a token that there shall be famine, pestilence, and great distress among the nations, and that the coming of the Messiah is not far distant'" (*Joseph Smith* [manual], 252).

A few centuries later, however, the promise was forgotten, or not trusted, by a cult who built the tower of Babel in order that they might not perish in another flood (see commentary at Genesis 11:1–9). The earth will indeed be cleansed again but not by water. Next time it will be a baptism of fire: Malachi 4:1; Doctrine and Covenants 29:9; 64:23–24; 133:64.

In Genesis 9 and in corresponding Joseph Smith Translation passages the covenant is iterated and reiterated numerous times. God renews the covenant with his children through every prophet heading every dispensation of the gospel. It is a *new* and everlasting covenant because it is *renewed* in every dispensation, though in this final dispensation it has been renewed to remain on this sphere forever—ultimately and finally *everlasting*.

Genesis 9:18–27

The sons of Noah, first mentioned in 5:32, are here mentioned as the forefathers of all who inhabit the earth (see Moses 8:12 concerning the birth order of Noah's sons). Japheth was forty-two years older than Shem, and Shem eight years older than Ham. Just what Ham did to cause a restriction of his priesthood privileges is not made clear in the incident of the garment. Later, one of his descendants, through his daughter, Egyptus, laid claim to authority through Ham's "right" to the priesthood, but he could not hold it. As to the spiritual reasons for such a restriction, see Alma 13:3–7. For ancient legends about the violation Ham committed to merit such punishment, see commentary at Genesis 3:21. The mother of Egypt was the Canaanite wife of Ham, who came through the time of the Flood on the ark, thus preserving the blood of the antediluvian Canaanites, according to Abraham 1:21–22, 27 (see also Nibley, *Lehi in the Desert and The World of the Jaredites*, 160–64). The episode needs more authoritative explanation to be intelligible.

Genesis 9:28–29

Note the length of Noah's life. If the chronology proposed by Irish archbishop James Ussher were correct, Noah would have lived long enough to overlap Abraham's life by several decades. Ussher's chronology tries to establish a history of the world from a close literal reading of the Bible, but the chronology cannot be substantiated. After Noah's time, however, men were said to have lived only about half as long as before the Flood, and after the Babel episode life spans were again cut in half. We do not have any definitive answers to questions about the very long life spans of those who lived during the first two millennia of earth's history and the much shorter life span for all of us who come afterwards, though the Jewish historian Josephus did propose some curious explanations for the phenomenon. He wrote:

"Let no one, upon comparing the lives of the ancients with our lives, and with the few years which we now live, think that what we have said of them is false; or make the shortness of our lives at present an argument that neither did they attain to so long a duration of life; for those ancients were beloved of God . . . and because their food was then fitter for the promulgation of life . . . and besides, God afforded them a longer time of life on account of their virtue and the good use they made of it in astronomical and geometrical discoveries. . . . Now I have for witnesses to what I have said all those that have written Antiquities . . . that the ancients lived a thousand years" (*Antiquities of the Jews*, bk. 1, chap. 3, para. 9).

Before leaving our discussion of Noah and his times, we

should emphasize that this great prophet—under his mortal name, Noah, and under his alternate name, Gabriel (Hebrew, *gever*, meaning "man," and *El* meaning "God," thus "man of God")—has through the ages appeared as an angelic messenger to Daniel and prophesied to him of the Messiah (Daniel 9:21ff), to Zacharias (Luke 1:11–19), to Mary (Luke 1:26–38), and likely to Joseph (Matthew 1:19–25), and even, according to other faith traditions, to Saint Jerome in Bethlehem and to Muhammad near Mecca.

Genesis 10:1–5

This chapter is commonly called the Table of Nations because of its description of the many different peoples who descended from the three sons of Noah and their wives: the three basic branches of Japhetic (Indo-European and possibly Asian), Hamitic (African and some Levantine), and Semitic peoples. The terms *Japhetic*, *Hamitic*, and *Semitic* are derived directly from the names of Noah's sons and appear in scholarly writings by the end of the eighteenth century.

The descendants of Japheth are called "Gentiles" in verse 5, but the Hebrew word is *goyim*, which means simply "peoples" or "nations." Indeed, the same word is rendered as "nations" at the end of the same verse. Names of some of these Japhetic peoples, who resided *northward* from the land of Canaan, are mentioned by the prophet Ezekiel as being among those who will come against Israel in the last days, after the gathering of Israel; they will be led by Gog, chief prince of the land of Magog, and his associates (Ezekiel 38).

Following are other possible identification of lands:
Madai: Media, land of the Medes
Javan: Greece
Kittim: island of Cyprus
Dodanim, or Rodanim: island of Rhodes

Genesis 10:6–20

The descendants of Ham, those who resided *southward,* are listed commencing with his four sons: Cush (Ethiopia),

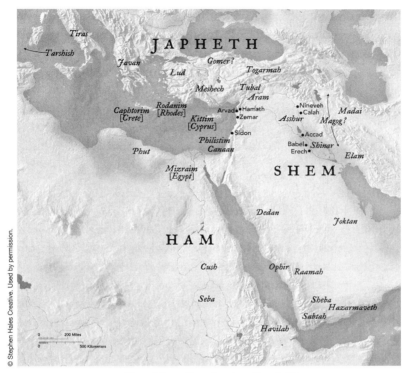

Map of the nations, based on Genesis 10

Mizraim (Egypt; the word has a dual meaning, referring to the two parts, Upper and Lower Egypt), Phut (Libya) and Canaan. Additional details about the names of the nations derived from each of the three sons of Noah may be found in Josephus, *Antiquities of the Jews,* bk. 1, chaps. 4–6.

Nimrod was from the family of Cush. Genesis 10:5 in the Joseph Smith Translation says he was a "mighty hunter *in the land.*" In the next chapter, he appears as the leader in the building of the tower of Babel in his kingdom in the land of Shinar. He is also mentioned in Ether 2:1. Babel, Erech, and Accad are otherwise known as Babylon, Erech or Uruk, and Akkad.

Notice also the many tribes of the Canaanite peoples (vv. 14–18); most of these names will appear from time to time in the history of the interaction of Israelites with their neighbors in the remainder of the Old Testament. Recall that the name Canaan was apparently preserved from the name of the rebellious people before the Flood who would not hearken to Enoch, according to the book of Moses. This was the blood line of the descendants of the wife of Ham (see Abraham 1:21–22; Moses 7:6–8). In the book of Moses, carefully distinguish between the righteous people of Cainan (Moses 6:18–19, 41ff) and the rebels of Canaan.

Genesis 10:21–32

The biblical account deals mostly with the descendants of Shem, who resided *eastward*. The descendants of Shem are the Shemites, or Semites, and the descendants of Shem's great-grandson Eber (or Heber) are called "Hebrews" (perhaps from the Hebrew verb *'avar,* "to cross or traverse").

Of the three major divisions of descendants of Noah's family, the lands of the Semites are best known to students of the scriptures because they include the writers of the Bible and the Book of Mormon. Elam is the region of southwest Persia, or southwest Iran. Asshur represents Assyria, and Aram is the Hebrew name for the Greek Mesopotamia.

A son of Eber was named Peleg (v. 25), whose Hebrew name means "division." In his day the one, great landmass was divided into separate continents. From scripture given in modern times, we know that the continents will one day return to the conditions that existed in the earth "before it was divided" (D&C 133:24; see also Topical Guide, "Earth, Dividing of").

President Joseph Fielding Smith wrote: "There can be no question to contradict the fact that during the flood great changes were made on the face of the earth. The land surface was in the process of division into continents.

"The dividing of the earth was not an act of division by the inhabitants of the earth by tribes and peoples, but a breaking asunder of the continents, thus dividing the land surface and creating the Eastern Hemisphere and Western Hemisphere. . . . Of course, there have been many changes on the earth's surface since the beginning. We are informed by revelation that the time will come when this condition will be changed and that the land surface of the earth will come back as it was in the beginning and all be in one place" (*Answers to Gospel Questions* 2:94; 5:73–74).

Elder Bruce R. McConkie further explained: "It is an interesting speculative enterprise to look at a map or a globe of the world and to wonder how, with modest adjustments involving the rising and sinking of various areas of the earth, the continents and islands might fit back together again. There is much to indicate they once were joined and would easily fit back in their former positions" (*Millennial Messiah*, 623).

"When the Millennium is ushered in, there will be a new heaven and a new earth. It will be renewed and will receive again its paradisiacal glory. The islands and continents will come together again, and there will be one land mass, as it was in the days before it was divided. It will become a terrestrial sphere. As it was baptized in water in the days of Noah, so it shall be baptized by fire in the day of the Lord Jesus Christ" (*Millennial Messiah*, 356–57).

According to verse 32, from these forefathers—Shem, Ham, and Japheth—proceeded all the nations of the earth after the Flood.

Genesis 11:1–9

According to Genesis 10:8–10 and the writings of Josephus about Babel, this tower to heaven was a project of Nimrod's people. The generalization is made that "the whole earth was of one language" and that as a result of this ill-conceived building project "the Lord did confound the language of all the earth." Just how and why all nations would be affected by the event in Babel is not made clear. One family that did not suffer the confounding of language is introduced in the Book of Mormon, in the book of Ether. Some interesting statements about the language, its preservation, and its superiority to other languages may be seen in Ether 1:33–37; 3:22–28, and 12:24–25. We might wish the book of Ether preserved more details, but Moroni says he did not include the history from the beginning to the great tower because at his time it was available in the records "among the Jews" (Ether 1:3).

The promise from God that the earth would not be destroyed by water again was at this time either forgotten, unknown, or mistrusted, for Nimrod "gradually changed the government into tyranny,—seeing no other way of turning men from the fear of God, but to bring them into a constant dependence on his power. He also said he would be revenged on God, if he should have a mind to drown the world again; for that he would build a tower too high for the waters to be able to reach! and that he would avenge himself on God for destroying their forefathers!" (Josephus, *Antiquities,* bk. 1, chap. 4, para. 2).

The name "Babel" evidently was taken by the ancient writers to mean "confusion," according to verse 9. Popular etymology derives the name from the root *balal,* meaning to "mingle, mix, confound." Others have seen it as a boastful name, "Gate of God," from *bab* ("gate") and *el* ("God"). From this point in history, over four thousand individual languages have developed from one hundred language families. It is probable that the tower of Babel is to be identified with one of the many step-pyramids built in ancient Mesopotamia (modern Syria and Iraq). These step-pyramids had a shrine or holy place on top and were called ziggurats (from Akkadian, *zaqaru,* "to build on a platform"), the remnants of which can be seen today. Ancient Mesopotamian city-states were dominated by temple complexes, each with one or more ziggurats, or false temples, dedicated to a particular deity. The step design made it easier, in the popular mind, for the gods to descend from heaven. Mesopotamian ziggurats were given names that reflected their purpose and function as staircases to and from heaven, names such as the House of the Link between Heaven and Earth (found at Larsa); the House of the Mountain of the Universe (at Asshur); and the House of the Foundation Platform of Heaven and Earth (at Babylon) (see *NIV Archaeological Study Bible,* 20, note for Genesis 11:4). Little wonder that the city-state of Babylon itself was given its name (Akkadian, *bab-ili,* "gate of the gods").

Genesis 11:10–26

Some added details are mentioned in this repetition and extension of the lineage of Shem.

Genesis 11:27–32

The next major character introduced is Abram, whose name was later expanded to Abraham. Abram's ancestry has been briefly traced by a few chapters covering two thousand years to this point, and whose descendants will be presented in more detail in all of the rest of the Old Testament, covering a period of another fifteen hundred years. Abraham's seed became the writers and major characters of the rest of the Old Testament, the New Testament, the Book of Mormon, the Doctrine and Covenants, and the Pearl of Great Price. All of these scriptures contain history, doctrine, and prophecy of the missions of Abraham and his seed. Included among them is the central figure of all time, Jesus of Nazareth, the Messiah and Redeemer.

Abram's father was Terah, and his two brothers were Haran and Nahor. Haran died, and his daughter, Milcah, became the wife of Abram's other brother, Nahor (Abraham 2:1–2). The first stage of the migration of Abram's family, including Terah, took them from Ur to Haran, in what later became known as Aram, or Syria. There the great call of Abraham came, and his significant life story unfolded.

Notice on Bible Map 9 the many hundreds of miles Abraham journeyed from Mesopotamia to Egypt. He did not go directly west across the great Arabian Desert but north and then south along what is now known as the Fertile Crescent, staying near sources of water. The traditional route has

Abraham leaving his hometown, Ur of the Chaldees, traveling northward parallel with the Euphrates River to Haran in the land of Padan-aram, later turning south past Damascus, through Canaan, across northern Sinai, into Egypt, and then back to Canaan.

There has been some academic debate as to the location of Ur of the Chaldees. Incidentally, the name Chaldees, Hebrew *kasdim,* begins with "ch" as it is spelled in English but is always pronounced as a hard "k". Some have sought the city in southern Mesopotamia and some in northern Mesopotamia, today's southeastern Turkey (for the north, see, for example, Gordon, *Biblical Archaeology Review,* June 1977, 20–21, 52; Hoskisson, *Ensign,* July 1991, 62–63; for the south, see Millard, *Biblical Archaeology Review,* May/June 2001, 52–53, 57; Selman, in Harrison, *Major Cities,* 275ff). For the time being, our conclusion regarding the whereabouts of biblical Ur must be "we don't know."

As we begin our study of the life and ministry of our father Abraham, we emphasize the honor and significance attached to his name in scriptures written hundreds and even thousands of years after his lifetime. For instance, two thousand years later, some people in Jesus' time thought it sufficient for their salvation that they were merely "descendants of Abraham" (Luke 3:7–8). When Jesus accused some Jewish leaders of doing evil works of their "father," the devil, they remonstrated with hurt pride, "Abraham is our father!" To this Jesus replied, "If ye were Abraham's children, ye would do the works of Abraham" (John 8:31–40). Matthew's genealogy of Jesus Christ begins with David and goes back immediately to Abraham to make sure everyone understood his rightful claim to be the Messiah. In Paul's day, Abraham was remembered as the "father of the faithful," and in fact all who had faith in Christ, whether they were originally Gentiles or otherwise, were counted as "Abraham's seed" and heirs to his promises (Galatians 3:7–9, 29). A modern prophet, eighteen hundred years after Paul, echoed the same message (D&C 84:33–34;

103:16–17; 109:62–67; 132:30–31). In addition, James 2:23 calls Abraham the "Friend of God," as does Islamic tradition (Arabic, *khalilullah*), sometimes just *el-Khalil,* the Friend.

The man we know as Abraham was first known as Abram; his wife, Sarah, was formerly known as Sarai. We shall soon consider the occasion and the reason for the name changes.

There are very few comments about Isaac in other scriptures, but some of these are quite significant. He is included, for instance, as an exemplar of faith in a brief overview of noteworthy patriarchs in Hebrews 11:17–19. First Nephi 17:40 recalls the fact that the Lord covenanted with Isaac. Doctrine and Covenants 133:55 lists him among the worthy ones in the presence of the Lamb of God. Jesus (as recorded in Matthew 22:32) mentions in his day that Abraham, Isaac, and Jacob were still "living" and not "dead," hundreds of years after their mortal life was over.

During our study of the Patriarchs you may want to consult the following entries in the Bible Dictionary: "Melchizedek"; "Abraham"; "Abraham, covenant of"; "Circumcision"; "Birthright"; "Firstborn"; "Patriarch"; "Tithe"; "Jacob"; "Israel"; "Angels"; "Esau"; see also articles on Melchizedek and Abraham in the *Encyclopedia of Mormonism.*

Genesis 12:1–3

Abraham 1:16–19 and 2:6–11 greatly enhance the concept in the Bible of the call of Abraham. They clearly tell what Abraham was to do for the Lord and for the people of the world in teaching about the true and living God and making known the benefits of administering his power that all might attain salvation. But note that Abraham instigated the process by which the Lord bestowed great blessings and power. He actively sought peace, righteousness, sacred knowledge, the blessings of the faithful fathers, and the right to administer those blessings. He had become a high priest (Abraham 1:2). He had been promised a new homeland and had been called on a

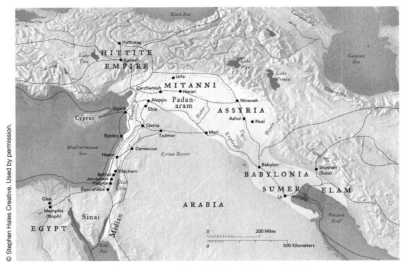

The ancient world at the time of the patriarchs

mission. He, and his righteous posterity, would bring blessings to all the families of the earth (Abraham 1:19; 2:6, 9–11).

Abraham came from a "less active" home. His "fathers" had turned from righteousness, had set their hearts to do evil, and had even sunk so low as to offer their children as human sacrifices. Abraham himself was almost killed upon an altar dedicated to the false gods of the region (Abraham 1:5, 7, 12–15). His life shows us how each of us can be determined to be faithful, regardless of environment and circumstance. Abraham 1:1–2 and 2:1–2 explain in some detail why he was willing, even desirous, to leave his homeland of Chaldea. The rest of Abraham, chapters 1 and 2, gives us an amplified account of what Abraham learned about God's great covenant and what he learned and experienced in Egypt.

Genesis 12:4–9

Abram left Haran with "the souls that they had gotten," or converted to the Lord. Abraham 2:15–16 confirms that the patriarch's covenant with God was one of missionary work. He worked to "win" souls for the Lord, and "eternity" was his "covering" and his "rock"—his assurance that his effort was worth it. The terms *covering* and *rock* are pregnant with divine meaning as they relate to the Atonement (Hebrew, *kippur*, "covering") of him who is the Rock of our salvation.

When Abram and his followers arrived in the promised land and the Lord appeared to confirm the promise, he offered a sacrifice to show his gratitude to God for his blessings. He regularly built such altars and called upon the name of the Lord wherever he went; for example, in Sichem (Shechem) and on a hill between Bethel and Hai (later called Ai in the conquest narrative). He continued journeying "toward the south" (v. 9; Hebrew, "toward the Negev").

Genesis 12:10–20

When famine forced Abram's group to go to Egypt for a time, he asked his wife to identify herself to the Egyptians by their blood relationship rather than their marital status (see Abraham 2:22–25). He did that because the Lord thus instructed him, and he was strictly obedient—as the Prophet Joseph Smith would later explain: "I made this my rule: *When the Lord commands, do it*" (*History of the Church*, 2:170), and "whatever God requires is right, no matter what it is, although we may not see the reason thereof till long after the events transpire" (*History of the Church*, 5:135).

Concerning their actual blood relationship, whereby she was called his "sister," see again Abraham 2:2, in connection with Genesis 11:29 and 12:5. Notice also that in Genesis 13:8, Abram spoke of his nephew Lot as his "brother." One reason for this terminology is the lack of early Hebrew words for "nephew," "niece," "granddaughter," etc. Sarai was the granddaughter of Terah but was called his "daughter" and would have been called the "daughter" of any of her more distant ancestors. Besides, Haran (Sarai's father) had died, so Terah took Sarai into his family, and she became a "sister" to Abram. Thus Abram says truly according to their idiom "and yet indeed she is my sister; she is the daughter of my father, but not the daughter of my mother; and she became my wife" (Genesis 20:12).

Eventually, Pharaoh, after taking Sarai to be included in his harem, learned from a divine communication that she was also Abram's wife and restored her. Why did he not punish Abram, or kill him, as Abram originally feared he might? (Genesis 12:12). What caused him to respect Abram and the God he worshiped enough to send Abram away a rich man? (see Facsimile No. 3 in the book of Abraham as to the status Abraham gained in Egypt and the evidently friendly relationship between him and Pharaoh).

It is important to note that the Lord was with Abraham in *all* that he did. Before he went down to Egypt the Lord gave him a powerful vision of the universe and the eternal nature of spirits so that he could "declare all the words" of the Lord to those descendants of Noah who could not hold the priesthood yet desired to understand the truths of eternity (Abraham 3:15).

Genesis 13:1–18

The story of Abram's clan settling in their promised land tells something about the character of Abram and of Lot, especially when a conflict arose between the herders of their many flocks. Verse 10 gives a hint about why Lot went to the region of Sodom to live.

It appears that the Lord again gave recognition to Abram's generosity and reassured and rewarded him. The locations of Bethel and Hebron are on Bible Map 10. The name Bethel in Hebrew literally means "house or place of God." It is both striking and revealing to note how many times Abraham built an altar and worshiped God. In this regard, Abraham and Lot present a telling contrast: the first thing Abraham did after arriving in his new area was build an altar; the first thing Lot did was pitch his tent toward Sodom.

An important Joseph Smith Translation addition is found in verse 14. God reminded Abraham of the everlasting covenant he had made, and in so doing solidified the patriarch's link with the great seer Enoch.

Genesis 14:1–12

One of the crucial decisions in the lives of two contemporaries, Lot and Melchizedek, was their selection of where to live. Lot "pitched his tent toward Sodom" (Genesis 13:12), and later "dwelt in Sodom" (Genesis 14:12). That decision cost him his family. Lot had apparently made the decision based on the attractive nature of the properties down in the Jordan Valley: "it was well watered every where . . . even as the garden of the Lord" (Genesis 13:10). Melchizedek, on the other hand, lived with his people up in the top of the hill country in a city called "Peace" (Salem, which was later called Jerusalem).

This is a significant contrast between the two men. Lot chose to live at the bottom of the world (the Jordan Rift Valley around the Dead Sea is literally the lowest spot on earth), while Melchizedek chose to live up in the highest part of the land with his people who eventually became righteous enough to be translated from the earth (see JST Genesis 14:34). Lot, along with his wife and children, were subjected to the lowest kind of life, in Sodom, while Melchizedek, along with his wife and children, as we suppose, lived on higher ground and enjoyed the blessings of being closer to God, physically and spiritually, likely enjoying the highest blessings available to God's children on earth, in the holy sanctuary, or Temple, in Salem (see Galbraith, Ogden, and Skinner, *Jerusalem*, 30–31, 36).

The lesson seems clear: choose the higher ground to avoid evil. Don't pitch your tent *toward* Sodom—don't even approach the evil. Lot's daughters later committed gross immorality (Genesis 19:30–36). And when did they learn that kind of behavior? Probably when their father pitched his tent toward Sodom.

Genesis 14:13–16

After Lot's capture in the Rift Valley near the Dead Sea, Abram took immediate action to save Lot and his family and possessions, showing little concern for his own safety. Why did he do so? You might be surprised to read in verse 14 that Abram had 318 trained servants on his estate that he could arm for battle. The Septuagint (the Greek Old Testament) uses the word *basileus* in referring to Abram, which means "king," "prince," or "commander." We probably have more to learn about this great man (interestingly, Enoch, Mormon, and Joseph Smith were also military commanders).

Notice that Abram is here the first one to be called "the Hebrew." Refer back to commentary at Genesis 10:21–32 for the possible origin of that term.

A geographical detail appears in verses 14–15: Abram and those under his command pursued their enemies to Dan (later known as the northernmost Israelite town in their promised land) and on to Hobah, which is on the "left hand" of Damascus. All directions in the Bible are given as if a person is facing east, so the "left hand" would be *north* of Damascus.

Genesis 14:17, 21–24

Look for two or three additional indications of Abram's character in the things he did in the process of rescuing and returning with Lot and the other captives, along with the booty, and in his refusing any rewards from the king of Sodom.

Genesis 14:18–20

Melchizedek "brought forth bread and wine," being "a priest of the most high God." Later, in Moses' time, bread and wine became important elements in the ceremonial feast of the Passover; and in the New Testament we learn that Jesus, in partaking of the last Passover with his apostles, adopted the Passover bread and wine as symbols of his own atoning sacrifice. Elder Bruce R. McConkie stated that with Melchizedek and Abraham the ordinance of the sacrament was "prefigured, some two thousand years before its formal institution among men" (*Promised Messiah*, 384).

Note that King Melchizedek of Salem, later to be known

as Jerusalem (see Psalm 76:2), blessed Abram. Modern revelation indicates that Abram at some time in his life received the high priesthood from Melchizedek. It was likely earlier than this event, however, according to Abraham 1:1–4 (see D&C 84:14 concerning the priesthood given to Abraham).

The king of Salem was "king of righteousness" (the literal meaning of *Melchizedek*), while the king of Sodom was king of wickedness. For more information about Melchizedek, who was called a "prince of peace," "king of Salem," "great high priest," etc., see Hebrews 7 (and JST Hebrews 7:3 in the Bible Appendix) and Alma 13:14–19 in the Book of Mormon. Of this extraordinary person it is written that "there were many before him, and also there were many afterwards, *but none were greater*" (Alma 13:19; emphasis added). The greatest power in the universe came to be called by the name of Melchizedek (for how this came about, read D&C 107:2–4). On his role as "the keeper of the storehouse of God" and the translation of Melchizedek and his people to join the city of Enoch, see Joseph Smith Translation Genesis 14:25–40 in the Bible Appendix. The Prophet Joseph Smith added remarkable new knowledge about Melchizedek; to the four verses in Genesis 14 he added sixteen verses (see more about Melchizedek in the commentary at Genesis 22:1–19).

Abram paid tithes (one-tenth of his possessions) to Melchizedek. This is the first biblical mention of tithing, a law which is still observed in God's kingdom on earth.

The parallels between Melchizedek and Jesus Christ are pronounced: both were called a "Prince of Peace;" both were "Kings of Righteousness;" both were "Prophet, Priest, and King;" both administered a sacramental meal; both had the higher priesthood named after them. In addition, the Prophet Joseph Smith said that Melchizedek held "the key and the power of endless life" (*History of the Church*, 5:555), which is the power the Savior made possible. There is no question that Melchizedek was a similitude, type, and foreshadowing of Jesus the Messiah.

Genesis 15:1–6

After eighty-five years of life, Abram was wondering about the promised progeny and whether in compliance with the custom of his times his chief steward, Eliezer of Damascus, would have to become his heir. Since Eliezer was from a city between Haran and the land of Canaan, it may be that he was another of those "souls he had won" referred to above (Genesis 12:4–9).

In response to Abram's inquiry, the Lord assured him again that a son begotten of his own body would be his heir. He believed the Lord, and this faith was "counted to him for righteousness" (see JST Genesis 15:9–12 in the Bible Appendix; compare Galatians 3:6).

Genesis 15:7–21

In answer to Abram's desire for confirmation of a "land of promise" for his descendants, he was instructed to offer an unusual sacrifice of three animals, two of them female, and one male, each three years old—and in addition a turtledove and a pigeon. The reasons for this selection and the unusual manner of sacrificing them have not been revealed to us, although the number three can signify completeness or perfection, as well as the Godhead.

A prophetic promise was then given pertaining to the descendants of Abram (through his future grandson, Jacob, or Israel) concerning their sojourn in Egypt. Not only is the duration specified but also the reasons for the delay in a foreign land, under conditions of affliction, until the time for their eventual inheritance of the land. As to who received the blessing and privilege of living in a "land of promise," then or now, see Leviticus 18:28; Deuteronomy 4:25–27; 1 Nephi 17:33–35; and Ether 2:7–10, which pertains to the Western Hemisphere.

You may notice in reading these passages that the Genesis account indicates that "the iniquity of the Amorites [was] not yet full" (15:16), but later, in the days of Moses, the "people had rejected every word of God, and they were ripe in iniquity" (1 Nephi 17:35). Scripture and archaeology testify of the total depravity of the Amorites and Canaanites inhabiting the land; with all their adultery, incest, homosexuality, and sodomy, they had polluted the land (see summary in Leviticus 18:27). The Lord always gives plenty of warning; then, if people do not obey God, they will be removed. "And it is not until the fulness of iniquity among the children of the land, that they are swept off" (Ether 2:10).

Incidentally, in verse 15 we see a curious phrase, "go to thy fathers." It is a euphemism meaning "you will die," but it also suggests, as several Jewish and Christian scholars have noted, going into the spirit world, to be with the fathers, or ancestors.

Abraham's posterity would be given a large territory as the land of their inheritance, from the "river of Egypt" (Wadi El Arish in northern Sinai; footnote 18*c*) to the river Euphrates (v. 18). This is where his posterity seem to be concentrated in the Eastern Hemisphere. Of course, his posterity through Joseph is found in the Western Hemisphere.

Genesis 16:1–3

Abram and Sarai still faced some problems: they were growing older (Genesis 12:4) and still had none of those descendants who were to be as numerous as the stars of the heavens and the sands along the seashore. Sarai consented that her husband take her handmaid also to wife (Genesis 16:3). This practice, as is known from such Near Eastern sources as the Nuzi and the Mari tablets, was not a new social invention but was quite customary. The clay tablets from these upper Mesopotamian sites reflect such marriage practices by neighboring peoples of antiquity. Doctrine and Covenants 132:34 and 65, however, give the command of the Lord as the reason for this act.

Genesis 16:4–16

Conflict and near-tragedy arose from this new union. The situation was alleviated only by the gracious intervention of the Lord. Hagar's attitude in looking upon her barren mistress as cursed, while considering herself blessed with an expected child, is understandable. It was an attitude common to those times and later too, as we shall see (for example, Genesis 30:1; 1 Samuel 1:1–7). Sarai's finding the status and relationship intolerable is also understandable. Abram gave her leave to do whatever was "good in her eyes" (as the Hebrew idiom reads), and Sarai dealt harshly with Hagar so that she fled. It is interesting that Hagar's name means "flight."

But God was concerned for the individual souls of his children, as evidenced in the attention and instructions he subsequently gave to Hagar through a divine messenger. With gratitude for what God had done, Hagar named the place "the well of him who liveth and seeth me" (Hebrew, *Beer-lahai-roi*).

Hagar received the divine promise of a numerous posterity, which promise, like that given to Jacob, or Israel, was later fulfilled in the birth of twelve "princes," or sons, to Ishmael (Genesis 25:16). The Lord also described for Hagar the future circumstances of Ishmael and his posterity: "And he will be a wild man; his hand will be against every man, and every man's hand against him; and he shall dwell in the presence of all his brethren" (Genesis 16:12; note 12*a*).

Hagar returned and bore Abram's firstborn son, Ishmael (meaning "God will hear"), when Abram was eighty-six years old. But Ishmael was not to bear the birthright; he was not the fulfillment of the Lord's original promise.

Genesis 17:1–8

A great challenge was given to Abram thirteen years later, when he was ninety-nine years of age. God appeared again, identifying himself as *El Shaddai* ("God Almighty"), and charged Abram: "Walk before me, and be thou perfect."

THE CONCEPT OF PERFECTION IN THE SCRIPTURES

Perfection even as God is perfect is the ultimate goal of every true disciple of the Lord, but here in mortality perfection does not mean to be "without sin"; there was only One without sin. The scriptural usage of the word will become apparent by examining the following five Hebrew and Greek terms, all translated "perfect" in the King James Version of the Bible:

Term	Language	Definition	Scripture Reference
shalem	Hebrew	finished, perfect, whole	1 Kings 8:61 1 Kings 15:14 2 Kings 20:3
tam	Hebrew	plain, undefiled, upright	Job 1:1
tammim	Hebrew	plain, whole, complete	Genesis 6:9; Moses 8:27 Genesis 17:1 Deuteronomy 18:13
artios	Greek	fitted, complete	2 Timothy 3:17
teleios	Greek	finished, wanting nothing necessary to completeness	Matthew 5:48 Matthew 19:21 Ephesians 4:13 James 3:2

Doctrine and Covenants 107:43 indicates also that Seth was a perfect man, as was his father, Adam. Adam, Seth, Noah, Abraham, Job, and others were certainly not perfect in the same measure as Christ, but they were pure and righteous and therefore perfect in the finite, or mortal, use of the term. One who is "perfect" as a mortal will, when he sins, immediately correct the wrongdoing, repent, return to God, and be whole, complete, or "perfect" once again.

After his salutation and stout challenge, the Lord reiterated the terms of his everlasting covenant with Abram and also gave him a new name, Abraham, signifying that kings should come of him and a multitude of peoples. But was the relationship with the Lord, often described as the Abrahamic covenant, really Abraham's covenant? After all, the Lord had established that covenant with Adam, Enoch, and Noah. Actually, the sacred covenant came to be called the Abrahamic covenant because Abraham was the father of the Hebrew peoples and was renowned for his faithfulness. There are other examples of labeling sacred doctrines, laws, ordinances, and practices after great individuals, for instance, the *Adamic* language, the Order of *Enoch*, the *Melchizedek* and *Aaronic* Priesthoods, the law of *Moses*, the Spirit of *Elijah*, the Book of *Mormon*, etc.

The covenant was sacred. God accepted each person entering the covenant as a partner, not just a subject. The covenant was available to all. The chosen people were not favored in the sense of receiving blessings and privileges exclusively theirs, but they had certain responsibilities and expectations, the fulfillment of which would bring corresponding blessings. If they accomplished the necessary service to all of humankind, they would merit the blessings, while at the same time inviting others outside the covenant people to come and join with them (be "adopted" or "grafted" in) and participate in these same blessings:

1. Become a great nation
2. Have a numerous posterity
3. Spread the blessings of God to all families of the earth
4. Enjoy the gospel and priesthood
5. Witness blessings come to those who bless, and curses to those who curse
6. Receive a land inheritance
7. Find kings among their descendants
8. The Messiah would also come as Abraham's descendant

9. Non-Hebrews could be adopted into the covenant lineage
10. The covenant would be everlasting

Genesis 17:9–14

The new sign of the covenant was to be the circumcision
of all males, performed at eight days of age, to remind them of
baptism at eight years of age (JST Genesis 17:11). Latin *circumcision* means to "cut around" and was performed on the
male organ of procreation, the portal of the seeds, whence begins the fulfillment of the sacred covenant of eternal posterity.
There is a sacred concept involved here: Hebrew *zer'a*, Greek
sperma, and Latin *semen* all mean "seed," and the promise to
Abraham—and to all the children of Abraham—is that our
seed may eventually be as numerous as the sand on the seashore or as the stars in the heaven. The blessings of exaltation include "a fulness and a continuation of *the seeds* forever
and ever" (D&C 132:19; emphasis added). For more on the
meaning and symbolism of circumcision, see Deuteronomy
10:16; 30:6; Romans 2:25–29. Interestingly, circumcision
did not originate with Abraham but was practiced by peoples
before his time. The Lord reoriented it as a symbol for his
purposes.

While baptism had been the sign of the covenant of salvation in Adam's time (Moses 6:59–66) and was also known
later in New Testament times, apparently it had fallen into
abuse and disuse, and unauthorized substitutions had sprung
up by the time of Abraham. The Lord told Abraham that
the people had not only perverted the ordinance of immersion baptism by substituting "the washing of children and
the blood of sprinkling" but had begun to view Abel's spilt
blood as an atonement for sin, thus confusing him with the
true Messiah to come in the meridian of time. On this point,
see Joseph Smith Translation Genesis 17:3–7 and 17:11–12 in
the Bible Appendix. The restoration of baptism in Abraham's
time is not mentioned but should be assumed.

Though the covenant itself was eternal, circumcision as a sign of the covenant was discontinued in New Testament times, according to Acts 15:1–28; Galatians 5:6; 6:15; Colossians 2:10–12; see also Moroni 8:8. Modern prophets and commentators explain that baptism and circumcision do not serve the same purpose (see Smith, *Teachings of the Prophet Joseph Smith*, 266, 314; Smith, *Doctrines of Salvation*, 2:323, 332–33; and Talmage, *Articles of Faith*, 121–22, 127).

Genesis 17:15–21

The name "Sarai" is somewhat difficult to translate, but the new name "Sarah" is plainly Hebrew for "princess"; the significance of it is seen in verse 16: "kings of people shall be of her."

Why did Abraham laugh when he received the renewed promise of a son to him and Sarah? Compare his response (17:17) with hers later (21:6). The meaning of the Hebrew words and the Joseph Smith Translation footnotes tell the more complete story: they *rejoiced* in it.

Ishmael and his posterity received an inheritance, but the birthright covenants and responsibilities would be perpetuated through Isaac and his posterity. Note that all sons received inheritance gifts, according to Genesis 25:6.

Genesis 17:22–27

The initiation of circumcision is recorded. Note the ages of Abraham and Ishmael; since Isaac was born one year later than the events here recorded, he would have been fourteen years younger than Ishmael.

Genesis 18:1–8

In this unique visit to Abraham, three persons brought a divine message giving Abraham and Sarah reaffirmation of the promise of a son. The nature of these "men," or "angels," who could bathe, eat, talk, walk, and so forth is probably not as mysterious as some have supposed. See the Joseph Smith Translation notes for 3*a* and 22*a* about the three men being mortals and "brethren" of Abraham. The word "angels" in Hebrew is *malakhim*, which simply means "messengers." The messages brought by these three, who were likely the presiding authorities of the Lord's kingdom then on the earth—possibly Melchizedek and his counselors—were messages directly from the Lord (see McConkie, *Doctrinal New Testament Commentary* 3:235; Sperry, *Improvement Era*, Aug. 1931, 583, 585).

In verse 4 we note the custom of hospitality known as the washing of the feet. Jesus later transformed this custom into a sacred ordinance (see JST John 13:10; McConkie, *Doctrinal New Testament Commentary*, 1:708).

Genesis 18:9–15

Note that Sarah's laughter in response to the surprising promise that a child would yet be born to her in her old age corresponds to that of Abraham (Genesis 17:17–19). Sarah laughed this first time in some disbelief and bitterness of soul. However, she would laugh again in joy (Genesis 21:6). The child's name would correspond to their response, for *Isaac* means "he laughs" or "he rejoices" (Genesis 21:6 and footnote; see commentary at Genesis 21:1–34).

Genesis 18:16–33

The statement of the Lord indicating why he could trust Abraham and why he desired to let him know about the catastrophe coming to Sodom and Gomorrah demonstrates God's esteem for a good man. It is a profound thing to be worthy to be trusted. President David O. McKay, ninth president of the Church, taught that "it is better to be trusted than to be loved" (*Ensign*, May 1999, 46). The lesson is clear: greater revelation and greater closeness to God come when we can be trusted in all things. Verse 19 explains why God could trust the great patriarch and therefore promise such marvelous blessings. He knew him. He knew that Abraham would teach his children, have their equivalent of family scripture study and family prayer, and be a catalyst for the promised blessings to his posterity. He knew Abraham well enough to know that he could make those promises and that Abraham and his posterity would fulfill them.

Regarding this episode, President Spencer W. Kimball said that Abraham's "life is a model that will lift and elevate any father in this Church who wishes to become a true patriarch to his family. . . . Abraham's faithfulness in all things qualified him to receive revelation for his family; indeed, he often spoke with the Lord 'face to face' (Abraham 3:11). . . . Abraham's desire to do God's will in all things led him to preside over his family in righteousness. Despite all his other responsibilities, he knew that if he failed to teach and exemplify the gospel to his children he would have failed to fulfill the most important stewardship he had received. Abraham's instruction and example in his home led the Lord to say of him 'For I know him, that he will command his children and his household after him, and they shall keep the way of the Lord, to do justice and judgment' (Gen. 18:19.)" (*Ensign*, June 1975, 4–5).

The mercy of the Lord in considering Abraham's feelings about the destruction of the cities wherein Lot dwelt is also gratifying (vv. 22–33). Consider why he let Abraham go through the long process of bargaining with him or persuading him to spare those wicked places, knowing all the while (as is implied later in 19:29) that it was Lot and his family about whom Abraham worried.

Another lesson we learn is that Abraham knew that just a few righteous souls can keep the world safe (see Helaman 13:12). The corollary is true: the wickedness of a few can contaminate the whole (see Deuteronomy 21:1–9). Some may wonder why the Lord does not release through death aged men and women who have lived righteous lives and passed the tests of mortality, yet linger on in a deteriorating condition. Some of these venerable old souls may be staying for the sake of the world—their righteousness is needed to protect the world from Satan's ravages.

Genesis 19:1–29

Three messengers came to visit with Lot in Sodom, as they had visited with Abraham, as recorded in Genesis 18. Lot moved *into* Sodom from a place first *facing* Sodom. This is significant. As we examine the immoral climate of the wicked cities near the Salt Sea, down at the lowest place in the world, and Lot's predicament, we recall the warning words of Alexander Pope in his *Essay on Man*:

> Vice is a monster of so frightful mien,
> As to be hated needs but to be seen;
> Yet seen too oft, familiar with her face,
> We first endure, then pity, then embrace.
> (in Monson, *Ensign,* May 2006, 18)

Let's say it again, for emphasis: If we expose ourselves to immorality very long, it begins to dull our abhorrence for sin. First we are shocked, then we tolerate and accept, then we experiment, and then we embrace. One of our students re-phrased it in this down-to-earth way: First we kick it out the door, and then we let it sit on the porch. Soon enough, sin is inside warming itself by the fire, and our home is corrupted.

The explanatory footnote to verse 5 is important in under-standing the immoral context of this episode at Sodom, and the Joseph Smith Translation correction in the story gives quite a different slant on the integrity of Lot in dealing with his daughters. This picture of the gross condition of the men of Sodom and the spiritual lassitude of members of Lot's fam-ily make it evident that mercy could not overrule justice and permit the cities to escape the results of their way of life, nor indeed could the hesitant family of Lot take sanctuary without some test of worthiness. One of them did not pass the test.

Lot's family was warned to flee for their lives and not "look back." Lot's wife disobeyed and was caught up in the holocaust of the wicked cities. A reading of Luke 17:29–32 suggests that she did not just "look back"; she apparently went back. Interestingly, the Qur'an also refers to Lot's wife, she being "*of those who stayed behind*" (xxvii:57; emphasis added; see also xxvi:171; xxix:32, 33; xv:60).

The theory has been advanced and is widely supported that the cities of Sodom and Gomorrah are under the shallow southern end of the Dead Sea. The northern bay of the Dead Sea is thirteen hundred feet deep, but the southern bay is shallow, averaging only eight to ten feet deep or less. Today the region consists almost entirely of evaporation pans for the extraction of minerals, mainly salt and potash. If Lot's wife went back to a city that is now under the Dead Sea, then she is a "pillar of salt" for sure.

God overthrew Sodom and Gomorrah (vv. 25, 29). The Hebrew verb used here is always used with reference to the cities of the plain. It is well known that the plain where the five cities were located (including Sodom and Gomorrah), was itself situated in the great Rift Valley, one of the longest and deepest cracks in the earth's surface, an earthquake fault zone. The overturning or overthrowing of Sodom and Gomorrah could have been caused by, or at least accompanied by, an earthquake. Deuteronomy 29:23 gives a vivid description of the region that is true even to this day.

Ezekiel 16:49–50 is a pointed two-verse commentary on *why* the Lord had to destroy the twin sin-centers, but *how* were the cities destroyed? "The Lord rained upon Sodom and Gomorrah brimstone and fire from the Lord out of heaven." The description of the obliteration of the city-sites notes that "the smoke of the country went up as the smoke of a furnace" (v. 28; see also cross-references). An almost identical description is given in Exodus 19:18 of the Lord himself coming down on Mount Sinai. Apparently Sodom and Gomorrah were destroyed by the Lord and/or other celestial beings appearing with their glory and consuming the depraved citizens of these cities. Jude 1:7 records simply that they were destroyed by "eternal fire." The Prophet Joseph Smith used the phrase "eternal fire" to describe the unparalleled glory God possesses as well as the environment in which he dwells in order to teach that all corruption is consumed by it: "God Almighty Himself dwells in eternal fire; flesh and blood cannot go there, for all corruption is devoured by the fire. 'Our God is a consuming fire'" (*History of the Church*, 6:366).

Genesis 19:30–38

It appears that Lot's daughters must have been imbued with the spirit of the times and the place from which they came; their rationale for getting children to perpetuate their family line looks as if they chose an opportune and bizarre way rather than the proper way to accomplish the objective. Joseph Smith's translation of Genesis 19:30 and 33 makes it clear that the daughters did *wickedly* in perpetrating their sin.

It should not be thought that this indelicate story has been preserved to impugn the background or character of the Moabite and Ammonite people who descended from the incestuous union of Lot's daughters with their father. It will be found later that equally scandalous stories are preserved about some links in the most famous biblical lineages. People and deeds, then as now, were good and bad, and both kinds are recorded in order to teach important lessons to covenant people.

Genesis 20:1–18

The story of Abraham and Abimelech is told with several parallels to that of Abraham and Pharaoh found in chapter 12. Sarah, in her old age, was at this time expecting her first baby; how Abimelech could claim to have taken her for his harem in integrity of heart and innocence of hands is not clear. Nevertheless, the Lord himself intervened, apparently to spare him from sinning in ignorance, and to give him correct information so that he could right the conditions that were wrong. Evidently Abimelech, like Pharaoh, learned through his experience to respect the God of Abraham and not to oppose his will.

Genesis 21:1–34

The chapter break is an artificial one, for the next verses of chapter 21 are intended to go with verses 17 and 18 of chapter 20. Just as the Lord opened the wombs of the house of Abimelech, so too he visited Sarah. She bore a son to Abraham—the covenant son through whom the fulness of God's promises were to be meted out. Note Sarah's reaction: God made her laugh again, this time in joy as opposed to her previous laugh in bitterness over her childless condition (Genesis 18:12). The wordplay throughout these chapters is quite skillful.

After Isaac was born, named, and weaned and Ishmael had become an older youth, trouble again arose between Sarah and Hagar. It originated when Sarah saw Ishmael doing something *with* or *to* Isaac he shouldn't have been doing. The Hebrew word *mitzaheq,* translated as "mocking" (v. 9) has a range of meanings. It is the same root as the word "laugh" as well as the root for the name Yitzhaq, or Isaac. But another meaning of the root has a physical connotation, as in Genesis 26:8, where "sporting" is sometimes translated as "caressing." Also, the meaning of the root word when used to describe the false accusations of Potiphar's wife against Joseph is clearly sexual (see "mock" in Genesis 39:14, 17). Whatever the meaning of the word here, it is clear that Sarah found Ishmael's actions bad enough to warrant his being sent away. Sarah was extremely sensitive about the welfare of her son and perhaps a bit callous to the welfare of the handmaid-wife and the first son of Abraham.

Abraham was naturally grieved by the demand of Sarah that Hagar and Ishmael be sent away, and it was only after a revelation about the boy's destiny, reassuring him all would be well, that he consented. Apparently the provisions he gave them were inadequate, and once again it was only by the Lord's intervention that tragedy was averted. The Lord "heard the voice of the lad" (v. 17) and showed compassion.

Abraham and Abimelech made a covenant of peaceful coexistence with seven lambs at a well Abraham had dug: *Beer-sheva* (anglicized, *Beer-sheba*), meaning "Well of the Covenant." There is a play on the last word because the

Hebrew root *sheva* means both "seven" and "swearing" an oath in making a covenant.

Owing to the giant aquifer under the ground around Beer-sheba, Abraham was able to plant a grove and there called on the name of God (v. 33). This recalls another sacred grove.

Genesis 22:1–19

The first verse opens a new episode in Abraham's life and has God tempting Abraham. The Hebrew verb used here is *nissah,* which means "to test, try, or prove," not "tempt" in the sense that Satan does. What was the test? "Take now thy son, thine only son Isaac, whom thou lovest, and get thee into the land of Moriah; and offer him there for a burnt offering upon one of the mountains which I will tell thee of" (v. 2). What was so extraordinary about this test? Abraham himself had nearly been sacrificed earlier in his life to the idolatrous gods in his old Chaldean homeland. He himself had been laid out on a sacrificial altar, with the cold blade raised to shed his blood, when the angel of the Lord appeared to rescue him (Abraham 1:7–16). Abraham knew how repulsive human sacrifice was and how foreign such a practice is to the true worship of our Heavenly Father. But Abraham knew something else, too. He knew that one of God's expressed purposes for his children during mortality was to "prove them herewith, to see if they will do *all things* whatsoever the Lord their God shall command them" (Abraham 3:25; emphasis added).

Abraham was called on to sacrifice, to give up, the best he had, as our Heavenly Father gave the best he had. The Book of Mormon prophet Jacob taught that Abraham's poignant trial, the offering up of his son Isaac, was a "similitude of God and his Only Begotten Son" (Jacob 4:5; see also Moses 5:7; D&C 138:12–13). Abraham and Isaac not only experienced the same kind of ordeal, feeling similar deep and agonizing feelings, but accomplished it at the same place where the Father would later sacrifice his Beloved Son. Genesis 22 does not give many details regarding time and place; the message is of paramount importance. But then why is the one detail included: "thine *only son* Isaac, *whom thou lovest*"? It is clear that God himself was aware of the magnitude of the trial. Paul wrote that "by faith Abraham, when he was tried, offered up Isaac: and he that had received the promises offered up his *only begotten son*" (Hebrews 11:17; emphasis added).

Abraham was instructed to go to the "land of Moriah" for the offering of his son. This is the first biblical reference to a place called Moriah. In October 1983, Brother Ogden, along with about twenty students in the Brigham Young University Jerusalem Study Abroad program, began a three-day journey in the footsteps of Abraham and Isaac from Beersheba to Mount Moriah in Jerusalem. That first morning as they rode the bus to Beersheba to begin the 53-mile walk, they asked themselves, "Why did the Lord send Abraham, who was well over a hundred years old by this time, more than fifty miles away and *uphill?* Why not send him to one of the nearby hills in the Negev desert? What was so special about Mount Moriah to the Lord or to Abraham?" The more they thought about it, the more likely it seemed that Moriah was already a significant and sacred spot in the days of Abraham—perhaps Melchizedek had a holy Temple or sanctuary at Salem there, or perhaps Abraham knew something about the great expiatory drama that would unfold there in the meridian of time.

Numerous and long-standing Jewish and Christian traditions, as well as the historian Josephus, all support the thesis that Moriah is the same place as Jerusalem's Temple Mount. The biblical record itself indicates that "Solomon began to build the house of the Lord at Jerusalem in mount Moriah, where the Lord appeared unto David" (2 Chronicles 3:1).

Partly because of the previous sanctity of the place, then, David purchased the rock threshing floor on Moriah to build an altar to the Lord (2 Samuel 24:18–25), and he instructed Solomon to construct the holiest edifice in ancient Israel at that spot. But what about Abraham? Was he making the long strenuous trek to that same hill to consummate one of the most stirring and emotional scenes in all of human history because there was something sacred about that place prior to *his* time?

Abraham had met with Melchizedek sometime before "at the valley of Shaveh, which is the king's dale," identified in Bible times and today as the confluence of the Kidron, Tyropoeon, and Hinnom valleys on the southeast of the city of David—Old Testament Jerusalem (Genesis 14:17). Melchizedek ruled over his people at Salem, later to be called Jerusalem. An ancient Israelite psalmist used the names interchangeably, "In Salem also is his tabernacle, and his dwelling place in Zion" (Psalm 76:2). Melchizedek was a type of the Savior: both are called "King of Righteousness" (the meaning of the name-title *Melchizedek*), and both are referred to as "Prince of Peace" (JST Genesis 14:33; Isaiah 9:6). Melchizedek reigned as king in Salem, reigning under or after his father (Alma 13:18). Jesus was of royal lineage, and if the country had not been under Roman subjugation at the time, Jesus might have been king in Jerusalem, reigning after his mortal stepfather; he was accepted by the righteous as their true King. Melchizedek established such peace and righteousness among his people that they "obtained heaven"; they were translated to join the city of Enoch (JST Genesis 14:34); Jesus provided the way for all mankind to obtain heaven and be exalted. We suppose, then, that Melchizedek and the Savior both accomplished their mortal missions at the same place.

Melchizedek was not only king but also God's high priest and keeper of the "storehouse of God" at Salem (JST Genesis 14:37). Abraham paid tithes to that storehouse. How could a great high priest function in his priesthood without a Temple? Or how could a people establish such righteousness as to be transferred from this telestial world without first having the blessings of the Temple, where holy ordinances are performed? (Alma 13:16). The Prophet Joseph Smith explained that the main object of gathering the people of God in any age of the world was "to build unto the Lord a house whereby

He could reveal unto His people the ordinances of His house and the glories of His kingdom, and teach people the way of salvation; for there are certain ordinances and principles that, when they are taught and practiced, must be done in a place or house built for that purpose" (*Joseph Smith* [manual], 416).

Thus, it is likely that a Temple existed on the site of Moriah during the early life of Abraham. Josephus wrote that "[Melchizedek] the Righteous King, for such he really was; on which account he was [there] the first priest of God, and first built a temple, [there,] and called the city Jerusalem, which was formerly called Salem" (*Wars of the Jews,* bk. 6, chap. 10, para. 1).

We may conclude that for Abraham, Moriah was already a place with some prior holy associations when he took Isaac there to be bound and offered up, though by that time, Melchizedek and his people had apparently already been taken up to Zion, the City of Enoch—and may have taken their Temple with them. To be sure, the mount was to be a place of centuries of sacrifices in anticipation of the Great Sacrifice which would be accomplished at that place in the future.

As with Bethel ("house of God") and Gethsemane ("oil press") and other place names which have particular meaning for the historical events occurring at those places, so the name of Abraham's mount is significant. *Moriah* is composed of two words: *-iah* or *-jah* is a contraction of the divine name *YHWH* (Jehovah), and *ra'ah* comes from the verb "to see," having also a host of other renderings, including "to provide." The name of the place, Moriah, could have something to do with where the Lord himself would be seen or provided.

ABRAHAM'S THREE DAYS' JOURNEY TO MORIAH

"And Abraham rose up early in the morning" (v. 3). Three days was a lot of time for Abraham to think about what was going to happen. On day two the father and son passed through the area where a future town would be called *Hebron* or *El Khalil,* meaning "the friend," referring to Abraham, "the Friend of God" (James 2:23). Then "on the third day" (compare Luke 24:46) Abraham "lifted up his eyes [as one would do while walking along], and saw the place afar off" (v. 4). The region of the Mount of Olives-Moriah can be first seen about ten miles away when approaching from the south on the Road of the Patriarchs.

Abraham took the wood and laid it upon Isaac (compare John 19:17), just as Jesus would also carry the wood, the cross, to the place of his death. Isaac asked the heart-rending question, "My father . . . Behold the fire and the wood: but where is the lamb for a burnt offering?" (v. 7). Abraham prophetically responded, "My son, God will provide himself a lamb for a burnt offering" (v. 8). "God" is translated from *Elohim* and "provide" from the Hebrew *jir'eh*. A "burnt offering," an *olah* (from the verb *la'alot,* "to go up") is literally that which goes up to heaven from the altar. The offering had to be a perfect male (*zakhar tammim*). Later, a male lamb without blemish was offered by individuals and the nation of Israel as atonement for sins. According to Leviticus 1:11 when a lamb was slain on the great altar of the Temple, it was slain on the north side of the altar. Golgotha, the place of Jesus' execution, is on the north side of the ridge of Moriah.

THE BINDING OF ISAAC

When they came to the designated place, Abraham built an altar, laid the wood on it, and bound Isaac; Jesus, too, was bound on the wood of his altar of sacrifice, the cross. Isaac was willing to carry out the sacrifice, just as the Savior was willing to suffer and accomplish his sacrifice. Upon their arrival at Moriah and after constructing an altar, it was probably late in the afternoon; Temple procedure later stipulated that passover lambs had to be slain late in the afternoon.

When Abraham had passed his test and the angel of the

Lord halted the sacrifice of his son, a ram (not a *lamb*) was substituted. "Abraham called the name of that place Jehovah-jireh: as it is said to this day, In the mount of the Lord it shall be seen" (v. 14).

In verse 8, Elohim (the Father) had promised to provide a lamb for sacrifice. Now, in verse 14, Jehovah (the Son) will appear; Jehovah will be seen or provided. The final phrase in Hebrew is *b'har YHWH yera'eh*. The English words 'of' and 'it' do not appear in the original, and the verb is a third-person masculine passive imperfect: it should read, "In the mount [and many manuscripts read *b'har hazeh*—in *this* mount, meaning Moriah] the Lord shall be seen, or, the Lord shall be provided."

All of this clearly signifies that Abraham knew something of the meaning of his similitude-sacrifice. He had uttered prophetically—not unintentionally or accidentally—that our Heavenly Father would provide a lamb as a sacrifice or atonement for sin, and he knew that his Son would be that sacrifice, to be made at that very place. Said Jesus, "Your father Abraham rejoiced to see my day: and he saw it, and was glad" (John 8:56).

Our original question was "Why did the Lord require Abraham in his old age to journey so far as the land of Moriah to perform his sacrifice of Isaac?" It seems that the mount of Moriah was already a spiritually important location to Abraham, and the similitude or representative sacrifice he was to make was meant to be done on the very same mountain where Jesus would suffer in the meridian of time. Moriah is *the* mount of sacrifice. There have been altars on it from the days of Melchizedek, Abraham, David, and Jesus. All sacrifices offered on Moriah were supposed to be a type of the Great Sacrifice.

If a Temple, altar, and holy place of offering existed on Moriah two thousand years before Christ and during the meridian of time, then what about two thousand years after Christ, in our own day? We cannot help but believe, knowing how history, prophecy, and divine symbolism always come full circle (God's course is "one eternal round"), that there will once again be a holy Temple on that same sacred parcel of ground. The object of gathering in any age is to build a Temple. Where father Abraham unwaveringly offered his beloved son and where the Father in heaven offered his Beloved Son, at that same mountain the Lord will *again* be seen, when "the Lord, whom ye seek, shall suddenly come to his temple" (Malachi 3:1).

Thus, we may summarize the ways in which Isaac stands as a type and foreshadowing of Jesus Christ and Abraham as a type of God the Father.

1. Relationship: As Paul notes, Isaac was Abraham's only begotten son (Hebrews 11:17) just as Jesus was the Father's Only Begotten Son (John 3:16).
2. Locale: The sacrifice of Isaac took place (v. 2) where the sacrifice of Jesus Christ occurred—Mount Moriah, the site of holy Temples (2 Chronicles 3:1).
3. Donkey: Just as Isaac rode to the place of sacrifice on a donkey (v. 3), Jesus rode into Jerusalem, the place of his condemnation and sacrifice, on a donkey (Matthew 21:1–7).
4. Wood: Isaac carried the sacrificial wood (v. 6) just as Jesus carried the cross (John 19:16–17).
5. Lamb: Isaac was the lamb provided (v. 8), just as Jesus was the Lamb chosen (1 Peter 1:19).
6. Nothing withheld: Just as Abraham did not withhold his son (v. 12), so too the Father did not spare his Son (Matthew 27:46).
7. Seen on the mount: Just as Isaac's obedience and sacrifice were seen on the mount, so too were Jesus' (v. 15).
8. Descendants: Just as innumerable descendants came through Isaac to bless the whole world (vv. 17–18), so too innumerable spiritual descendants came through Jesus Christ to bless the whole world (Mosiah 14:10–12; 27:25–26).

Now take a few minutes to really ponder for your own life the following five statements:

"Therefore, they needs must be chastened and tried, even as Abraham, who was commanded to offer up his only son. For all those who will not endure chastening, but deny me, cannot be sanctified" (D&C 101:4–5).

"All intelligent beings who are crowned with crowns of glory, immortality, and eternal lives must pass through every ordeal appointed for intelligent beings to pass through, to gain their glory and exaltation. Every calamity that can come upon mortal beings will be suffered to come upon the few, to prepare them to enjoy the presence of the Lord. If we obtain the glory that Abraham obtained, we must do so by the same means that he did. If we are ever prepared to enjoy the society of Enoch, Noah, Melchizedek, Abraham, Isaac, and Jacob, or of their faithful children, and of the faithful Prophets and Apostles, we must pass through the same experience, and gain the knowledge, intelligence, and endowments that will prepare us to enter into the celestial kingdom of our Father and God. How many of the Latter-day Saints will endure all these things, and be prepared to enjoy the presence of the Father and the Son? You can answer that question at your leisure. Every trial and experience you have passed through is necessary for your salvation" (*Discourses of Brigham Young*, 345).

"It is recorded that Jesus was made perfect through suffering. If he was made perfect through suffering, why should we imagine for one moment that we can be prepared to enter into the kingdom of rest with him and the Father, without passing through similar ordeals?" (*Discourses of Brigham Young*, 346).

"I heard the Prophet Joseph say, in speaking to the Twelve on one occasion: 'You will have all kinds of trials to pass through. And it is quite as necessary that you be tried as it was for Abraham and other men of God, and . . . God will feel after you, and He will take hold of you and wrench your very heart strings, and if you cannot stand it you will not be fit for an inheritance in the Celestial Kingdom of God" (John Taylor, *Journal of Discourses,* 24:197).

"Did the Lord actually want Abraham to kill Isaac? . . . He did not, but in that thing was the grand thread of the Priesthood developed. The grand object in view was to try the people of God, to see what was in them. . . . How can the Priesthood judge the people if it does not prove them. If you are ever brought into the presence of God, and exalted to a seat in His celestial kingdom, it will be by virtue of the Holy Priesthood, therefore you have got to be proved, not only by being tempted by the devil, but the Priesthood will try you—it will try you to the core. If one thing won't try you, something else will be adopted, until you are like the passive clay in the hands of the Potter. If the Lord our God does not see fit to let the devil loose upon you, and mob you, He will employ some other means to try you as in a crucible, to prove you as gold is tried seven times in the furnace" (Jedediah M. Grant, *Journal of Discourses,* 2:14).

Genesis 22:20–24

News reached Abraham about the children and grandchildren of his brother Nahor, who had stayed at Haran when Abraham migrated to Canaan. One of the granddaughters, Rebekah, here introduced, later became the wife of Abraham's son Isaac.

Genesis 23:1–20

Years after the episode involving the sacrifice of Isaac, when Isaac had reached the age of thirty-seven and his mother was one hundred twenty-seven, Sarah passed away. In the story of Abraham's purchase of the cave of Machpelah as a burial place for her, there is again opportunity to see something of the character and reputation of Abraham. The process of bargaining in order to make a purchase is still common in the Near East, except that the seller usually overstates rather than understates the desired price.

A shrine exists to this day at the site of Machpelah, in

Hebron, with cenotaphs (monuments or empty tombs to honor someone) for three patriarchs and their wives—revered by Jews, Christians, and Muslims.

The sons of Heth (v. 3) are the Hittites, who are part of the pre-Israelite population of the land of Canaan. Thus, Abraham describes himself to them as "a stranger and a so-journer" (v. 4), or resident alien. The Israelites were later told not to oppress or vex strangers (Exodus 22:21), perhaps because their very progenitor had been one himself.

The care taken by Abraham to buy a final resting place shows his love for Sarah as well as his desire to secure all his possessions legally in perpetuity. Because buying the entire area or field would have made Abraham responsible for additional obligations under Hittite law, such as yearly property taxes, he purchased only "the cave of Machpelah . . . which is in the end of the field" (v. 9). The original owner of the field continued to assume the tax burden. Consistent with what we know about business and legal transactions as well as religious discussions, Abraham's business was ratified at "the gate of the city" (v. 10).

Upon closer examination, despite Ephron's pretense of generosity (v. 15), four hundred shekels was a high price for a small piece of property (compare Jeremiah 32:9). Some scholars believe Ephron was taking advantage of Abraham during a time of grief and pressure to find quickly a suitable burial place.

Genesis 24:1–9

In his old age Abraham had been blessed with all things, except a suitable wife for his covenant son (the Lord also promises all things to the faithful in our day; see D&C 50:26–30). Abraham's concern over the wicked and corrupting influences of those outside the covenant led him to place his servant under oath to find a righteous wife and, in turn, to promise to his servant that the Lord would guide him (vv. 1–9). An oath is a solemn promise to fulfill a pledge—even to the point of swearing by one's own life or by the God of all life that the promise will be fulfilled.

The manner of procuring a proper wife for this birthright son is instructive: notice from whom she was to be chosen, and from whom she must not be chosen; and note also who must choose her. Yes, the wishes of the young woman involved were, of course, considered. But the help of the Lord in the process was critical. She had to believe in the true God and be able to bring up children in the faith, to carry on the covenant mission.

We will see that for more than one generation the posterity of Abraham or their messengers will be sent beyond the land of Canaan for wives. Why didn't they make a shorter trek to Salem, to the people of Melchizedek for righteous wives who would perpetuate the covenant? They didn't go to Salem because Melchizedek and his people were no longer there; they had been taken up to the city of Enoch (JST Genesis 14:32–34).

Genesis 24:10–27

The procedure of the servant of Abraham in humbly addressing the Lord as "Lord God of my master Abraham" and asking for help in fulfilling the charge of his master is noteworthy. In this whole process Eliezer, Abraham's servant, shows himself to be a man of great faith. Like the brother of Jared, Eliezer turned to the Lord. But instead of asking God to solve his problem he presented a plan for God to confirm (Ether 2:23; 3:1–4; D&C 9:8–9).

In answer to the servant's request for a very practical and helpful sign from the Lord to help him identify the right woman for his master's son, the proper one indeed appeared. The word picture of her shows that she was industrious, charitable, virtuous, courteous, very fair to look upon, and—most important—she was a virgin (v. 16). She seemed to be the ideal wife. Rebekah's name (Hebrew, *Rivkah*) derives from the root meaning "to trap, noose, or entrap." Perhaps she was thought to be an entrapment because of her beauty. We wonder about the conversations at the well and in her home. Did Rebekah know more than the Bible tells us? She is clearly a spiritually minded woman because she later received personal revelation regarding her sons.

Genesis 24:28–49

When he had given her a symbolic gift and had been accepted as a guest by her father's household, the conscientious servant would not even sit down to eat a meal until he had told of his errand, his instructions, his supplication of the Lord, and his success—thanks to the Lord's blessings—so far. For more on the custom of washing the feet (v. 32), see commentary at Genesis 18:1–8.

Verse 40 reminds us that angels go with all those who are on the Lord's errand, fulfilling the Lord's tasks: "And whoso receiveth you, there I will be also, for I will go before your face. I will be on your right hand and on your left, and my Spirit shall be in your hearts, and mine angels round about you, to bear you up" (D&C 84:88).

Genesis 24:50

Their response shows Bethuel and his family to be respectful of the Lord's will. They were obviously still true worshipers of Him. This fact was undoubtedly the most important factor in the selection of a proper bride for Isaac. How could the next patriarch bear his birthright and pass it on to his descendants unless he had a believing wife who could bring up his children in the true faith? It is almost impossible to overestimate the importance of the character of a wife and mother in the upbringing of her children.

Genesis 24:51–58

As you read how the ancient marriage contract was concluded, do not miss the respect shown for the desires of the woman in the matter, as specifically mentioned by Abraham in his instructions to the steward charged with the negotiation.

Do not suppose that the camel laden with goods for the father of the bride-to-be implies that the bride was bartered for or bought. It is true that compensation for her upbringing

in the house of her father was given, but she was not purchased in the ordinary sense and was not by any means the
property of the husband. This can be discerned by watching
her demeanor in her home in these and later stories, thus giving reflections of domestic life and respective status of husbands and wives.

Genesis 24:59–67

The best wish her family could express in blessing their
daughter and sister, as she departed for her new home, was
that she would become the mother of "thousands of millions"
(v. 60). Since it was through Rebekah that Abraham's seed
would bring blessings to all the families of the earth, perhaps
their blessing was more prophetic than they knew. This is still
the blessing given by Jewish fathers to their daughters before they wed. Note that Rebekah's family also expressed the
hope that her descendants would be free from oppression and
would prevail over their enemies.

There is even a bit of romance in the account of the young
couple's meeting and marriage. The details are quite nicely
told, including the conclusion: "and he [Isaac] loved her
[Rebekah]" and was comforted by her after the death of his
mother. So Rebekah follows Sarah as a covenant woman of
faith.

Unfortunately, no details are given us about the marriage
ceremony; but that may be understandable, for in our dispensation details of priesthood marriages in the Temple are also
not made public.

Genesis 25:1–6

It would be interesting to have a detailed account of
Abraham's additional family of six sons by Keturah and the
account of the presentation of the holy priesthood to members of that family line. In the book of Exodus we will see
that Moses married a daughter of a man named Jethro, (high)
priest of Midian, who was also a descendant of Abraham
through Keturah. According to modern revelation, he actually

held the high priesthood and ordained Moses to the same (D&C 84:6; Exodus 2:15–16, 21; 18:1–12).

Abraham gave to the sons of the other wives "gifts" and sent them to seek their fortune in the east country but gave charge and responsibility for all else to Isaac. This was the birthright blessing, which involved a double inheritance from the father. That birthright blessing always went to the firstborn *righteous* son. Thus, note the number of times the birthright did not go to the firstborn because of their unrighteousness. For more about the birthright, see "The Life of Joseph: A Typology of the Messiah" following commentary at Genesis 50:15–21.

The perpetuation of the Abrahamic covenant with Isaac is made explicit in the beginning of the next chapter (Genesis 26:1–5) and later with Jacob (Genesis 28:10–15). Surely it is more than coincidence that the hand of the Lord in these commissions is emphasized more than the hand of man.

Genesis 25:7–10

It is good to see that Isaac and Ishmael set aside their old rivalry and came together to perform the burial rites for their father, Abraham, at his death.

It is significant that the narrator says not only that Abraham died but also that he was "gathered to his people." This shows that Abraham and his clan knew the essential elements of the gospel and that they had a concept of the spirit, upon the death of the body, entering the presence of those loved ones who had gone before.

Genesis 25:11–18

Verse 11 features a concise characterization of the good relationship that Isaac maintained with the Lord. In the list of Ishmael's descendants, the twelve "princes" (what we might call the "twelve tribes of Ishmael") are memorialized by the writer. The death of Ishmael is described, as is the death of Abraham.

THE NUMBER 12 IN PATRIARCHAL RECORDS

The number 12 is found frequently in the genealogical records of the early patriarchs, but it is not accidental. Consider the following:

- 12 descendants of Nahor (Genesis 22:20–24)
- 12 princes of Ishmael (Genesis 25:13–16)
- 12 descendants of Esau (Genesis 36:10–14)
- 12 tribes of Israel (Genesis 49:28; Numbers 1; 36; Deuteronomy 33)

It is interesting to note that the twelve tribes of Israel are counted differently in the different narrative sections of the Old Testament.

	Genesis 29:31 and ch. 49	Numbers 1 and ch. 36	Deuteronomy 33
Leah	Reuben	Reuben	Reuben
	Simeon	Simeon	—
	Levi	—	Levi
	Judah	Judah	Judah
	Issachar	Issachar	Issachar
	Zebulun	Zebulun	Zebulun
Bilhah	Dan	Dan	Dan
	Naphtali	Naphtali	Naphtali
Zilpah	Gad	Gad	Gad
	Asher	Asher	Asher
Rachel	Joseph	Ephraim	Ephraim
	—	Manasseh	Manasseh
	Benjamin	Benjamin	Benjamin

Genesis 25:19–26

There are great similarities between the introductions to Abraham's narrative (Genesis 11:27–32) and Isaac's narrative here (vv. 19–26). Abraham's brother Haran died before his father; Isaac's half-brother Ishmael died before his other half-brothers (v. 18). Abraham took a wife who was barren (11:30); Isaac took a wife who was barren (25:20–21). Both lives contained an element of struggle between brothers. Abraham was accompanied from birth by Lot and separated from him (13:9, 11, 14), and Isaac's son Jacob was accompanied from birth by Esau and separated from him (25:23). Formulas or patterns of writing were followed by ancient authors.

Typical excerpts from genealogical books of remembrance in Genesis always begin with "These are the generations of" (as in 25:12 and here in 25:19). Isaac's "generations" did not start until twenty years after his marriage, and like Abraham and Sarah, Isaac and Rebekah had to wait for the Lord's blessing before starting their family.

When the firstborn children, twins, were expected, Rebekah asked the Lord why she felt strife within and received an important answer indicating the destiny of the two sons to be born to her. She learned by personal revelation that "the elder shall serve the younger." It appears later, in Genesis 27, that she felt she had to help the younger child reach his destiny and took action with this in mind.

The first child born was named Esau (from a Hebrew root meaning "hairy"), but his descendants were usually called *Edom* (Hebrew, "red"); both names recall his appearance as a newborn. The second twin was named Jacob, which can be literally translated as "he shall follow at the heel," a Hebrew idiom meaning "he shall assail, overreach, or supplant" and was so named by his mother because of her knowledge that he would get the birthright rather than the firstborn, Esau. The law of primogeniture stipulated that it was the exclusive right of the firstborn to a double portion of the inheritance, though a higher spiritual law of inheritance usually took precedence: that is, the greatest blessings and inheritance would default to the oldest *righteous* son. Note that in the line of great patriarchs and prophets, Shem, Abraham, Isaac, Jacob, Joseph, and

Ephraim, not one of them was the oldest by birth, and each received the birthright.

Righteousness is a supreme qualification for blessings. According to Origen, the fourth-century church father in Palestine, Jacob must have been "beloved by God, according to *the deserts of his previous life,* so as to deserve to be preferred before his brother" (*Origen De Principiis,* bk. 2, chap. 9, para. 7, in *Ante-Nicene Fathers;* emphasis added).

Isaac was forty years old when he married Rebekah. She was barren for twenty years. Isaac was sixty years old when the twins were born. Anyone who has tried to keep up with younger grandchildren can certainly appreciate Isaac's challenges.

Genesis 25:27–28

Descriptions of the babies when they were born and subsequent characterizations of them when grown suggest that one was very manly and the other a mama's boy. Esau was described as a hunter or a man of the field, while Jacob was called a "plain" man. The translators could have used a more illustrious adjective than "plain," as the Hebrew word used here has the same root as that used in describing Noah in Genesis 6:9 and Abraham in Genesis 17:1, where it is translated "perfect" in both of those cases. Be that as it may, the interests of the two boys were different, and Jacob definitely was interested in continuing the pastoral way of life with the flocks and herds.

So far as parental favoritism is concerned, we hope and believe that both parents loved both sons, in spite of the division of favor indicated in these verses. Rebekah's promoting of Jacob's welfare derived from her prayer and the consequent revelation before the boys were born (25:23).

Genesis 25:29–34

Esau must have exaggerated his condition of hunger upon returning from the hunt when, upon smelling Jacob's lentil soup cooking, he reasoned, "I am at the point to die, and what profit shall this birthright do me?" A person generally dies from hunger after a long period of emaciation, rather than dropping over suddenly from strongly stimulated appetite! The writer was impressed, according to verse 34, with the fact that Esau must have "despised his birthright" to trade it for a bowl of soup. There is no question that Jacob took advantage of the opportunity to bargain for the birthright, but to characterize him as a hard, cruel man who would not feed a starving, dying brother without compensation hardly fits the picture. Esau's passing off his birthright was certainly not just for hunger; the real reason was that intrinsically it meant nothing to him. Hebrews 12:16 uses strong, negative words in describing Esau's character. In modern times an English idiom has been used from this biblical episode to describe something that means little or nothing to us: "selling our birthright for a mess of pottage."

The picture or even caricature of Esau that emerges at this stage of his life is of the older brother who was worldly—thinking of physical concerns before spiritual matters—dull, and easily outwitted on an empty stomach. Like some young people today, Esau recognized the value of what he lost only after it was gone. His chronological superiority did not translate into spiritual superiority or maturity. As went the boys, so went the nations. Israel is described as gaining ascendancy over Edom even though Edom became a nation first (2 Samuel 8:12–14; 2 Chronicles 25:11–14; compare Genesis 36:31–39).

Genesis 26:1–5

Because one of the cyclical droughts had caused a famine, Isaac went to Gerar, about ten miles from the Mediterranean seacoast, in the Philistine Plain (see Bible Map 10). The Lord appeared to Isaac and assured him it would not be necessary to take refuge in Egypt and officially confirmed the former blessings of Abraham upon him as to land, posterity, and the mission to take blessings to all the nations of the earth. As with Abraham, however, Isaac's whole blessing was conditioned upon his faithfulness. It was precisely because Abraham had remained faithful that his blessing had come down to Isaac, for as the Lord said, "Abraham obeyed my voice, and kept my charge, my commandments, my statutes, and my laws." And Isaac had to do likewise.

Genesis 26:6–11

Isaac also employed the ruse of telling the people of a foreign place that his wife was his "sister." Rebekah was actually Isaac's double first cousin once removed, but recall that biblical Hebrew customarily describes all the descendants of a common forefather as "brothers" and "sisters." The incident here is much like that of Abraham and Sarah in Egypt and in the land of Abimelech, as told in Genesis 12:9–20 and 20:1–18. Whether the same Philistine king was involved in both instances is not indicated, but since a time interval of sixty to eighty years is involved, it would seem likely that they were two different kings of the same royal line and name-title. The name Abimelech may be translated "my father is king" and could plausibly be the title of a dynastic family, given to each king in succession, just as the title "pharaoh" was used in Egypt.

Genesis 26:12–33

Isaac's blessings and prosperity aroused jealousy, fear, and some acts of vandalism against him in spite of the king's proclamation of protection (v. 11). Isaac's behavior in this situation illustrates a great trait of his character. He evidently followed the law of patience and forbearance under persecution, which law was given to him and to others in those ancient times (D&C 98:23–32). It impressed the Philistines who "saw that the Lord was with him." This is, of course, a good way to make known the name and nature of the Lord.

One of the great sermons given on a single verse of scripture in the Old Testament was delivered years ago by Elder Theodore Tuttle of the Seventy on verse 25 and entitled

"Altar, Tent, Well" (*Ensign,* Jan. 1973, 66–67). Ponder this powerful excerpt:

"Isaac did not become an Abraham or a Jacob. He did not reach the heights of Abraham, called the 'father of the faithful.' Nor was he as impressive as his son Israel, father of the twelve tribes. Yet Isaac is loved and revered. He worshiped God, cared for his home, and pursued his work. He is remembered simply as a man of peace. The eloquent simplicity of his life and his unique ability to lend importance to the commonplace made him great.

"Altar, tent, and well: his worship, his home, his work. These basic things of life signified his relationship to God, his family, and his fellowmen. Every person on earth is touched by these three.

"Isaac worshiped at an altar of stone. He sought there answers to life's questions: Where did I come from? Why am I here? Where am I going? . . .

"To know the word and works of God, Isaac knelt in his day at his altar. His tent, a home for himself and family, was sacred to him, as our homes are to us. . . .

"Kneeling at his altar, mindful of his family in his tent, Isaac found most of his working hours consumed in watching over wells he had caused to be digged. His flocks were nourished by them. His simple dependence upon the water and the soil and the forage that grew is little different in our day, for man must work. . . .

"Let a man choose an occupation in balance with the other two elements of the triumvirate of which I have spoken. Learn to give an honest day's work for an honest day's pay. In the farm or shop or office, let that man know that work is not an end in itself, but a means to a noble end.

"How little things have changed since Isaac's day—the things that really matter. There is the same God of Abraham, Isaac, and Jacob, the same family roles to fill, the same need to work.

"Altar, tent, and well: these things are essential. Placed in proper perspective by God's revealed word, they provide at once our greatest challenge and achievement."

Genesis 26:34–35

Esau married Hittite women, who were descendants of Heth, the son of Canaan, the son of Ham (Genesis 10:15). In light of this, and the information already considered in Abraham 1:27, his parents' "grief of mind" is understandable, for the mission of Abraham could not be accomplished by people spiritually or culturally disqualified.

Genesis 27:1–29

Details of the change of the birthright blessing are described beginning with Isaac's decrepit condition, which all of us, even prophets, must face.

Was Rebekah right in desiring the birthright blessing for Jacob? Recall the basis for her motivation; she must have known Esau's unfitness for it. What Jacob's motive was is not immediately evident. It is true that a "double portion" of the material property of the father was apparently the normal heritage of the birthright son, while the others received a "single portion" only. But the double portion was to be used to help the rest of the family, to ransom those in trouble. Remember the birthright itself is a type and foreshadowing of the Messiah and his ability to ransom and redeem family members in trouble.

But the major item of importance in the succession was the right of leadership in the mission of Abraham. Why Rebekah chose this dangerous and seemingly deceptive way to alter the procedure when she heard Isaac's plan to give the blessing to Esau is not known. It is also not known whether she had ever tried to inform Isaac of her revelation in answer to prayer, received years before. It is not likely that Isaac would have willingly flouted the will of the Lord.

It is also unlikely that Jacob could have profited by a blessing procured under false pretenses (compare D&C 130:20–21). Righteous power and privilege are predicated on worthiness. There are evidences later in the story about how Jacob had to prove worthy and that he got the blessings in spite of his seemingly deceitful act and not because of it (even as we get some blessings in spite of our faults, not because of them).

In sum, what can we say about this episode?

1. The record itself does not seem to be complete.
2. Rebekah knew by personal revelation that Jacob was the son chosen by the Lord to guard the covenant (25:22–23). What if the Lord told Rebekah to do what she did owing to Isaac's condition?
3. Jacob was reluctant to participate in the ruse (27:12–13), but he was obedient.
4. The fact that this story is told with all the characters' human blemishes lends credibility to its main points.
5. Isaac could have undone or revoked the blessing, but he did not (27:33). Perhaps he realized that it was right.
6. Following the story we see that the Lord, as well as Isaac, sanctioned the blessings as they stood (28:1–4; 11–15).

It is interesting that everyone in the family will endure some painful struggles after this event. Esau was ready to murder. The relationship between Isaac and Rebekah may have been a little strained. Rebekah would never again on earth see her favored son. Jacob, the home lover, went into exile. Laban later deceived Jacob: just as Jacob had displaced his brother, so Laban put one daughter in place of the other. Jacob's own children later deceived him, too.

"Although the early patriarchs and their wives were great and righteous men and women who eventually were exalted and perfected (see D&C 132:37), this fact does not mean that they were perfect in every respect while in mortality. If the story is correct as found in Genesis, Isaac may have been temporarily shortsighted in favoring Esau. Or Rebekah may have had insufficient faith in the Lord to let him work his will and therefore undertook a plan of her own to ensure that the promised blessings would come to pass. These shortcomings do not lessen their later greatness and their eventual perfection" (*Old Testament* [manual], 85).

Genesis 27:30–33

When Isaac realized it was Jacob to whom he had given the blessing, he could have rescinded it and replaced it with a curse (27:12). He did not, however, but said, surprisingly, "Yea, and he shall be blessed." It was as if he realized that the blessing was given to the right son in spite of the circumstances.

Genesis 27:34–46

Esau was also blessed with the bounties of the earth and with the potential to cast off the yoke of oppression, but like most of us, he valued what he had lost after it was gone and rued the day he had traded the birthright to Jacob. He bitterly resolved to get revenge by fratricide when he saw the blessing of the birthright actually confirmed upon the head of Jacob, to whom he had bartered the right to it. The alert and resourceful Rebekah averted a double tragedy (loss of both sons: one by murder and the other by execution, as the law of Genesis 9:6 would require) by proposing to Isaac that they send Jacob away to find a proper wife in Rebekah's homeland. Thus she would remove him from harm while Esau's feelings cooled. The proposition that he be sent to find a proper wife apparently was approved immediately by Isaac, because he realized that it was true, as Rebekah said, that their life's mission would be frustrated if Jacob married as Esau had. Verse 46 captures the authentic, anguished sigh of every parent who wants the best, eternally, for their children but sees the world standing in opposition and children choosing the latter.

Genesis 28:1–5

Before Jacob went away, Isaac called him in and officially confirmed what he had formerly unwittingly done, blessing Jacob with the blessings of Abraham. The instructions for selecting a wife were like those Abraham gave to his steward for selecting a wife for Isaac.

Genesis 28:6–9

Esau seems to be trying to make amends in some degree by marrying "within the family"—with descendants of his half-uncle Ishmael. Incidentally, there is a discrepancy in the name of one wife as listed here and as given in Genesis 36:2–3. But this marriage could not have helped him fulfill the birthright. Recall the lineage of his wife according to Genesis 21:21 and then recall again Abraham 1:27. Indeed, Esau missed the point all the way around. It wasn't just having a wife from what he thought was an acceptable group. It was the covenant in the first place. It was Esau's whole attitude toward sacred things. It was as if Esau were saying, "Well, to please Dad I'll take a wife from some part of the Abrahamic family so that I'll be okay in his eyes."

Genesis 28:10–22

Alone on top of one of the seemingly endless hills he had to traverse, with the day's last tired steps up the limestone terraces behind him, Jacob must have slept the sleep of exhaustion on his bed and pillow of stone. From Beersheba to Bethel is a hike of over sixty miles (see Bible Map 10). As he slept, he dreamed a dream doubtless more refreshing to him than his sleep. Jacob's dream, or vision, was God's will and desire to pass on to Jacob the call of Abraham. Notice the promises and reassurances the Lord offered, and what Jacob resolved to be and to do in response. Like Abraham, Jacob resolved with gratitude to pay tithes to the Lord.

Jacob was near the ancient city of Luz. Because his dream was on a hill that seemed to be the very entryway of God's house, he named a little shrine which he built there *Bethel,* meaning "House of God."

President Marion G. Romney taught: "Pondering upon the subject of temples and the means therein provided to enable us to ascend into heaven brings to mind the lesson of

Jacob's dream. You will recall that in the twenty-eighth chapter of Genesis there is an account of his return to the land of his father to seek a wife from among his own people. When Jacob traveled from Beersheba toward Haran, he had a dream in which he saw himself on the earth at the foot of a ladder that reached to heaven where the Lord stood above it. He beheld angels ascending and descending thereon, and Jacob realized that the covenants he made with the Lord there were the rungs on the ladder that he himself would have to climb in order to obtain the promised blessings—blessings that would entitle him to enter heaven and associate with the Lord.

"Because he had met the Lord and entered into covenants with him there, Jacob considered the site so sacred that he named the place Bethel, a contraction of Beth-Elohim, which means literally 'the House of the Lord.' He said of it: ' . . . this is none other but the house of God, and this is the gate of heaven.' (Gen. 28:17.)

"Jacob not only passed through the gate of heaven, but by living up to every covenant he also went all the way in. Of him and his fore-bear[ers] Abraham and Isaac, the Lord has said: ' . . . because they did none other things than that which they were commanded, they have entered into their exaltation, according to the promises, and sit upon thrones, and are not angels but are gods.' (D&C 132:37.)

"*Temples are to us all what Bethel was to Jacob.* Even more, they are also the gates to heaven for all of our unendowed kindred dead. We should all do our duty in bringing our loved ones through them" (*Ensign*, Mar. 1971, 16; emphasis added).

In the *History of the Church* we have the following declaration from the Prophet Joseph Smith: "Paul ascended into the third heavens, and he could understand the three principal rounds of Jacob's ladder—the telestial, the terrestrial, and the celestial glories or kingdoms" (5:402).

The Hebrew word behind the English "ladder" is *sulam*, which means a "stairway." Angels (Hebrew, "messengers") of God were going up and down this stairway between heaven and earth. Jacob's exclamation "How dreadful is this place!" is rendered better with the words "How awesome is this place!" He sensed a degree of reverence and awe because of his own spiritual encounter at the place where his grandfather Abraham had conversed with the Lord. This hill at Bethel could be considered as sacred a site as Mount Sinai, the Sacred Grove, the Kirtland Temple, and other such locations of contact between God and man. Later, when the Israelites entered Canaan, they immediately set up a holy place, a sanctuary to the Lord at Bethel, where their progenitors had learned from the Lord.

Genesis 29:1–12

Upon his arrival at Haran in Upper Mesopotamia, Jacob found his relatives, and the Lord guided the meeting of Jacob with Rachel. It was too fortunate to be coincidental. Compare all this with the meeting of Abraham's steward with Rebekah, Jacob's own mother, in Genesis 24:10–27.

The protection of the source of water in arid lands by a huge stone that could only be rolled away by several shepherds together was ingenious. Additionally, it seems that local customs prevented use of a well by a single person without others being there to ensure that all got their fair share. Thus, a covering bigger than one man could normally lift guaranteed some equality. But with strength born of eagerness to be of service (and a desire to make a good impression), Jacob rolled the stone away and watered Rachel's sheep himself. He was a bit forward in making himself acquainted with her with an introductory kiss, and the romance appears rather unconventional for the times. However, he did follow his father's instructions to seek out his mother's family to choose his wife.

Genesis 29:13–20

He who had taken into his own hands the matter of gaining a birthright had nothing but his own hands to produce the needed compensation for a bride. Jacob had no camel train laden with riches as had the negotiator for a wife for Isaac. His first seven-year work contract seems to have succeeded rather well. A modern fiancé would probably have difficulty waiting seven years while he worked to deserve a bride. But "they seemed unto him but a few days, for the love he had to her."

Genesis 29:21–35

Since it was known from the beginning of the contract that it was the younger daughter for whom Jacob was working, Laban contrived to have him marry the older, less fair, and "tender eyed" Leah. Indeed, the Hebrew idiom employed here, *'aynay Leah rakkot*, probably means Leah was "lackluster or plain." Just as Jacob had deceived (one brother in place of another), so Jacob was now himself deceived (one sister in place of another). Jacob was allowed to marry Rachel also after Leah's normal week of wedding festivities and was "allowed" to work another seven years for her.

A contest developed between the two wives, which eventually gave Jacob four wives and twelve sons. And interestingly, half of the sons as well as one daughter, Dinah, were mothered by the faithful but less-favored Leah.

Genesis 29:30–31 says that Jacob loved Rachel and hated Leah. Luke 14:26 records Jesus saying, "If any man come to me, and hate not his father, and mother, and wife, and children, and brethren . . . he cannot be my disciple." In neither of these cases is the word *hate* to be taken literally, of course; nowhere in all of scripture is there a command that the disciple of Christ is to hate any of his or her fellow human beings. Rather, this is an example of the ancient literary device we call hyperbole, which intentionally exaggerates and strongly contrasts emotions for emphasis. The intent of the Genesis passage is to show that Rachel was favored and loved and Leah was cared for less, and likely neglected, in comparison with her sister. The Luke passage features an intentional exaggeration for effect. You cannot love someone else *more* than you love God; you must place your greatest affection on him. In these cases "hate" is merely an idiomatic way of saying "love less."

Some have wondered how Jacob could have been duped on his wedding night. However, both sisters could have been of similar height, weight, and general appearance, and it was dark. Also, the bride came into the wedding tent veiled (Genesis 24:65).

Genesis 30:1–24

This chapter opens by emphasizing that there was great competition among the wives (see 29:31–35; 30:14–16). In the conflict that ensued over their sons the pattern is set for the remainder of the patriarchal narratives in Genesis.

Again, as in the previous two generations, the birthright son was born only after some delay, soul searching, and supplication to God. Rachel turned to her husband to demand children and was called to repentance. She turned to Leah for help and saw her become the mother of yet another son instead. Finally she turned to God. God hearkened to her request, and she bore a son.

Meanings of the names of all the sons born to Jacob and his wives are given in the footnotes to Genesis 29, 30, and 35. On the tradition of fertility potency in mandrakes, see Bible Dictionary, "Mandrake." It is the root of a potato-like substance considered to be an aphrodisiac, a substance that is believed to excite sexual desire.

It was perhaps with a thought to the future and a hope for more sons to come that she named her firstborn Joseph, meaning "He [God] shall add." The name was more prophetic still, for it may be derived from a verb meaning, "He shall gather." That concept seems implied in statements in later scriptures (for example, Deuteronomy 33:17; D&C 58:45).

At this point we insert some explanation about the fact that three generations of covenant patriarchs had more than one wife. The Prophet Joseph Smith taught, "I have constantly said no man shall have but one wife at a time, unless the Lord directs otherwise" (*History of the Church,* 6:46). Occasionally the Lord did direct otherwise in ancient and in modern times. Monogamy has been the rule since the time of Adam and plural marriage the exception. The latter is to be practiced only when the Lord authorizes it, as in the case of the patriarchs Abraham, Isaac, and Jacob. The reason for the law of plural marriage is clearly stated in the Book of Mormon: to "raise up seed unto me" (Jacob 2:30). One illustrated Bible atlas features an article entitled "Polygamy in the Bible," which says: "Throughout the Old Testament we read of patriarchs taking several wives. . . . Such polygamy was most likely motivated by the need to produce sufficient children to control the tribe's principal asset[s]. . . . Childbirth was fraught with danger for both new mothers and infants. Many children were carried away by disease while still in their infancy, and many women died during childbirth. Tribes practiced polygamy as a way of sustaining themselves and ensuring the survival of the clan" (Isbouts, *Biblical World,* 64). In modern revelation the Lord has elaborated on the reasoning behind any man's being instructed to take more than one wife: "They are given unto him to multiply and replenish the earth, according to my commandment, and to fulfil the promise which was given by my Father before the foundation of the world, and for their exaltation in the eternal worlds, that they may bear the souls of men; for herein is the work of my Father continued, that he may be glorified" (D&C 132:63).

Genesis 30:25–43

Though Jacob's acquired birthright included the right to a double portion of the family property, he did not want to wait for his inheritance to bring him security. He showed admirable initiative and self-reliance in assuring Laban that he need not *give* him anything but that the off-color animals among Laban's livestock should be his wages.

Laban wanted Jacob to stay and continue as his foreman because he had learned by experience that God blessed Jacob, and that he, Laban, profited because of him. Jacob also knew that. Jacob's use of striped and spotted willows to engender conception of striped and spotted animals was based on superstition; it still persists today in some areas. Jacob gave credit to the Lord for his increases in livestock (Genesis 31:6–10).

Again we see Laban's deceptive and conniving personality. He secretly removed all the goats earmarked for Jacob before Jacob could receive his fair and agreed share.

Genesis 31:1–16

Here we find the reasons for Jacob's decision to leave Laban's service and return home, including the influence of the Lord and of his wives. Laban's attitude toward Jacob changed; Laban's daughters, Jacob's wives, were disaffected toward their father, feeling disinherited; and the Lord himself revealed that it was time for Jacob to return home. When Jacob prospered, Laban became even more envious and upset. Despite their rivalry, both sisters agreed that Jacob was justified in leaving Laban, who had spent or withheld their dowry (v. 14). Jacob's story here mirrors his grandfather Abraham's: "Get thee out from this land" (v. 13).

Genesis 31:17–55

A dramatic conflict arose with Rachel's theft of Laban's *teraphim* ("images"; see Bible Dictionary, "Teraphim") and Jacob's secret departure, passing over the Euphrates and trekking to Gilead in ten days, where Laban overtook him in seven days. Also included in this episode were Laban's revelation from "the God of the father of Jacob"; Laban's accusation of Jacob and Jacob's remonstrance, with neither one knowing of Rachel's perfidy; the final nonaggression pact and boundary set up between them; and the invocation of God's surveillance of the acts of both.

Regarding the stolen images and why they were so important, W. W. Phelps stated that "the word *Teraphim* . . . might with more propriety, be rendered spectacles or spy-glass, and actually mean the Urim and Thummim." These instruments of

revelation were markers of power and authority in the leadership of the family, and Laban seems to have lost that place.
Brother Phelps went on to say that the "Urim and Thummim,
Seer stones, Teraphim, and Images, [or] whatever name is
given to them; are found in the United States of America. And
when Israel . . . shall seek the Lord their God in the latter
days, the same instruments of the holy offices of God, will be
used as formerly. We are coming back to the light ages" (*Times
and Seasons* 2, no. 7 [Feb. 1, 1841]: 298).

Genesis 32:1–2

Revelations were frequently granted to Jacob; here is a
brief account of one. His vision of the angels of God's host
came to him in a place Jacob named significantly "The Two
Camps" (*Mahanaim*) and was probably to reassure him about
the fulfillment of the promise the Lord had made to him
twenty years before. Soon afterward, Jacob pleaded with the
Lord to make good his promised protection while anticipating
meeting his brother, Esau, after twenty years' separation.

Genesis 32:3–21

Messages and gifts were sent by Jacob to Esau as he approached the reunion with his family. It is as if he wanted it
known that he was not returning to claim the birthright property. When Jacob learned that Esau was coming out to meet
him with four hundred men, he naturally thought the worst
was going to occur and contrived a strategy to try to protect his company. Who can blame Jacob for feeling great fear
and distress? The brothers had parted twenty years earlier with
Esau vowing to kill Jacob (27:41–42). Ponder his prayer for
help (vv. 9–12).

Genesis 32:22–32

It seems that nighttime magnifies our concerns, perhaps
because the prince of darkness does his best work in the absence of light. Jacob was not able to sleep that night and rose
up and sent all his company over the river Jabbok (*Jabbok*

means "the wrestler," named for this occasion.) Meanwhile, he tarried alone and "wrestled" with a man who had the power to bless him—indeed from whom he tried to force a blessing, suffering even a physical injury but persistently holding on. The Hebrew word for "wrestled" is *yea'abek,* which can also mean "embrace." This leads us to believe that there is, in this fragmentary text, the suggestion of ritual embrace, new name, and priestly and kingly power bestowed, which has a parallel in the holy endowment. The man had power to change Jacob's name, and from this struggle *Jacob* ("he shall supplant") emerged as *Israel* ("let God prevail"). Some see a real change in his nature and way of life from this time on; watch for evidence of this.

During this experience, he "saw the face of God" and named the place "Face of God" (*Peniel*), marveling that his life had been spared (compare Alma 8:10; Enos 1:2, 10). Thus, we may now paint the complete picture. At Bethel, twenty years earlier, Jacob had received his endowment, according to President Marion G. Romney. At Peniel, Jacob received a visitation from God and a guarantee of the blessings of the endowment.

Genesis 33:1–16

The acts and words of both of the twins, Esau and Jacob, were aimed at creating good will. The twenty years of separation seem to have mellowed Esau since he apparently was not intent on fulfilling his old threat, but his heart was softened en route from Mount Seir, another name for Edom. Surely prayers to the Lord had something to do with the change.

Jacob's act of putting handmaids and children, defenseless members of the family, in the front of the array may have been a calculated message intended to emphasize Jacob's desire to avoid violence and plead for sympathy and peace. The practice of bowing seven times before one's superiors, as Jacob did before Esau, is a well-documented custom in the ancient Near East, signaling honor and peace. The meeting of the twin brothers, their embrace, and their tears is one of the most touching scenes in scripture—the epitome of forgiveness, restitution, and fellowship.

Genesis 33:17–20

The green valley of the Jabbok and the broader green valley of the Jordan must have looked good after the long trip, the worry, and the struggle were over. Jacob and family settled just east of the city of Shechem ("before the city" means east), on ground purchased from the local inhabitants. He built an altar, showing gratitude to God. He also dug a well there, which was still used in Jesus' time (John 4:1–12), and from which visitors may drink to this day.

Genesis 34:1–31

The peace of the first settlement described in Genesis 33 and the first established "land of Israel" near a city of peace ("Shalem"; 33:18) was soon shattered through an act of carelessness followed by an act of lust, an attempt at recompense, an agreement made in duplicity, and a violent assault. Note the factors on both sides, in both the family of Hamor and the family of Israel, in this tragic interchange. Jacob's sons responsible for the murder of the men of Shechem, according to the Septuagint, were Simeon and Levi (see footnote 14a).

Simeon and Levi were justified in their fury over the rape of their sister (the Hebrew word translated as "defiled" implies violence). Perhaps also distasteful to Jacob's sons is the implication that these Canaanites (Hivites) wanted to absorb Israel (vv. 9–10, 16) in order to benefit from and control Israel's strength. This was a danger Israel constantly faced—either assimilation or hostility. However, Simeon and Levi were not justified in their deceitful plan to slaughter all the males of the city based upon the pretext of establishing the covenant of circumcision among them.

Jacob was obliged to move on for fear of vengeance by other local inhabitants. Though his condemnation of the guilty sons who had supposedly defended the honor of their sister sounds mild at this point, the deep and lasting effects of their deeds are later recorded (Genesis 49:5–7).

Genesis 35:1–15

At God's command, Jacob took his family southward, back to the hills of Bethel. There he tried to purify their ways and dedicate all to God, who had surely fulfilled all that was promised. He built an altar there also, as was his custom, and named it "God of the House of God" (*El-Bethel*). Both the former blessings promised at that place and those in connection with his new name, Israel, were renewed to him by the Lord at Bethel.

It seems that Rebekah's nurse of a generation before (Genesis 24:59) had died and was buried there, and an "Oak of Weeping" marked the place. It doesn't seem likely that Jacob's mother's nurse was somehow traveling with the company and died at the time of these other events related.

Genesis 35:16–21

Another death took place as Jacob's family journeyed southward, beyond the site of Jerusalem, near to the place that would be called Bethlehem (then called Ephrath, "fruitful," with valleys that still merit the name). Jacob's first love, Rachel, died in childbirth and was buried alongside the way to Ephrath, which is Bethlehem. The little son of her suffering, whom she called *Benoni*—"Son of my affliction"—lived, but he was called by his father Benjamin, "Son of my right hand." No husband could bear to be reminded of his great loss in the death of his wife at the mere mention of her son's name. There is, to this day, a monument to Rachel near the entrance to Bethlehem.

Genesis 35:22–26

Here is recorded a breach of the moral law by Reuben, and it would affect his destiny—losing his birthright—as noted in the patriarchal blessings Jacob would give to his sons (Genesis 49:3–4).

The family roster is recorded in verses 23–26. There were twelve sons, twelve potential patriarchs. The discussion of the family tree at this seemingly odd juncture is purposeful, for it sets the stage for the coming story of Joseph (Genesis 37–50).

Genesis 35:27–29

Father Isaac, who had felt "old" twenty years before as he gave the birthright blessing (Genesis 27:1–2), did not die until he was one hundred eighty years old, many years after Jacob returned. Jacob settled his family at Mamre, in Hebron (or, in Hebrew, *Kiriath-arba,* "the city of Arbah"). Esau and Jacob, still at peace with each other, joined in performing the burial rites for their father, Isaac.

Genesis 36:1–43

A page of the family pedigree of the descendants of Esau is also presented at this juncture. Notice that there were kings in the land of Esau, or Edom, long before Israel was ruled by kings. The "Horites" with whom they intermarried could have been the first dwellers in the rock-hewn caverns of the marvelous, later cliff-carved, city called "The Rock"— *Sela,* or *Petra.* Today, visitors to that secluded city are shown carved temples and treasuries and all kinds of dwellings left by the Byzantines, and by the Romans before them, and the Nabateans before them, and the holes in the rocks perhaps inhabited by Edomites and Horites before them.

Unfortunately, the spirit of the meeting of Esau and Israel at Peniel didn't prevail between Edomites and Israelites. Most of the accounts of contact between the two peoples from the time of this narrative onward for a thousand years, from Moses to Malachi, show strife and contention. Some of the prophets used the name of *Edom* or its Latin form, *Idumea,* as a symbol and synonym for "the wicked world" (Isaiah 34:5–6; Ezekiel 35:15; 36:5; D&C 1:36; and the whole book of Obadiah, "the prophet of Edom's doom").

Genesis 37:1–11

The narrative of Joseph, son of Jacob, now unfolds—the last cycle of patriarchal narratives—and is often the favorite of students of the Old Testament. In his teen years, Joseph enjoyed a favored status with his father which put him in disfavor with his brothers. Note what he did, as a somewhat immature youth might do, in telling his dreams to them, which aggravated their disfavor (compare Joseph's challenging teenage years to those of his descendant, another Joseph [Smith], who also lamented the foibles of youth, in Joseph Smith–History 1:28). The dreams needed no particular revelatory expertise to be interpreted. His father "observed" the dreams and apparently realized their significance. But to Joseph's brothers his seeming braggadocio was an offense since some of them undoubtedly felt they should inherit Reuben's forfeited birthright. Perhaps Reuben himself may not have accepted the fact that he had lost the birthright even though he clearly acted immorally by defiling his father's bed (35:22). Perhaps Simeon was expecting that all the others should do obeisance to him since he was Leah's second son. Probably Judah felt entitled to the family leadership since Simeon and Levi had slaughtered the Shechemites and he was Leah's next oldest after them. Maybe Dan felt entitled because he was Rachel's firstborn (but by Bilhah). Because of the spiritual weakness of the brothers, none could comprehend God's requirements to hold the birthright, as well as his intents and purposes.

The Hebrew words for "coat of many colours" are *ketonet passim,* which mean, according to the Brown-Driver-Briggs *Hebrew Lexicon* (509), a "tunic with long skirts and sleeves" (see also footnote *c* for that verse). The Septuagint and Josephus apparently perpetuated the notion of *ketonet passim* having something to do with colors. The one other use of the term in the Bible, in 2 Samuel 13:18, relates how Tamar (who was raped by her half-brother Amnon) had "a garment of divers colours [*ketonet passim*] upon her: for with such were the king's daughters that were virgins apparelled," suggesting that the long garment or coat was meant to modestly cover the whole body. The coat may also have signaled some birthright blessing. Regardless of its actual or symbolic meaning, it was a source of contention and jealousy with the other brothers.

Genesis 37:12–36

Joseph found his brothers herding sheep in the Dothan valley, about eighty miles north of Hebron. As he approached, "they conspired against him to slay him." Evil promptings motivated the brothers to eliminate this source of irritation. Years later, however, Joseph gave the Lord credit for taking him into Egypt and giving him high status there. It is evident that the Lord helped to bring good out of an otherwise evil situation. Even though the brothers' callous treatment of their younger brother and their aged father was not caused by the Lord, he could have influenced them through Reuben not to kill Joseph. Reuben, as the eldest, was responsible for his younger brother and would have to answer to his father. Thus, Judah thought of selling him rather than abandoning him in the pit. The traders unknowingly took him to his trials and opportunities in Egypt. Since two of Joseph's brothers, Simeon and Levi, had already murdered people at Shechem, it is evident that at least they were capable of murdering him.

Verse 22 informs us that Joseph was thrown into a "pit" (which is *bor* in Hebrew; the same word is used for the dungeon he was later thrown into in Egypt). The pit was in "the wilderness." Although there are desolate regions of wasteland in the Near East, notably the Sahara and parts of the Arabian Desert, there is no place in the land of Canaan that could be designated utter wasteland. There is a surprising amount of animal life and flora even in the desert lands. As a point of clarification, the words *desert* and *wilderness* are used interchangeably in English translations of the Bible, both in the Old and New Testaments. All Hebrew and Greek words used signify deserted or uninhabited places. The most frequently used Hebrew word is *midbar,* which is a tract for pasturing

"And the Midianites sold him into Egypt" (Genesis 37:36)

flocks. When Joseph's brothers wanted to kill him and decided instead to throw him into a pit, the account says, "shed no blood, but cast him into this pit that is in the wilderness" (Genesis 37:22). The brothers were herding sheep in the Dothan Valley, which is fertile agricultural and pastoral land just south of the great Jezreel Valley. The word "wilderness" used here fits the definition of unsettled pasturage area perfectly.

Judah proposed the sale of Joseph for twenty pieces of silver, the price of a slave. Centuries later, another man named Judah (now using the Greek form, Judas) proposed the sale of another great person for the price of a slave, by then increased to thirty pieces of silver.

The two related peoples involved in the transaction that took young Joseph into slavery in Egypt were the Ishmaelites and Midianites ("Ishmeelites" in 37:28 and 39:1 is a misspelling in the King James Version). In later history the names of these peoples were used interchangeably (see Judges 8:22–24). They were descendants of two of Abraham's sons.

Genesis 38:1–30

Here is another sordid episode. Judah married a Canaanite wife, which he should not have done. They had sons who were rebellious and perished in their wickedness. A young widow left uncared for contrived to conceive a son by her father-in-law, Judah, without divulging her identity until a later strategic moment. Judah was thereby brought to realize that there is no double standard of morality, for his sin was worse than hers. Out of it all, twin sons were born to him and the young widow, Tamar. The story is not told because it memorializes what was good, or proper, or even permissible in ancient society but perhaps because it preserves a genealogical truth: from this very family came the ancestry of David, the kings of Judah, and Jesus of Nazareth (see Ruth 4:18–22; Luke 3:23–38). Perhaps it has great positive value in alleviating anyone's supposition that because of some sin or disgrace of his forefathers he cannot excel; that is shown not to be true. Ancestry does not determine personal righteousness.

Genesis 38 is dropped into the beginnings of the Joseph story. Some, including biblical scholar E. A. Speiser, viewed this chapter as an interruption, as a completely independent unit, having no connection with the drama of Joseph (p. 299). But is that true? Is it mere coincidence that chapters 38 and 39 both deal with moral temptation to which two now-famous sons of Israel, Judah and Joseph, were subjected? If you were to analyze the two accounts using the Book of Mormon principle "And thus we see . . . ,"—what would you write?

It appears to us that both the story and its placement are purposeful. First, it indicates why Judah did not receive the actual birthright even though he and his tribe took the de facto leadership of the family (see Genesis 43:8 for example). Second, in the context of the whole story of Joseph, a number of powerful lessons emerge.

1. Joseph remained virtuous under the most trying and testing circumstances, while Judah engaged in illicit relations of his own free will.
2. We see how two brothers in the covenant used their moral agency, and we contrast the moral bankruptcy of Judah with the absolute integrity of Joseph.
3. Judah was a lineal heir to the blessings of the Abrahamic covenant. Thus we see that lineage and family position guarantee neither blessings nor righteousness.
4. Jesus Christ's genealogical lineage comes through the illicit relationship described in chapter 38. Interesting!
5. It is not necessary to come from a righteous family to be righteous.
6. Not even Judah's wicked behavior thwarted prophecy that the Messiah would come through his lineage.
7. Man's use of agency cannot thwart God's foreordained plan or purposes.
8. We see clearly a double standard operating in Judah's mind, for he was ready to punish the woman by death until his own wickedness was revealed.

Genesis 39:1–6

How quickly Joseph was elevated to the status of steward over all the operations of the estate of Potiphar, captain of Pharaoh's guard, is seen in (1) Potiphar's acquisition of him, (2) Potiphar's prosperity because of God's blessing him "for Joseph's sake," and (3) the delegation to Joseph's management of all that Potiphar had.

Potiphar was probably of the foreign, Semitic, ruling

class called the Hyksos, who were the fifteenth through the seventeenth dynasties of pharaohs of lower Egypt, between 1720 B.C. and 1550 B.C. This period would almost certainly include the period of Joseph's lifetime. If true, this is a significant factor in aiding us to understand certain important developments later.

The Hebrew terms characterizing Joseph—"goodly person" and "well favoured"—have much more meaning than the weak English translation. The Hebrew text describes Joseph as having "nice form and nice appearance," or in other words, he was well built and handsome, which sets the stage for the encounter with Potiphar's wife, which follows.

Genesis 39:7–18

It is disgusting that Potiphar's own wife, the mistress of the house, should be a person so lacking in marital loyalty, so sensual, so undignified, and so lacking in social standards as to become a young man's temptress. Perhaps it is surprising that Joseph would have the knowledge, the standards, and the will to resist temptation from such a person, who could presumably give him certain advantages through sin. But he recognized it as such, and his thoughtful rationale as to why he could not do to his master and to God such "great wickedness and sin" fortified him against her day-by-day attempts at seduction, until the time came when he could only escape the temptress by fleeing while she clung to his outer robe. Joseph's question ought to be the motto of every true Saint of God of every age: "How then can I do this great wickedness, and sin against God?"

In our day the adversary uses modern technology to speak to us "day by day," luring us toward lustful temptations (compare also Delilah doing the same with Samson, in Judges 16:16). As Elder Neal A. Maxwell once remarked, "Joseph had both good sense and good legs in fleeing from Potiphar's wife" (*Notwithstanding My Weakness*, 102). He refused to hearken to her or "to lie by her, or *to be with her*"

(v. 10; emphasis added). The message is clear: don't even get near to anything or anybody tempting. As the bumper sticker says, "Keep your distance!"

Genesis 39:19–20

Unlike true love, which "suffereth long and is kind," the woman's lust, when frustrated, turned to hate. Naturally, Joseph had no defense against the accusation which she leveled against him to her husband. But why wasn't Joseph put to death for such a violation of his master's trust? Did the Lord temper Potiphar's feelings so that he merely cast Joseph into prison? And, furthermore, might Potiphar have known something about his wife's character?

Genesis 39:21–23 and 40:1–23

It is a hallmark of Joseph's greatness that he did not become bitter over his incarceration or blame the Lord for the injustice done to him. As a result, the Lord prospered Joseph again in prison, and the prison keeper put him in a position of responsibility. And instead of oppressing his fellow prisoners, he is seen in the exemplary act of giving them advice from the God whom he served. Such behavior soon brought him an opportunity to rise to new heights.

A modern parallel to Joseph is Corrie Ten Boom, who was a Dutch victim of the Nazi Holocaust, as told in *The Hiding Place*, in that both were faithful to God despite the severe injustice of their imprisonment.

In interpreting the dreams of Pharaoh's chief butler (40:13), Joseph used a familiar idiom, "[Pharaoh will] lift up thine head," to indicate that the butler would be delivered or restored (compare 2 Kings 25:27; Jeremiah 52:31). But for Pharaoh's chief baker Joseph turns the idiom into a grisly pun, "[Pharaoh will] lift up thy head from off thee" (40:19).

Genesis 41:1–36

Patient servitude was required of Joseph for two more years (he was in prison for a total of at least three years). His years as slave and prisoner must have helped to temper his faults and weaknesses and prepare him for service to the Lord. Finally the butler whom he had helped remembered to help him, but he remembered only after Pharaoh himself had some troublesome dreams. When Joseph was called before Pharaoh to interpret, he cleaned himself up before appearing. He humbly corrected Pharaoh's information concerning his powers. Joseph was apparently quite aware of, and active in, the work of the mission of Abraham, for he bore testimony of the Lord's name "in a strange land" (Abraham 2:6). He explained that it was not he but God who could give an interpretation of the dreams. Pharaoh was converted at least to the authenticity of the dream-revelation, Joseph's interpretation of it, and God's power to fulfill it.

In the story of the dream and the interpretation, the King James English words referring to the "ears" and "stalks" of "corn" need to be rendered in modern American English with the words "heads," "stems" and "grain." What we know as corn is indigenous to America and was, of course, unknown to biblical peoples. The "corn" they spoke about was wheat. Evidence of this are the stores of wheat that have been found among the foodstuffs buried in royal Egyptian tombs dating back to Old Testament times.

A few cultural observations regarding this part of the narrative might be helpful. Pharaoh seeing cattle coming up out of the river in his dream harmonizes with scenes today along the Nile. Cattle often submerge themselves up to their necks to escape oppressive heat and annoying insects (41:2). The "east wind" that blasted the wheat (41:6) is still witnessed in modern times. In the Holy Land it is the dreaded *khamsin* which blows in from the desert (see Hosea 13:15) in late spring or early fall and often withers vegetation (see Isaiah 40:7; Ezekiel 17:10). The "magicians of Egypt" (41:8) were probably leaders of the old Egyptian religion who claimed special knowledge of the occult, thus implying a showdown between the true God of Joseph and the false gods of Egypt.

And finally, when Pharaoh called for Joseph's release, the latter shaved himself (41:14) so as not to offend anyone since many Egyptians followed the practice of being clean-shaven in contrast to those from the north (especially Abraham's posterity) who wore beards (see 2 Samuel 10:5; Jeremiah 41:5).

Genesis 41:37–45

Pharaoh found impressive qualifications in Joseph: discretion, wisdom, and possession of the Spirit of God, and he immediately entrusted special powers and privileges to him.

The wife given to Joseph was Asenath, daughter of Potipherah, priest of On, who presumably would have been also of the Semitic ruling class, the Hyksos, mentioned before. Joseph would not have married into the Hamitic group of people who could not hold the priesthood (Abraham 1:27). In view of all the emphasis on proper marriage in the preceding generations, it is unlikely that the important patriarchal link provided by Joseph would be joined with impunity to peoples heretofore forbidden. Asenath must have been converted to the true God of Israel to become the wife of a prophet of God and the mother of Manasseh and Ephraim.

The Egyptian name Pharaoh gave to Joseph, Zephnathpaaneah, fits with the practice among the Hyksos, the "foreign lords," to adopt Egyptian royal throne names. A translation of the name yields, "the god speaks and he [the one who bears the name] listens." It has also been translated from late Egyptian as "revealer of secrets" or "the man to whom secrets are revealed." No wonder Pharaoh made Joseph ride in the second chariot. Later Joseph will be called "lord of the land" and "lord of the country" (42:30, 33).

Genesis 41:46–49

The young minister, Joseph, proceeded to do what he had recommended to Pharaoh, initiating a massive food storage program. He took twenty percent of the crops during the seven good years (v. 34) and stored a large stock of supplies in the cities in preparation for the time of need.

Genesis 41:50–57

His work for Pharaoh, his marriage, and his children must have been a joy and a blessing to Joseph after many years without love and appreciation. The name of one son, Manasseh, may mean "causing to forget," for God had helped him forget toil, trouble, and bereavement. The other's name, Ephraim, is from the word for "fruit," here used in the dual form, "double fruit." Of him Joseph said, "God hath caused me to be fruitful in the land of my affliction." As far as we know, these two sons—from whom many in the Church today descend—lived their entire lives, died, and were buried in the land of Egypt, never having resided in the land of promise. Thus, members of the Church whose lineage goes back through Ephraim are, in a sense, children of Egypt.

Joseph had charge of food distribution when the famine began. Although at first glance his selling the grain rather than giving it away might seem unjust, anyone experienced in welfare assistance knows the problems and dangers inherent in a dole.

Genesis 42:1–38

The preceding chapters recorded Joseph's rise to power; the following ones detail the divine purposes behind that spectacular rise—to save Israel. Joseph's brothers came among many foreigners who, along with the native Egyptians, were allowed to buy grain because of famine, and they bowed themselves before Joseph, unknowingly fulfilling the old prophetic dream of years earlier (compare Genesis 42:6; 37:7; 44:14). Joseph recognized them but controlled himself and remained unrecognized by them. To try their integrity, he seized upon any statement they made to test them. He challenged their assertion that they were not spies but the sons of one man, and that another son remained at home. Three days in jail must have terrified them, and they must have been surprised when they were released by this capricious governor who said piously that he did it because he reverenced God.

Notice how conscious they were of their guilt over what they had done to their brother many years before. Does it ever appear that Joseph enjoyed their suffering and soul-searching in the course of the tests to which he subjected them? We see that Joseph had forgiven them because he understood God's purposes.

His taking Simeon rather than the firstborn, Reuben, as hostage is interesting; it appears that Reuben's efforts to save him years before and his calling the brothers to repentance again at this later date may have constrained Joseph not to impose undue suffering upon him.

Even the return of their money was looked upon suspiciously by the brothers as a method whereby God sought to punish them.

Verses 29–38 describe the brothers' retelling of events in Egypt when they returned home. The continuing sorrow of aged Jacob over the loss of his beloved Joseph years before is poignant and felt by us, the readers. We see how Jacob must have thought that insult was being added to injury as Reuben sought to persuade his aged father to entrust them with Benjamin on their next trip in order that they might get food and redeem Simeon, a second son who now also appears lost.

Genesis 43:1–14

Jacob would not permit the brothers' return to Egypt with Benjamin until they were in dire need of more food. Recalling the loss of Joseph and apparently of Simeon, his apprehension over the safety of Benjamin is understandable.

Judah became the spokesman for the brothers from this point on and took the leadership of the family (vv. 3, 8–10; 44:13–34; 46:28). His offer to act as "surety" for Benjamin speaks to some redeeming qualities of Judah (v. 9).

In verse 11 we have a list of the best fruits of the land they would carry with them into Egypt: balm, honey, spices, myrrh, nuts (probably pistachios; they are mentioned only here in the Bible), and almonds. Because they require little rain, balm, some spices, and myrrh all produce even in drought years. Giving gifts was a customary practice when approaching one's superiors, whether political (1 Samuel 16:20), religious (2 Kings 5:15), or military (1 Samuel 17:18).

Genesis 43:15–34

When the brothers returned to Egypt, they must have been mystified when they were treated at once as honored guests, even having their feet washed before dinner, and being seated according to priority of age. The money they had found in their sacks and brought back was not accepted because the steward said he had been paid (v. 23). And what must they have thought when Benjamin was given a portion five times that of anyone else. In all these encounters Joseph had difficulty hiding his true feelings. Notice also in verse 23 that Joseph's servant responds to the brothers with the traditional greeting to allay fear and consternation as well as restore harmony, *shalom aleichem*, "Peace be unto you!" This was used by the Savior at a moment of great anxiety (Luke 24:36–37).

Verse 32 implies that native Hamitic Egyptians were servants under the Hyksos rulers. Thus, they would not eat with Joseph, a representative of those who had subjugated and humiliated them. To eat with any of these Semitic Shepherd Kings would be to acknowledge their humiliation. In addition, the Hyksos were herdsmen who slaughtered and ate cattle—which were symbols of several native Egyptian deities. Thus, to eat with the Shepherd Kings would be an abomination.

Genesis 44:1 to 45:15

In the final test he contrived to put them through, Joseph caused Benjamin to be detained in Egypt. Judah proved true to his pledge—and more compassionate than he had been years before. He volunteered to take Benjamin's place rather than cause his father further grief. Joseph wept a third time as the brothers pleaded before him.

Apparently after being satisfied that they would not do to

their youngest brother what they had done to him—that they would not abandon Benjamin to be killed nor to be imprisoned—Joseph divulged his identity. He hastened to give them his whole-souled assurance that though they had meant to do him evil when they sold him, God had brought good out of it for him, for Egypt, for Pharaoh, and for the whole family of Israel.

In this section, the narrative focuses our attention on the personalities of two leaders of the family of Israel. We see that Judah had changed over the years. It is significant and perhaps evidence of true repentance that the one who originally wanted to get rid of Joseph by selling him as chattel (37:26–27) now became the protector and guarantor of Benjamin's safety (44:18–34). In Joseph's case, reunification with his family was a very emotional experience, accompanied by much weeping (see 45:2, 14–15; 46:29). There was no bitterness or malice, only recognition of God's hand in their situation (45:4–8).

This was all part of Joseph's Christlike nature, and when he made himself known to his brothers, we are reminded powerfully how he was a type, similitude, and foreshadowing of Jesus Christ—the great *Savior* and *Deliverer* (see especially 45:7). As the apostle Paul implied, "without seeing Jesus everywhere in the Old Testament, there is no understanding of the Old Testament at all" (Pearson, *Ensign*, June 1986, 17). All of the prophets and patriarchs were types of Christ, and "many of them lived in special situations or did particular things that singled them out as types and patterns and shadows of that which was to be in the life of him who is our Lord" (McConkie, *Promised Messiah*, 448). Joseph was a savior-deliverer in his day.

Genesis 45:16–20

Pharaoh's people reacted very positively when they learned about Joseph's brothers. The country had good reason to be grateful. Though the people had been obliged to give their land and even themselves into the hand of Pharaoh in exchange for food, they were the possessions of the king only in a general fatherly sense of guardianship, and seed was made available for them to return to their land and till it. Joseph had not only saved the nation from the famine but unified the whole land under the strong monarch. Pharaoh was generous in urging that all of Joseph's family should come, and not worry about their property, since all the goods of Egypt were at their disposal if needed. Verse 18 is an echo of the blessing Isaac gave to Jacob (27:28).

Genesis 45:21–28

Wagons were sent to convey Israel's family to Egypt. The news that Joseph yet lived and was "governor" in Egypt was overwhelming to Israel. Only when he heard what Joseph had said and saw all that he had sent was Israel convinced that Joseph was indeed yet alive.

Genesis 46:1–27

Israel probably set out from the family estate at Hebron (35:27) with all that was his and went south to Beersheba to offer sacrifices. Abraham and Isaac had also worshiped the Lord there (21:33; 26:23–25). In Beersheba Israel still needed a revelation from God to reassure him that he should not hesitate to go down into Egypt. God spoke to Israel as he did to Abraham, calling Israel by name, and Israel answered exactly as Abraham had decades earlier: "Here am I" (46:2; compare 22:1, 11). Israel was told that he would there become "a great nation" and would be brought up from there again by the Lord according to his promise to Abraham. There's an interesting parallel. In a sense, God has said to all of us: "Fear not to go down" to earth. "I will go down with thee . . . and I will also surely bring thee up again."

The names of these forefathers of the nation of Israel are given—seventy souls in all, including Joseph's family. After this point in the Bible, organizational units will often be made to contain twelve or seventy people; doubtless this would commemorate, at least in part, this original group of twelve patriarchs who with their families made a clan of seventy.

The size of some families is a bit surprising, especially "young" Benjamin's.

Genesis 46:28–30

The scene of the reunion of Joseph and his father was joyous. One can hardly imagine their mutual feelings on such an occasion. Those who were raised in a close family environment can picture the scene—the feelings, the expression of relief, the joy, and satisfaction of such a family reunion. Verse 29 is especially poignant: "he fell on his neck, and wept on his neck a good while."

Genesis 46:31–34

In order that this clan of livestock-raising men might have good grazing lands, Joseph advised that they frankly tell Pharaoh that they were herdsmen. (The King James English word "cattle" included sheep and goats, as well as cattle; so does the Hebrew word it translates.) That "every shepherd" was repulsive (which the word "abomination" connotes) to the Egyptians is an allusion to the Hyksos, the Shepherd Kings who overran and humiliated the native Hamitic Egyptians. Israel could be sure of being granted the land of Goshen, as Joseph had hoped (Genesis 45:10). Goshen was situated in the eastern portion of the Nile delta (later called the land of Rameses by Moses). Joseph's headquarters, if they were at the Hyksos capital Avaris, would have been nearby.

Genesis 47:1–26

A delegation of brothers sent to Pharaoh did as Joseph had directed, and they were granted land as he had hoped; they were even given the work of caring for the Egyptians' livestock. When the old patriarch was brought in for an audience with the king, he told the king of his hard life and then gave him a blessing. Why did Jacob regard the days and years of his life as "few and evil"? In comparison with Abraham's life (175 years) and Isaac's (180 years), Jacob's 130 years were "few." As for "evil," the Hebrew here means "sorrowful, full of toil and trouble." Consider the following:

1. He had to flee to Haran to escape Esau's deadly wrath.
2. He toiled during years of hard labor under the supervision of deceitful Laban.
3. The tension between his wives, and then the death of Rachel, was a source of consternation and sadness to him.
4. The loss of young Joseph was a grief almost greater than he could bear.

Jacob, like Jesus, was a man of sorrows and acquainted with grief (Isaiah 53:3), someone who models for us faith in the face of adversity.

Genesis 47:27–31

For the remaining five years of the famine (45:6, 11), and an additional twelve years afterward, Jacob lived with his clan in Egypt. They grew in wealth and numbers. Then as he neared death, Jacob called for Joseph to hear his last request: that he be buried in the old family tombs in the cave of Machpelah, at Hebron, in Canaan (23:9, 19; 25:9; 49:30).

Genesis 48:1–22

At this time Joseph brought in his two sons for patriarchal blessings, and Israel reviewed for Joseph the promises made to the fathers concerning the land of Canaan. When the boys stood before their grandfather and were identified for him, Joseph performed the symbolic act of bringing them from between Israel's knees, representing their new status as though they were literal sons of Israel. The boys were then given blessings. Once again it was not priority of birth that determined the choice for the leadership. Joseph took both boys and faced them toward Israel, with Manasseh on his left side (toward Israel's right hand) and Ephraim on his right side (toward Israel's left hand). But Israel crossed his hands and put his right one on Ephraim. Joseph tried to correct his father, but the birthright went to the younger Ephraim. Manasseh, though, did receive a powerful blessing. The blessing of Joseph's sons would fulfill the double blessing of the birthright—Ephraim and Manasseh would now be numbered among the twelve tribes of Israel.

President Joseph Fielding Smith clarified the symbolism of the right hand: "Showing favor to the right hand or side is not something invented by man but was revealed from the heavens in the beginning. . . . There are numerous passages in the scriptures referring to the right hand, indicating that it is a symbol of righteousness and was used in the making of covenants" (*Answers to Gospel Questions,* 1:156–57; see Topical Guide, "Right Hand").

Ephraim's place of leadership is especially significant in the latter days. It is the privilege of the tribe of Ephraim to be the first to hear and then bear the message of the restored gospel to the world, to begin to gather scattered Israel before the millennial reign of Christ. "And they [the other tribes] shall bring forth their rich treasures unto the children of Ephraim, my servants. . . . And there shall they fall down and be crowned with glory, even in Zion, by the hands of the servants of the Lord, even the children of Ephraim" (D&C 133:30, 32). The latter statement surely has reference to Temple ordinances administered by those who hold the keys (often members of the tribe of Ephraim).

In a bit of poetry (vv. 15–16), notice the intensity of Israel's feeling of gratitude for the God who had preserved and redeemed him and his supplication that God's provident power would preserve and prosper the seed of his grandsons, Ephraim and Manasseh. Note that the "Angel" in verse 16 is capitalized, and the Hebrew *malakh* ("messenger, angel") can also mean God.

Genesis 49:1–2

Notice the chapter summary at the head of chapter 49; it would likely startle other Bible-loving Christians to realize the significance of some of the patriarchal blessings Jacob gave to his sons. The patriarch prophetically foreshadowed their destinies. The symbolic words in the blessings of several of them also anticipate the locations and occupations of their tribes later in Canaan. Some blessings pertained to the individual being blessed; other blessings, only to their descendants.

Genesis 49:3–4

A sad blessing was given to Reuben, who had proved himself "unstable" in his sin with Bilhah years before (Genesis 35:22).

Genesis 49:5–7

Gloomy blessings were also given to Simeon and Levi, whose shameful and sinful slaughter at Shechem is recalled (Genesis 34:26). Their descendants would remain among the others of Israel, but they themselves would not be distinguished; Levi's descendants were appointed to priesthood functions through all the tribes of Israel. Jacob indicated that he would not want to trust himself to these two impulsive and vengeful men.

Genesis 49:8–12

The first two positive and noteworthy blessings were also the longest, given to Judah and Joseph, who became the leaders of southern and northern Israel, respectively. Unlike the preceding three sons, Judah heard nothing of his personal sins or qualifications. He was told about the status of leadership that his descendants would attain. Judah's brethren would praise and bow down to him, and he would prevail over his enemies. He was compared to a lion's cub. The "lion" was a symbol of rulership, and allusions to the "sceptre" and to a "lawgiver" are unmistakable hints of the position Judah's tribe would have among the other tribes. Those born from him ("from between his feet"), even a royal lineage, would not cease until *the* Ruler (*Shiloh*) would come—him to whom the kingdom belongs (notice footnote 10c: the Hebrew term is rendered "whose right it is [to reign]"; the same expression appears in Ezekiel 21:27 and D&C 58:22). The prophetic imagery continued: the royal colt upon which he would ride and the "blood of grapes" that would stain his clothing identify the same figure mentioned in Isaiah 63:2 and Doctrine and Covenants 133:48—the Redeemer of Israel. He trod the winepress alone; he became red as wine when he bled from every pore in Gethsemane (Luke 22:44). At his second coming he will be "red in his apparel, and his garments like him that treadeth in the wine vat" (D&C 133:48).

Modern revelation complements and completes Israel's blessing to Judah and declares the final destiny of the tribe: "And they also of the tribe of Judah, after their pain, shall be sanctified in holiness before the Lord, to dwell in his presence day and night, forever and ever" (D&C 133:35).

Genesis 49:13–18

See Bible Map 3 showing the inheritance of each tribe. Zebulun's and Issachar's lands in and around the great Jezreel Valley were particularly productive and "pleasant." That region is mentioned in Isaiah's prophecy of the ministry of the Messiah (Isaiah 9:1–4). Dan's name means "judge," and Jacob prophesied that Dan would, like a judge, be "a serpent by the way, an adder in the path." "Geographically this had come to pass with Dan's tribal inheritance of land in southern Canaan, which stretched from the Judean Shephelah [low hills] to the Mediterranean coast, strategically intersecting the ancient international travel route known as the Way of the Sea. When the Danites of Judges 18 conquered Laish in the far north it also placed them in a strategic position where the Way of the Sea crosses the Upper Jordan Valley. In spite of their move, these Danites had remained 'an adder in the path'!" (Ogden and Chadwick, *Holy Land*, 292).

Genesis 49:19–21

Some reference to the ultimate triumph of Gad, the prosperity of Asher, and the freedom and speaking ability of Naphtali are anticipated, but when and how these are to be fulfilled is not certain. Galilee, the region occupied by Naphtali, was also envisioned by Isaiah: "the people that walked in darkness have seen a great light" (Isaiah 9:2).

Genesis 49:22–26

The two branches of Joseph's descendants were to be numerous and prosperous (Joseph would prove to be "a fruitful bough") and their territories extensive, even beyond the confines of the vineyards of Israel. Joseph's branches or posterity "run over the wall" and their blessings extend "unto the utmost bound of the everlasting hills." Ephraim and Manasseh would receive the double portion in land also: North and South America (for a detailed explanation of this remarkable prophecy, see Ogden and Skinner, *Book of Mormon*, 1:124–27). Only in the western hemisphere can we find a match for the geographical designation of "everlasting hills," to which the blessings of Joseph would extend. Spanning the continents of the Americas, there is a continuous chain of mountains—from Alaska to Patagonia—where the descendants of Joseph would come to be established. Indeed, today there are stakes of the Church from the northernmost reaches of North America to the southernmost reaches of South America, which the patriarch Israel obviously had in mind when he described the extent of the habitat of Joseph's posterity.

We begin to see the fulfillment of Israel's prophetic blessing in the words of Nephi, who was speaking in the New World: "Behold, I say unto you, that the house of Israel was compared unto an olive tree, by the Spirit of the Lord which was in our father; and behold are we not broken off from

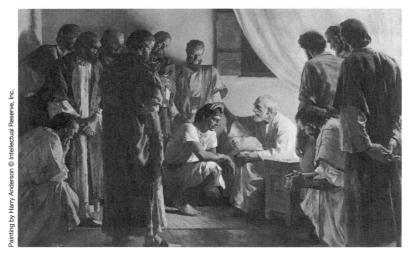

Painting by Harry Anderson © Intellectual Reserve, Inc.

Jacob blessing Joseph (Genesis 49:1, 22–26)

the house of Israel, and are we not a branch of the house of Israel?" (1 Nephi 15:12).

The adversaries of Joseph's descendants would harass them severely but would not prevail against them, because God would help them and send the Shepherd, the Stone of Israel. Joseph (meaning his descendants) would be strengthened by "the mighty God of Jacob."

To be sure, the Redeemer would be from Judah, as is prophesied in verses 8–12, but later prophets foresaw eventual cooperation between the two great leading tribes, Joseph and Judah. See, for example, Isaiah 11:12–13.

Israel's blessings, which were above and beyond those of his forefathers, were invoked upon the head of Joseph. On Joseph's birthright and leadership status read also Deuteronomy 33:13–17; 1 Chronicles 5:1–2.

Genesis 49:27

The blessings of Benjamin indicated that his people would be fighters, but when or how is difficult to tell from the vague wording. Israel's King Saul and the apostle Paul were descendants of Benjamin.

Genesis 49:28–33

Jacob's request to be buried in Canaan is repeated, then he is "gathered unto his people." Verse 31 lists patriarchs and wives, some of our most revered personalities from Bible times, who were all buried in the cave of Machpelah at Hebron.

Genesis 50:1–14

Jacob's request was honored. After forty days of embalming and seventy days of mourning in Egypt, the grand entourage made the journey to Hebron in Canaan.

Genesis 50:15–21

The magnanimity of Joseph in responding to his brothers' entreaty for forgiveness and in providing for them after the old patriarch was dead (whose presence they had considered a restraint upon Joseph's taking deserved vengeance) is noteworthy. The characterization of Joseph continues to elevate him in our esteem. He reiterated for his brothers his own conviction and understanding of the meaning of the course of his life: "God meant it unto good, to bring to pass, as it is this day, to save much people alive." Joseph knew what so many of us need to learn: the Lord's ways are different than man's ways because he knows all things (Isaiah 55:8–9; 2 Nephi 2:24). Joseph saved the people of Israel in that day, and so it would be again. Descendants of Joseph (including a latter-day Joseph) offer the fruits of the covenant and salvation to all the children of Israel and to those outside the covenant of Israel who would be grafted, or adopted, in. The whole narrative of Joseph was often seen by later writers as a type of things to come (see JST Genesis 50:24–38; 2 Nephi 3 and 4:2; and Ether 13:6–10).

THE LIFE OF JOSEPH: A TYPOLOGY OF THE MESSIAH

1. Joseph was a firstborn son and holder of the birthright in a great family (Genesis 30:22–24; 37:3; 43:33). Jesus Christ was *the* Firstborn and held the birthright (D&C 93:21). In

ancient times and under the patriarchal order, the birthright carried certain prerogatives, obligations, opportunities, and blessings and was passed from father to firstborn son (Genesis 43:33). With it came an extra portion of the family inheritance and the right to preside. As the possessor of these benefits, the birthright holder was expected to govern the family in justice and equity, to redeem family members in trouble, to recover forfeited property of a kinsman, or to purchase the freedom of a kinsman if he had fallen into slavery. The birthright itself was a type and similitude of the Firstborn of the Father, Jesus Christ (see LDS Bible Dictionary, "Birthright").

2. Joseph was the favored son of his father (Genesis 37:3). Jesus was the well-beloved Son of the Father (Matthew 3:17).

3. Joseph was rejected by his brothers, the house of Israel (Genesis 37:4). Likewise, Jesus "came unto his own, and his own received him not" (John 1:11).

4. Joseph was betrayed and sold into the hands of the Ishmaelites and then to the Egyptians as a result of Judah's urging (Genesis 37:25–27). Jesus was betrayed and sold out to the Jews and Romans through the work of another Judah (Greek, *Judas*) (Matthew 27:3).

5. Joseph was sold for twenty pieces of silver—the price of a slave in his day (Genesis 37:28). Jesus was sold for thirty pieces of silver (Matthew 27:3)—the price of a slave in his day as outlined in the law of Moses (Exodus 21:32). Elder James E. Talmage noted: "Under the impulse of diabolic avarice, which, however, was probably but a secondary element in the real cause of his perfidious treachery, [Judas] bargained to sell his Master for money . . . 'and they covenanted with him for thirty pieces of silver' [Matthew 26:15]. This amount, approximately seventeen dollars in our money, but of many times greater purchasing power with the Jews in that day than now with us, was the price fixed by the law as that of a slave; it was also the foreseen sum of the blood-money to be paid for the Lord's betrayal" (*Jesus the Christ,* 592).

The Old Testament prophet Zechariah foresaw Judas's perfidy in vision centuries before it occurred. "And I said unto them, If ye think good, give me my price; and if not, forbear. So they weighed for my price thirty pieces of silver. And the Lord said unto me, Cast it unto the potter: a goodly price that I was prised at of them. And I took the thirty pieces of silver, and cast them to the potter in the house of the Lord" (Zechariah 11:12–13). Exactly as Zechariah had foreseen, Judas tried to return the thirty pieces of silver after experiencing overwhelming remorse. The chief priests refused the money. Judas then threw down the money in the house of the Lord, and the Jewish leaders subsequently purchased the potter's field with it (Matthew 27:3–10).

6. In their attempt to destroy Joseph, his brothers actually set up the conditions that eventually brought about their own temporal salvation. In parallel fashion, Jewish leaders, in their attempts to destroy Jesus, arranged for the sacrifice of Jesus—which led to the Atonement and their own possibility of redemption as well as the potential temporal and spiritual salvation of all of Israel and all humankind.

7. Joseph was unjustly accused and punished (Genesis 39:14–20), but he did not become bitter or blame God. He was submissive and even offered to help his fellow convicts (Genesis 40:6–8). Likewise, Jesus was unjustly accused and punished (Matthew 26:65–67; 27:19–50) but did not blame God. He was submissive and offered to help his fellow convicts (Luke 23:39–43). Concerning Jesus' submissiveness, President Boyd K. Packer reminds us that what happened to Jesus happened not because Pilate or the Jewish leaders had the power to impose it but because he was willing to accept it (*Ensign*, May 1988, 69).

8. Joseph began his mission of preparing for the salvation of his brothers and sisters at age thirty (Genesis 41:46). Jesus officially began his ministry of preparing the salvation of his brothers and sisters at age thirty (see commentary at Luke 3:23–38 in Ogden and Skinner, *Four Gospels*).

9. When Joseph was finally raised to his exalted position in

Egypt, all knees bowed to him (Genesis 41:43). All will eventually bow the knee to Jesus (D&C 88:104).

10. Joseph provided bread for Israel and saved them from death, all without price (Genesis 47:12). Jesus, the Bread of Life, did the same for all mortals (John 6:48–57). As the Book of Mormon prophet Jacob said of the Savior's offer: "Come, my brethren, every one that thirsteth, come ye to the waters; and he that hath no money, come buy and eat; yea, come buy wine and milk without money and without price" (2 Nephi 9:50).

Genesis 50:22–26

Joseph's experiences throughout his life may be summarized in the words of Romans 8:28: "We know that all things work together for good to them that love God, to them who are the called according to his purpose." His last fifty-five years are described in a sentence or two indicating that he and the rest of the Israelites enjoyed a good life during these early decades in Egypt. His grandsons on his knees is an appealing word picture. Before he died, Joseph recalled to the people of Israel the promise of God that one day they would go to the land of promise.

Beginning at verse 24, a latter-day Joseph—the Prophet Joseph Smith—restored material that Joseph of Egypt originally spoke before his death, including major prophecies relating to two future periods of Israelite history. A sampling of this material shows that it was not lost to everyone, for a good deal of it appears in the Book of Mormon via the brass plates, which was another Old Testament record (see 2 Nephi 3, for example). Consider the following:

1. Joseph of Egypt testified that the Lord had visited him.

2. The Lord promised Joseph that a future prophet, though not the Messiah, would deliver his people

out of Egyptian bondage, and Joseph knew his name would be Moses.

3. Joseph saw a scattering of his people, the first coming of the Messiah, and the American sojourn of a branch of the Israelite family.
4. Joseph saw another choice seer raised up by God, also named Joseph, who would bring forth a record to complement the Judahite record.
5. Joseph prophesied that the other Joseph would have great power to convince the remnant of Israel's posterity of God's revealed word.

Many other things did Joseph of old say that demonstrated his leadership of the family of Israel and his tremendous gift of seership.

Joseph's final request was that his remains be taken with them to the promised land and buried there in due time.

Thus ends the mortal story of one of the noble and great ones, born in Padan-aram and died in Egypt, living ninety-three years (from age seventeen to one hundred ten) in the land of pyramids, tombs, and temples. The people of Israel would remain in Egypt until the Lord called them out under the direction of another great prophet.

Interestingly, literary and archaeological evidence from ancient Egypt sheds light on the biblical record at this juncture. First, ancient Egyptian records indicate that one hundred and ten years, the lifespan of Joseph (v. 26), was considered to be the ideal—thus showing how divine favor smiled upon Joseph. Second, the Khu-Sebek inscription dating from the nineteenth century B.C. at Abydos in Egypt, presents the first-person account of Khu-Sebek, servant of the Pharaoh. It describes how he, a servant, came to the notice of the Pharoah, was taken and then elevated to high position within the government. The proof of Khu-Sebek's assertions is the erection of a memorial in his honor (*NIV Archaeological Study Bible*, 82–83). Thus, biblical mention of the elaborate funeral of Joseph's father, Israel, and Joseph's embalming are given credence by physical evidence.

Not only was there a scroll of Abraham, which now exists, at least in part, in translation as the book of Abraham, but there was also a scroll of Joseph. Scripture scholar Daniel H. Ludlow wrote: "Evidently some of the writings of Joseph are still in existence but have not been published to the world. Joseph Smith said that he received some papyri scrolls that contained the record of Abraham and Joseph at the same time he obtained the Egyptian mummies from Michael Chandler. Concerning this record, Joseph Smith has written: 'The record of Abraham and Joseph, found with the mummies, is beautifully written on papyrus, with black, and a small part red, ink or paint, in perfect preservation' (*History of the Church,* 2:348). The Prophet next describes how the mummies and the record came into his possession and then concludes: 'Thus I have given a brief history of the manner in which the writings of the fathers, Abraham and Joseph, have been preserved, and how I came in possession of the same—a correct translation of which I shall give in its proper place' (Ibid., 2:350–51).

"The record of Abraham translated by the Prophet was subsequently printed, and it is now known as the book of Abraham in the Pearl of Great Price. However, the translation of the book of Joseph has not yet been published. Evidently the record of Joseph was translated by the Prophet, but perhaps the reason it was not published was because the great prophecies therein were 'too great' for the people of this day" (*Companion to Your Study of the Book of Mormon,* 130–31).

Some of Joseph's prophecies, however, have been preserved and published for us in the Joseph Smith Translation Genesis 50:24–35 and in 2 Nephi 3.

EXODUS

The English title of the second of the five books of Moses is derived from the Greek *exodos,* meaning "exit" or "departure." The Hebrew name of the book, *ve'elleh shemoth,* is taken from the first two words of the Hebrew text of the book and translates as "And these are the names" of the sons of Israel who went to Egypt with Jacob. The same phrase occurs in Genesis 46:8, which also lists the names of those who went down into Egypt with Jacob, or Israel. Thus, it is readily seen that Exodus was originally intended to be not a separate, stand-alone book but a continuation of the narrative begun in Genesis.

In Genesis we saw the inspired author telling Israel who they are and where they came from. It ended with Israel remaining in Egypt after the passing of the old guard, the patriarchs Jacob and Joseph. Exodus picks up the story there and sets the stage for the rise of the great deliverer-lawgiver, Moses. After detailing Moses' leadership of Israel's escape from bondage, Exodus describes Moses' attempt to make the people of Israel into a kingdom of priests and a holy nation.

Evidence, both internal and external to the book of Exodus, indicates that Moses was largely, though perhaps not wholly, responsible for its composition (see Exodus 17:14; 24:4). The ancients themselves believed that Moses was the author of Exodus. Indeed, the later author, Joshua, referred to a command about the construction of altars found in Exodus 20:25 as "written in the book of the law of Moses" (Joshua 8:31). And Jesus certainly upheld the Mosaic authorship of

Exodus, or certain portions of it at the very least (see Mark 7:10; 12:26; Luke 2:22–23).

As to the time of the composition and appearance of the book of Exodus, various statements in the Bible have led to conflicting views. According to 1 Kings 6:1, the Exodus occurred four hundred and eighty years before "the fourth year of [King] Solomon's reign over Israel." This would put the event sometime in the mid-fifteenth century B.C. (around 1450 B.C.). Some scholars believe that the oppression and exodus of Israel took place under the reigns of New Kingdom pharaohs Thutmose III and his son Amenhotep II.

The appearance of the name Ramses in Exodus 1:11, however, has led others to place the oppression and exodus of Israel during the reigns of the nineteenth dynasty pharaohs Seti I and his son Ramses II. Since the latter reigned from 1279 to 1213 B.C., the Exodus would have happened after 1279 but before 1213 B.C. This placement accords well with the earliest, and only, Egyptian archaeological evidence mentioning the name Israel—the Victory Stele of Merneptah (a stele is a column featuring an inscription). This pharaoh, a son of Ramses II, ruled from 1213 to 1203 B.C. The victory stele is pure propaganda that mentions Merneptah's conquest of various groups living north of Egypt, one of whom was Israel. The stele states: "Israel is wasted, bare of seed." The hieroglyphic language in which the stele is written makes clear that the term *Israel* referred to a group of people and not a country. Since the stele is dated to 1209–1208 B.C., it means Israel as a distinct group or tribal confederation was back in the land of Canaan toward the end of the thirteenth century B.C.

Critics of this view of the dating of the Exodus point out that the name Ramses mentioned in Exodus 1:11 also appears in Genesis 47:11 and is very likely the result of editorial updating of the text in both passages, undertaken centuries after Moses lived. However, it is also possible that the mention of Ramses in Exodus is original whereas his mention in Genesis is a later update.

*Stele of Merneptah mentioning Israel
on display in the Egyptian Museum of Antiquities in Cairo*

Inscription on the Stele of Merneptah claiming that "Israel is wasted, bare of seed"

Overall, the book of Exodus is a primer on revelation, from listening to the inspiration of heaven in order to save young Moses' life, to encountering Deity and learning his name and attributes, to learning how to save Israel at the Red Sea, to understanding the meaning and purpose of sacred space—the Tabernacle—where more revelation could be given, to realizing the consequences of rejecting revelation, to preparing a loosely organized tribal family to become a mighty nation, to preparing Israel to inhabit the Abrahamic lands of promise. As a textbook on revelation, Exodus should thrill Latter-day Saints for its instructional value. The Prophet Joseph Smith undoubtedly appreciated it, as can be seen from the references to it in the Doctrine and Covenants.

In addition, one can see four predominant subthemes in Exodus:

1. The roles and greatness of Moses—prophet, mediator, deliverer, gatherer, and lawgiver, all of which single him out as one of the most pronounced types and foreshadows of Jesus Christ
2. Deliverance—God's involvement in Israel's history to preserve them
3. The covenant—including the covenant code which informed Israel's daily behavior as a society of laws
4. The Tabernacle—the supreme place of holiness on earth and forerunner of the Temple

Exodus is a masterpiece in its own right. But it is also a foundation stone for the modern revelations in this dispensation.

There are two main divisions in the book of Exodus: chapters 1–19 consist of the historical narrative, and chapters 20–40 present the legislative code by which Israel must live.

During your study of the book of Exodus, you may also want to consult the following entries in the Bible Dictionary: "Exodus, book of"; "Moses"; "Jehovah"; "Burning Bush"; "Commandments, the Ten"; "Egypt"; "Cloud"; "Peculiar"; "law of Moses"; "Feasts"; "Inheritance"; "Gentile"; "Leprosy";

"Ephod"; "Altar"; "Ark of the Covenant"; "High Priest"; see also articles in the *Encyclopedia of Mormonism* on Moses and the law of Moses.

Exodus 1:1–5

Joseph and all his brethren had returned to Egypt after journeying to the northeast to bury their father in the cave of Machpelah in Hebron, which is about twenty miles south of Jerusalem (Genesis 50:13–14).

The names of the twelve sons of Jacob are given again. By Moses' time their families had become very large tribes. Although only seventy souls were counted among those who came into Egypt, Genesis 46:26 says these were "besides Jacob's sons' wives." Obviously, there would also have been husbands and wives for some of the grandsons and grand-daughters because the sons of Jacob would have been 50 to 70 years old by the time he was himself 130 years old (Genesis 47:9). Some commentaries on the Bible estimate that the total number of those who entered Egypt could have been several hundred.

Exodus 1:6–14

With the death of Joseph, the people of Israel, who had become very numerous, may have felt adrift since their direct connection to the Hyksos leaders of Egypt, who had accorded them their special status in society, was ended. Things went from bad to worse as a new pharaoh arose who "knew not Joseph," meaning, as we understand it, that a complete regime change occurred. The Hyksos, the Semitic shepherd kings, were overthrown, the Second Intermediate Period in Egyptian history ended (roughly 1720–1540 B.C.), and native Hamitic pharaohs retook the throne of a united Egypt. This monumental change began as a war of liberation under Kamose in the south. It was completed by his brother Ahmose who finished the expulsion of the Hyksos in the north, re-unified Upper and Lower Egypt into one empire, established himself as the first pharaoh of the new eighteenth dynasty, and inaugurated the New Kingdom period of Egyptian history. It was a natural strategic move that the Israelites, the now numerous friends of the former Hyksos rulers, be enslaved and afflicted by harsh taskmasters, who made their lives bitter.

Several conditions made Israelite slavery difficult, and we do not know how long the slavery lasted. Some have wondered if Paul (in Galatians 3:17) is accepting a statement from the Hebrew text and the Greek Septuagint in Exodus 12:40 that says 430 years had passed from the time Abraham received the covenant until the Mosaic law was given. This would then mean that Israel was in Egypt about 215 years. Since the clan lived there in peace for some 71 years of Joseph's life after Jacob and the family arrived, only about 144 years remain. Part of their sojourn of 215 years was under the pharaohs of Joseph's time, and the remainder was under the pharaohs "who knew not Joseph." Though the approximate date of the overthrow of the Hyksos is fairly well established (ca. 1550 B.C.), we do not know for sure which of the later pharaohs was the pharaoh of the Exodus. The phrase "land of Rameses" (perhaps used anachronistically in Genesis 47:11) can hardly mean that Israel entered Egypt in the days of Pharaoh Rameses; however, the names of the treasure cities "Pithom and Raamses" (v. 11) are sometimes taken as evidence that the Israelites' slave labor was used in construction work during the administration of Rameses II. There is insufficient internal evidence, and more conclusive external evidence is still needed, but the circumstantial evidence confirming the historical truthfulness of Exodus is impressive.

The footnote 11d notes four different names for the same site or vicinity where Israelites lived and worked, including Avaris/Tanis—the former Hyksos capital in the north.

Exodus 1:15–22

The behavior of two midwives who refused to fulfill Pharaoh's order to kill all male babies is particularly courageous and shows there was still some knowledge of the true and living God, some faith in him, and some inclination to serve him in preference to serving an earthly king. It was especially courageous since Pharaoh was regarded as a living god on earth by almost everyone else. The Lord "dealt well" with the midwives and "made them houses" (meaning that he blessed them with families; see 2 Samuel 7:10–11), indicating that there was still some contact between Israel and God.

Pharaoh issued an edict of infanticide. It was only against males because the men were the ones who might revolt against the new regime and also because in the absence of Israelite men, the women would then be forced to marry Egyptian men and thereby be assimilated.

Could the Egyptian pharaohs also have known of the prophecies of the rise of Israel's deliverer, Moses? Abraham knew (Genesis 15:13–16); Jacob knew (Genesis 46:3–4); and Joseph knew (2 Nephi 3:9–10, 16–17). Since these great patriarchs taught much of what they knew in Egypt, it is indeed possible that the pharaohs knew of the Hebrews' beliefs and may have tried to remove the threat by force (as Herod did later in Bethlehem).

Exodus 2:1–10

Chapter 2 opens by giving us Moses' pedigree as a pure Levite (v. 1). Amram was the name of his father, and Jochebed the name of his mother (Exodus 6:20). Moses was "goodly," meaning handsome or, as Josephus calls him, "beautiful" (*Antiquities,* bk. 2, chap. 9, para. 6). In this respect, he was like Joseph before him (Genesis 39:6). What's more, he apparently resembled Jesus Christ in a special way. Elder Bruce R. McConkie provided this fascinating insight: "Moses was in the similitude of Christ, and Christ was like unto Moses. Of all the hosts of our Father's children, these two are singled out as being like each other. All men are created in the image of God, both spiritually and temporally. . . . And all men are endowed with the characteristics and attributes which, in their eternal fullness, dwell in Deity. But it appears there is a special image, a special similitude, a special likeness where the man Moses and the man Jesus are concerned. . . . That is to say, Moses bore the resemblance of his Lord. In appearance, guise, and semblance, they were the same. The qualities of the one were the qualities of the other" (*Promised Messiah,* 442–43).

Moses came into the world under the decree of death by drowning, just as Jesus was born under a decree of death (Matthew 2:13–17). It was through courage and ingenuity that Moses' parents kept him hidden for a time and then "cast him in the river" in a basket coated with pitch so that he could be found, rescued, and preserved by Pharaoh's own daughter. Her compassionate desire to save the baby is commendable, but it is likely that the Spirit of the Lord influenced her as well.

Moses received his education from his mother-nurse, from the Egyptian princess, from the teachers of Egypt, and from his experiences as a prince (see Stephen's summary in Acts 7:21–25). More detailed descriptions are given by Josephus about, for example, Moses leading a triumphant battle against Ethiopians and becoming a national hero, but the authenticity of Josephus's sources has not as yet been corroborated. Josephus's story of Moses marrying an Ethiopian princess is supported by Numbers 12:1.

English "bulrushes" is equivalent to the Greek *papyrus,* from which we derive our word *paper.* "Pitch" is bitumen (asphalt, tar).

The list of famous pharaohs during the period of this New Kingdom begins with Ahmoses, Thutmoses, and Ramses, and all three names include the Egyptian root word *m-s-s.* This word, derived from the verb "to give birth," combined with one of the names of the gods means "child of [the god]. . . ." The name *Thutmoses* means "child of Thoth" (the moon god); *Ramses* means "child of Ra" (the sun god). The fact that Moses was given this name leads us to believe that he was being groomed for Egyptian leadership, but he was not the son of one of the false gods of the land. Rather he was a son of the true and living God, as God himself declared (Moses 1:6), and the God that the Egyptian leaders would ultimately re-fuse to acknowledge. Of course, the origin of Moses' name in the Hebrew writings was given a Hebrew etymology (v. 10), *m-sh-h,* to "draw out of the water." Like the Egyptian root word indicates, the Hebrew prophet Moses gave new birth— to the Hebrew nation.

Exodus 2:11–15

Moses' hour of decision came when he "went out unto his brethren, and looked on their burdens" and smote a task-master who was smiting one of the slaves. The same verb is used to tell what both the taskmaster and Moses did. "Smote" and "slew" in King James English are both translated from Hebrew *nakkah,* meaning "to beat down"; it is the word used in describing the action taken by soldiers in combat against each other. It would be correct to say that Moses *slew* a man who was slaying another, or that he took a life in saving a life. He knew that the Egyptians would not condone his defense of a slave as shown by his looking "this way and that" or his attempt to settle strife between two Hebrews the following day. From these two acts, Stephen says Moses "supposed his brethren would have understood how that God by his hand would deliver them: but they understood not" (Acts 7:25).

Being learned in all the wisdom of the Egyptians, Moses had access to royal archives. Perhaps he knew of the teach-ings and prophecies of the patriarchs, Abraham and Joseph, recorded when they sojourned there, and was thus inspired to reflect on the burdens of his own people. Both the Qur'an (the Muslim holy book) and traditional Jewish commentar-ies on the Old Testament indicate that Moses was justified in his action. We may rest assured that the Lord would not have called a murderer and deceiver to be his prophet and liberator (Petersen, *Moses,* 42).

Naturally he had to flee from Egypt and find refuge else-where from that time on. Some might even have accused him of aspiring to become pharaoh and of harnessing the forces of Ethiopia in the south and the forces of the Hebrews in the north in a move to control the government.

Soon, Pharaoh "sought to slay Moses," and he fled to "the land of Midian" in the Sinai Peninsula. This, too, proved to be a providential move.

Exodus 2:16–22

In Midian, Moses was blessed to find refuge with a true high priest of God, Reuel, or Jethro (called Raguel the Midianite in Numbers 10:29). From him Moses received the Melchizedek Priesthood (D&C 84:6–7). Recall that Abraham and Keturah had a son named Midian (Genesis 25:1–4). Moses married one of Jethro's daughters named Zipporah, and they had two sons.

Exodus 2:23–25

After Moses' forty years in Sinai, the time had arrived for Israel to be redeemed. The pharaoh who had sought Moses' life was dead, and the supplications of the people of Israel were reaching God, who began to fulfill the covenant he had made with Abraham.

MOSES: A TYPE AND SHADOW OF JESUS CHRIST

From the very beginning of Moses' life we see specific episodes that foreshadowed episodes from the life of the future earthly Messiah, Jesus of Nazareth. Both were born in perilous times. Both survived kings who attempted to kill babies around the time of their birth (Exodus 1:15–16; Matthew 2:16–18), and both were saved by their families who were helped by God (Exodus 1:20–2:8; Matthew 2:12–15).

Both Moses and Jesus Christ spent time in Egypt, and both came forth out of Egypt, led by God (Exodus 13:18; Matthew 2:15, 19–21). Both Moses and Jesus were tempted by Satan and had to engage in spiritual combat, so to speak, with the actual personage of Satan (Moses 1:12–22; Matthew 4:3–10).

In studying Moses' experience with Satan, it becomes clear

that the great prophet-deliverer was conscious that he was a living similitude of Jesus Christ. Knowing for himself the nature of God and his Only Begotten Son, Moses could tell the difference between God and Satan, between truth and error, between light and darkness, between transfigured glory and the natural man. Knowing that he was in the similitude of the Son of God, Moses became a mighty prophet of the Messiah. The spirit of prophecy is "the testimony of Jesus" (Revelation 19:10). Moses possessed this spirit, and thus the power of his prophetic mantle, to the very end. During his final days with Israel, Moses delivered the last three speeches of his mortal life on or near Mount Nebo as the twelve tribes stood poised to cross over into the promised land. In this setting, Moses declared: "The Lord thy God will raise up unto thee a Prophet from the midst of thee, of thy brethren, like unto me; unto him ye shall hearken. . . . And the Lord said unto me, . . . I will raise them up a Prophet from among their brethren, like unto thee, and will put my words in his mouth; and he shall speak unto them all that I shall command him. And it shall come to pass, that whosoever will not hearken unto my words which he shall speak in my name, I will require it of him" (Deuteronomy 18:15–19).

Few scriptures in the standard works are as important as this one, at least judged on the basis of where this passage is subsequently quoted and who uses it. It is quoted by Nephi (1 Nephi 22:21), Peter (Acts 3:22–23), Stephen (Acts 7:37), and Moroni (Joseph Smith–History 1:40), always as a special testimony that Jesus is the literal fulfillment of Moses' words. As the ultimate validation of Moses' declaration, the resurrected Lord himself quoted them: "Behold, I am he of whom Moses spake, saying: A prophet shall the Lord your God raise up unto you of your brethren, like unto me; him shall ye hear in all things whatsoever he shall say unto you. And it shall come to pass that every soul who will not hear that prophet shall be cut off from among the people. Verily I say unto you, yea, and all the prophets from Samuel and those that follow after, as many as have spoken, have testified of me" (3 Nephi 20:23–24).

During his leadership of the tribes of Israel as they sojourned in the wilderness, Moses used one of the most profound and enduring symbols of the Messiah's atonement in all of the Old Testament—the brass serpent (Numbers 21:9). The brass serpent was a type and a symbol of the redemption of Christ, which he, in part, worked out on the cross.

Other parallels, similitudes, and foreshadowings of Jesus Christ in the life of Moses are plentiful:

Like Jesus Christ, Moses was foreordained to perform prophetic and redemptive ministries in behalf of our Heavenly Father's children (JST Genesis 50:24–29; 1 Peter 1:18–20).

Like Jesus Christ, Moses viewed the lands and kingdoms of the earth (Moses 1:27–29; JST Matthew 4:8).

Like Jesus Christ, Moses was meek "above all the men which were upon the face of the earth" (Numbers 12:3; compare Matthew 11:29 and 1 Peter 2:22–23).

Like Jesus Christ, Moses controlled the waters and elements (Exodus 14:21–22, 26–27; Matthew 8:26; 14:26; Mark 4:38–39).

Just as Moses provided manna from heaven (Exodus 16:15), so Jesus Christ was the living manna, the Bread of Life sent down from heaven, as Jesus himself testified. Note how he linked himself to Moses:

"Then Jesus said unto them, Verily, verily, I say unto you, Moses gave you not that bread from heaven; but my Father giveth you the true bread from heaven.

"For the bread of God is he which cometh down from heaven, and giveth life unto the world. . . .

"And Jesus said unto them, I am the bread of life: he that cometh to me shall never hunger; and he that believeth on me shall never thirst. . . .

"Verily, verily, I say unto you, He that believeth on me hath everlasting life.

"I am that bread of life.

"Your fathers did eat manna in the wilderness, and are dead.

"This is the bread which cometh down from heaven, that a man may eat thereof, and not die" (John 6:32–50).

Just as Moses was the mediator of the Old Covenant, so Jesus Christ was the Mediator of the New Covenant (Hebrews 8:5–6; 9:15–24; 12:24).

There are many other ways in which Moses paralleled and prefigured the life and ministry of Jesus Christ. Both are judges, lawgivers, and miracle workers, and it is clear that Moses understood that his roles were a similitude of the Messiah, the Lord Jesus Christ. More important, Jesus Christ left his witness that he, as the mortal Messiah, knew that Moses had been called and chosen to stand through the ages both as his type and shadow and also as his second witness. As he said, "Do not think that I will accuse you to the Father: there is one that accuseth you, even Moses, in whom ye trust. For had ye believed Moses, ye would have believed me: for he wrote of me. But if ye believe not his writings, how shall ye believe my words?" (John 5:45–47).

Exodus 3:1–6

As keeper of the flock of Jethro, God's true high priest, Moses was led by inspiration to God's mountain, Horeb, or Sinai. But this was not the same mountain on which Moses received the profound visitations recorded in Moses 1. That mountain was not known among mortals (Moses 1:42), and the events there happened after Moses' initial encounter with Deity here on Horeb (see Moses 1:17).

A manifestation was given to Moses by a messenger of light who caused a bush to appear to burn. After Moses' attention was drawn to the bush, the voice of the Lord spoke to Moses, who responded in awe and reverence.

The word "angel" could have been better translated as "messenger," which is the basic meaning of the Hebrew word *malakh*. A flame in a bush, a mighty wind, a small voice, a great thundering, or other phenomena, including a tender feeling, may herald a message from God. However, Joseph Smith Translation Exodus 3:2 indicates that the flame of fire signaled the actual presence of the Lord, whose glory was described by Joseph Smith as eternal fire (*History of the Church*, 6:366), thus requiring Moses to be transfigured so as not to be consumed (Moses 1:2, 11).

Exodus 3:7–12

The Lord described Moses' mighty act of deliverance as though he (God) was personally performing it: "And I am come down to deliver them" (v. 8). The implication constitutes a profound lesson: when we are on the Lord's errand, we are acting as he would.

The call required a great mission for which Moses humbly felt incapable. The Lord reassured him, saying, "Because I shall be with thee, this shall be the sign to thee that I have sent thee" (v. 12, literally translated).

Exodus 3:13–15

Perhaps Moses remembered being rejected by some of the people, who asked, "Who made thee a prince and a judge over us?" (Exodus 2:14), so he asked the Lord for credentials of his call which he could present to the people if they asked the name of the God that sent him. The Lord's response was the sacred name of Jehovah, whom righteous men had called upon since the days of Adam. The name had been used by Abraham, Isaac, and Jacob. For instance, see the word "Lord" in Genesis 22:14; 27:27; 28:13. Later, while identifying himself (Exodus 6:3), the Lord told Moses that he was known to the patriarchs as the Almighty, but, as our common translation reads, "by my name JEHOVAH was I not known to them." However, if this sentence is punctuated with a question mark, as it was by the Prophet Joseph Smith in his inspired revision (see Exodus 6:3, footnote *c*), it is more clear: "by my name JEHOVAH was I not known to them?"

In Hebrew, the name *Jehovah* derives from the verb which means "I am" in its active form, "I cause to be" (i.e., "I create") in its causative form, and "I will be" in its future form. It is called in Greek the Tetragrammaton because of its four-consonant construction, *YHWH*. Study Exodus 6:3, John 4:26 (see the footnote), and John 8:58 for evidence that identifies "I AM." Then turn to the direct statements in 1 Nephi 19:10; 3 Nephi 15:5; Isaiah 63:8–9 and 49:26 that identify the God of Moses as Jesus the Savior (see also D&C 29:1; 38:1; 39:1). Our common translation substitutes the word LORD in small capital letters wherever the four-letter sacred name *YHWH* (Jehovah) appears in Hebrew. It appears only as the four consonants YHWH because ancient Hebrew was written without vowels.

Exodus 3:16–22

Apparently the patriarchal organization of family and social life had been perpetuated because "elders" of Israel were called to help Moses prepare the people. As the Israelites left Egypt, they were to ask not only for freedom but also for some compensation for their long service. The word "borrow" is here translated from the Hebrew word for "ask," which does not mean requesting temporary use of a thing. It is related to "spoil," which is King James English for a Hebrew word meaning "empty out." Indeed, when Israel left Egypt they took with them many riches and "emptied out" Egypt (Exodus 11:2; 12:33–36).

Exodus 4:1–9

In order to help Moses persuade both the Israelites and the Egyptians that he represented the true and living God, the Lord allowed him to use "signs and wonders" to persuade the people, although later, in Christ's own mortal life, he said it was a "wicked and adulterous generation" that asked for a sign of divine authority. Although such signs were sometimes permitted for those who had little knowledge of God and little faith in him, we, like the people who lived in Jesus' day, are not justified in asking for signs. Miracles are given as a reward of faith, not to satisfy curiosity (D&C 63:9–10).

The symbol or image of the serpent represented deity in most cultures of the ancient world. The king of the very Egyptians before whom Moses would stand wore the *Ureas* (cobra image) on his headdress—symbol that he was a living god on earth. Ironically, the serpent image really did represent God but not the false gods of other civilizations. Rather, the serpent was ultimately a symbol of Jesus Christ, his power to heal and bless (see commentary at Numbers 21:1–9; see also John 3:14–15). This is why Satan tried to usurp the image of the serpent in the Garden of Eden—to deceive our first parents by passing himself off as God through the use of one of his symbols. Some symbols were instituted in our premortal existence, but the symbol or sign of the dove is the only one that the devil cannot duplicate, usurp, or use (*Joseph Smith* [manual], 81). See commentary at Genesis 3:1–3.

Exodus 4:10–17

Moses was reproved for his lack of confidence and his excuse that he could not speak well, because the God who created all things could surely put words in his mouth. Nevertheless, upon Moses' further hesitation his brother, Aaron, became his spokesman. This is the beginning of the call of Aaron. More will be seen concerning his call and ordination in Exodus 7:1–2, Leviticus 8, and Numbers 3. Aaron's call was from God, as Hebrews 5:4 says—no man takes the honor of the priesthood authority upon himself, but each must be called of God, as was Aaron.

Moses' response to the Lord's call is typical. He felt he had a particular weakness which could hinder his accomplishing the Lord's will: "I am not eloquent; I am slow of speech and of a slow tongue." It cannot be thought that Moses was unable to speak well, since we know he "was mighty in words" and "learned in all the wisdom of the Egyptians" (Acts 7:22). He was probably expressing a genuine concern that his mother tongue was Egyptian and not the Northwest Semitic dialect spoken by the Israelites.

Others have likewise been reluctant to accept seemingly overwhelming assignments in the face of what they supposed were insurmountable personal deficiencies, and they offered excuses. For example, Enoch responded to the Lord's call with "[I] am but a lad, and all the people hate me; for I am slow of speech" (Moses 6:31), or "I'm just a youth, and nobody likes me." Gideon replied, "My family is poor . . . and I am the least in my father's house" (Judges 6:15), or "I'm a nobody." Saul felt similarly: "My family [is] the least of all the families of the tribe of Benjamin" (1 Samuel 9:21), or "I'm of low birth; I've been raised in rather humble circumstances." Jeremiah expressed the same fears as Enoch and Moses, "I cannot speak: for I am a child" (Jeremiah 1:6), or "I haven't matured enough yet to handle this." Furthermore, a modern prophet, Spencer W. Kimball, heard a voice inside him saying, "You can't do the work. You are not worthy. You have not the ability" (Conference Report, Oct. 1943, 16).

There are many more excuses: "I'm not smart enough. I'm not spiritual enough. I'm not strong enough." Maybe the Lord is trying to teach us something with all these examples. It doesn't necessarily take great speaking ability, high birth, the wisdom of age, popularity, knowledge, or physical strength to fulfill a calling from the Lord. It does take faith and determination to make of ourselves more than we are. Actually, the Lord makes us what we can become, as Moses would learn.

Out of this interaction between Moses and God came the Lord's final decree: Aaron would become spokesman. But notice the authority and position the Lord ultimately ascribed to both (v. 16). Aaron would act as prophet; Moses would be as God (Hebrew, *Elohim*). Can we truly appreciate the towering greatness of Moses?

Exodus 4:18–23

Moses finally accepted the calling, took leave of Jethro, the high priest of Midian, and set out with his wife and sons for Egypt.

Moses was forewarned that Pharaoh would have a hard heart, and he gave a warning to Pharaoh. The phrase "I will harden his heart" that appears in our common English version is an idiomatic expression which could also be rendered: "I will show him to be hard of heart," or "I will permit or suffer his heart to be hardened." The Joseph Smith Translation changes all such passages to indicate that it was Pharaoh himself who hardened his heart.

Incidentally, in the Book of Mormon, though there is much heart hardening that goes on, it never says that God hardened anyone's heart.

In verse 22 we encounter the first of several passages that begin to lay out the doctrine of Israel's foreordained election and preeminent status in terms of the covenant. "Israel is . . . my first born," which we can make sense of only with a knowledge of the doctrines of the premortal existence of all spirits, their preassigned roles in mortality (see Acts 17:26), and Israel's chosenness and preappointment as the guardian of the covenant—a chosenness of obligation and responsibility and not of elite privilege.

Exodus 4:24–26

The statement that as Moses proceeded toward Egypt, "The Lord met him and sought to kill him" is confusing in our translation. Obviously, if the Lord sought to kill a man, he would not have failed. The Joseph Smith Translation (in the Bible Appendix) indicates that the Lord was angry with Moses because he hadn't kept the law of circumcision with respect to his sons. The circumcision was performed, and Moses went on. Zipporah met the demands of justice, spared Moses further upset from the Lord, and ransomed him, as it were, giving him a fresh start. Understood this way, the episode foreshadows and points us to Jesus Christ, whose shed blood makes him "the bridegroom of blood." The Hebrew and explanatory footnotes on 25*b* suggest that further light on this episode is needed for understanding. Zipporah evidently returned with the children after this incident and stayed with her father until Moses completed his mission of bringing Israel out of Egypt; then she rejoined him at Mount Sinai (Exodus 18:5).

Many peoples in the ancient Near East practiced circumcision. Its earliest attestations portray it as a puberty rite, a rite of passage, or as an initiation rite before marriage. It initiated a young man into the common life of the clan. God, however, reinforced its meaning as a sign of the covenant and a reminder to his people of the saving ordinance of baptism, by which they were made full and functioning members of his community. The English term "uncircumcised," therefore, is a metaphorical reference for something not part of the covenant community and out of harmony with God's purposes.

Exodus 4:27–31

Aaron was "called of God" and went out to meet Moses. When they arrived in Egypt, they assembled the elders and instructed them of God's intent. They became a truly dynamic duo, speaking powerful words, and performing miraculous signs. The message of deliverance was received with gratitude and hope.

Between Exodus chapters 4–5, Moses was transformed from a recently called excuse-giver to a confident, powerful prophet. Moses had been given the vision, perhaps the glorious revelation recorded in chapter 1 of the book of Moses. Moses knew the ultimate outcome of his encounters with Pharaoh.

Exodus 5:1–23

Freedom was requested from Pharaoh, but he naturally responded: "Who is the Lord, that I should obey his voice?" Pharaoh would learn the answer to this question by much sad experience. In the meantime, he sought to show who was boss by increasing Israel's burdens and expectations.

Disappointed and embittered because they only received increased burdens instead of freedom, the people of Israel complained to Moses, and Moses complained to the Lord.

Exodus 6:1–8

The Lord reassured Moses and renewed his promise, telling him of God's identity, his power, and his intent to deliver Israel and keep the covenant he had made with Abraham, Isaac, and Jacob. Recall what was said earlier about their knowledge of the divine name in Exodus 3:13–15.

Exodus 6:9–13, 28–30

Moses obediently repeated the promises to the people, but in their misery they were unimpressed. This is the great test of mortality for all of us—to learn to listen to the voice of the Lord in our extremity and our trials, and heed that voice. Moses himself was also discouraged and broken in spirit until the Lord again spoke to him. The prophet's humility would turn his weakness into strength; he became a man "mighty in words and in deeds" (Acts 7:22).

Exodus 6:14–27

This passage is an overview of the four generations of Moses' lineage in Egypt. Recall the promise of the Lord to Abraham (Genesis 15:13–16) that deliverance would come in the *fourth generation*. For the total time involved, recall the commentary at Exodus 1:6–14.

Moses was a pure Levite and three years younger than his brother, Aaron. Their mother's name, Jochebed (Hebrew, *Yo-kheved*), means "Jehovah praised." This is obvious evidence that the divine name of Jehovah was known before Moses' time.

Aaron married a woman named Elisheba, a name that later came into Greek and then English as Elizabeth or Elisabeth (compare Luke 1:5)—which, with all its derivatives, is one of the most common female names in the world.

Exodus 7:1–7

See Joseph Smith Translation footnotes for important changes in verse 1. Recall the commentary on "hardening hearts" in Exodus 4:18–23 to see why miracles and plagues were used. Although Jesus refused to use such tactics when he was fulfilling his mission (Luke 9:51–56), it is clear that conditions sometimes alter approaches.

Moses' life can be divided into three forty-year stages. The first constitutes the period of his birth, upbringing, education, and training. The second is his forty years in Sinai, and the third begins with his efforts to deliver Israel, noted in verse 7.

Here we see the character of a mighty prophet forged in the furnace of affliction, concern for God's children, and spiritual battle against the mightiest mortal king on earth—Pharaoh.

Exodus 7:8–13

Moses and Aaron showed their divine calling and power, but Pharaoh was unimpressed. His astrologers and sorcerers, the magicians of Egypt, were able to duplicate the first miracles. (On the symbol and imagery of the serpent, see commentary at Exodus 4:1–9 and Genesis 3:1–3). Doctrine and Covenants 84:21 explains that faith-promoting miracles can only be done through righteous use of the priesthood of God. How then were the magicians seemingly able to perform the same miracles? (You will find answers in Matthew 7:21–23 and Doctrine and Covenants 63:7.) Pharaoh had to be educated about many other facets of God's omnipotence before he finally acceded to the demands of the unseen God. Watch the development of this process in Exodus 9:17 and 10:3.

Exodus 7:14–25

The plagues came in cycles of three. The first plague in each cycle was announced to Pharaoh at the river in the morning. When the first plague was announced, its purpose was clarified, and it was performed. But Pharaoh, impressed with the powers of his own magicians, resisted Israel's request.

Exodus 8:1–15

The second plague was announced and performed, but it was also imitated. However, Pharaoh did finally supplicate Moses' aid to remove it and made his first promise to let the Israelites go. Though Moses repeated the purpose of the plague when he removed it, Pharaoh hardened his heart and retracted his promise.

Exodus 8:16–19

The third plague was sent without warning and could not be duplicated by the Egyptians' magical powers; in fact, they identified what Aaron did under Moses' direction as a manifestation of "the finger of God." From this point on the magicians were "out of the contest." However, Pharaoh was still adamant and made no concession whatever.

Exodus 8:20–32

With the fourth plague, Moses again met Pharaoh in the morning at the river and warned him what would happen if he did not yield to the Lord's request to free Israel. Again there was no concession until the plague came. This plague demonstrated that God could distinguish between the Egyptians and the Israelites. Pharaoh conceded, and Moses warned him against retracting his promise. However, when the "swarms" were removed, Pharaoh's promise was withdrawn.

Moses asked to go into the wilderness to offer a sacrifice. This was because the blood sacrifice of an animal sacred to the Egyptians (the cow) would be considered an offense, and they might stone the Israelites.

Exodus 9:1–7

The fifth plague was also preceded by a warning. The cattle of the Egyptians were affected and those of Israel were not, but Pharaoh made no concession before or after the plague came.

Exodus 9:8–13

The sixth plague came without warning. The magicians themselves suffered, but Pharaoh was still adamant and made no concession.

Exodus 9:14–35

The seventh plague continued until Pharaoh finally did make a humble confession and ask for intercession with the Lord. However, he once again recanted when the plague was removed.

The words "cause" and "in" in verse 16 are in italics, meaning that their equivalent was not in the Hebrew account at all, and they were added to the account. The meaning of the verse is quite different if these words are left out: "For this

I have raised thee up, for to show thee my power," signifying that God would show His power not *in* Pharaoh but *to* him.

"Hail" in Hebrew is *barad,* which, according to some scholars, has connection to the Hittite word for iron, meaning "metal from stars" and the Egyptian word for iron, meaning "metal from heaven."

Exodus 10:1–20

The eighth plague was preceded by a warning, and as usual it came when Pharaoh would not yield. The purpose was again made clear, that the plague was so the Egyptians would know the power of the Lord. Again to get relief, Pharaoh supplicated Moses and the Lord for forgiveness, but when the plague was gone he reverted again to his obstinacy.

Exodus 10:21–29

The ninth plague came without warning, and Pharaoh asked for relief again but would not grant the full request of Moses. He even threatened Moses' life, whereupon Moses responded ominously, "Thou hast spoken well; I will see thy face again no more."

Exodus 11:1–10

Instructions to prepare for the final plague were given to Moses and Aaron, and the purposes of the earlier plagues were reviewed. The first instructions concerning the Hebrews' release were also given. The Lord sent nine plagues to Egypt in order to try to persuade Pharaoh to let his people go free. But the real audience, the most important audience, was Israel. Each of the plagues demonstrated Jehovah's power over Egypt's gods and, thus, over the many and varied aspects of life. Remember, the Egyptians were obsessed with life in the present and obtaining eternal life in the future. Thus, when Egypt would not hearken, there was one plague more—and this one, too, centered on life.

TEN PLAGUES

FIRST PLAGUE centered on the Nile (Exodus 7:20).

- This was a direct challenge to Egypt's existence—the Nile was the source of all life and fertility in the land.
- Pharaoh went to the Nile each morning to worship this major deity.
- "Both time and place are of significance here. Pharaoh went out in the morning to the Nile [Exodus 7:15; 8:20], not merely to take a refreshing walk, or to bathe in the river, or to see how high the water had risen, but without doubt to present his daily worship to the Nile, which was honoured by the Egyptians as their supreme deity" (Keil and Delitzsch, *Commentary on the Old Testament,* 1:478).

SECOND PLAGUE centered on the goddess Heqet, the frog (Exodus 8:6–8).

- The frog was sacred—a symbol of life springing forth, of childbirth, and thus a symbol of resurrection.
- Heqet presided over the birth of kings and queens, as a divine, unseen midwife. She had assisted Osiris to rise from the dead. Among Egyptian Christians the frog would become the symbol of the resurrection (Keil and Delitzsch, 2:90).
- A sacred animal was now manipulated by Israel's God.

THIRD PLAGUE, stinging gnats, centered on the soil or the earth (Exodus 8:17).

- Stinging gnats issued from the very soil worshiped by Egyptians.
- Again, one of their own gods was now controlled by Israel's God.

FOURTH PLAGUE, swarms of flies, was related to the scarab (Exodus 8:24).

- The "fly" has been identified as an Egyptian beetle or scarab— emblem of the sun-god Ra (one of the greatest and most enduring of the gods).
- "In the fourth plague (see Ex. 8:21–32) the fly or beetle—

sacred emblem of the sun-god, Ra—became a torment by swarming the Egyptians and their possessions and ruining the land" (Vorhaus, *Ensign*, Sept. 1980, 65).
• Another example of Israel's God controlling an Egyptian god.

FIFTH PLAGUE, involving the livestock, centered on both the sacred bull god, Apis, and the cow goddess, Hathor (Exodus 9:6).
• The sacred nature of both is well-documented. Among other things, they symbolized strength, power, life, and fertility (which helps to explain why, later, the Israelites made a golden calf).
• Thus, these Egyptian deities were also overpowered by Jehovah.

SIXTH PLAGUE of boils showed Jehovah's power over personal health.
• This highlights the personal relationships between Israelites and their God.
• Egyptian religion did not promote the idea of a personal god who could heal from sickness or even prevent it—no one-to-one relationship with the gods.

SEVENTH PLAGUE demonstrated Jehovah's power over the gods of Egypt—hail and fire from the sky (Exodus 9:22–26).
• The lightning god, Min, was one of Jehovah's targets.
• The result of this plague was the destruction of all crops, animals, and men that were in the fertile fields of the Nile.
• Osiris was also a target since he was a personification of the overflowing of the Nile and the rebirth of vegetation which comes from the flooding of the Nile.

EIGHTH PLAGUE had as its object a demonstration of Jehovah's power over the Nile and life (Exodus 10:12–13, 20).
• This was a double plague involving the "east wind" *and* locusts (grasshoppers).
• Famous Egyptologist Wallis Budge noted: "Ideas of religious enjoyment seem to have been associated [with the grasshopper], for in the *Book of the Dead* . . . the deceased says, 'I have rested in the Field of the Grasshoppers.' . . . The grasshopper

is mentioned as early as the VIth Dynasty, and in the text of [Pharaoh] Pepi II . . . the king is said to 'arrive in heaven like the grasshopper of Ra'" (*Gods of the Egyptians,* 2:379).

- The destructive power of the *khamsin,* or the east wind, is well known from the scriptures (contrasted with the west wind, which is beneficent).

NINTH PLAGUE was darkness (Exodus 10:21–22).

- The target was Ra, the great sun-god, *and* Osiris. For obvious reasons, the sun was worshiped in ancient Egypt.
- Every king upon accession adopted the god's name, and those kings who became the sons of Ra by taking his name became his equal and took their place side by side with Ra in heaven. Perhaps the most famous pharaoh of all was *Rameses.*
- One scholar points out why the darkness and/or control of light would have a devastating effect on the Egyptians: "The Egyptians formed the conviction that human life is a close parallel to the course of the sun: man is born like the sun in the morning, lives his earthly life and dies, like the sun, which emits its life-giving rays the whole day and sets in the evening; but the analogy requires that his death should not be final, and that in a certain sense it does not take place at all" (Cerny, *Ancient Egyptian Religion,* 83).

Each succeeding plague came closer and closer to the very existence of the individual. Each time Pharaoh rejected the command to release Israel. The final plague touched their deepest, ultimate concern with the perpetuation of life as it also pointed to the death of another Firstborn.

TENTH PLAGUE. The death of the firstborn (Exodus 11:1–6).

- Preparation for the tenth plague is the Passover.
- Passover is at the heart of the Exodus.

Exodus 12:1–13

Israel would be spared the tenth plague by participating in the ordinance of Passover, Hebrew *pesach*, from the verb meaning "to skip by or spare." Instructions were given concerning the sacrificial lamb and the "passover" of the angel of death who was to bypass the homes of the faithful and obedient who marked their doors as instructed. The qualities and specifications concerning the male lamb without blemish are mentioned (vv. 5, 46; compare John 19:36). Observe the lamb's significance as anticipatory of the great atoning sacrifice which was to come. Consider the interpretation of such things in the New Testament: 1 Peter 1:18–19; Galatians 3:24–25; and in the Book of Mormon: 2 Nephi 11:4; Mosiah 3:14–15; 13:30–31; 16:14–15.

Exodus 12:14–20

Unleavened bread, a symbol of the haste of the Israelites' departure, was to be eaten for a week, beginning with the night of the slaughter of the paschal lamb on the fourteenth day of the month of Aviv and continuing until the twenty-first. Those dates became "fixed sabbaths" to be observed every year on the same dates and during them no work was to be done.

Exodus 12:21–28

Moses passed these instructions on to the people to prepare them for the first Passover. The purpose of the Passover was to teach the children in the future. Jewish families still keep this celebration and review these events, showing the meaning of freedom to their children. Christians also take lessons from these stories as Paul suggested in his letter to the Corinthians (1 Corinthians 10:1–11).

Exodus 12:29–51

Verse 33 has the frightened Egyptians claiming, "We be all dead men"; however, the Joseph Smith Translation reads: "We have found our first-born all dead; therefore get ye out of the land lest we die also."

The exodus of the Israelites is unique in all of history. The Israelites left with treasures of Egypt. A great "mixed multitude" went forth, for there were non-Israelites who went with them, probably including some Egyptians. By undergoing the proper initiatory ordinance of circumcision, the "stranger" could also qualify to partake of the Passover, and later it is specified that there is one law for all, whether an Israelite or a gentile convert.

The Exodus began with 600,000 men, besides women and children (JST), moving into a wilderness area. Some have argued that the Sinai Peninsula could not sustain that number of people, but the point of the biblical text is to show that only the Lord, in miraculous ways, could help so many people survive in such desolate terrain.

Concerning the "four hundred and thirty years," see the commentary at Exodus 1:6–14 about whether the Israelites were "sojourners" in Egypt for that whole period or whether Abraham and his descendants were really "sojourners" wherever they were from the time the promise was made until it was fulfilled when they inherited a land of their own. "Strangers" and "sojourners" are called *gerim* in Hebrew, meaning "temporary dwellers," in contrast to *toshavim,* meaning "permanent inhabitants."

SYMBOLISM BEHIND THE PASSOVER

Verses	Action or Activity	Symbolism
12:2	Passover represents a new beginning	Atonement and Resurrection of Jesus Christ provide a new beginning
12:3, 5	A lamb without blemish became the sacrifice	Jesus Christ is the Lamb without blemish (1 Peter 1:18–19)
12:6–7	Blood was put on door posts of dwellings	Identifies the participant as a follower of God
12:8–10	A whole lamb roasted with fire, nothing remaining	a. The whole lamb signified God's unity with his people as well as his glory b. Jesus as the Lamb was "wholly consumed"—he gave all

Verses	Action or Activity	Symbolism
12:12	Firstborn die	Jesus Christ is the Firstborn who died (D&C 93:21–22)
12:13	Blood of the paschal lamb caused physical death to pass by	Blood of Christ causes physical and spiritual death to pass by (2 Nephi 9)
12:14	Passover kept as a memorial feast throughout generations	Always remember the Lamb; eternal nature of ordinances (D&C 20:77, 79)
12:15–19	Feast of unleavened bread lasted seven days	"Leaven"—corruption (Luke 12:1; Mark 8:15)—is done away eternally in Christ's sacrifice
12:21	The Passover killed	Christ, our Passover, is killed for us (1 Cor. 5:7)
12:22–23	Hyssop used	Foreshadows the Crucifixion (John 19:29)
12:26–27	Children asked questions during the first Passover	During the Seder meal four questions are asked by children. Symbolizes parents' obligation to teach salvation to children (D&C 68:25)
12:36	Israel received good things through God's intervention after many long years of unjust treatment	Through the Atonement justice becomes our friend; see the parable of Lazarus (Luke 16:19–26)
12:43	No stranger eats the Passover (commitment required)	No stranger is to partake of the sacrament (meaning someone unworthy; 3 Nephi 18:28–30); it is a covenant requiring commitment
12:46	No bone broken of the Paschal lamb	No bone broken of Christ (John 19:36)
12:48	Covenant making allowed some to be adopted as Israelites—children of the covenant	Acceptance of gospel covenants allows all to become children of Christ (Mosiah 5:7; 27:25)

Exodus 13:1–16

In grateful memory of their deliverance and because of the "ransom" of the firstborn of Egypt, the Israelites were to consecrate their firstborn with a sacrifice, the nature of which will be noted later. Certain animals were substituted for the firstborn of the family.

The meaning of the "sign" and "memorial" in verse 9 and "token" and "frontlets" in verse 16 is discussed in commentary at Deuteronomy 6:6–25 and 11:18–32. The Hebrew term for these frontlets is *totafot*, which is the same as the Greek *phylacteries*. Verses 1–10 and 11–16 are two of the four passages included inside each phylactery.

Exodus 13:17–22

Israel's route was indicated by a pillar of cloud by day and a pillar of fire by night, signifying the presence of the Lord going before them (compare the Lehite colony's Liahona and our fire, the gift of the Holy Ghost). Their journey would have been short if they had been ready and capable of following the coastal route through the Philistine lands to Canaan. Since there were Egyptian army posts along that route, however, they could have found themselves with Egyptian soldiers in front and in back of them. See Bible Map 2 for a possible route of the Exodus.

Moses, acquainted with Joseph's writings, took the bones of Joseph with them, as the former patriarch and ruler had made them promise (Genesis 50:25).

Exodus 14:1–9

The problem of labor in the Egyptian economy was part of the reason Pharaoh didn't want to let Israel go. Thus, after the Israelites had begun their exodus, Pharaoh once more retracted the concessions he had made and tried to recover the slaves. The Egyptian army, with their thundering war horses and chariots, pursued the Israelites who were on foot and no match for battle-hardened warriors—at least as man measures such things.

Exodus 14:10–18

The Israelites were frightened by the threat and became sarcastic and critical. But Moses stood firm in faith to strengthen them. When man can of himself do nothing more, he must simply put his trust in God and "stand still, and see the salvation of the Lord" (v. 13).

Moses was in his extremity; he was backed up against the sea. He had to rely on the spirit of revelation to know how to fulfill the Lord's intention that Israel be saved. The spirit of revelation involves having faith enough to take the next step into the unknown. Modern revelation provides important insight for all of us on this principle: "Yea, behold, I will tell you in your mind and in your heart, by the Holy Ghost, which shall come upon you and which shall dwell in your heart. Now, behold, this is the spirit of revelation; behold, this is the spirit by which Moses brought the children of Israel through the Red Sea on dry ground" (D&C 8:2–3).

Exodus 14:19–31

The miracle of the crossing of the sea showed supernatural as well as natural forces responding to God's command (see Nephi's comment on this miracle and confirmation of it in 1 Nephi 17:25–27). Miracles and supernatural occurrences are really nothing more or less than manifestations of higher laws and principles understood by God, who instituted them, who "governeth and executeth all things . . . [and] hath given a law unto all things" (D&C 88:40, 42).

The Lord "overthrew the Egyptians" not because he hated them but because they would not free Israel nor prevent them from languishing and degenerating in bondage. In this regard, a foundational principle has been emphasized in modern times: "it is not right that any man should be in bondage one to another" (D&C 101:79).

Exodus 15:1–19

Moses, in addition to being a prophet, was also a songwriter and singer (see also Deuteronomy 32) and wrote a poetic song of praise and triumph commemorating the gifts of freedom, salvation, and victory over opposition.

Hebrew poetry is characterized by parallelism of thoughts expressed in short couplets (see further in Psalms). This parallelism appears in our translation, but other characteristics of Hebrew poetry, such as alliteration and a rhythm pattern, are almost impossible to preserve in translation. Poetry is frequently used in prophecy in the Old Testament and predominates in Job, Psalms, Proverbs, Ecclesiastes, and the Song of Solomon.

Verses 1–19 constitute Moses' actual song of triumph composed in poetic form. The next verses (20 and following) are written in prose. Verse 2 speaks of the Lord: "he is become my salvation." The word "salvation" in Hebrew is *Yeshua,* which is also the name "Jesus." Verse 3 articulates a true principle, though it may offend the peaceful sensibilities of some people: "The Lord is a man of war: the Lord is his name." (This construction also demonstrates parallelism in Hebrew composition.) Verse 16 refers to the Lord's people, "which thou hast purchased"—a concept amplified in the New Testament. Though most of this song contains imagery which is noble and beautiful, some lines admittedly express thoughts and feelings we find neither noble nor beautiful, as in the outcries for vengeance. The poets wrote of things they felt strongly about—supplication, blessing, praise, prophecy, thanksgiving, or calls for condemnation and chastening.

Exodus 15:20–27

Miriam is one of several prophetesses mentioned in the Bible. Some others are Deborah (Judges 4:4), Huldah (2 Kings 22:14), Anna (Luke 2:36), and the daughters of Philip (Acts 21:9). That these women should possess the gift of prophecy and revelation is in perfect harmony with restoration scripture (Alma 32:23). However, only one man on earth at a time is designated as the prophet-leader of the

Lord's people, possessing all the keys of the priesthood (D&C 132:7).

After the singing and dancing were finished, the mundane need for food and drink began to press upon the Israelites, and their voices turned from singing to murmuring but not to supplicate in faith for God's help. However, the Lord heard them patiently and provided water for them. He tried to teach a lesson with the water and give them a promise if they would be obedient; but alas, the children of Israel did not pass the test after one lesson.

The powerful promise preserved in verse 26 (see also Exodus 23:25) applies dramatically to our own day: If we will diligently obey God's commands, he will spare us the increasing array of social and sexual diseases (what modern revelations may be referring to when they speak of overflowing and desolating "scourges" and "sicknesses"; D&C 5:19; 45:31). "I am the Lord that healeth thee" can be literally translated "I am your physician" (compare Matthew 9:12; Luke 4:23; Moroni 8:8).

Exodus 16:1–7

The lack of food again brought murmuring among the Israelites, who appeared to prefer slavery with sustenance over freedom with responsibility after about six weeks' experience in the wilderness. The Lord even said he would provide ("rain down") bread from heaven, which was a type and foreshadowing of the Bread of Life. But even that did not completely satisfy some murmuring hearts.

Exodus 16:8–36

It is remarkable that the Israelites' supplies from Egypt sustained them as long as they did. The merciful Lord miraculously provided sustenance in a desert region where the alternative for so many people was either a miracle or death. It is useless to guess what the food was; even the original Hebrew name they called it, *man-hu*, means "what is it?" Thus it came to be called "manna." From then on a miracle was specially prepared every day, except the Sabbath, for nearly forty years—more than 12,000 times! The quails provided at this time do not seem to be a regular part of their provisions; they were seasonal or occasional. Verse 12 reflects the custom in ancient Israel of eating two meals per day.

The instructions for keeping the Sabbath constitute the first recorded instruction on this practice since it was mentioned in connection with the creation periods. Some followed the instructions; some did not.

Exodus 17:1–7

Lacking water to drink, the Israelites again complained and pessimistically "tempted" the Lord. The word "tempted" is translated from the Hebrew word meaning "test," "try," or "prove." They were testing the Lord to see whether he could be depended upon to help them when they needed help. This is the same idea Jesus seems to have had in mind when he said, "Thou shalt not tempt the Lord thy God," quoting Deuteronomy 6:16 (see Luke 4:12; Matthew 22:18; and compare Acts 5:9).

At every sign of trouble the people of Israel wished to be back in Egypt. There seems to have been a lot of murmuring, which is half suppressed or muttered complaint or grumbling. Sometimes we do this when we are not openly critical but disloyal behind the scenes. We might wonder at this point why Moses continued as their leader.

The "rock in Horeb [Sinai]" was another symbolic representation of Christ, the spiritual rock of their salvation (1 Corinthians 10:4).

Exodus 17:8–16

Israel again showed their lack of confidence in the Lord's constant help in their first war. Only when they could see Moses' hands uplifted, apparently in communication with God, did they fight with courage and prevail. However, "Moses' hands were heavy," and he needed support. Aaron was his brother, and Hur his brother-in-law (married to

Miriam). Compare in the modern-day Church the role of two counselors in supporting and sustaining the president or bishop. The young leader Joshua is first introduced in this event. His name was originally Oshea, but Moses gave him a new name by which he became known to future generations (Numbers 13:8, 16).

Moses was commanded to write about these events in a book. This is only one example of many internal evidences that Moses wrote down the information which has been preserved in the books of Moses (see also Exodus 24:4, 7). At this point, Israel traveled to the wilderness of Sinai (Exodus 19:1–2), traditionally the southern part of the Sinai Peninsula.

Exodus 18:1–12

Moses was reunited with his wife and family, whom he had sent back to be with his father-in-law, the high priest Jethro. Appropriate to the occasion, Jethro offered a sacrifice of thanks for the Lord's deliverance of Israel and ate a ceremonial meal with Moses and Aaron and the elders of Israel.

The names of Moses' and Zipporah's sons were Gershom ("an alien [or stranger] there") and Eliezer ("my God is my help")—given to them for the reasons indicated. There is not much information about Moses' family, but his descendants are listed in 1 Chronicles 23:14–17.

Exodus 18:13–27

Jethro made a valuable suggestion to Moses that he organize leaders over groups of ten, fifty, one hundred, and one thousand who would instruct and judge the people in all but the most difficult matters. Matters requiring greater attention could go through a system of inferior and superior courts, if necessary, until they reached Moses at the head. This is the first recorded leadership training using principles of delegation, chain of command, and sharing of burdens with others (delegation has been dubbed the art of executive sanity).

Moses showed commendable humility and wisdom in accepting the old priest's advice. The use of the same type of organization in a modern exodus may be seen in Doctrine and Covenants 136:2–3ff. Also, the general Church organization today is comparable. There are those who preside over the thousands (stake presidents), over the hundreds (bishops and branch presidents), over the fifties (high priests group leaders and elders quorum presidents), and finally those who labor with the tens—home teachers.

Exodus 19:1–6

Arriving at Mount Sinai three months after being freed, they would stay there for eleven months, which corresponds in our Bibles to Exodus 19:1 through Numbers 10:11–12. The revelation of the Lord to Israel once they arrived at Mount Sinai was monumental: one of four watershed revelatory episodes in salvation history (the others being the inaugural revelation given to Adam in the beginning, the revelation of Jesus Christ in the meridian dispensation, and the revelation of the Restoration in the fulness of times). The revelation at Sinai is linked to the other three episodes in terms of what the Lord was attempting to accomplish—exalting his people.

At Sinai, Moses made a number of trips up the mountain to communicate with God, the first being recorded beginning in verse 3. This mountain was regarded as a temple, just as the Lord's Temples were regarded as his mountains (see, for example, Isaiah 2:2). In beautiful verbal imagery Moses heard of God's personal interest in his people: "I [personally] bare you on eagles' wings, and brought you unto myself" (v. 4). Israel learned of God's great plans for their nation: they were to be *a peculiar treasure, a kingdom of priests,* and *a holy nation* for the benefit of all families of the earth. This was essentially Abraham's mission and the mission of his descendants. The covenant was again confirmed through Moses.

The Lord wanted a "peculiar treasure" (see also Deuteronomy 14:2). "Peculiar" (Hebrew, *segulla*) means "special or valued possession, purchased or private property, or treasure" and always refers (in all occurrences in the Old

and the New Testaments) to the people of Israel. In Malachi
3:17 the term is translated "jewels" (see also D&C 60:4).
The people of the Lord were purchased through the blood
of Christ, as Peter notes (1 Peter 1:18–19), and thus were
the Lord's "peculiar people" and "holy nation" (1 Peter 2:9).
Sadly, the Lord's special treasure made themselves worthless, as the Hebrew of 2 Kings 17:15 indicates ("vain" really
should be rendered as "empty" or "worthless").

In sum, the Israelites could have become a kingdom of
Melchizedek Priesthood "priests," for there was no Aaronic
Priesthood yet. Elder Bruce R. McConkie stated that those
who are "ordained kings and priests . . . will bear rule as exalted beings during the millennium and in eternity" (*Mormon
Doctrine*, 599). Furthermore, "whenever the Lord has a
people on earth he offers to make them a nation of kings and
priests—not a congregation of lay members with a priest or
a minister at the head—but a whole Church in which every
man is his own minister, in which every man stands as a king
in his own right, reigning over his own family-kingdom. The
priesthood which makes a man a king and a priest is thus a
royal priesthood. To ancient Israel the offer was made in these
words: 'If ye will obey my voice indeed, and keep my covenant, then ye shall be a peculiar treasure . . . And ye shall be
unto me a kingdom of priests, and an holy nation.' (Ex. 19:5–
6.)" (McConkie, *Doctrinal New Testament Commentary*,
3:294). This was Jehovah's intended destiny for Israel.

Exodus 19:7–13

At this point the Lord wanted to reform the Israelites'
lives, bestow upon them the greater, or Melchizedek, priesthood, establish a holy Temple, and give them a sacred endowment. Had the Israelites followed the Lord's instructions and
accepted all the privileges offered them, they could have received the grandest of all revelations: they could have seen the
Lord, heard him speak to Moses, known for themselves about
his will and his law, comprehended Moses' future revelations

from God (Deuteronomy 4:10), and been translated as other communities had (JST Genesis 14:32–34). There was a need for cleanliness and dedication in preparing for this great spiritual experience.

At first Israel accepted and committed themselves to the Lord's intended plan. "All that the Lord hath spoken we will do" (v. 8). But something was amiss—a fact we are not made aware of until the next chapter, when we see Israel retreating or shrinking from their opportunities (Exodus 20:19).

Exodus 19:14–25

At the prearranged signal, the sounding of the trumpet "exceeding long and loud" (see also D&C 29:13), the people trembled in anticipation and awe. But apparently they were not fully ready to come up "in the sight" of the Lord on the mount where Moses was, because the Lord told Moses to go down and warn them not to come up. The Lord warned that if they broke through and gazed on Him, they would perish. (Mortal bodies must be transfigured to endure the presence of celestial beings; see Moses 1:11).

President Spencer W. Kimball explained: "It must be obvious . . . that to endure the glory of the Father or of the glorified Christ, a mortal being must be translated or otherwise fortified. . . . There is a protective force that God brings into play when he exposes his human servants to the glories of his person and his works. . . . In heavenly glorious vision, Moses 'beheld the world . . . and all the children of men. . . . ' (Moses 1:8). He was protected then, but when the protection from such transcendent glory was relaxed, Moses was left near helpless" (*Faith Precedes the Miracle*, 86).

An explanation of why all this happened at the mount is found in Doctrine and Covenants 84:21–24, which constitutes some of the most important verses in all the standard works for understanding Israel's plight for the next 1200 years or more (see also Hebrews 4:1–3). Although their hearts were not fully prepared to endure his presence, they did hear his voice as the Ten Commandments were given. (Moses' review of these great events is recorded in Deuteronomy 4:10, 12, 33, 36; 5:22–26.)

Thunderings, lightnings, fire, smoke, and a "thick cloud" accompanied the Lord's descent upon Mount Sinai. (For a fascinating study of light, fire, and cloud phenomena at the appearance and disappearance of celestial beings, see Ogden and Skinner, *Acts through Revelation,* 383–86.)

The presentation of the Ten Commandments (the Decalogue) on the stone tablets is related in Exodus 31:18; 32:15, 19; the second set of tablets, prepared after the first set was broken, is discussed in Exodus 34:1ff. Adam and Eve had the Ten Commandments, which are eternal laws, from the beginning.

Exodus 20:1–6

The Ten Commandments, revealed by God, are essentially the basic laws of civilization and the foundation, even precursor, of any and all constitutions of nations. Israel's constitution was based on the Ten Commandments and was laid out following them (v. 22–23:33). These commandments are so fundamental to the Lord's plan that they are revealed again in every dispensation. For example, Adam received them, Abinadi gave them, the Savior included them in his teachings, and the Doctrine and Covenants reiterated them. The first half of the commandments center on man's relationship to God; the second half govern man's relationship to his fellow man.

The First Two Commandments. The first two commandments are essentially one. The Lord declared his identity as the One who freed the Israelites from bondage and also declared "Thou shalt have no other gods." The restriction is against worshiping any other "god" and is emphasized again in verses 4 and 5 by the commandment against making an image or likeness of anything in heaven, on earth, or under the earth or bowing down and worshiping them.

*Brigham Young University student reenacting Moses
with the tablets on the traditional Mount Sinai* (Jebel Musa)

The phrase "before me" in the familiar translation "Thou shalt have no other gods *before me*" is from the Hebrew phrase *'al-panai*, which means "in front of"—either to the exclusion of another or "in preference" or "in addition to." The meaning is clear: those who worship the Lord should not make or adopt any other object to worship.

Moses had grown up seeing a pharaoh regarded as a god. The Lord made a point of teaching Moses that "there is no God beside me." Moses responded, "This *one God only* will I worship" (Moses 1:6, 20; emphasis added). The Lord knew Canaan, and he knew the Israelites, so he warned them in no uncertain terms to make him their first priority in life.

The Second Commandment forbids the making of graven images of things above, things in the earth, and things beneath the earth. The Egyptians did such things. They worshiped the sun, moon, sky, earth, hawk, falcon, vulture, beetle, crocodile, jackal, cobra, monkey, baboon, bull, cow, ram, lion, and more as gods or as physical manifestations of the gods. Did God forbid these images for selfish or jealous reasons, insisting on

210

our full attention and loyalty? (Notice the definition of "jealous" in footnote 5*b*.) The Lord does have sensitive and deep feelings, but he also knows that we can only become as he is if we develop his attributes. We must focus our energy on worshiping him.

Making figures, images, figurines, or statuettes which were not for the purpose of worship (that is, not to be an idol) was allowed. In fact, later we find instructions for making certain symbolic forms to be placed on the Ark of the Covenant or to adorn the Tabernacle and later the Temple.

The Lord will "visit the sins of the fathers upon the heads of the children" generation after generation as long as the children continue to hate or oppose him (2 Nephi 25:9), but he will show mercy to anyone who will learn to love him and keep his commandments. Sometimes suffering is imposed on people because of some status, condition, or characteristic transmitted to them from their father or mother ("the fathers have eaten sour grapes, and the children's teeth are set on edge"; Ezekiel 18:2), but our parents' sins cannot be used as an excuse or justification for our own actions because we believe we will be punished for our own sins and not for those of our fathers when it comes to God's punishments (see Article of Faith 2; D&C 124:50; Deuteronomy 24:16; Ezekiel 18).

Exodus 20:7

The Third Commandment. We are not to swear, profane, or invoke the name of God for false or vain purposes. The concept of "vain" means in an "empty" or "worthless" way. Common profanity is no doubt our most usual violation of this command. President Spencer W. Kimball often said, "Profanity is the effort of a feeble brain to express itself forcibly" (*Ensign*, Nov. 1974, 7). However, this commandment warns against not only profane language but also taking the Lord's name upon us in sacred covenants (as the sacrament and Temple ordinances) and then not honoring it by living up to those covenants. Read the warning to that effect in Doctrine and Covenants 63:61–64.

Exodus 20:8–11

The Fourth Commandment. We are admonished to remember God's rest after the six days or periods of creation by also ceasing from our ordinary work and sanctifying one day in seven. "Rest" does not mean cessation of all activity, rather it is to turn wholly to the Lord's holy will and ways, to sanctify our activity. Of course, there is no way to sanctify a day except by letting the day sanctify us. To sanctify means "to make saintly" or "to make holy." We do not know how the Lord originally sanctified the day when he rested, but this is a commandment everyone ought to obey joyfully and be thankful that God has made a Sabbath for man.

Remember that work is ennobling and that "six days shalt thou labour" is also part of the commandment.

Exodus 20:12

The Fifth Commandment. If parents teach children (as urged in Genesis 18:17–19, or as specifically admonished in our dispensation in Doctrine and Covenants 68:25–28), and if the proper relationship is maintained between parents and children (as suggested, for example, in such passages as Ephesians 6:4; Colossians 3:21; Matthew 18:1–6, 10, etc.), it is only natural that each succeeding generation will preserve the best of the heritage of the generations before. Thus the home is established as the base where good living is taught and learned. It is when the rising generation rebels against the best, and indulges in the worst, that society deteriorates.

This commandment to honor one's parents is a transition between the commandments pertaining to relations with God and those pertaining to relations with others.

Exodus 20:13

The Sixth Commandment. This is a continuation of the commandments that regulate how we should behave toward our fellow human beings. Behind them is the principle of the "second great commandment" (Leviticus 19:18), which is quoted by Jesus in Matthew 22:36–40, that one who loves a neighbor would not do any of the things forbidden by the commandments.

The sixth commandment is specifically against murder. The evils of murder were known, of course, from the beginning. Recall the warnings to Cain and his subsequent punishment (Genesis 4:8–15); recall the punishment of the one who sheds human blood (Genesis 9:5–6); and recall the awareness of Joseph's brothers of the evil they plotted against him. The revelation to Moses on Mount Sinai reiterated a known law.

Jesus, in his review of the law against murder, added a warning against even getting angry or inciting anger which could result in violence and murder. Similar advice was given in later dispensations (Matthew 5:21–22; D&C 42:18–19; 59:6).

Willful destruction of the life of anyone is an infringement upon the rights of other humans and the prerogatives of God. Shedding innocent blood by someone who has been sealed in the new and everlasting covenant is a most grievous sin (see D&C 132:26).

Participation in warfare is not murder in defensive circumstances (Exodus 17:8–16; Alma 43:47; D&C 98:33–37).

Unnecessary slaughter of animals is a related matter but is not murder (D&C 49:21a; JST Genesis 9:11).

Joseph Smith commented about reconciling different commands from the Lord to preserve and to destroy: "God said, 'Thou shalt not kill'; at another time He said 'Thou shalt utterly destroy.' This is the principle on which the government of heaven is conducted—by revelation adapted to the circumstances in which the children of the kingdom are placed. Whatever God requires is right, no matter what it is, although we may not see the reason thereof till long after the events transpire" (*History of the Church*, 5:135).

Exodus 20:14

The Seventh Commandment. Like the sixth, this commandment involves tampering with God's domain as well as the dignity and rights of people. God has specified how children should be brought to this earth. It is the privilege of men and women to participate in this creative process when properly married, but if the process is abused or prostituted and proper responsibility is not accepted in connection with it, it is a "great wickedness and sin against God" (Genesis 39:9). The unauthorized giving or taking of life carries significant consequences.

Furthermore God has said in three different dispensations that this sin, or "anything like unto it," must be avoided (for example, Leviticus 20:10; D&C 59:6). During his mortal ministry, Jesus added a higher law: Don't even lust after another person or you have already committed adultery with that person in your heart (Matthew 5:27–32).

Adultery is punishable on earth and in heaven, but it is not unpardonable because complete repentance can bring forgiveness (John 8:3–11; D&C 58:42–43; 61:2; 64:7).

Exodus 20:15

The Eighth Commandment. This commandment forbids all stealing. Such a prohibition against robbery, burglary, shoplifting, plagiarism, embezzlement, cheating, or any other form of self-aggrandizement at the expense of others is essential for any stable society. Sins and crimes involving stealing are punishable both in this life and in the life to come unless corrected by repentance (Deuteronomy 24:7; Zechariah 5:3; D&C 42:20).

Exodus 20:16

The Ninth Commandment. This commandment specifically forbids giving false testimony, but it is expanded in other scriptures to include all forms of lying, misrepresentation, or falsehood. The liar at the judgment bar is listed with the "abominable, and murderers, and whoremongers, and sorcerers, and idolaters" who "shall have their part in the lake which burneth with fire and brimstone" (Revelation 21:8; 22:15). The unrepentant liar cannot be trusted, and trust is an indispensable attribute of godliness.

Exodus 20:17

The Tenth Commandment. This commandment does not end with the words "thou shalt not covet." Instead, it continues with examples of things we should not covet. To covet is to desire or take pleasure in somebody or something. Some things we *should* covet, such as spiritual gifts and other blessings. However, this commandment is against coveting, or taking illicit delight in and feeling desire for, things we cannot legally or morally have, such as another's property, status or position, or spouse. This commandment is a safeguard against breaking the other commandments.

About the Ten Commandments in general, President Thomas S. Monson has taught: "Although the world has changed, the laws of God remain constant. They have not changed; they will not change. The Ten Commandments are just that—commandments. They are *not* suggestions. They are every bit as requisite today as they were when God gave them to the children of Israel. If we but listen, we hear the echo of God's voice, speaking to us here and now. . . .

"Our code of conduct is definitive; it is not negotiable. It is found not only in the Ten Commandments but also in the Sermon on the Mount, given to us by the Savior when He walked upon the earth. It is found throughout His teachings. It is found in the words of modern revelation" (*Ensign,* Nov. 2011, 83).

Elder L. Tom Perry spoke powerfully of the need to live the Ten Commandments today:

"For much of the civilized world, particularly the Judeo-Christian world, the Ten Commandments have been the most accepted and enduring delineation between good and evil.

"In my judgment, four of the Ten Commandments are

taken as seriously today as ever. As a culture, we disdain and condemn murder, stealing, and lying, and we still believe in the responsibility of children to their parents.

"But as a larger society, we routinely dismiss the other six commandments:

- If worldly priorities are any indication, we certainly have 'other gods' we put before the true God.
- We make idols of celebrities, of lifestyles, of wealth, and yes, sometimes of graven images or objects.
- We use the name of God in profane ways, including our exclamations and our swearing.
- We use the Sabbath day for our biggest games, our most serious recreation, our heaviest shopping, and virtually everything else but worship.
- We treat sexual relations outside marriage as recreation and entertainment.
- And coveting has become a far too common way of life.

"Prophets from all dispensations have consistently warned against violations of two of the more serious commandments—the ones relating to murder and adultery. I see a common basis for these two critical commandments—the belief that life itself is the prerogative of God and that our physical bodies, the temples of mortal life, should be created within the bounds God has set. For man to substitute his own rules for the laws of God on either end of life is the height of presumption and the depth of sin.

"The main effects of these depreciating attitudes about the sanctity of marriage are the consequences to families—the strength of families is deteriorating at an alarming rate. This deterioration is causing widespread damage to society. I see direct cause and effect. As we give up commitment and fidelity to our marriage partners, we remove the glue that holds our society together. . . .

"God reveals to His prophets that there are moral

absolutes. Sin will always be sin. Disobedience to the Lord's commandments will always deprive us of His blessings. The world changes constantly and dramatically, but God, His commandments, and promised blessings do not change. They are immutable and unchanging" (*Ensign,* May 2013, 87–88).

Exodus 20:18–20

As mentioned in Exodus 19:14–25, the people were awestruck and fearful when they heard the voice of God speaking the commandments, and they fled from his presence. But Moses comforted them, explaining that God's purpose was to impress them and to prove them so they would not sin later. Sadly, this fear was symptomatic of a deep-seated problem—a lack of faith in the true and living God and his prophet. This retreat from God's intended blessings led to tragic consequences. The Prophet Joseph Smith taught that the moment we reject blessings and opportunities that come from God the devil takes power and is able to increase his control over us (*Joseph Smith* [manual], 214). In other words, when Israel pulled back or retreated from the Lord, Satan increased his control, the people hardened their hearts and began to receive less and less until they knew little or nothing of the Lord's mind and will (Alma 12:9–11). They then committed the gravest act of apostasy, manifested in the golden calf episode (Exodus 32).

Exodus 20:21–26

Moses "drew near" (or as the Septuagint reads, "entered into") the "thick darkness" (or as the Hebrew is translated, "heavy cloud"), which was the cloud of the divine Presence. He was then instructed to remind the people that God had spoken to them and that they were to worship Him properly by their behavior, their lives, and their sacrifices.

Verse 23 warns against making gods of silver or gold, and the warning was given just before they did that very thing! Verse 26 mentions that indecent exposure of priests ascending steps to the great altar was to be avoided by the use of a ramp.

Exodus 21:1–11

From this point through Exodus 23, specific provisions of the covenant code (or what we might label a constitution of theocratic laws) are detailed. The Book of Mormon prophet Abinadi referred to this code as the law of ordinances and performances. All laws of the Mosaic code were types of higher things to come.

Regulations are given concerning servants and the provision for freeing them in the seventh year, the sabbatical year. It may be difficult for some today to understand why slavery, usually some form of indentured servitude, ever existed among the Lord's people. At that time it would have been remarkable to find a nation or people who did not practice some form of slavery, and the Israelites also adopted some of the customs of the times. Many of the laws Israelites lived were "lower" laws; thus it was necessary to gradually upgrade Israelite spirituality.

In ancient Israel, permanent ownership of servants was not permitted unless an individual chose to be a slave for life (vv. 5–6). These servants were almost on an equal footing with their masters in Israel. Some were willing to forfeit freedom for security. Certain legal guarantees were invoked for female servants in Israel, in contrast to surrounding nations (vv. 7–11).

Exodus 21:12–25

Laws governing capital offenses and some lesser crimes are set forth. Compare, for example, premeditated murder as opposed to accidental death due to negligence (v. 13, which also refers to appointed cities of refuge). One oft-repeated law of that time—"an eye for an eye and a tooth for a tooth"—some wrongly suppose characterized their whole way of life, but it was really applicable only in very specific cases. Some may see this as a law of retaliation, but it was actually a law requiring equal compensation—a law of restitution or reparation. Our modern justice systems often provide no recompense for the victim and often leave a heavy burden on the victim. For example, for involuntary manslaughter, the guilty party goes to prison (and we pay) and both families go on welfare (and we pay). Under the Mosaic law the burden was on the guilty. The law demanded more than punishment; it encouraged restitution as part of repentance. We should view the Mosaic laws as part of the handiwork of God, bearing the marks of a just and perfect God, rather than as primitive laws.

Exodus 21:26–36

These verses have good principles for any society in dealing with responsibility for hazards connected with one's property, animals, or premises. The numerous "if . . . then" laws (called casuistic laws) stipulate that *if* a certain thing happens, *then* this is what the consequence should be. Verse 32 indicates the standard price for a slave: thirty pieces of silver. It was also the number of silver pieces Judas was willing to settle for in betraying Jesus (Matthew 26:14–15; Zechariah 11:12–13).

Exodus 22:1–20

Particular ways "thou shalt not steal" are mentioned, especially the responsibility involved in borrowing and lending. Verses 1–13 are sometimes referred to as the five cases of embezzlement. Ratios of restitution lay at the heart of all these rules.

The "witch" of verse 18 was anyone who practiced sorcery or communion with evil spirits. The Hebrew word also connoted seduction and harlotry. Sorcery was common and was considered as serious as idolatry before God. Notice the Joseph Smith Translation change to "murderer." This parallels the Septuagint translation which uses the word "poisoner" here. Verse 30 may seem harsh, but given all that Israel had been through, and what they would yet encounter, this sternness is understandable. Technically, this verse invokes the *herem* (Hebrew, "utterly destroy"), which plays a tremendous role in Israelite life when they enter the promised land.

The total destruction of the thoroughly corrupt Canaanite nations was later commanded by the Lord (Numbers 21:2; Deuteronomy 2:34, 3:6; 7:2; 13:15; 20:17; Joshua 2:10; 6:17, 21; 8:26; 10:1–40; 11:11–12; Judges 1:17).

Exodus 22:21–31

These are samples of what some call the "higher" moral laws, which admonish love, kindness, consideration, mercy, gratitude, respect, and dedication. Verses 25–27 outline laws dealing with interest on loans (see Bible Dictionary, "Usury"). Verses 26–27 outline kindness to the poorest of people, for if all one could offer as a pledge was the clothes off his back, he was poor indeed.

Exodus 23:1–9

The Israelites were warned against letting mob hysteria or other group fads or trends influence one to "follow a multitude to do evil," an appropriate warning for modern cultures also.

"Countenance" in verse 3 means "favor"; judgment should not be biased by fear, influence, bribe, or favor on behalf of either the rich or the poor (see the Joseph Smith Translation footnote for a different rendering).

Doing good to one's enemy, or to "him that hateth thee," is a principle usually associated with Jesus' teachings (Matthew 5:43–48), but it was part of the teachings of Moses' dispensation, too. Verse 9 is a variation of the Golden Rule.

Exodus 23:10–13

Sabbatical years of "rest" for the land allowed it to lie fallow to renew itself, but it also provided food for the poor (see Bible Dictionary, "Sabbatical Year"). Sabbath days were a blessing for people and their animals.

Exodus 23:14–19

The three major annual feasts were those of the unleavened bread in early spring (*Pesakh*, or Passover), the harvest of the first fruits of the late spring (*Shavuot*, or Pentecost), and the ingathering of the late harvest of the fall (*Sukkot,* or Tabernacles). These were all for thanksgiving to God.

The Feast of Weeks (*Shavuot*) was so called because it came seven weeks after the Feast of Unleavened Bread/Passover (usually coming between mid-May to mid-June), during the first wheat harvest. In the Judaism of Jesus' day, it also celebrated the giving of the Law on Mount Sinai. In the New Testament it is called Pentecost (Greek, "fifty"; see Acts 2:1; 20:16) because it was held fifty days after Passover. The Feast of Tabernacles (Leviticus 23:43), or Booths, was so called because the Israelites lived in makeshift shelters when God brought them out of Egyptian bondage (usually celebrated sometime between mid-September to mid-October) and commemorated the Exodus as well as the joyous fall harvest.

These celebrations came to be known as pilgrimage or sanctuary festivals because they were the designated times when all males of the covenant were to come, from close or far, and appear before the Lord, which was at first the Tabernacle and then the Temple in Jerusalem. This perhaps helps to explain why Joseph and Mary went to be taxed (or enrolled for the Roman census) at springtime when she was so close to giving birth. They would take care of both government and religious obligations at the same time (Luke 2:1).

The strange law prohibiting the cooking of a young goat in its own mother's milk is probably related to fertility cult practices of the peoples round about Canaan. It became a basic tenet of *kashrut,* or proper ("kosher") dietary practice of Judaism. To this day, orthodox Jews keep dairy products and meat products strictly separated (no cheeseburgers and no pepperoni pizzas, etc.); they never combine the two in one meal and never use the same utensils for both dairy and meat meals. For the basic reason behind these strict regulations, see Mosiah 13:29–30.

Exodus 23:20–33

The angel of the Lord sent to guide and guard Israel reminds us of the gift of the Holy Ghost to guide, prompt, and comfort the faithful. The obedient will be protected and the Lord will fight their battles. This is the first of several such promises. The divine help as Israel approached and entered the promised land is best understood in light of the Lord's principle of blessing the worthy and letting the wicked suffer the consequences of their evil ways (for example, 1 Nephi 17:25–43). Another great promise was health and fertility—a tremendous blessing to a pastoral people. The reason for forbidding integration of the Israelites with the inhabitants of Canaan is seen in verses 32–33.

Exodus 24:1–8

The people of Israel, in anticipation of having Moses and the seventy special witnesses go up to the presence of the Lord, were instructed in all the laws and judgments of God. The theocratic constitution of Israel as a nation was presented and accepted by the citizenry. They accepted the laws, covenanted to keep them, and preserved a copy of them as a binding witness. Then their covenants were sanctified by a sacrifice. The people promised, "All the words which the Lord hath said will we do." In Exodus 32 we read about what they eventually did shortly after Moses was gone.

Notice the mention of writing and written records in verses 4 and 7. Also notice reference to the "blood of the covenant," which is symbolic of Jesus' mortal life and his instituting a "new testament," or covenant (Matthew 26:28). Indeed, "Moses alone," the only one allowed to "come near the Lord," describes Moses' role as mediator between God and the people of Israel, and clearly parallels Jesus Christ, who is the "mediator of the new covenant" (Hebrews 12:24).

Exodus 24:9–11

A marvelous revelation was granted to the Israelite priesthood leaders, including seventy of the elders of Israel. They actually saw God. They were not smitten by being in his presence as mortals normally would be (see commentary at Exodus 19:14–25; 33:13–23). They were still "in the body" because "they saw God, and did eat and drink," but their physical bodies must have been in a transfigured state (see Moses 1:11). It is important to remember that Moses, Aaron, Nadab, Abihu, and the seventy elders held the higher, or Melchizedek, priesthood. They saw God before the institution of the Aaronic order. But when the law of carnal commandments was added because of transgression (Galatians 3:19), Aaron and his sons were chosen to lead the lesser priesthood by which the lesser law was administered. This concept is not hard to understand since we have an analogous situation: in modern times the bishop of a ward, a Melchizedek Priesthood holder, is also the president of the Aaronic Priesthood in that ward.

Exodus 24:12–18

After the group of special witnesses returned, Moses and Joshua again ascended the mount where Moses was to commune with God. Moses was in the Lord's presence for forty days (five to six weeks) and received "tables of stone, and a law, and commandments which I have written," so he could teach them to the people (v. 12). Meanwhile, Aaron and Hur were to administer the affairs of the congregation.

The contents of this first set of tablets included instructions on holiness, particularly the plans for how to construct the Tabernacle (Exodus 25–31), which was to be the holiest place on earth.

The fiery manifestation of the glory of the Lord on top of Mount Sinai must have been an awesome sight for the people, and it should have kept them from the apostate revelry in which they soon engaged.

Exodus 25:1–9

Moses was to gather from all who would willingly give their precious metals, fabrics, and materials to build a sanctuary according to the pattern shown to him, where the presence of the Lord could abide with them. Chapters 25 through 31 constitute the plans for the Tabernacle, or Tent of Meeting. The actual construction is recorded beginning in chapter 35.

Exodus 25:10–22

The sacred Ark of the Covenant was a box made of acacia wood (KJV, "shittim wood") overlaid and adorned with gold and equipped with a kind of throne on top, called the mercy seat, that was guarded by two cherubs with wings. The Lord could sit, symbolically, on the mercy seat and give further revelations and commandments. Its dimensions were about 27 x 27 x 45 inches. The mercy seat was regarded as the throne of God, the heavenly king (1 Samuel 4:4; see Bible Dictionary, "Mercy Seat.") On the possible significance of the cherubim's wings, see Doctrine and Covenants 77:4 and Isaiah 6:2. And for the purpose of the veil with cherubim, consider Doctrine and Covenants 132:19: "They shall pass by the angels . . . which are set there."

Exodus 25:23–30

The gold-covered, acacia-wood table held the "bread of presence," or shewbread (pronounced SHOW-bread). The Tabernacle was all about God's literal presence on earth. Twelve fresh loaves (one for each tribe of Israel) were placed upon it every week and left as a thank-offering to the Lord for his provision of daily bread (see also Leviticus 24:5–9).

Exodus 25:31–40

The seven-branched lampstand (*menorah,* or light fixture) was made of solid gold and had seven cups containing oil with wicks for burning. It thus signified wholeness or perfection, and the light it provided in the Tabernacle and later in the Temple symbolized the perfect Light, which God is. It was a type or symbol for spiritual light. Pure olive oil was to be used in the menorah. (The plan recorded in 25:31–40 was carried

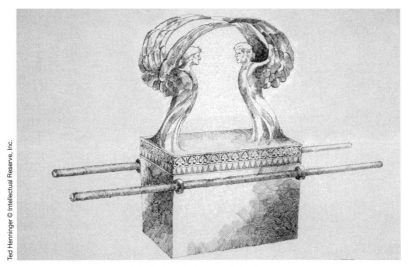

A depiction of the Ark of the Covenant

out in 37:17–24.) The flowerlike cups of the menorah were patterned after the almond tree, the first of the trees in the ancient Near East to blossom in spring. We know verse 40 is important because of the number of times the Lord uses the wording to remind his servants of how revelation came, according to the pattern or manner shown them (see Exodus 26:30; 1 Nephi 17:8; Ether 2:16).

The menorah is still one of the best-known symbols in Judaism. Its ancient appearance is depicted on the Arch of Titus in Rome, showing part of the triumphal procession of booty from the Roman overthrow of Jerusalem and destruction of the Temple in A.D. 70. The menorah is frequently found carved on structures all over the Mediterranean world, wherever Jews were residing.

Exodus 26:1–30

The Tabernacle, a portable Temple, was about 15 x 15 x 45 feet and was placed toward the western end of the court which was 75 x 150 feet. The holiest place within the Tabernacle, or "dwelling" as it was called in Hebrew, was a

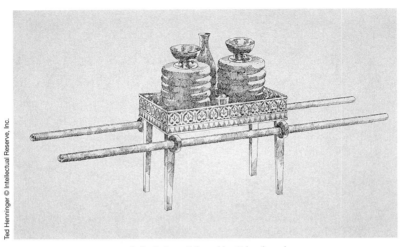

A depiction of the table of shewbread

cubical structure at its west end, 15 x 15 x 15 feet. See further detail in Bible Dictionary, "Tabernacle."

The "blueprints" for the construction were received by Moses "in the mount." Compare the plans for Nephi's ship, also received from the Lord on a mountain (1 Nephi 17:7–8).

The description of curtains to be used in the Tabernacle occupies significant space. Linen was not just a nice fabric but also symbolic of purity. The colors of blue, purple, and red symbolize power, royalty, and redemption (see also Exodus 25:4).

The Lord repeatedly mentions goats' hair as one of the several coverings for the Tabernacle (Exodus 26:7; 35:6, 23, 26; 36:14). Ancient peoples of the Near East (as well as the Bedouin still today) were aware that making tents from the hair of their goats protected items inside the tent from becoming wet during the heavy rains of wintertime. Upon getting wet, goats' hair immediately becomes impermeable, thus sealing off the tent covering and preventing rains from penetrating inside.

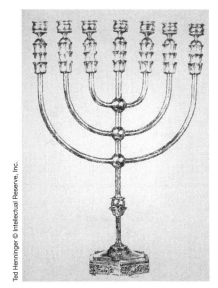

The menorah, *or lampstand,*
of the Tabernacle and the Temple

Exodus 26:31–37

The holiest place of the sanctuary (Hebrew, "Holy of Holies"), where the Ark of the Covenant was placed, must have been richly adorned. Apparently then, as now, things of value and beauty were used in such places to remind us of God's goodness and to sacrifice our best in worshiping him.

Exodus 27:1–8

The acacia-wood altar was not large: 7½ x 7½ x 4½ feet. All of its implements and utensils were of brass. We are not certain how this altar with its bronze grate in its hollow interior was used in offering the burnt offering. There were horns at each of the four corners. One meaning of the Hebrew *qeren* (horn) is power—in this case, priesthood power. Blood applied to altar horns represented the Atonement, and the Messiah, the Anointed One, is the horn of our salvation (Psalm 18:2). Horned altars from ancient Israel have been discovered at Megiddo, Beersheba, and other biblical sites.

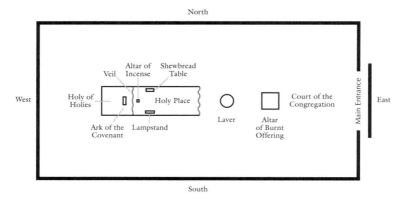

Floor plan of the ancient Tabernacle

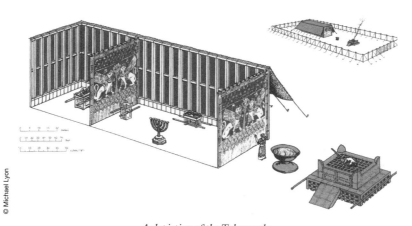

© Michael Lyon

A depiction of the Tabernacle

Exodus 27:9–19

Specifications are given for the 75 x 150 foot courtyard mentioned before, where the "sacred dwelling, or Tabernacle, was placed. Its curtain-fence was seven and a half feet high. This area was open to all worthy members of the congregation of Israel.

228

Exodus 27:20–21

The menorah, the olive oil lamp, was to burn constantly, being tended by Aaron and his sons in the Tabernacle of the congregation, or the "tent of meeting." The continual burning of the menorah symbolized the eternal nature of God. Pure olive oil was the only acceptable oil. It symbolized Jesus Christ and his atoning sacrifice (see Skinner, *Gethsemane*, 77–91). The tent of meeting was a place not of regular congregational worship but rather where God met with his people according to his timetable and will.

Exodus 28:1–4

This chapter details revelations regarding Aaron's and his sons' roles in Aaronic Priesthood leadership. Aaron and his four sons were to have special clothing, holy garments "for glory and for beauty," including a breastplate, an apron (Hebrew, *ephod*), an inner garment, an outer robe, a sash, and a cap. Those who made them were those specially endowed with the "spirit of wisdom." From the days of Adam onward, special garments have been a sign of God's covenant with his children and symbolize higher levels of commitment and desired holiness on the part of the wearer.

For more on sacred clothing and garments worn in holy places, read the following scriptural passages with their respective commentary in this volume: Exodus 28:31–43; 29:1–46; 39:1–43; 40:1–15; Leviticus 8:1–36; 16:1–4; and Numbers 15:37–41.

Exodus 28:5–29

Particulars on the materials and colors for the garments and the breastplate are set forth. Compare the Israelite breastplate with the Nephite breastplate mentioned in Joseph Smith–History 1:35 and Doctrine and Covenants 17:1.

Exodus 28:30

The Urim and Thummim (meaning "Lights and Perfections") was an instrument used by Aaron for receiving

Ted Henninger © Intellectual Reserve, Inc.

A depiction of the altar of burnt offering

revelation in judging the people (see Topical Guide and Bible Dictionary, "Urim and Thummim"; see also Ogden and Skinner, *Book of Mormon,* 1:378–80). Abraham used the Urim and Thummim to receive revelations about the astronomical universe. The Israelites used it for judgment and to discern worthiness of lineage. The Nephites called the device "interpreters," and modern prophets have used it to translate unknown languages and receive revelation in general. Their exact appearance and their mode of operation are known only to the seers who are divinely appointed to use them. Verse 30 clearly indicates that the Urim and Thummim worn "upon his heart" was a type and symbol of the Savior's judgment upon our hearts.

Exodus 28:31–43

More details about the garments, the cap, and the crown for Aaron, which bore the words "Holiness to the Lord." The priests officiating at the altar in all sin offerings were to "bear the sins" of the people unto the Lord and show the people's repentance through a sacrifice, that it might be accepted by the Lord and the people forgiven.

Garments of the priests

Exodus 29:1–46

Instructions concerning the preparatory ordinances of washing, anointing, and clothing the priests who ministered at the altars are set forth, as well as the initiatory offerings for the installation of the priests. According to the great Jewish rabbinic commentator, Rashi, the Hebrew verb in verse 4, translated as "wash," signifies immersion of the whole body (*Soncino Chumash*, 527). The word *baptism*, which is of Greek origin, was of course unknown to the Israelites. They used *rakhatz*, which is usually translated as "wash" or "wash away."

Verses 10–14 describe the sin offering of the priests. Specific requirements for sacrifices associated with the consecration of the priests (vv. 19–21) involved daubing blood on certain parts of their bodies in symbolic gestures:

- the tip of the right ear because the ear was the organ of hearing by which one hearkened to the word of the Lord;
- the thumb of the right hand, the hand by which one acted and made covenants, to remind them to act in the right or proper manner;
- the right great toe, an organ of walking, to remind them to walk in the ways of the Lord.

In this ancient era only priests were so anointed; they represented the people to the Lord. In modern times, each person may be anointed to stand before God. Notice that Aaron and his sons laid their hands on the head of the ram, by which the sacrifice became personal.

Verses 38–46 present instructions for the daily morning and evening "continual burnt offering," as a supplication in behalf of the whole congregation of Israel.

Exodus 30:1–16

The altar of incense stood before the veil that separated the Holy Place from the Holy of Holies. The fragrant smoke of the incense symbolized prayer ascending to heaven (see Psalm 141:2; Luke 1:10; Revelation 5:8; 8:3–4).

The half-shekel atonement offering was required of everyone, rich and poor. These performances were types or symbols of things to come and did not of themselves bring salvation. The sacrifices did not take away any sins; they were done in similitude of the Savior's sacrifice that could take away sins. These rituals taught principles to the people and strengthened their faith in him who was to come and make effective Atonement for all humankind (Alma 25:15–16).

Exodus 30:17–21

The laver, or wash basin, was placed in the courtyard between the altar of burnt offerings and the entrance to the Holy Place. Aaron and his sons could ceremonially wash their hands and feet in it before entering the Tabernacle or ministering at the altar. The laver could also have been used for ritual immersions. The concept of outward washing was a symbol of inner cleansing. The same symbolism is found in baptism.

Exodus 30:22–38

Recipes are given for preparing the aromatic anointing oil and the incense spices. Things pleasant to the smell as well as things pleasant to the eye were used in all of these worship facilities. See commentary at Leviticus 8:1–36.

Exodus 31:1–11

Certain men were called and spiritually endowed to do work on the Tabernacle. Compare the "spirit of God, in wisdom, in understanding, and in knowledge," to the functions of the gifts of the Spirit as enumerated later in the New Testament. Peter says the Holy Ghost operated in Old Testament times because holy men of God wrote scriptures "as moved upon by the Holy Ghost" (2 Peter 1:21).

Exodus 31:12–18

Sabbath observance is for rest, for worship, for remembering blessings, and blessing the lives of others. Those who keep it holy discover that the Sabbath is a sign of keeping our covenants with the Lord and the Lord's sanctifying us. In Moses' day, defilement of the Sabbath could result in physical death. In our day, it can result in spiritual death.

At the conclusion of his communion in the holy mount, Moses received the tablets of testimony, or tablets of stone, "written with the finger of God."

Exodus 32:1–6

Growing impatient and hopeless concerning Moses' return, the Israelites demanded an image of a god that they could see—a golden calf. They knew about the holy Hathor cow or the sacred bulls involved in Egyptian religious observances. From the bull cult of the eighteenth and nineteenth dynasties, we have the remains in Egypt of the *Serapeum*, long

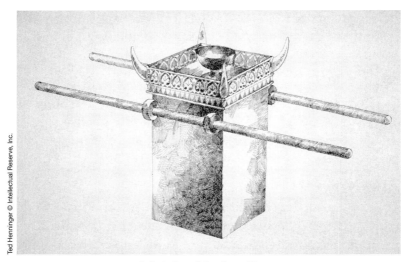

A depiction of the altar of incense

corridors under the sand with rooms containing huge granite coffins for embalmed apis bulls.

Aaron, whom Moses left in charge (Exodus 24:14–18), tried to rationalize that it was a "feast to the Lord" (Jehovah) whom they would celebrate by their offerings, their eating and drinking, and their "play" before the calf (vv. 5 and 6). It may have been Aaron's original intent to provide a visual image to try to turn the people's faith back to the true and living God, but we really do not know why Aaron acted as he did. It was certainly not wholly out of righteousness. Apparently it was a far greater challenge to get Egypt out of Israel than to get Israel out of Egypt.

Exodus 32:7–10

Aware that the Israelites had "corrupted" (Hebrew, "debased") themselves, God instructed Moses and Joshua to return and warn the people that failure to keep their covenants would make them subject to destruction. They had been clearly taught the first two of the Ten Commandments, and recall from Exodus 24:3 their promise to do all that the Lord had instructed them to do. They were now doing the very things for which the Canaanites were about to be destroyed.

Exodus 32:11–14

Moses humbly but firmly declined the Lord's offer to substitute him and his posterity in the covenant which apostate Israel seemed now to be abandoning. Moses pleaded that God would not summarily reject Israel but would still remember the covenant and give them another chance. Our King James text says God "repented," but remember the Hebrew meaning of the word translated in Genesis 6:6; *nikham* means basically to "sigh," and thus to express either regret, exasperation, or concession and compassion. Note Joseph Smith Translation changes in verses 12 and 14. In mercy the Lord allowed them another trial period. This was a great test of Moses' integrity— to have pleaded for the lives of the Israelites while refraining from exalting himself, his name, or his posterity. True disciples plead for others, as did Abraham (Genesis 18:23–33), Enos (Enos 1:9), and Mormon (Mormon 3:12).

Exodus 32:15–24

Angered by his people's failure to be worthy of high and holy covenants with God, Moses broke the tablets of stone he had received. In the ancient Near East, to "break tablets" on which promises were made between countries was to nullify the treaty, to cancel the promises. That is essentially what God and his prophet were saying symbolically to Israel. Moses challenged Aaron to answer for his part in the affair. Later, we will see that Aaron would have perished for his guilt if Moses had not supplicated the Lord for mercy on his behalf (Deuteronomy 9:20).

Aaron weakly excused his action as something demanded by the pressure of the people. The difference between inspired leadership and indulgent leadership is obvious.

Exodus 32:25–30

Moses separated those who were "on the Lord's side" from those whom Aaron had made "naked." The Hebrew word used here may mean "bare, uncovered," "unruly, broken loose," or "exposed in guilt before God's wrath" (compare the feeling of Alma as he described such exposure in Alma 36:14–21). That Israel had "broken loose" and become "unruly" under Aaron's lead was quite evident. These conditions were shameful for a people who were supposed to be holy. Foreshadowing their dispersement throughout the tribes of Israel in their lands of promise, the Levites were sent throughout the camp of Israel at Mount Sinai to destroy the recalcitrant.

Exodus 32:31–35

Moses asked the Lord to forgive Israel if possible, but if not possible, to blot Moses' own name also out of his "book" (see Topical Guide and Bible Dictionary, "Book of Life"). The reply of the Lord is based on the principle that each man will be punished for his own sins, and Moses was not considered responsible for Israel's instability. He had tried to take sufficient precautions before leaving for the top of the mount to assure their fidelity while he was gone.

Exodus 33:1–11

The Lord further punished Israel and threatened not to accompany them into the promised land because of their stiffneckedness.

The people had forfeited the privilege of having the Lord in their midst, so Moses moved the Tabernacle, symbolizing the Lord's presence, outside the camp, and the people observed with awe that the Lord communicated only with Moses out there, although Joshua was sometimes with Moses.

Exodus 33:12–23

The Lord's people were to be "separated" but not in a physical sense as some later Essenes and some Orthodox

Jewish groups today still believe. Israel was to be separated in a spiritual sense, living *in* the world but not being *of* the world.

Encouraged, and having already spoken face to face with the Lord "as a man speaketh with his friend," Moses requested the supreme privilege, saying to the Lord: "Show me thy glory" (as the brother of Jared requested centuries before: "Lord, show thyself unto me"; Ether 3:10). The Lord denied his request with a brief reminder, "No man shall see me and live." The Lord related this to Israel's sinful condition (read JST Exodus 33:20 in the Bible Appendix). Moses had once before received the plain explanation: "No man can behold all my works, except he behold all my glory; and no man can behold all my glory, and afterwards remain in the flesh on the earth" (Moses 1:5). He had, on that occasion, said that "now mine own eyes have beheld God; but not my natural, but my spiritual eyes, for my natural eyes could not have beheld; for I should have withered and died in his presence; but his glory was upon me; and I beheld his face, for I was transfigured before him" (Moses 1:11). Mortal, natural man must be "transfigured" or transformed, specially prepared through the priesthood of God and the Spirit of God to be able to behold the Lord in his glory (D&C 84:19–24). However, a certain privilege was accorded Moses (vv. 21–23), and in "the natural man" he was allowed to see the Lord's departure. See also Joseph Smith Translation footnote 23*c*.

Exodus 34:1–10

Before reading this chapter, read Joseph Smith Translation Exodus 34:1–2 in the Bible Appendix. Read also Doctrine and Covenants 84:18–27 and then proceed with Exodus 34.

Having prepared new stone tablets as instructed, Moses returned a seventh known time to Mount Sinai to receive a new law, known as the "law of Moses": a law that was a carnal, or temporal, order of things. This Mosaic law was intended to be a "schoolmaster" to turn Israel to Christ (Galatians 3:24;

Romans 10:4; 2 Nephi 11:4; Jacob 4:5; Mosiah 3:13–15). It was a "law of performances and ordinances" to keep Israel in remembrance of God and to strengthen their faith in the Messiah (Mosiah 13:30–33; Alma 25:15–16). The Lord again proclaimed his name and nature to Moses. Many facets of his divine personality are mentioned.

Notice that something is left out at the end of verse 7 and only one word, "generation," in italics, has been supplied. The statement should probably be as it was in Exodus 20:5; otherwise it seems that the Lord punishes us not only for our sins but also for our fathers' transgressions.

Moses again pleaded for the Lord's mercy and grace to help the children of Israel, and the Lord promised to do marvelous and awesome (KJV, "terrible") things with Israel.

Exodus 34:11–17

Certain warnings and principles are repeated with reference to keeping Israel uncontaminated from the evil ways and false religions of others.

The word *jealous* (considered briefly in Exodus 20:4–6) is used to translate the Hebrew *qanah,* meaning "to become very red," or envious, jealous, etc. Thus, God is not nonchalant about us; he is pleased, sensitive, wrathful, or sad in response to the behavior and attitude of his covenant children. Notice in the footnote to verse 14 that the Joseph Smith Translation changes "Jealous" to *Jehovah.*

Exodus 34:18–26

Reminders are given about the offerings to show gratitude for the things the Lord was doing for them (compare Exodus 23:14–19 on the three principal feasts of the year, the Sabbath, and so on).

Exodus 34:27–35

Moses was on the mount five to six weeks and was fasting the entire time. There he received revelations and a reiteration of commandments on the new stone tablets suitable to the new law of Moses. The Lord's presence and glory were physically sustaining to the prophet's person (see D&C 84:33).

After such prolonged time and such experiences in God's presence, it is no wonder that Moses' face shone with divine glory when he returned, and the people fell back in fear of him. This phenomenon of light radiating from heavenly beings and earthly beings who are under heavenly influence is not unique. Compare the descriptions of the apostles on the day of Pentecost, when "tongues of cloven fire" radiated from them (Acts 2:3); see also the experience of Abinadi, which is specifically compared to that of Moses (Mosiah 13:5).

In the fifth century A.D., Jerome was given permission by the Roman Catholic Church to translate the Hebrew and Greek biblical manuscripts into Latin for use in churches. After attaining some mastery of the two languages, he produced the Latin Vulgate Bible, which is used in some churches to this day. From his work came a mistranslation in Exodus 34:29–30 that has been immortalized in one of the world's great works of art. The scripture says that Moses came down from Mount Sinai and "the skin of his face shone." The Hebrew word for "shone" is *qaran*, a verb from the root that can also mean "horn"; that is, beams of light, like the "horns" or rays of morning seen over the horizon before the sun rises. Jerome understood *qaran* in its primitive sense "horn," and thus translated the scripture as "horns formed on his face." A thousand years later, using the Latin Vulgate translation, Michelangelo created his sculpture of Moses, a heroic and imposing figure which had two horns extending from his forehead!

Exodus 35:1–29

Here are more instructions about making the Sabbath a day of rest and a holy day unto the Lord. Emphasis is placed on offerings made by "whosoever is of a willing heart."

Moses repeated the instructions concerning the construction work to be done on the Tabernacle. Then follows

Michelangelo's Moses

the response of the "wise hearted and the willing hearted" in actually doing the work. The people were generous with their time, talents, and material goods. This is a bright spot in Israel's history.

Exodus 35:30–35; 36:1–7

Two of the men who were inspired and filled with the Spirit of God were made leaders: Bezaleel and Aholiab. They taught others to do the fine art and craft work associated with the Tabernacle. Construction began, and for once the people did better than they were required to do, and more than enough precious material was contributed.

Exodus 36:8 to 38:31

The Tabernacle was made according to instructions previously received, as recorded in Exodus 26.

Leaders of the workmen reported the volume of precious things used in the structure. It would be difficult to estimate the worth of gold and gems today, but it was a surprising amount.

240

Exodus 39:1–43

The garments of the priesthood were made according to the plans revealed. The colors, the fabrics, and the gems made them beautiful.

The particulars of all the work were reviewed. The phrase HOLINESS TO THE LORD was a constant reminder to the people of the Tabernacle's preeminent purpose and consecrated status. The words, "all the work . . . [was] finished" seem to hark back to the completion of the Creation (Genesis 2:1). When all was done as commanded, Moses blessed the workers. What a tremendous lesson: obedience with exactness brings divine approbation.

Exodus 40:1–15

Instructions were given for setting up, preparing, and dedicating the Tabernacle for worship and for the washing, anointing, and clothing of the priests to officiate in the holy ordinances.

Exodus 40:16–33

Moses had everything prepared as directed. The testimony was placed in the Ark of the Covenant and set up in the Holy of Holies. Altars, lavers, and other implements were all put in their places, ready for the dedicatory services. After ordinances of washing, the Tabernacle was set up on the first day of the second year after the Exodus. The Lord's acceptance of the Tabernacle resembles the future acceptance of Solomon's Temple (see 1 Kings 8).

Exodus 40:34–38

The Tabernacle was accepted as a dwelling of God on earth and a place of worship and communication for man. This was manifested by the cloud showing God's presence and by his glory filling the Holy of Holies so that even Moses could not enter (compare similar phenomena at the dedication of the Kirtland Temple recorded in *History of the Church*, 2:427–28).

Thereafter, the children of Israel were guided by the divine cloud as they traveled through the wilderness. When the cloud stopped, they stopped, and when and where it moved, they followed. They should have felt very secure under such divine accompaniment.

Thus ends Exodus, the record of the exit of Israel from Egypt. With many impressive, spiritual blessings and teachings, the Lord prepared the children of Israel for their mission and life in the promised land. Just so will he prepare any who accepts him for life, service, and joy in his kingdom.

With the Tabernacle and the priesthood in place, the Lord was ready to reveal the rituals and ordinances to be performed. This was done while Israel was still encamped at Mount Sinai and is recorded in the book of Leviticus.

LEVITICUS

The third book of the Pentateuch, Leviticus, gets its name from the Septuagint (Greek translation of the Old Testament) and means "pertaining to the Levites." Its Hebrew title, taken from the first words of the text, is *va-yiqra'*, "and he [the Lord] called [to Moses]." Its theme is making Israel a holy nation through the ordinances of worship administered by the Aaronic priests. Though organized as a distinct book, its contents are actually a continuation of the priestly rules found at the end of Exodus.

Leviticus, which is really a priesthood handbook for ancient Israel, is important to us as it teaches "atonement" (a word that appears forty-nine times). The ritual sacrifices were types of the Savior's future Atonement, and they continued until they were fulfilled by him at Gethsemane, Golgotha, and the Garden of the Resurrection. It is essential to understand the meaning of sacrifices, and the general principle of sacrifice, in order to understand *the* Sacrifice. The book of Leviticus is, therefore, a book about how to make the Atonement effective and central in ancient Israel and, by similitude, in modern covenant Israel.

Some of the best commentary on Leviticus is by Paul (Hebrews 9–10) and by Abinadi (Mosiah 13:29–32; 16:14–15). Jehovah frequently taught that he is holy, so he expected his disciples to be holy. Everything was holy for possessors of the holy priesthood: the laws, the sacrifices, the commandments, the holy days, and so on. Chapters 1–7 detail the laws and regulations governing sacrifices, which point to Jesus

Christ; 8–10 describe the consecration and activities of priests, which taught Israel about priesthood governance and service; 11–15 deal with ritual purity (the clean and unclean), to teach Israel how to stay clean physically and spiritually; 16 is devoted to Yom Kippur, the Day of Atonement, which taught Israel to evaluate their lives yearly in preparation for final judgment; 17–26 set forth laws for Israel as a holy people, another holiness code, which taught Israel to be a separate and peculiar people among the nations; and chapter 27 constitutes an appendix on religious vows, which reminded Israel that an eternal relationship existed between them and the Lord. These laws and regulations were given during the year that Israel camped at Mount Sinai.

During your study of Leviticus, you may want to consult the following entries in the Bible Dictionary: "Leviticus," "Levites," "Sacrifices,"and "Clean and Unclean."

Leviticus 1:1–17

Some people may feel that sacrificial offerings involving the slaughter and burning of animals is repulsive, but there is nothing primitive or barbaric about animal sacrifice. (We slaughter thousands of animals every day in order to feed millions of people.) For the covenant people, each animal's death on the altar of the Tabernacle or Temple had religious significance and was part of the true worship of God. The sacrifice described here is a continuation of the commandment given to Adam, Enoch, Noah, Abraham, Isaac, and Jacob. The purpose was to remind the people that "this thing is a similitude of the sacrifice of the Only Begotten of the Father" (Moses 5:7).

The word "offering" in verse 2 is used to translate the Hebrew word *corban*. The term is used later by the Savior in his mortal teachings (see Matthew 15:5; Mark 7:11; Bible Dictionary, "Corban"). The whole burnt offering was consumed, signifying complete dedication and sacrifice or surrender to the Lord's will. Note the necessary qualities of the animal offered and the requirement that the worshiper offer it "of his own voluntary will," and it be the offerer's own property (Deuteronomy 23:18). A burnt offering was offered every morning and evening for all Israel (Exodus 29:39–42). Extra burnt offerings were given on Sabbaths and feast days. Individuals could offer special burnt offerings to express devotion to the Lord. One is struck by the requirement that a man must lay his hands on the head of the offering to transfer sins and imperfections (v. 4), thus pointing to the core principle of substitution, or proxy, as it pertains to the Atonement of Jesus Christ (2 Corinthians 5:21). Also, by the laying on of hands, the sacrifice becomes personal: one "owns" the sacrifice.

Directions are given for offering a bullock (vv. 3–9), for a sheep or goat (vv. 10–13), and for fowls (vv. 14–17). Sacrifices were offered on the north side of the great altar (v. 11), which was probably a similitude of the location of the Crucifixion (see "Abraham's Three Days' Journey to Moriah" in commentary at Genesis 22:1–19). Apparently the ascending aroma of the roasting meat symbolized the communication of the good will of the worshiper to the Lord.

SACRIFICIAL OFFERINGS UNDER THE LAW OF MOSES

1. Burnt offering (Leviticus 1, 6): voluntary gift of a whole male bullock (young bull), ram, or goat without blemish, burnt on the altar to make payment for sin. This is the type of sacrifice Adam and Eve first offered (see Moses 5:5–8).

2. Meal offering (Leviticus 2, 6): voluntary gift of grain, oil, and incense; also referred to as grain (KJV, "meat"), or cereal offering (with no blood involved); some placed on the altar, some eaten by priests; to honor, revere, and worship God.

3. Peace offering (Leviticus 3, 7): voluntary gift of cattle, sheep, or goats, to make peace with God and express gratitude to him.

4. Sin offering (Leviticus 4–6): required sacrifice of cattle, sheep, goats, birds, or grain; some offered to God, some

given to priests; to make payment for unintentional sins of
uncleanness, neglect, or thoughtlessness.

5. Trespass offering (Leviticus 5–7): required sacrifice of a
ram without blemish, along with compensation to anyone
injured, to atone for or make payment for sins against God
and others; also called guilt offering.

Leviticus 2:1–16

Specifications are given concerning "meat" (meaning
"meal" or "grain" in modern English) offerings. Only token
portions of the grain, flour, and cake offerings were burned
upon the altar; the remainder of it was eaten by the men of the
priesthood. In our day we would consider such offerings as a
sort of "maintenance fund" contribution. In Hebrew these
offerings are called simply by the word *minkhah,* meaning "a
gift." Grain and flour are often mentioned in the Bible in connection with these offerings. Grain symbolized, among other
things, the effects of the Atonement as described by Christ
just days before his great and last sacrifice (see John 12:23–
25). Oil symbolized the blood of Christ shed in Gethsemane,
the place of the "oil press" (Luke 22:44), and on Golgotha's
cross. Fire symbolized God's eternal glory.

The "salt of the covenant" was symbolic as a preserva-
tive, signifying that the covenant was to endure and not decay.
Jesus called true disciples "the salt of the earth" (Matthew
5:13), those who preserved his words and works in the earth.

Leviticus 3:1–17

As will be seen later, in Leviticus 7, the "peace offering"
was an unblemished male or female animal that was offered
in times of distress to supplicate for relief and in times of
plenty to show thanksgiving; in the latter case, it was sometimes called a "thank offering." Since only a portion was
burned and the rest was eaten by the priest and by the family
of the worshiper, this sacrifice was a communion meal eaten
and "shared" with the Lord. Other specific types of the peace

offering were the vow offering and the freewill offering (see also Leviticus 7:11–34).

Again we see the qualities requisite in the animals, whether cattle, sheep, or goats; all of these specifications anticipated the Atonement of the Savior. The phrase "carnal" offerings (Latin, meaning "flesh"), refers to the involvement of flesh and blood in the sacrifice (see Hebrews 9:6–14).

Leviticus 4:1–35

This chapter outlines requirements of the sin offering. All have sinned and come short of the glory of God (Romans 3:23). Even sinning in ignorance of the law—whether done by priests, by the congregation, by a ruler, or by one of the people—required offerings by the shedding of blood and burning of flesh on the altar before such sins could be forgiven. Naturally, if the sins were committed in ignorance, this repentance procedure could be undertaken only when the violations became known. Verse 4 reiterates three core principles of sacrifice:

1. Substitution (the bringing of the animal to the Tabernacle door).
2. Identification and transference (laying on of hands).
3. Death of the substitute.

Verse 7 calls attention to the horns of the altar, symbolic of power, especially power in Christ, to be saved through the blood of his sacrifice. Many hundreds of years later Zacharias would praise God for raising up "an horn of salvation for us in the house of his servant David" (Luke 1:69). The purpose of sin offerings, after true repentance, was to prepare people to receive forgiveness and renew their covenants. The same blessings are available by partaking of the sacrament (JST Matthew 26:24).

From Hebrews 13:11–13 we learn that taking the animal outside the camp was a type and foreshadowing of the Savior's sacrifice outside the walled city of his day. It was only the sacrifice for the high priest that was taken outside the wall, making it even more symbolic of Christ.

Leviticus 5:1–13

Special instructions are given for gaining forgiveness in cases of concealing knowledge of blasphemous swearing or of touching unclean things. The substitution of less costly things was acceptable if the offerer was too poor to afford the lamb or even the two turtledoves.

Leviticus 5:14 to 6:7

Compared to the punishment for sins and trespasses committed in ignorance, those committed knowingly—such as lying or deceiving—were, of course, subject to more severe punishment. The sacrifice to be offered in this circumstance is called the trespass or guilt offering. It also covered offenses committed against others such as false testimony, stealing or unlawfully possessing property (vv. 2–4), disrespect for sacred things, and errant acts of passion.

Leviticus 6:8 to 7:38

These paragraphs of what may be called the priesthood handbook of ancient times instruct the Levitical priests in the offering of burnt offerings, meal offerings, sin offerings, trespass offerings, etc. Portions called heave offerings were lifted up in a gesture of giving them to the Lord; likewise, wave offerings were moved back and forth as if being offered to him. After the gesture was complete and thanks to God was given for the offerings, they were then consumed by the priests. The prohibition against consuming blood (Genesis 9) was a reminder of life and the great and last sacrifice of the Perfect Life by the shedding of his blood. In the resurrection, all will receive an incorruptible body, quickened by spirit and not by blood (*Doctrines of Salvation*, 1:76–77).

Leviticus 8:1–36

Aaron and his sons were prepared for priesthood service, particularly the washing, anointing, and clothing of the priests. Blood offerings followed and then a ceremonial meal. These consecrational proceedings took seven days.

Regarding the significance of anointing oil, President Joseph Fielding Smith taught: "The use of olive oil in anointing is from very ancient times. It was the custom to anoint prophets, kings, and holy messengers as a stamp or token of their official calling. In Leviticus, 8:6–12, is an interesting account of the calling of Aaron, and how Moses not only anointed Aaron, but likewise the altar and the vessels, and sanctified them with holy oil. Samuel also anointed Saul and proclaimed him king in Israel, and when Saul transgressed, David was anointed in his stead to be king of Israel. This custom continued in Israel until they were rejected by the Lord and scattered.

"The olive tree and its golden oil were among the greatest treasures of Israel. . . .

"No other kind of oil will do in anointing. It is very apparent that the oil from animal flesh would never do, and there is no other kind of oil that is held so sacredly and is more suited to the anointing than the oil of olive; moreover, the Lord has placed his stamp of approval on it" (*Answers to Gospel Questions*, 1:152–53).

Leviticus 9:1–24

The Lord had promised that he would appear in a manifestation of acceptance when Aaron and his sons made their first offerings after being consecrated. Accordingly, fire from the Lord came and consumed the offering; the people responded with a cry of joy and prostrated themselves in reverence.

Leviticus 10:1–7

Two of Aaron's sons violated the procedures for burning incense and were themselves smitten with fire (the glory of the Lord) and died. Two hundred and fifty others would also be consumed by "fire from the Lord" later (Numbers 16:35).

"Strange fire" is opposite of that which is holy, legitimate, or authorized sacrifice. Thus, those consumed were engaged in an unauthorized form of worship, mimicking in a blasphemous way the sacred fire kept burning at the altar that had been lit by God.

Leviticus 10:8–20

The insertion of this seemingly unrelated rule about intoxicating drinks into the midst of the narrative of the death of Aaron's sons has caused some to think that it was intoxication which caused the two to fail to discern right from wrong, clean from unclean, holy from unholy. In any case, this "word of wisdom" about the need for priestly abstinence from wine and strong drink, which impair the senses of discernment and discretion, is interesting and valuable, although Israelites as a whole were not under the same injunction as Latter-day Saints.

Moses instructed Aaron and his two remaining sons, Eleazar and Ithamar, to make an offering and partake of it in a certain way to be acceptable. Aaron was excused while he mourned the loss of his two disobedient sons.

We note that an important responsibility of the priests was to teach the people the law and statutes of God. Even today, priesthood holders have an inherent responsibility to teach.

Leviticus 11:1–47

Lists of clean and unclean animals distinguish what may or may not be eaten. The unclean beasts and fowl were either carnivores or scavengers or both.

People may forget to pray, to work, or to play, but they seldom forget to eat. Thus the Lord used eating practices and foods to teach symbolically. While sanitary and nutritional considerations may have been part of the Lord's reasons for this revelation (certain creatures more easily carry diseases, for example), the main lesson for the Israelites was that they should not defile themselves in any way and should keep themselves pure and holy because the Lord, our ideal, is holy. Whatever God requires, even regarding culinary matters, is right (see reference at Genesis 12:10–20). Thus, Israel could easily and immediately preserve its distinctive status as people of the one true God, Jehovah.

Verses 1–8 define meat that is kosher (Hebrew, "appropriate, acceptable, fit"). Verses 9–12 define sea creatures that are kosher; 13–20 describe kosher fowl; and 21–25 refer to creeping things. Later on, the Jewish sages and rabbis established a very elaborate and detailed construct of rules and regulations governing *kashrut* ("kosherness")—what could be eaten, cooked, taxed, or used, based on the laws in Leviticus. Jesus inveighed against these traditions of the elders.

Leviticus 12:1–8

There were also purification procedures for the mother of a new baby. If the child was male, the mother's purification was for the week prior to his circumcision and for thirty-three days thereafter, totaling forty days. If the baby was female, the purification was for two weeks plus sixty-six days, totaling eighty days in all. Why the time of purification was longer for a female child is unknown.

The purposes of such ceremonial purification are not clear. The health of the mother may have been one consideration, or perhaps it is reminiscent of the fall of woman and man and anticipatory of the Atonement. In fact, Joseph and Mary were fulfilling this old Mosaic law when they went to the Temple to offer "two turtledoves, or two young pigeons" after the period of purification (Luke 2:22–24). Nowhere, however, is it indicated that childbearing was itself considered a sin, so the ceremonial cleansing was not a punishment. These rituals do, on the other hand, teach about the value of life and the purity God expects.

Leviticus 13:1–14:57

These chapters concern a variety of diseases of the skin; any blemishes, mildew, and mould in cloth or clothing; and even the scaling or crumbling of mortar between the stones of a house—all called by the English word *leprosy.* The Hebrew word used here denotes a "stroke" or "being stricken." Some forms of "leprosy" could be cleansed and the person afflicted could become "clean" and acceptable in society again. However, the form of leprosy known today as Hansen's disease had no cure, except by a miracle. Leviticus 13 covers diagnosis and isolation; Leviticus 14 deals with remedies. These chapters possibly show how revelation helped prevent epidemics from which the Israelites would otherwise have had no protection.

Leviticus 15:1–33

Normal and abnormal discharges of the body and procedures for cleansing them are detailed. Not only was ritual cleansing symbolically meaningful but it was practical basic hygiene.

Leviticus 16:1–4

Certain restrictions regarding Aaron's entry into the Holy of Holies and instructions about the holy garments he should wear were given in preparation for the Day of Atonement. The special garments of the priesthood included linen underclothing ("breeches"), a robe ("coat"), sash ("girdle"), and cap ("mitre"). This teaches us an important pattern we still follow to this day: a special change of clothing is required for the most sacred times of worship.

The Day of Atonement is the most solemn of Israelite commemorations. It is the holiest day of the year, a sacred fast; the phrase "afflict your souls" (Leviticus 23:27) was interpreted to mean complete fasting. If commemorated with full purpose of heart, the people of Israel were restored to a state of full fellowship with God. The Hebrew word *kippur* derives from *kaphar* and means "to cover." In this commemoration we see most clearly the typology or symbolism of Christ's work, to cover the sins of his people.

Leviticus 16:5–34

On the annual Day of Atonement (*Yom Kippur*) the people sought forgiveness of sins for which they had repented.

The sins were put upon the head of a "scapegoat" (an actual goat) which was then driven out into the wilderness, symbolically bearing away their sins. The term "scapegoat" is substituted for the peculiar Hebrew word *azazel,* which apparently designates the adversary of the Righteous One.

On the calendar, *Yom Kippur* falls near the solemn celebration of *Rosh Hashanah* (New Year's Day) and comes just before the week of *Sukkot* (Feast of Tabernacles) and *Simkhat Torah* ("Rejoicing in the Law"). Of course, since the destruction of the Temple in A.D. 70, animal sacrifice has not been a part of any of these observances.

These practices were highly symbolic. Verse 17 mentions that only one man alone could enter the Holy of Holies, just as Jesus accomplished the Atonement alone in Gethsemane and on the cross. Also, verse 30 explains that the priest made an atonement to cleanse the people. However, the ritual that the priest performed did not actually cleanse them any more than a piece of bread or cup of water cleanses us—it is the repentance that accompanies the ordinance, in concert with God's power to forgive and make pure, that cleanses.

Leviticus 17:1–16

Loyalty is demanded by God—no sacrifices are to be offered to false gods. The phrase "go/gone a whoring" was a well-known concept in ancient Israel: Jehovah was the husband to whom Israel was married (see Isaiah 54:5). When Israel looked to false gods (idolatry), she was unfaithful to the relationship she had with the true God and was thus depicted as playing the prostitute or harlot, which was spiritual adultery (see Jeremiah 3:6, 8, 9). In the New Testament the same imagery was used: the Church was the bride of Christ (2 Corinthians 11:2; Revelation 19:7).

More on the symbolism of blood is presented, indicating that there was something significant about blood. It was not to be consumed in any way on pain of excommunication from the congregation of Israel. Some ancient religions had their worshipers drink blood ceremonially in hopes that ingesting the life-essence of the victim would extend the worshiper into eternal life. Such a concept may be a corruption of the revelation to Adam that the blood of a sacrificial animal was in similitude of the Savior's blood and by his blood humankind could gain eternal life. Apparently some of Adam's descendants much later received fragmentary knowledge of the idea and perverted it. The sole ritual use of blood by the Israelites was in sprinkling it on the altar after the sacrifice; it was symbolic of "the blood that maketh an atonement for the soul" (v. 11).

President Joseph Fielding Smith explained the significance of blood being shed: "The reason that the blood of Christ had to be shed is because Adam was without blood before the fall. The blood came into his body afterwards. Therefore, it was necessary that the blood which came by the fall should be shed in the atonement. . . . Since it was by the creation of blood that mortality came, it is by the sacrifice of blood that the redemption from death was accomplished, and all creatures freed from Satan's grasp" (*Answers to Gospel Questions,* 3:207; 3:103).

Leviticus 18:1–30

A list of abominations is articulated, including such sexual aberrations as homosexuality and bestiality. Notice the parallel between the admonition not to uncover the nakedness of anyone you are not legally and lawfully married to and the admonition of Jesus not to look upon a woman to lust after her (Matthew 5:28).

In verses 24–30, especially verse 28, the Lord discussed the consequences for immorality. He said that no blessings would be extended to Israel if they did abominations like others in the land of Canaan had done. If they did, they would suffer what the Canaanites were about to suffer. (Recall Genesis 15:16 and 1 Nephi 17:33–35.) Behavior and the land are linked. The earth is a living creation that recoils from wickedness (Moses 7:48).

Leviticus 19

This chapter is the heart of the ethics of the book of Leviticus; it epitomizes the principles and practices that would indeed make a nation of Saints.

Verses 1–4: The first four verses can be compared to the first five of the Ten Commandments. The word "fear" is translated from a Hebrew word meaning both "revere" and "fear." You can tell by the context which is meant. To fear God and fear one's parents, while still loving them, is to respect and revere, not to have anxiety and apprehension.

Verses 5–8: Proper consumption of the peace-offering meats during the two days they were to be eaten.

Verses 9–10: A welfare law permitting gleaning by the poor and needy. More on this later, in the book of Ruth.

Verses 11–14: Laws on avoiding injury of others and on not taking advantage of the weak, the poor, the needy, or the maimed.

Verses 15–16: Justice must be impartial, and gossip and false witness are not to be tolerated.

Verses 17–18: No hatred of people is permissible, not even when righteous rebuke is necessary. Love thy neighbor as thyself is the "second great commandment"; the first great commandment appears in Deuteronomy 6:5. Compare the teachings of Jesus (Matthew 5:43–44; 19:19; 22:39) and similar principles taught in this last dispensation (for example, D&C 121:45–46).

Verses 19–32: Familiar rules to follow and trespasses and sins to avoid. Protect virtue, be reverent in the sanctuary of the Lord, be courteous to the aged, avoid superstitions and spiritualistic practices. Verse 27 shows the origin of orthodox Jews' practice of growing side curls (side curls are *pe'ot* in Hebrew).

Verses 33–34: Love of neighbor includes also the stranger,

resulting in the "golden rule" principle: treat others the way you would like them to treat you.

Verses 35–37: More on justice, fairness, and honesty in all dealings. Throughout this chapter is the oft-repeated clause: "I am the Lord your God." It serves as a stamp of authority upon these principles and admonitions. Moral law is not the product of man; it originates in God because he cares about how we treat each other.

Leviticus 20:1–27

Punishments were prescribed for such evils as those mentioned in chapter 18. Molech was the worst of all idolatrous fertility gods; infants were sacrificed to him by being cast into the open, fire-belching mouth of a monstrous furnace, and abominable sex orgies and perversions were celebrated around this god. Again the warning was given that if Israel ever behaved like the people in the land they went to possess, Israel would also be wiped out.

The word rendered "familiar spirit" is *'ov* in Hebrew, denoting some sort of instrument or implement for necromancy, or spiritualistic divination used to call forth messages from the spirits of the dead (see commentary at 1 Samuel 28:3–25).

Leviticus 21

Priests were to adhere to a high standard of holiness in many ways:

Verses 1–9: A priest was not to defile himself by preparing dead bodies for burial (except his own family members) or by cutting and marking the flesh (as some ancient cults did). His wife and daughters must be virtuous.

Verses 10–15: A priest was to marry a worthy woman, a virgin. There was to be no celibacy of the priesthood.

Verses 16–24: Officiating priests, like the symbolic sacrifices they offered, were to be without blemish as symbols of Jesus Christ. In our dispensation, however, physically impaired men are not denied the priesthood nor the opportunity to function in any priesthood ordinance, in or out of the Temple.

Leviticus 22:1–33

More qualifications of the priests and of their families who eat the sacrificial foods are outlined in these verses, as well as more information concerning reverence for God and sacrificial animals.

Leviticus 23:1–44

This chapter on the seasonal feasts and the festivals is the chief source for information on the fixed-date holy days celebrated annually. The feasts of the Passover and Unleavened Bread, the First Fruits (or "Feast of Weeks," which is *Shavuot* or Pentecost), the New Year (*Rosh Hashanah*), the Day of Atonement (*Yom Kippur*), and the combined feasts of Ingathering and Tabernacles (*Sukkot*), have all been introduced before (Exodus 12; 23; Leviticus 6). Celebrations such as *Hanukkah, Purim,* and *Tisha b'Ab* came later (see Bible Dictionary: "Calendar," "Fasts," and "Feasts").

HOLY DAYS, FEASTS, AND FESTIVALS
UNDER THE LAW OF MOSES

Three times a year all males of the covenant people were required to present themselves before the Lord at his holy Temple. These three pilgrimage festivals were Passover (including its Feast of Unleavened Bread), Pentecost (Feast of Weeks), and Sukkot (Feast of Tabernacles).

1. Sabbath (Hebrew, *Shabbat*): weekly holy day of rest, to worship and do good; remembering the completion of God's work of creation and his redeeming Israel from Egypt (Deuteronomy 5:15)
2. Passover (Hebrew, *Pesakh*): one-day commemoration (Leviticus 23:5) of God's passing over Israelites' firstborn and facilitating their exodus from Egypt
3. Feast of Unleavened Bread: seven days (Leviticus 23:6–8), plus Passover day, to celebrate their quick departure from Egypt (symbolized by use of unleavened bread)
4. Feast of Weeks (Hebrew, *Shavuot*): one-day festival

(Leviticus 23:15–21) celebrating the grain harvests, occurring fifty days after Passover (later called Pentecost, from the Greek term *pent,* meaning "fifty")

5. Feast of Trumpets (Hebrew, *Rosh Ha-Shanah*): one-day celebration (Leviticus 23:23–25) marking the beginning of the civil new year

6. Day of Atonement (Hebrew, *Yom Kippur*): one-day solemn fast (Leviticus 23:26–32) to recall and honor God's removal of sin from his people

7. Feast of Tabernacles (Hebrew, *Sukkot*): seven-day joyful celebration (Leviticus 23:33–43) of God's guidance and protection in the wilderness while Israelites lived in temporary dwellings (booths, shelters, or "tabernacles"); also called Feast of Ingathering (of the final fruit harvest)

Leviticus 24

Verses 1–4: Laws concerning tending the perpetually burning menorah, the seven-branched lamp of the Tabernacle, are set forth (also in Exodus 27:20).

Verses 5–9: More rules about the shewbread, or bread of the presence, are given.

Verses 10–23: This is one of the few narrative passages in Leviticus. It concerns one who had blasphemed and was killed for his breach of divine law. Other laws were reviewed.

Leviticus 25

Verses 1–7: Details are presented about sabbatical years to give rest to the land and the people and provisions from volunteer crops for sustenance of the poor.

Verses 8–22: The jubilee year, a sabbath of sabbatical years—that is, on the fiftieth year—was to bring freedom to all Israelites in bondage to fellow Israelites, to provide for the return of ancestral properties sold because of poverty, and to give liberty to all the inhabitants throughout the land. The words from verse 10, "proclaim liberty throughout all the land unto all the inhabitants thereof" are inscribed on the Liberty Bell in

Independence Hall, Philadelphia, Pennsylvania. In truth, the culture of colonial America was filled much more with references from, and allusions to, the Old Testament than the New Testament. Leviticus 25 was well known to Americans of the colonial and Revolutionary War period.

The land of Israel itself was also to be guaranteed some rest. It was to lie fallow every seventh year. This raised the practical question: "what shall we eat the seventh year?" It was a test of faith, because the Lord himself would provide. Nephi later bore testimony of the principle involved: where a commandment is given, the Lord will provide a way for it to be accomplished (1 Nephi 3:7).

Verses 23–55: Laws were given concerning the sale and redemption of land and other properties. In the jubilee year, redemption was available even if no one could be found to redeem the land. Laws were given protecting the poor from slavery among fellow Israelites and providing for redemption of those enslaved by outsiders.

Leviticus 26

Blessings and cursings, both physical and spiritual, were promised to Israel upon conditions of obedience or lack of it. Underlying these blessings or cursings, again, was the link between the commandments and the land, especially rain and fertility (see footnote 4*b*). The chapter discussion breaks into two parts:

Verses 1–26. The principle of moral agency lets one choose one's way but not in ignorance or with impunity. Some ways lead to blessings, and some to cursings; one must learn the laws of cause and effect and exercise faith and discernment in choosing which way to go. The consequences of different ways of life are noted—both natural consequences and divinely decreed consequences. (Deuteronomy 28 has similar lists.) It is significant that here, too, pride seems to be the root of most other problems (v. 19).

Verses 27–46. The nation of Israel will be blessed when

obedient to God and cursed when disobedient. In the latter days, many from the covenant lines will return to God.

Leviticus 27:1–34

Laws are explained concerning things dedicated to the Lord, for example, money, houses, land, or animals. The law of tithing is outlined. Every tenth animal or item of produce, without selection or discrimination, was to be given to the Lord.

NUMBERS

The book of Numbers is so named because it begins and ends with a census, a numbering, of the people of Israel. In Hebrew it is called *b'midbar*, or "in the wilderness" because these are some of the first words in the Hebrew text. The history of most of Israel's forty-year sojourn in the wilderness is covered in this book. Thus, the main purpose of Numbers is to describe Israel's condition, physically and spiritually, as they stood poised to enter the promised land. Another purpose is to reiterate and solidify instruction already given—laws and principles also found in Exodus and Leviticus. Yet another is to demonstrate practically the effects of Israel's disobedience but also to show that God did not abandon his people. One principle to keep in mind throughout your study of Numbers is that it wasn't geographical distance that caused the Israelites' forty-year sojourn in the wilderness—it was the distance between their hearts and God's.

Moses certainly authored the core of the book of Numbers, but portions bear the stamp of later contributors. Numbers 12:3, for example, can hardly be Moses' own comment about himself: "Now the man Moses was very meek, above all the men which were upon the face of the earth."

The three main divisions of Numbers are as follows:

1. The camp of Israel at Mount Sinai (1:1–10:10).
2. Israel's thirty-eight-year journey from Sinai to the plains of Moab (10:11–22:1).
3. Israel's camp on the plains of Moab (22:2–36:13).

During your study of Numbers, you may want to consult

the following entries in the Bible Dictionary: "Numbers," "Aaron," "Aaronic Priesthood," and "Wilderness of the Exodus."

THE SIGNIFICANCE OF CERTAIN NUMBERS IN THE SCRIPTURES

The Lord and his prophets teach unique lessons by giving special emphasis and meaning to certain numbers. "Numbers possess *qualitative* meaning in addition to their more obvious *quantitative* function. Like all symbols, they also possess layered meaning" (Brinkerhoff, *Day Star,* 1:43). Following is a sampling of specific numbers that have received scriptural attention, along with examples of their usage and application.

Three

The number three represents divine fulness. The Godhead (the Father, the Son, and the Holy Ghost) serves as the perfect Council of Heaven and apparently the model for all earthly councils: the First Presidency of the Church, stake presidencies, ward bishoprics, and every priesthood quorum presidency. Other uses of the number three are the three days of light as a sign of the Messiah's coming into the world (Helaman 14:4) and three days of darkness signaling his departure from the world (Helaman 14:20). His mortal ministry lasted three years. He experienced three particular temptations in the Judean desert (Matthew 4:1–11). Peter denied knowing Jesus three times (Matthew 26:34, 69–75), and then he reaffirmed his testimony and love for Jesus three times (John 21:15–17). Jesus was crucified at the third hour (Mark 15:25), and darkness covered the execution scene for three hours (Matthew 27:45). On the third day he was resurrected and perfected (Luke 13:32). The scriptures also mention wise men with three gifts (Matthew 2:11), three Nephite apostles who were translated (3 Nephi 28:12), three witnesses of the Book of Mormon (Ether 5:3), and three degrees of glory (D&C 76).

Seven

The number seven is the most used symbolic number and signifies completion, wholeness, perfection, and the covenant. It is used fifty-four times in John's book of Revelation; there are seven churches, seven candlesticks, seven stars, seven angels, seven vials, seven thunders, seven heads on the beast, seven kings, seven mountains, and seven seals to open the seven one-thousand-year periods. The revelation that Joseph Smith received with the Lord's answers to his questions about John's Revelation is now recorded as Doctrine and Covenants 77 (an appropriate number for elaboration of that revelation).

The Lord organized this world in seven "days," or time periods, making the seventh period a sacred day of divine rest and worship (Moses 3:1–3; Abraham 5:1–3).

Jacob worked two seven-year periods for his two brides (Genesis 29:20, 27), and his son Joseph forecast for Egypt seven years of plenty followed by seven years of famine (Genesis 41:28–30). During Israelite history, the seventh year was a special, sabbatical year, and seven times seven plus one was a jubilee year (Leviticus 25:8–10). Seven priests walked around the city of Jericho seven times, in seven days, blowing seven shofars on the seventh day (Joshua 6:4–16). Naaman, the Syrian army officer, was told by Elisha to immerse himself in the Jordan River seven times (2 Kings 5:10). There were seven wounds in Jesus' crucified body (hands, wrists, feet, and side).

According to Doctrine and Covenants 77:6–12, our world is on a schedule of seven one-thousand-year time periods, or millennia, the last of which, the seventh and greatest Millennium, will be the closing, culminating chapter in our earth's temporal history.

The Savior will come here to rule and reign after the opening of the seventh thousand-year period (see Revelation 7 and 8 and their chapter headnotes; D&C 77:12–13), then he will move this sphere along toward its eventual completion, wholeness, and perfection—the celestialization of our earth (D&C 77:1; 88:18–20; 130:9).

Eight

The number eight denotes spiritual renewal or rebirth, the beginning of a new era or new order. Circumcision, a sign of God's covenant with his people, was performed when a baby boy was eight days old, and it served for a time as a foreshadowing of a covenant person's baptism at eight years (JST Genesis 17:11). Also, eight souls would regenerate life on earth after being saved in Noah's ark (1 Peter 3:20); the Jaredites sailed to their new life in eight vessels (Ether 3:1); Lehi's colony journeyed for eight years in the wilderness as they began a new life for those Israelite tribes (1 Nephi 17:4); and eight additional witnesses testified of the Book of Mormon (Introduction to the Book of Mormon). After the seven thousand years of earth's temporal existence, the eighth thousand years commences its celestialization (D&C 77:6; 88:18–22, 26; 130:9).

Ten

The number ten symbolized completeness of order. Ten percent of one's income was the ancient law called tithing, meaning "tenth" (D&C 119:4). There were ten plagues in Egypt (Exodus 7–12) and Ten Commandments given in Sinai (Exodus 20:3–17). Ten tribes were lost to the world's knowledge (D&C 110:11; Article of Faith 10), ten lepers were involved in a miracle (Luke 17:12–17), and ten virgins were the subject of a parable of Jesus (Matthew 25:11–13).

Twelve

The number twelve signifies perfection in governance and witness. Jacob had twelve sons whose descendants became known as the twelve tribes of Israel (Genesis 49:28), and twelve gems were set in the priestly breastplate representing those twelve tribes (Exodus 28:21). In Solomon's Temple, as in modern Temples, there are twelve oxen supporting the baptismal font (1 Kings 7:25)—again representing the twelve tribes of Israel. Jesus made his first public appearance at age twelve (Luke 2:42), and today young men may be privileged to enter priesthood service at twelve years of age. Jesus called twelve apostles in both the Eastern (Matthew 10:1) and Western Hemispheres (3 Nephi

12:1). The original twelve apostles chosen in the Holy Land will sit on twelve thrones judging the twelve tribes of Israel (Matthew 19:28; 1 Nephi 12:9–10). There are twelve members of a high council and twelve members of a deacons quorum, with multiples of twelve for each of the other quorums (D&C 107:85–89). The divine city of the New Jerusalem will feature repeated use of the number twelve: twelve gates, twelve angels, twelve foundations, and twelve pearls—some of which are associated with the twelve tribes and the twelve apostles (Revelation 21:10–21). Also there are twelve witnesses of the Book of Mormon (Three Witnesses + Eight Witnesses + the Prophet himself = twelve).

Forty

The number forty is a most interesting number in biblical scripture, often associated with a time of testing, trial, or preparation. The patriarch Jacob was embalmed for forty days (Genesis 50:3). The twelve spies were gone for forty days (Numbers 13:25; 14:34). Goliath presented himself to the Israelites for forty days (1 Samuel 17:16). Nineveh was to be overthrown after forty days (Jonah 3:4). After Jesus' birth, Mary spent forty "days of purification" in isolation (Luke 2:22–39), according to requirements of the law of Moses. Jesus returned after his Resurrection to give instruction for forty days (Acts 1:3).

For forty days and forty nights, rain and flood waters came upon the earth (Genesis 7:4, 12). Moses was on Mount Sinai forty days and forty nights (Exodus 24:18; 34:28; Deuteronomy 9:9, 11, 18, 25; 10:10). Elijah went fasting to Horeb/Sinai for forty days and forty nights (1 Kings 19:8). Jesus fasted forty days and forty nights (Matthew 4:2; Mark 1:13; Luke 4:2).

Isaac married at forty years of age (Genesis 25:20), as did Esau (Genesis 26:34). Moses was a shepherd for forty years (Acts 7:30). Israelites remained in the wilderness forty years (Numbers 14:33–34; 32:13; Deuteronomy 8:2; 29:5; Joshua 5:6). Caleb was forty when sent to scout out the land (Joshua 14:7). The land rested for forty years (Judges 3:11; 5:31). The land was in quietness forty years (Judges 8:28). The land was in the hands of Philistines for forty years (Judges 13:1). Eli judged forty years (1 Samuel 4:18). Ishbosheth was forty when he started his reign (2 Kings 2:10). Saul reigned forty years (Acts 13:21). David reigned forty years (1 Kings 2:11). Solomon reigned forty years (1 Kings 11:42). Jehoash reigned forty years (2 Kings 12:1). Egyptian cities would be desolate forty years (Ezekiel 29:11–12). In this final dispensation it took forty years to build the Salt Lake Temple (from 1853 to 1893).

In some cases the number forty appears to mean exactly that amount, or duration, of time. In other cases it seems to be simply figurative for a long period of time.

Seventy

The number seventy is a multiple of seven times ten, therefore signifying completeness or perfection of order. During his mortal ministry, Jesus sent out seventy special missionaries, along with the twelve apostles, to teach in his name (Luke 10:1, 17). Likewise, in our day there are quorums of the Seventy among the general and area authorities of the Church (D&C 107:25, 34), undoubtedly an echo of the seventy elders who accompanied Moses and saw God on Mount Sinai (Exodus 24:9–10; Numbers 11:16). The modern Seventy are usually released or given emeritus status at age seventy.

Jesus also taught that we should be willing to forgive "seventy times seven" (Matthew 18:22).

For additional material on numbers in the scriptures, consider Bullinger, *Number in Scripture;* Peacock, *Unlocking the Numbers;* and Brinkerhoff, *Day Star,* especially 38–48.

Numbers 1:1–46

The book begins with a phrase found throughout, one that emphasizes the Lord's closeness to his prophet: "The Lord spake unto Moses . . ." Moses was commanded to assemble a census committee with a representative prince from each tribe to count all of Israel.

The number in each tribe was accounted for. Judah was larger than others of the tribes, although Joseph, composed of Ephraim and Manasseh added together, was also large in numbers. The census did not count females of any age, old men, or boys under twenty years of age.

The total, 603,550 men twenty years old and older (those who could go to war), excluding the Levites, made a total census of two to three million when the probable number of women and children was added. This is not impossible in view of the starting figure (Genesis 46:26–27). Most commentators think it is too large a group to be sustained in the wilderness, or to cross the Red Sea in a night, or to be governed in camps, and several theories have been put forward to adjust the numbers downward, more in line with human assumptions. But the Lord made the point several times that their deliverance from Egypt and their maintenance in Sinai were *miraculous,* and no conclusive, objective evidence is available to contradict the census count reported. Whatever the actual number of Israel's population, there can be no debate about one thing: Moses had an incredible task on his hands! All those listed in the census, all 603,550 would die in the wilderness, except for Joshua and Caleb and, of course, Moses who was translated.

The order of encampment and march was laid out very specifically by the Lord. Immediately it became clear that he wanted the Tabernacle, the symbol of his presence, to be at the center, physically and spiritually, of life. In the early days of this dispensation the Lord wanted the Temple to be at the center in Kirtland, Ohio (see D&C 94:1; 95:8). Later on, Salt Lake City was to be laid out in relation to the Temple, which was at the center. Spiritually and symbolically, should not the Temple be at the center of our lives?

Numbers 1:47–54

The Levitical tribe was exempt from military service and hence excluded from the census because it only concerned the number of men "able to go forth to war" (v. 45). The Levites were to be in charge of the Tabernacle—to staff it, to move it, and to guard it.

Numbers 2

Verses 1–9: Judah, accompanied by Issachar and Zebulun (a total of 195,000), were to camp on the east side of the Tabernacle and to be first in the line of march.

Verses 10–16: The people of Reuben, with those of Simeon and Gad (a total of 125,000), were to occupy the south side.

Verse 17: Next in line of march were the Levites (from Merari, Gershon, and Kohath) and Moses and Aaron with the Tabernacle and the Ark of the Covenant.

Verses 18–24: On the west side of the Tabernacle in camp, and following it in the march, was Ephraim, accompanied by Manasseh and Benjamin (a total of 120,000).

Verses 25–31: On the north was Dan, accompanied by Asher and Naphtali (a total of 160,000).

ARRANGEMENT OF THE CAMP OF ISRAEL

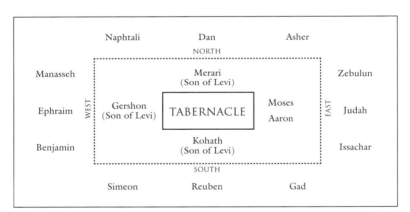

The groupings were by family, according to the mothers of the original sons. Those in the east and south camps and in the center were all children of Leah, except for the addition of Gad, child of Zilpah, the handmaid of Leah. Those on the west side were all descendants of Rachel's two sons, Joseph and Benjamin, but constituted three tribes because of the division of Joseph into the tribes of Ephraim and Manasseh. On the north were the descendants of the two sons of Bilhah, the handmaid

of Rachel, plus Asher, the remaining son of Zilpah. This genealogical arrangement is interesting, but the significance is unclear
except that Judah leading the procession and Ephraim following
the Tabernacle seem to have been positions of honor.

Verses 32–34: The arrangement is summarized. (Compare
a recurrence of such organization in modern times; D&C
61:24–25.)

Numbers 3

Verses 1–4: Of the four sons of Aaron anointed to be
priests, two died through abuse of their office, leaving only
two; one of these later succeeded his father, Aaron, as the
"high priest" (in Hebrew, literally "great priest"). These were
priests of the Aaronic order, not of the Melchizedek order
(D&C 84:18, 26, 30; also D&C 13; 107:13–14).

Verses 5–13: The Levite males were appointed by revelation from God to be priests to replace the firstborn males
of all the tribes. Recall that Abraham, Isaac, Jacob, and others of the old patriarchal order officiated in ordinances and
sacrifices without the aid of specially appointed priests. After
the change of organization described here, the patriarchal
leaders retained many of their former functions in the government of their families and tribes, but priestly functions such as
the offering of sacrifice were performed only by the Aaronic
Priesthood, and all facilities were cared for by the Levitical
order in a specifically organized body which is described later
in this chapter.

Verses 14–38: Names of the leading descendants of the
three sons of Levi. Gershon's descendants were given charge
of the Tabernacle, its curtains, hangings, etc. Kohath's descendants cared for and carried the sanctuary proper, the Ark, etc.
Merari's descendants carried, assembled, and disassembled the
boards, bars, pillars, etc. Moses and Aaron were descendants
of Kohath, so the priests also came of that family, because they

were all descendants of Aaron, and because of Moses' and Aaron's towering greatness.

Verses 39–51: The total number of the Levites in religious service (22,000) closely approximated the number of firstborn (22,273). The remaining 273 who were not "redeemed" man for man by a Levite replacement were redeemed by a five-shekel offering each.

Numbers 4:1–49

Verse 3 mentions thirty as the customary age to begin ministering in the priesthood; this is the age Jesus began his ministry (see commentary at Luke 3:23–38 in Ogden and Skinner, *Four Gospels*).

The Levites were responsible to keep the altar fire going; to offer meat, meal, and drink offerings each morning and evening; to place seven fresh loaves on the table of shewbread weekly; to burn incense; to keep the menorah always burning; to receive and offer various sacrifices; to receive and distribute tithes and offerings; to perform circumcisions; to perform immersions; to teach the statutes of the Lord; and on special occasions such as war and festivals, to blow the silver *shofars* (rams' horns).

At the time of the census, the total number of all Levites of the specified age to serve was 8,580.

Numbers 5:1–10

Numbers 5:1 through 10:10 constitutes a larger section devoted to commands regarding the maintenance of purity among the people. Chapter 5 follows a progression on the issue of purity, moving from the general to the personal: camp purity provides the context for personal purity, which provides the foundation for intimate marital purity.

Exclusion, or quarantine, outside the regular camp was required of all with diseases and other uncleanness. Leviticus 12 through 15 discuss the treatment of these people until they could be readmitted.

A law of recompense was given whereby one could repent

of sins and trespasses against other individuals and against the Lord. Verses 5–10 speak to the importance of inward purity, that which affects the spirituality of the camp.

Numbers 5:11–31

This law which outlined the test for unfaithfulness in order to determine the "guilt" of a wife whose husband was jealously suspicious seems strange to us. However, the chief difference from common "trial by ordeal" is that the ordeal (in this case drinking water with dust in it) was not of itself harmful or hurtful. Only if the woman were guilty did any suffering result from it. Perhaps it was a psychological tool, or perhaps it was based on faith that the Lord would reveal guilt or innocence. It appears that the intent, at least, was not simply to assuage the bruised feelings of a husband but to invite revelation regarding purity in what was the Lord's camp. Whether this passage actually preserves a revealed process is difficult to know now. Verse 21 is using figurative language to speak of the loss of childbearing capability.

Numbers 6:1–21

This chapter sets forth the Nazarite law. A Nazarite (from Hebrew *nazir,* "to separate") was a person who wished to dedicate part or all of his or her life unto the Lord and was thus set apart to do so. The Nazarite vow symbolized total, intense commitment to the Lord on the part of the one making the vow. It was voluntary and thus came with a great expectation that it would be observed. Today, missionaries are "Nazarites," in a sense, as they separate themselves for a time to do exclusively the work of the Lord, and "all the days of [their] separation [they are] holy unto the Lord" (v. 8).

There was a strict code of behavior, special diet, specific appearance, etc., but how or when these practices originated is uncertain. The Nazarite vow governed three areas of life: diet, appearance, and associations. Every Israelite life was regulated in these areas anyway, but the regulations became much more intensified with the taking of the Nazarite vow.

271

Samson was supposed to be a Nazarite from birth; Paul made a vow at least once (Acts 18:18); the Old Testament prophet Samuel and the New Testament prophet John the Baptist served as Nazarites all their lives (see also Bible Dictionary, "Nazarite"). Details were given whereby one's days of separation as a Nazarite could be ended.

Do not confuse "Nazarite" with "Nazarene," meaning an inhabitant of Nazareth. They are two different words with completely different meanings.

Numbers 6:22–27

The priestly benediction, pronounced at the end of synagogue services in our day, is a priesthood blessing for Israel that has been set to beautiful music in modern times. These lines are also one of the oldest biblical texts ever discovered in an ancient inscription. In 1979 archaeologist Gabriel Barkay was digging along the western slope of the Hinnom Valley in Jerusalem and unearthed the largest treasure trove from biblical Jerusalem ever found. About 1,000 items were taken out of family burial chambers from the First Temple period. The items that received most publicity were two solid silver amulets that contain this priestly benediction, almost identical in wording to verses 24–26, providing once again scientific corroboration and illustration of a biblical text. The name of God was etched several times onto the tiny amulets—the earliest mention of the name of God (*YHWH*) ever found in Jerusalem and one of the very rare times in 150 years of archaeological excavations that the Hebrew form of the name of God has been discovered. The priestly benediction text is the oldest biblical Hebrew inscription known today, half a millennium older than the Dead Sea Scrolls.

The three-fold repetition of the name Jehovah, "Lord," is to emphasize the force of the expression in verse 27, "they shall put *my name* upon . . . Israel" (emphasis added).

Silver amulets with the priestly benediction, found in Jerusalem

Numbers 7:1–89

The offerings are noted of each of the twelve princes of the twelve tribes of Israel on the day of the dedication of the altar specifically, and the Tabernacle generally, and the twelve days thereafter. The descendants of Joseph were divided into two tribes and named after his two sons; thus there were twelve tribes besides the Levites.

Numbers 8:1–26

A revelation came to Moses through a voice speaking from the mercy seat atop the Ark of the Covenant, giving directions concerning the lighting of the seven-branched menorah.

The cleansing of the Levites featured initiatory ordinances, complete with ceremonial sprinkling, washing of clothes, laying on of hands, and special sacrifices. The preparatory service of Levite men began at age twenty-five and their complete service was given from age thirty to age fifty.

Numbers 9:1–14

Men who wondered about partaking of the Passover after being defiled by a death in the family asked Moses for information about what they must do. Moses asked the Lord and received the answer, another example of continual revelation. Not breaking any bone of the passover lamb is emphasized again and points to Christ (compare John 19:36).

The same law and ordinance of the Passover applied to all. Strangers could also participate by qualifying as the Israelites did, after conversion and circumcision.

Numbers 9:15–23

The importance of the Passover and its observance is reiterated to all Israel by divine decree. Notice again how contact with the dead defiles the living by abrogating ritual purity.

The pillar of cloud by day and fire by night over the Tabernacle showed the presence of the Lord, and when the Israelites traveled, the same symbol guided them in the direction they should go; compare the Liahona in Lehi's company (1 Nephi 16). Today, we also have a fire to guide us: the gift of the Holy Ghost.

Later they also used Moses' brother-in-law as their guide for finding specific routes and for locating specific camping places (Numbers 10:29–36).

Numbers 10:1–28

Directions were given for departure from Mount Sinai at the sound of signals blown by silver trumpets, and the journey began, with the march organized as previously specified. Numbers 10:12 through 13:25 describe the journey from Mount Sinai to the camp of Kadesh-barnea, near the southernmost border of the promised land.

Numbers 10:29–36

Hobab, the brother-in-law of Moses, was persuaded to accompany Israel as a guide to choose routes and campsites. He and his family later became heirs to lands in Canaan (Judges 1:16; 4:11; 1 Samuel 15:6; 1 Chronicles 2:55; and Jeremiah 35, where they were cited for their exemplary integrity).

Numbers 11:1–9

Israel and the "mixed multitude" (literally, "rabble") with them grew tired of manna three times a day and recalled the juicy and flavorful foods they had once had in Egypt. Israel had lost sight of the symbolic and spiritual meaning of the bread (John 6). Here we see that the price of freedom is too great for those who love physical gratification more.

Numbers 11:10–23

Moses heard all the complaints of all the people. He was tired and said, in essence, "How long do I have to play nurse-maid to *your* chosen people? I need HELP! And if you are displeased with me, kill me outright." The Lord did understand, and he did provide help. Moses was accordingly authorized by the Lord to choose seventy elders (a quorum of seventy) to help him bear the leadership responsibilities.

In answer to the complaint about a steady diet of manna and no meat, the Lord instructed Moses to promise the people meat—which he did, after questioning the proposition.

Numbers 11:24–30

In answer to Moses' request for help, seventy men were chosen and endowed with the "spirit that was upon him," that is, the Spirit that was upon Moses, meaning that they were endowed with some of the same authority and spiritual gifts, so they were also able to "prophesy." When some people objected that two of the men were prophesying who did not attend the ceremony of installation, Moses said wishfully, "Would God that all the Lord's people were prophets and that the Lord would put his Spirit upon them!" He refused to forbid them to prophesy.

In our dispensation all members of the congregation of the Lord may have the gift of prophecy and other gifts, by virtue of the fact that all who are baptized are given the gift of the Holy Ghost. Some of us do not exercise our gifts, however.

Numbers 11:31–35

In fulfillment of the promise of meat, quail fell in the camp about three feet deep! People ate meat until they perished from overindulgence and were buried in the place, which thereafter was called *Kibroth-hattaavah*—"the graves of lust." What profound lessons can be learned from this episode. We must be careful about what we ask of the Lord. We must learn to keep our fallen urges, instincts, and impulses within the bounds the Lord has set. Lack of restraint is sometimes deadly. Greed is ugly!

Numbers 12:1–16

Motivated by jealousy for power, though ostensibly by a "holier than thou" attitude toward Moses because Moses had once married an Ethiopian (see commentary at Exodus 2:1–10), Aaron and Miriam spoke out against Moses. But the Lord taught them that since he found Moses worthy to be the leader of Israel, they should not presume he was unworthy, especially when their own motives were self-advancement. Having found blemish in the Lord's anointed, a blemish appeared in Miriam, and she had to remain outside the camp of Israel for seven days.

One of Moses' great qualities is mentioned in verse 3. Compare what Jesus said about such a quality in Matthew 5:5 and 11:29. Here is a likely example of later revision, because although Moses prepared these books, he *was* meek and undoubtedly would not have inserted such a characterization about himself.

Meekness is not the exact equivalent of humility. Though grounded in humility, meekness is that quality of character that is nonconfrontational, nonargumentative, calm in the face of challenges, and poised in the face of provocation. It is not a lack of "backbone," strength, or power. The meek are not doormats. They know what is right and they do it—no matter what (see Maxwell, *Ensign*, Mar. 1983, 70–74).

Numbers 13:1–25

Arriving within a few days at the southern border of the promised land, the Israelites established camp at Kadesh-barnea (see Bible Map 2), which served as the Israelites' main camp during the forty years of wilderness wanderings; they resided there much longer than at any other of the forty camps. Excavations have attested to the site's ability to sustain a large population for an extended period of time. Moses selected a representative of each of the twelve tribes to spy, or scout, out the land, its peoples, the settlements, the fortifications, the resources, and the fruits, in preparation for their penetration into the land. One of them was Oshea, the son of Nun, of the tribe of Ephraim (Joshua, or Jehoshua; each of the names is a form of the Hebrew word for "salvation"). Verse 20 hints at the time of year the scouts made their journey. The brook Eshcol was in Hebron, which even today is the heart of viticulture in the hill country. They found such big, luscious clusters of grapes that they attached one of them to a pole so as not to bruise it and carried it, along with pomegranates and figs, back to camp to show the productivity of the good land they were to inherit. The scene of two scouts—Joshua and Caleb, representing Ephraim and Judah—walking together bearing the pole with a cluster of grapes is the symbol of the Ministry of Tourism in the State of Israel today.

Numbers 13:26–14:10

The report of the land was good, but the report about the strong peoples and their walled cities frightened the host of Israel. Because of the negative majority report and the people's reaction to it, the Lord pronounced a curse on the Israelites: they would stay in the wilderness.

Thus came major provocation—doubt concerning the promises of the Lord and mutiny against Moses. Led by the ten fearful scouts, the whole people seem to have rebelled in spite of the good efforts of Caleb and Joshua to persuade them that with the Lord's help they could indeed conquer the land. Yet, even after all they had witnessed, the people of Israel still could not muster a small amount of faith or trust in God. Though the report was a negative exaggeration, it was a catalyst in bringing to light the deep-seated fear and spiritual laziness of the people. Faith and fear are incompatible, but they could have done something about decreasing their fear and increasing their faith. They did not. The national tragedy began to crescendo as the people promoted the negative report and murmured against Moses and the land.

Numbers 14:11–39

The Lord reacted to Israel's rebellion by threatening to abandon them all and make of Moses and his descendants a new chosen people. Moses pleaded for them and even reasoned that it would be a shame for the Lord to destroy them and thus let the other nations know that he could not bring them to the status that he intended.

Some clemency was granted, but the ten scouts who led the mutiny perished in a plague, and the rebellious older generation was all sentenced to perish during the years Israel would have to wait for entry into the land of promise.

We may take away some impressive lessons from this episode:

1. Moses' integrity is emphasized; he refused to put himself ahead of the people and seek his own fame and power through a tempting offer.
2. Like the future Savior, Moses acted as mediator on behalf of the people (see D&C 45:3–5).
3. Moses' meekness once again shone brightly as he responded with faith in God though provoked by the people.
4. Moses did not flinch in carrying out his duty. He boldly declared God's judgment against the very people who were angry with him and rebelling against him: they would wander in the wilderness, bearing the consequences of their "whoredoms" (v. 33), or spiritual adultery (Leviticus 17:7), and would eventually perish, being replaced by a new generation. This has profound implications for each of us. We might call it a parable of replacement.

Numbers 14:40–45

After hearing the sentence, some repented of their mutiny and confessed their sin, claiming to be ready to go to the promised land. But they were not sincere, and the second stage of the national tragedy unfolded. Some presumed to organize an assault on local enemy forces in the Negev. The devastating consequences are reported in these verses and in Deuteronomy 1:41–45.

Numbers 15:1–36

More details are recorded on offering sacrifices and keeping covenants, with provision for redemption from errors committed in ignorance, whether by Israelites or by strangers. "But the soul that doeth aught presumptuously," whether Israelite or stranger, was to be excommunicated, or cut off from the community, for he "despised the word of the Lord." This again points to the difference between the Lord's attitude toward the defiant and those who simply don't understand. This difference helps us understand the mercy that is available to those who sin in ignorance and the justice that applies to those who sin willfully. The Hebrew in verse 30 uses a descriptive idiom for willful or presumptuous sin—literally, "with a high hand."

The implication then is that the man who gathered sticks on the Sabbath was willfully defiant and belligerent in his disobedience.

Numbers 15:37–41

Israelites were to make marks, called fringes, in the borders or hems of their garments, suggesting to their minds that they do all the things God commanded and be holy (sanctified) unto God. As an Israelite would walk along, these fringes would swirl around and be seen—an excellent memory prod. Later some people were condemned for hypocritically observing the details of this practice even though their hearts were far from God (compare Matthew 23:5). In modern times, these ritual fringes (Hebrew, *tzitzit*) are crafted from strings, knotted in a certain way to represent the 613 individual commandments in the Torah. They are attached to the four corners of an undergarment worn by Jewish men, as well as an outer prayer shawl. Latter-day Saints can be grateful for their sacred clothing and other symbolic practices to help us remember covenants, commandments, and godly promises "and be holy" (v. 40).

Numbers 16:1–50

The willful mutiny and bid for power by a Levite leader, Korah (member of the important Kohathite group who were bearers of the Ark and other sacred things), along with two associates from the tribe of Reuben and "two hundred and fifty princes" of Israel, brought a severe rebuke from Moses. Their failure to appreciate their callings and Korah's lust for power—seeking "the priesthood also"—was the height of pride. The argument the rebels used against the Lord's anointed sounds disturbingly familiar: "You try to exercise too much power. You're not the boss of us. The whole congregation is holy; you have the problem!" (see v. 3). Since Korah was rebelling against Moses for "lifting himself above the congregation," it was obviously the high priesthood held only by Moses that Korah coveted (see JST footnote 10a). Moses reminded the rebels that though they thought they were rebelling against Moses and Aaron, it was really the Lord they were opposing. The rebels accused Moses of not fulfilling his promise of taking Israel into the land of plenty. The phrase "wilt thou put out the eyes of these men" is an idiom meaning "will you make slaves of men?" We will see this practice followed in Samson's era (Judges 16:21).

Though Moses denied any misuse of power or intent to oppress others through his priesthood, Korah gathered his forces for the showdown. Justice demanded that the rebellious be punished, but Moses pleaded for mercy for all except those immediately involved. Then the punishment fell, and in order that the people might know that it was a punishment from God, a "new thing" happened—the earth opened and swallowed them.

Some of those who were spared complained about the fate of those punished, and the punishment proceeded to include the new rebels. Does the chastisement sound too harsh? Read Hebrews 12:9–11.

A powerful lesson comes from modern American history. General George C. Marshall once told a discouraged staff:

"Gentlemen, it is my experience [that] an enlisted man may have a morale problem. An officer is expected to take care of his own morale" (in Uldrich, *Soldier, Statesman,* 216). In other words, morale problems are an enlisted man's privilege; they are not for the officers! As with General Marshall's officers and with the Israelite leaders, so it is with us: we have a duty to be loyal and positive; we have an obligation as God's covenant people to be faithful and strictly obedient.

Verse 48 teaches a powerful and important lesson for our day. Sometimes the only thing that stands between us and destruction is the Lord's anointed—his prophets and priesthood leaders.

Numbers 17:1–13

A sign was provided to show that Aaron was still the Lord's chosen leader of the Aaronic Priesthood. Some apparently continued to smart under the realization that they could not rebel without suffering consequences.

Numbers 18:1–32

Aaron and his priestly sons were responsible for any wrongs done in the sanctuary or by the priesthood leadership. Offerings could be used for the support of the priests, since they were to have no tribal lands as an inheritance. Because certain tithes and offerings were their "inheritance," they were to pay tithing themselves upon that income. Verses 22–23 help us to appreciate that the Israelites were to have physical mediators, the priesthood holders, to point them to their need for a spiritual mediator, the Messiah.

Numbers 19:1–22

The law of the red heifer is outlined. Ashes of a certain sacrificed animal were to be put into a vessel with water to be used to remove ritual impurity from Israelites who necessarily or inadvertently handled the body of a dead person. That the specified animal was a heifer (a young cow, a potential giver of life) and red (the color of blood) may have made her ashes a symbolic counteragent for contact with death.

Other symbolism behind the sacrifice of the red heifer is associated with spiritual death and redemption. One who defiled himself or herself through sin would necessarily undergo spiritual death whereby he or she would be cut off from the presence of God. Redemption from spiritual death is obtained by faith in Christ's atonement, his shed blood, symbolized by the death of the red heifer. Just as hyssop was used in the preparation of the burning of the red heifer, so hyssop was also used during the crucifixion of Jesus Christ (John 19:29). Just as Jesus was the perfect offering for sin, so too each red heifer had to be perfect. Even one non-red hair from the heifer disqualified the animal from being an acceptable sacrifice.

Numbers 20:1

The death and burial of Miriam, the older sister of Moses, who was referred to as "the prophetess" is mentioned (see commentary at Exodus 15:20–27). Probably too little has been recorded about this remarkable woman. We heard of her leading the dancers in thanksgiving to the Lord after the Red Sea crossing and heard of her short period of faultfinding. Recall that when she was punished for that, Moses pleaded with the Lord in her behalf that the punishing malady be removed from her, and it was (Numbers 12:13–15). The name Miriam, a common name in New Testament times also, is anglicized as Mary.

Numbers 20:2–13

The people once again accused Moses and the Lord of leading them into the desert to perish. One needs to visit the terrain of the Sinai, Negev, and Arabah—some of the most rugged, desolate landscapes in the world—to appreciate the desperate cry for water to drink.

To meet the need for water, Moses was commanded to *speak* to a rock to get water. But he disobeyed and instead struck the rock with his familiar instrument of divine power, his rod, as he had done before. The previous time had been in compliance with a command, however (see Exodus 17:6–7). Moreover, on this occasion he "took honor to himself" saying, "Must we fetch you water out of this rock?"

President Spencer W. Kimball explained: "Even Moses, like many of us, seemed to let his humility cloak wear thin and threadbare. The wanderers had come to the desert of Zin. . . . But Moses, undoubtedly annoyed to the limit of human endurance, forgot himself and said to them, ' . . . Hear now, ye rebels: must we fetch you water out of this rock?' The Lord was displeased with Moses in assuming to perform the miracle. I can imagine the Lord saying something like this: '*Who*, did you say? Who made the water? Who made the rock? Moses! Who brought the water from the rock?'. . . . Moses had integrity in great measure, but when he had presumptuously taken credit for the Lord's miracle, for a single moment he had forgotten" (*Humility*, 7; see also *Integrity*, 10).

As a result, Moses himself would be punished, and his punishment became a lesson to all that no one is exempt from obedience—even Moses, the prophet, must obey exactly. He was told that he could not lead the people into the promised land. Compare the operation of the same principle in modern times: read carefully Doctrine and Covenants 59:21 and 93:47–49. This is not pharisaism but submission. God doesn't want quite a bit from us—he wants everything, as represented by our hearts. All of us must learn to obey with strictness, with exactness.

EXACT AND STRICT OBEDIENCE

Eliza R. Snow was an exceptional writer in the latter-day Church. She was a poetess and wrote some of our best known and best loved hymns, for example, "O My Father," "Behold the Great Redeemer Die," "Truth Reflects upon Our Senses," and "How Great the Wisdom and the Love." In verse 3 of "How Great the Wisdom and the Love," Sister Snow wrote: "By strict obedience Jesus won The prize with glory rife" (*Hymns,* no. 195). Even Jesus, the greatest person ever to live on this earth, won the prize of eternal glory by strict obedience to the will of his Father. "Though he were a Son, yet learned he obedience by the things which he suffered" (Hebrews 5:8).

Elders and sisters in the missionary training centers are encouraged in talks, handbooks, bulletins, and memos to be "exactly" and "strictly" obedient. Those two adjectives are critical. The first law of heaven is obedience, and it is vital that those going out to represent the Lord Jesus Christ be *exactly* obedient and *strictly* obedient. Those two words may not be very popular out in the world these days. Young people demand freedom; they don't want to be restricted with mountains of rules. Yet hundreds of thousands of missionaries over the decades have been taught to be exactly and strictly obedient in all things.

In the holy Temple everything is also done in a specific and exact way, in clothing and ordinances. All things need to be in their proper place. The Lord is teaching us that his House is a house of order. He is teaching us to prepare to live in the most refined society in the heavens—to learn exact obedience to the God of heaven, because that is the only way we will become like he is. To Moses, and to all Israel, the Lord said, "Ye shall be holy . . . for I the Lord am holy" (Leviticus 20:26).

We have a host of examples preserved in sacred records of those who have demonstrated their willingness to obey all things the Lord commands. We have already seen that Adam was offering sacrifices to the Lord one day when a messenger from heaven appeared to ask him why he was doing it (Moses 5:5–7). Even though he didn't know why, Adam was willing to do exactly what the Lord asked of him. Of course, the Lord ultimately wanted Adam to understand the sacred symbolism involved in offering blood sacrifices, so he sent his angel to explain the meaning of the ordinance to Adam. But first he tested Adam's obedience, to see if he was willing to do precisely what the Lord asked, even without knowing the reasons up front. Adam strictly obeyed the commands of God and received the corresponding blessings. From the beginning, he and Eve provided an abiding example to their posterity.

Noah was another superb example. Long before the rains came, while it was still dry, the Lord commanded him to build a ship to save his family from a great flood. That would be like the Lord commanding Brother Ogden or Brother Skinner to take his family from Utah Valley and flee up the canyon eastward into Heber Valley and there build a spaceship because the world would soon be destroyed and that would be the only way for his family to be saved. The reaction, of course, would be, "But, Lord, I don't know how to build a spaceship." Noah likely felt the same way. But he responded by doing exactly as the Lord instructed him (the Lord providing the details after Noah demonstrated his willingness to obey), and, in the end, the prophet and his family were saved and thus perpetuated the human race. We all appreciate Noah's obedience: we are all descendants of Noah, and his obedience preserved our option to come here for this crucial mortal probation.

Abraham and Sarah are classic examples of faith and obedience. Elder Bruce R. McConkie wrote: "I would suppose that among faithful people in ancient Israel, through all the ages from Abraham's day onward, the favored illustration and the favored text to teach the people that the Only Begotten Son would be sacrificed to bring immortality to men would be the story of Abraham. There is nothing more dramatic than this in the whole biblical account" ("Promises Made to the Fathers," 57).

The command came to offer his beloved son as a burnt offering, as recorded in Genesis 22. Abraham knew how repulsive human sacrifice was and how foreign such a practice is to the true worship of our Heavenly Father. But Abraham knew something else, too. He knew that one of God's expressed purposes for his children during mortality was to "prove them herewith, to see if they will do *all things* whatsoever the Lord their God shall command them" (Abraham 3:25; emphasis added). God had commanded it; how could he not obey? As Joseph Smith declared, "Whatever God requires is right" (see commentary at Genesis 12:10–20; Exodus 20:13). Following Abraham's example, we will obey, no matter what the command, for we know that God gives no commandments to us without preparing the way for us to accomplish them (1 Nephi 3:7).

Nephi was instructed to make two sets of plates without knowing why. That was a big order because the Book of Mormon writers frequently remind us that it was hard work making metal plates and hard work carving on them. We don't know that Nephi ever learned the reason why he had to go to all that extra work to make a second set of plates, but he was willing to be expressly obedient to what the Lord, in his wisdom, directed his prophet to do.

Such marvelous scriptural examples teach us how to be exactly obedient. Sometimes the Lord tells us why we are to obey a commandment—although other times he does not—but we learn to trust him and carry out his will even if we don't understand why.

President Brigham Young said: "Truth is obeyed when it is loved. Strict obedience to the truth will alone enable people to dwell in the presence of the Almighty" (*Journal of Discourses*, 7:55).

Of Jesus verse 3 of Sister Eliza Snow's hymn says: "'Thy will, O God, not mine be done,' adorned his mortal life." Strict obedience is simply a matter of daily diligence; it is a habit of daily discipline.

We would err if we were to denigrate Moses because of his misstep. He was eventually translated so he could fulfill other missions for the Lord. He ultimately passed the tests of mortality and needed no more tests or trials. He proved his willingness to serve the Lord at all hazards. His exaltation became secure. As Joseph Smith stated: "When the Lord has thoroughly proved him, and finds that the man is determined to serve Him at all hazards, then the man will find his calling and his election made sure, . . . and the Lord will teach him face to face, and he may have a perfect knowledge of the mysteries of the Kingdom of God; and this is the state and place the ancient Saints arrived at when they had such glorious visions—Isaiah, Ezekiel" and, we may say, Moses (*History of the Church,* 3:380–81).

Numbers 20:14–21

In anticipation of a thrust into the middle of Canaan from the east, the Israelites journeyed into Edomite territory towards the King's Highway and were refused passage (see Bible Map 2). At this point we have two conflicting reports of their route. Numbers 33 seems to suggest they continued on through Edomite territory anyway. That suggested route is rather unlikely. The more likely course of travel forced the tribes into a nearly two hundred-mile detour south to the Red Sea and then northeast along the desert roads called "the way of the wilderness of Edom" and "the way of the wilderness of Moab," east of the King's Highway, thus circumnavigating the heartland of Edom and Moab. We will see what the Israelites felt about that route in Numbers 21:4–5.

Numbers 20:22–29

When the time for Aaron's death drew near, his priesthood garments were transferred to his son Eleazar, which signified the transmission of his call as presiding priest. The Israelites paused in their march for a month at Mount Hor to mourn and honor Aaron.

Numbers 21:1–9

A skirmish with the king of Arad and his southern Canaanite peoples ended in victory for Israel. Notice that the *herem,* the Hebrew word signifying the utter destruction of people of the Lord's choosing, was employed (see commentary at Exodus 22:1–20). Hence, the location was named Hormah, a variation on the term *herem.*

Another complaint about manna brought punishment in the form of venomous serpents. Escape from death was provided through a test of faith and obedience: Moses made a bronze serpent on a pole and instructed that all who looked up at it should be saved. Other Israelite writers later wrote that because of the simpleness of the cure, the obstinate refused to comply and receive salvation (1 Nephi 17:41; 2 Nephi 25:20; Helaman 8:14–15).

"Behold, he [the Messiah] was spoken of by Moses; yea, and behold a type was raised up in the wilderness, that whosoever would look upon it might live. And many did look and live. But few understood the meaning of those things, and this because of the hardness of their hearts. But there were many who were so hardened that they would not look, therefore they perished. Now the reason they would not look is because *they did not believe that it would heal them*" (Alma 33:19–20; emphasis added).

Still later, the apostle John reported that Jesus himself saw in that event a type or similitude in anticipation of the Messiah: "as Moses lifted up the serpent in the wilderness, even so must the Son of man be lifted up: that whosoever believeth in him should not perish, but have eternal life" (John 3:14–15).

Just as Israel had looked to the serpent on a pole to live, they were encouraged to look to their Redeemer, who would be lifted up, to gain eternal life. The serpent sometimes is a symbol of God. From the very beginning, however, there was a perversion of the true symbol. Satan usurped the image to represent himself. "The great dragon was cast out, that old serpent, called the Devil, and Satan, which deceiveth the whole world" (Revelation 12:9; 20:2). "The serpent beguiled Eve through his subtilty" (2 Corinthians 11:3).

Moses' serpent on a pole was able to heal, and the Savior lifted up on the cross is able to heal. The serpent's healing powers persisted in the mythologies of Near Eastern religions, even down to the Greco-Roman god Asclepius, the god of healing and medicine. Healing or medical centers were established throughout the Roman Empire, for example, the Asclepieum at Pergamum and the Asklepeion on the island of Cos where Hippocrates practiced for many years. The symbol of Asclepius was a serpent wrapped around a pole. Today it is the symbol of the American Medical Association. The parallel of serpent and God is present in other ancient cultures as well, for example, the Aztec god Quetzalcoatl, literally "Precious Serpent," who reputedly lived in Coatzacoalcos, or "sanctuary of the serpent."

Numbers 21:10–35

Sihon was king of some of the Amorite people living east of the Jordan Valley at the time of the Israelite incursion there. His capital was at Heshbon, up on the plateau east of the northern end of the Dead Sea, on the King's Highway. Once the Israelites crossed to the north side of the deep Arnon canyon, they were in Sihon's territory and had to deal with him (see Bible Map 2). Their next campaign was with more Amorites under Og, king of Bashan (east and south of the Sea of Galilee). Details of these conflicts are said to have been written in the "book of the wars of the Lord," but at present we have no such book nor substantial excerpts from it, except for a brief poem about the triumphs of the Israelites from the Dead Sea to the streams of Moab. Since Israel was in transjordanian country, these conquests provided lands for some of the tribes who later settled there.

Numbers 22:1–8

Israel's advance on Balak of Moab prompted Balak to send for one Balaam of Pethor in the valleys of the upper Euphrates (Deuteronomy 23:4), where Abraham once dwelt and from whence Rebekah, Leah, and Rachel came, to try to get Israel's own God to curse Israel. In this account, Balaam is not called a prophet. Yet, the Lord spoke to him, and he experienced significant interactions with heavenly messengers. His challenge and fall from grace are described by Elder Bruce R. McConkie:

"Let me tell you the story of a prophet, in some respects a very great prophet, but one 'who loved the wages of unrighteousness,' who 'was rebuked for his iniquity' in a most strange and unusual way, and whose actions (which included the uttering of great and true prophecies) were described by another prophet in another day as 'madness.' . . .

"Our story took place on the plains of Moab near Jericho; . . . the chief participants were Balak, king of the Moabites, and Balaam, a prophet from the land of Midian. Israel's hosts, numbering in the millions, had just devastated the land of the Amorites and were camped on the borders of Moab. Fear and anxiety filled the hearts of the people of Moab and Balak their king. Would they also be overrun and slaughtered by these warriors of Jehovah? . . .

"What a story this is! Here is a prophet of God who is firmly committed to declare only what the Lord of heaven directs. There does not seem to be the slightest doubt in his mind about the course he should pursue. He represents the Lord, and neither a house full of gold and silver nor high honors offered by the king can sway him from his determined course. . . .

"But greed for wealth and lust for honor beckon him. How marvelous it would be to be rich and powerful . . .

"Perhaps the Lord would let him compromise his standards and have some worldly prosperity and power as well as a testimony of the gospel. . . .

"I wonder how often some of us get our directions from the Church and then, Balaam-like, plead for some worldly rewards and finally receive an answer which says, in effect, If you are determined to be a millionaire or to gain this or that worldly honor, go ahead, with the understanding that you will continue to serve the Lord. Then we wonder why things don't work out for us as well as they would have done if we had put first in our lives the things of God's kingdom? . . .

"And don't we all know people who, though they were once firm and steadfast in testimony, are now opposing the Lord's purposes and interests on earth because money and power have twisted their judgment of what should or should not be?

"Balaam, the prophet, inspired and mighty as he once was, lost his soul in the end because he set his heart on the things of this world rather than the riches of eternity" (*New Era,* Apr. 1972, 7).

Joshua 13:22 calls Balaam a "soothsayer."

Numbers 22:9–36

Balaam could not curse Israel if God would not, but Balak the king tried again. This time he offered more enticing rewards to Balaam.

Balaam tried God again and won a concession; the Lord told him (JST Numbers 22:20): "If the men come to call thee, rise up, *if thou wilt go with them;* but yet the word which I shall say unto thee, shalt thou speak." In other words, Balaam had a choice. But Balaam overstepped his privilege, so he was warned and chastised by a dumb beast, which was made able to speak and to see the angel that his master could not see. It is possible that the words could have just appeared to have come from a donkey, similar to Moses with a burning bush; however, we should not restrict God's ability to perform any kind of miracle. We know that even animals, when filled with the Spirit of the Lord and celestialized, will be able to express themselves (Revelation 4:6, 9; D&C 77:2–4). The text uses an interesting word in verse 22 which translators rendered "adversary"; the Hebrew is *satan.*

Of the many lessons found in this episode, one wonders if some of us are like Balak or Balaam as we seek answers to our petitions. We ask the Lord for direction and when we receive it we want something different, either out of selfishness or social pressures.

Numbers 22:37 to 24:25

Though Balaam was warned that he could effectively speak only that which God authorized him to speak, Balaam also tried to serve Balak's desires. Sure enough, upon the first attempt, a blessing was spoken concerning Israel instead of a curse. The second and the third attempts were the same.

Balaam was unwilling to lose the offered rewards from Balak. It is impossible, however, as Jesus later said, to "serve two masters" (Matthew 6:24). Balaam became a symbol of perverting divine power to gain one's own end.

Later Balaam must have done with subtlety what he could not do with divine authority, because Moab nearly "conquered" Israel by seducing her sons with Moab's idols and daughters, through what was later called the "counsel of Balaam" (see Numbers 31:16; Deuteronomy 4:3; 2 Peter 2:15; Revelation 2:14). Balaam was a classic example of our human nature and disposition. As soon as we get a little authority, as we suppose, we begin to exercise unrighteous dominion and aspire to the honors of men and the things of this world (ponder D&C 121:34–40). At what point did Balaam begin to compromise? Where did he go wrong?

There is another lesson from this unusual episode. Though not called by God to serve as a prophet to the children of Israel, Balaam nevertheless was allowed to utter one of the most inspiring prophetic promises of the coming of the Messiah: "There shall come a Star out of Jacob, and a Sceptre shall rise out of Israel . . . Out of Jacob shall come he that shall have dominion" (24:17, 19; compare Caiaphas prophesying, John 11:49–51). This prophecy applies to the Second Coming as well: Israel's future deliverer will be a star to them, bringing victory over Israel's enemies (Revelation 22:16).

Don't miss the simple verse that says, "God is not a man, that he should lie; neither the son of man, that he should repent" (23:19). This statement justifies all the changes the Prophet Joseph Smith inserted into the last two hundred pages of the biblical text that God did *not* repent of this or that. Being sinless, God never needs to repent; only men need to repent.

Numbers 25:1–18

Shittim (pronounced she-TEAM) was another name for Israel's staging area before the conquest of Canaan. It was situated on the east side of the Jordan River opposite Jericho.

The twin sins of idolatry and adultery encouraged by the Moabites and Midianites required vigorous countermeasures which were undertaken under the leadership of Phinehas, grandson of Aaron and son of Eleazar. These sins tempted Israel away from her proper course again and again throughout Old Testament history.

Numbers 26:1–65

Numbers 26:1 through 27:23 report preparations for the conquest. The second military census was taken, preliminary to the conquest of Canaan proper. The first census had been taken over thirty-eight years earlier. All were numbered according to tribal affiliation again, and the total of military-age men was 601,730. Compared to the 603,550 at the beginning, the death rate had exceeded the birthrate, except in the single tribe of Levi which had grown from 22,000 to 23,000. The total number of descendants of Joseph was greater at this point than any other tribe (85,200). Significantly, the wicked sons of Judah were mentioned in the census, but they received no inheritance (see Genesis 38:1–10).

The land was apportioned according to two factors, which were influenced by the Lord: the population of tribes and the casting of lots.

None of the old generation was among those numbered except Caleb and Joshua and Moses, who remained a little longer to complete his mission.

Numbers 27:1–11

Through revelation, women were given the right to inherit their father's property if there were no sons. Recognition of women's rights is noteworthy in these early biblical times, since it was all but nonexistent elsewhere. Ancient Near Eastern law did not usually provide for women to inherit property.

Numbers 27:12–14

The Lord reiterated that Moses could *see* the land but not enter it because of his lack of exact obedience on the occasion of getting water from the rock (Numbers 20:2–13). From one of the peaks of the range east of the Jordan valley and the Dead Sea, Moses could gaze over at the choice but small "promised land." The particular peak of the Abarim range from which Moses would view the land was named Mount Nebo (Numbers 33:47; Deuteronomy 32:49).

Numbers 27:15–23

The procedure was given for naming and authorizing a successor to Moses. This section is important for our understanding of how calling and ordination were done anciently and how the restored gospel follows well-established principles and patterns. Joshua was "called of God," presented before the people, and approved and blessed by the laying on of hands with the spirit and authority to lead the people. However, he did not get all of the power of Moses and was admonished to ask counsel of the Aaronic Priesthood leaders, who would direct Israel in God's ways by the Urim and Thummim. Moses was instructed to "put some of thine honor upon him" (compare D&C 84:25). Joshua was also given a charge concerning his duties.

Numbers 28:1–31

The daily, weekly, monthly, and yearly offerings, the Passover regulations, and the offerings of the first fruits were reiterated.

Numbers 29:1–40

More offerings and annual feasts were reviewed (compare Leviticus 23). To understand the significance of commemorating things in cycles of seven, refer to the Creation story in Genesis 1, the references to the seven thousand years of the earth's temporal existence in Doctrine and Covenants 77:6, 12, and the whole structure of the book of Revelation. The number seven symbolized wholeness, completeness, even perfection (see "The Significance of Certain Numbers in the Scriptures," page 263). The Hebrew root from which the word for "seven" derives is also the root of the word for "oath." See Mosiah 13:29–30 and 16:14–15 for an explanation of the purpose of these many offerings and laws.

Numbers 30:1–16

This passage constitutes one of the main Old Testament passages on vows. Vows and oaths should be kept faithfully between man and wife, father and daughter, etc. The principle of integrity is at the core of behavior: a man "shall not break his word, he shall do according to all that proceedeth out of his mouth." We must keep our vows, just as God keeps his (D&C 82:10; 84:40).

Numbers 31:1–54

One of Moses' last actions as leader of the Israelites was to declare a holy war against a group who hindered Israel. The gory destruction of several Midianite tribes who had been involved in the corruption of Israel during the Balak and Balaam affair is reported. Balaam was killed in open war against the people he had unwillingly blessed. Some of the slaughter was punishment for the seduction of Israelite males by Midianite females "through the counsel of Balaam, to commit trespass against the Lord." The killing of women and children along with the men but keeping certain virgin girls along with some booty does not seem just nor in keeping with a law later clearly pronounced (Deuteronomy 24:16).

Numbers 32:1–42

The herdsmen and shepherds of Gad and Reuben requested inheritances in the lands already conquered east of the Jordan River. Moses counseled and warned them, testing their motives.

The tribes of Gad and Reuben denied any intent of leaving the body of Israel. Indeed, they planned to establish their families in conquered cities and then provide soldiers to help the rest of Israel conquer the land before settling down in their inheritances. Their request was granted. Moses also assigned half of the tribe of Manasseh to lands in those transjordanian regions (east of the Jordan River).

Numbers 33:1–49

Moses wrote a review of the Exodus and the Lord's efforts in behalf of the Israelites against the Egyptians; he also wrote concerning their travels, camping places, and major incidents during their journeys. This is further internal evidence that these things were written in the days of Moses and not eight hundred to a thousand years later, as some critics have claimed.

Numbers 33:50–56

The Lord again warned Israel to obliterate, not assimilate, the culture of Canaan, because if those apostate and perverted societies were not destroyed, they would be "pricks in your eyes, and thorns in your sides." This later proved to be the case.

Numbers 34:1–29

Moses gave advance description of the regions and boundaries of the land of Canaan. The description more or less parallels the Egyptian province of Canaan as defined in the Egyptian-Hittite peace treaty signed following the Battle of Kadesh in 1285 B.C. Compare Ezekiel 47:15–20 and 48:1, 28 for that prophet's description of the future borders of Israel.

Under the direction of Eleazar, the priest, and Joshua, the civil and military leader, and twelve princes from the twelve tribes (all called and named by revelation from the Lord), the land was parceled out to each of the tribes.

Numbers 35:1–34

Forty-eight cities were designated as those which the Levites could possess as their own and live among the people of all the other tribes.

Six of the Levitical cities (three to the east and three to the west of the Jordan River) were to be "cities of refuge," where one accused or guilty of bloodshed could flee until a jury of his peers could determine whether he had indeed committed murder and deserved punishment. This guaranteed the right of trial by careful examination and procedure rather than quick justice by vendetta.

Differentiation is made between murder and involuntary manslaughter. The laws of capital punishment and of witnesses were given. Another warning was issued against resorting to violence and bloodshed, for bloodshed pollutes the land. Latter-day Saints understand that the earth is a living entity and recoils at the wickedness perpetrated by her inhabitants (Moses 7:48).

Numbers 36:1–13

The question about land passing from tribe to tribe because of the marriage of female heirs (recall Numbers 27:1–11) was solved by the recommendation that women marry men of the tribe of their father.

DEUTERONOMY

Deuteronomy, the fifth and last book of the Pentateuch, is a reiteration, or repetition, of the law (*deutero,* "second"; *nomos,* "law, instruction"). Its English title comes from the Septuagint and Latin Vulgate, which, in turn, came from a mistranslation of the phrase "copy of this law" found in Deuteronomy 17:18. The Hebrew name for the book is *'elle ha-d'varim* ("These are the words"), or more simply, *D'varim* ("words," "matters"), some of the beginning words of the Hebrew text of Deuteronomy 1:1.

Whereas Leviticus and Numbers were, respectively, a technical manual for the priests and a historical treatise, Deuteronomy was for the people in general. It is composed, for the most part, of the final three sermons Moses delivered to the Israelites just before he was translated. Deuteronomy 1:5 describes the setting for the sermons. Moses and the Israelites were situated in Moab, latitudinally parallel with where the Jordan River flows into the Dead Sea. As they were assembled on that part of the plateau opposite the Judean wilderness with the Rift Valley and Jordan River in between, poised to enter the promised land, Moses undoubtedly looked over the congregation. He knew from experience their strengths and weaknesses. He knew by revelation what they needed to hear. He began his first sermon by summarizing important matters. Thus, the organization of the book proceeds straightforwardly.

In chapters 1–4, the first sermon, Moses recalls important

facts of Israel's forty-year wanderings and exhorts them to remember the covenant.

In chapters 5–26, the second sermon, Moses again sets forth important points of the law for Israel to follow.

In chapters 27–30, the third sermon, Moses renews the covenant with Israel.

Chapters 31–34 constitute an appendix.

Because it is largely Moses' sermons, Deuteronomy comes across in a more personal way than the somewhat stilted narrative style of Leviticus and Numbers.

In addition to the opening verses of the first chapter, indicating its origin as speeches by Moses "beyond Jordan," see also the following apparent references to this book of "the law of the Lord" and of Moses in the days of King Josiah of Judah (ca. 621 B.C.): 2 Kings 22 and 23, and 2 Chronicles 34, especially verse 14: "The priest found a book of the law of the Lord given by Moses."

During his mortal ministry, our Lord bore witness to Moses' authorship of Deuteronomy (Matthew 19:7–8; Mark 10:3–5; John 5:46–47). In fact, Jesus quoted more from Deuteronomy than from any other Old Testament book except Isaiah and Psalms, and he ascribes great authority to it (Matthew 4:4, 7, 10). Other New Testament figures also attest to Moses' authorship of Deuteronomy (Acts 3:22–23; 7:37–38; Romans 10:19). It is, however, almost certain that portions of the book, as well as the final editing process, are the work of later editors; see, for example, the book's prologue (1:1–5) and the report of Moses' "death" (chapter 34).

Although Deuteronomy has commonly been regarded as a composition of much later times by some scholars and commentators, there are still many, including the Latter-day Saints, who regard the book of Deuteronomy as the farewell teachings of Moses. And for one who had protested, "I am slow of speech," Moses seems to have made admirable progress; these are great speeches!

As you begin, you may want to read in the Bible Dictionary the entry entitled "Deuteronomy."

Deuteronomy 1:1–8

The opening sentence looks like the words of an editor, introducing the author and the setting for the book. The translators have rendered the location "on this side Jordan," but the Hebrew really says "beyond the Jordan"; that is, to the east of the Jordan River, which is in the great Rift Valley. In verses 2–5, an introduction follows, in the third person, relating that Moses "began explaining this doctrine" (translated in King James English as "began to declare this law"). In verse 6 Moses reminded the people of the words of the Lord directing them to leave Mount Sinai, or Mount Horeb, and journey to the promised land. *Horeb,* the other name for Sinai, derives from a Hebrew word meaning "desolate, barren"—and it certainly is! Verse 19 describes the whole Sinai peninsula as "that great and terrible wilderness." The parenthetical travel note in verse 2 is accurate: from Jebel Musa, the traditional Mount Sinai, to Dahab, to Kadesh-barnea, is indeed an eleven days' journey.

Deuteronomy 1:9–18

In recalling the reasons for setting up a government in the wilderness, Moses commented that the Lord had blessed and multiplied them and would still increase them a thousand times more (compare D&C 132:30). Then he reviewed the system of leadership and the type of officials he had chosen to lead them, as well as the instructions he had given them.

Deuteronomy 1:19–46

Moses summarized the events leading to the Israelites' wilderness sojourn. He placed the responsibility for their suffering and even for his own punishment—not being allowed to enter the land—squarely upon the people.

Verses 29–30 emphasize a major theme we see repeated throughout the period of the conquest of the Holy Land: do not fear but have faith, for the Lord will fight for his people Israel (compare Deuteronomy 2:25; 3:22: 20:1–4; Joshua 1:9; 10:14). Sadly, as Moses reminded his audience, "In this thing ye did not believe the Lord your God." In fact, because of their unbelief and unrepentant wickedness the Lord actually strengthened Israel's enemies against her (Judges 2:14; 3:12; 4:2). The Lord uses the wicked to punish the wicked (Mormon 4:5).

In this modern dispensation, living prophets have taught that if we, latter-day Israel, are righteous the Lord will again fight our battles. President Spencer W. Kimball wrote:

"We are a warlike people, easily distracted from our assignment of preparing for the coming of the Lord. When enemies rise up, we commit vast resources to the fabrication of gods of stone and steel—ships, planes, missiles, fortifications—and depend on them for protection and deliverance. When threatened, we become anti-enemy instead of pro-kingdom of God; we train a man in the art of war and call him a patriot, thus, in the manner of Satan's counterfeit of true patriotism, perverting the Savior's teaching:

"'Love your enemies, bless them that curse you, do good to them that hate you, and pray for them which despitefully use you, and persecute you;

"'That ye may be the children of your Father which is in heaven.' (Matt. 5:44–45.)

"We forget that if we are righteous the Lord will either not suffer our enemies to come upon us . . . or he will fight our battles for us (Exodus 14:14; D&C 98:37, to name only two references of many)" (*Ensign*, June 1976, 3–6; emphasis added).

Deuteronomy 2:1 to 3:11

Moses next reviewed the Israelites' contacts with other peoples, the conflicts, the routes taken to avoid molesting other people who were under God's protection, the provisions God had made to supply their daily needs, the ways in which the old rebellious generation had perished, and the steps by which Israel had finally proceeded up to the east side of the promised land, conquering some peoples there. Again, you may follow all these journeys on Bible Map 2. The Lord also declared that he was beginning to use psychological warfare against nations living in the land that Israel was about to enter in order to make their conquest easier (v. 25).

Lands of inheritance given by God to other specific groups are highlighted: Esau (2:5), Moab (2:9), and Ammon (2:19), thus teaching Israel that God is concerned for the welfare of all his children and blesses those who live uprightly. Moses also reminded his audience that the Lord raised up a new generation of Israelites through attrition. Modern readers note that by the time of Israel's encounter with Sihon the Amorite, the conquest had, for all intents and purposes, begun.

Deuteronomy 3:12–29

The conquest had already begun. The tribes of Reuben and Gad, along with half the tribe of Manasseh, had been established in the transjordan area (east of the Jordan River), and the pattern of conquest and settlement there was an example to Joshua and all Israel of what to expect in invading the region west of the Jordan. Again, Israel was told not to fear for the Lord was going to fight for his people.

Moses made a poignant plea to the Lord that he might go over into the promised land, but the Lord refused (we will see more on the reasons why at the end of Deuteronomy). The charge to Joshua is then reviewed.

Deuteronomy 4:1–4

A warning is given not to add to or take away from the words which Moses spoke and recorded. Revelation 22:18–19 contains an identical warning, and those verses are sometimes quoted by antagonists of the Church as a warning to Latter-day Saints or anyone else not to add to what is written in the Bible. These antagonists reject the whole idea of additional scripture, such as the Book of Mormon, feeling it is theologically scandalous to think that God has any more words for his children on earth. But a careful examination of John's inspired warning will reveal its real meaning. "If any man shall add unto these things"—the first caution is that no *man* should tamper with these things, though the Lord may certainly add more if he so desires. The second caution is not to add to "these things," and the antecedent to "these things" is "the prophecy of this book." John was warning against attempts to alter his revelation as he himself wrote it. He could not have been talking about the whole Bible because the Bible as we know it was not even in existence at the time John wrote his conclusion to the book of Revelation. Moses wrote his warning against adding to or diminishing from *his* revelations—the Torah (the first five books of the Bible). If the same reasoning were applied to Moses' warning as is commonly applied to John's, then we could accept nothing after the fourth chapter of Deuteronomy (for more on this point, see Brigham Young, *Journal of Discourses,* 1:242–43; 10:323–24).

Deuteronomy 4:5–40

In verses 5–8 an excellent statement is given on the mission of Israel and how it should be accomplished (compare Matthew 5:16).

Verses 9–40 constitute a powerful summary of the revelation given to the Israelites at Mount Horeb (Mount Sinai), where they had heard "the voice of the words" though they had not seen the Lord in person. One reason why they had not been permitted to see him was to avoid their ever attempting to make an image or likeness to represent him. But they had been permitted to hear his voice so that they might reverence the Lord forever, teach his law to their children and their children's children, and tell them of the great things he had done. No other people had ever had such a group privilege.

Notice one item among the blessings the people of Israel had received: the Lord had brought them forth "out of the *iron furnace,* even out of Egypt" (v. 20; emphasis added), an interesting epithet for the land of their bondage, where God "turned up the heat," in a sense, to test, try, and prove them.

Verses 25–31 constitute a prophecy of the scattering and then gathering of Israel in the latter days, not just the Jews but the whole house of Israel. Israel was told that if they behaved as the other corrupt nations they were commanded to destroy, they would be destroyed. Israel's scattering would force them to serve other gods, who could do nothing for them. But the Lord would not forsake his people. In the last days Ephraim would be gathered first (D&C 133:26–30). Modern revelation tells us the gathering is the work of the Father (3 Nephi 20:12, 13, 25–29).

The reason given for keeping God's commandments is simple but far-reaching: "That it may go well with thee, and with thy children after thee, and that thou mayest prolong thy days upon the earth."

Deuteronomy 4:41–49

Three cities east of the Jordan River were specified as cities of refuge (recall Numbers 35).

The repetition of an introductory setting for this review of the commandments leads some to wonder if this begins the second day's address by Moses.

Deuteronomy 5:1–21

The usual interpretation regards Deuteronomy 5 as the beginning of Moses' second sermon, the longest of the three (it ends in chapter 26), containing a summary of principles his people were to live by. Moses reminded Israel that the laws of God were as binding on those listening to him then as on those who heard them originally at Sinai. They are also valid for "us, even us [in the latter days], who are all of us here alive this day."

In verses 6–21 we have another version of the Ten Commandments, slightly different in the fourth, fifth, and tenth commandments as compared to the version in Exodus 20.

Deuteronomy 5:22–33

The revelation of the Ten Commandments, spoken by God unto Israel and then delivered to them on tablets of stone, was a great privilege for the Israelites. The testimony they should have derived from it is stated in verse 24 (compare the testimony of Joseph Smith and Sidney Rigdon in D&C 76:22). The rarity of the privilege is noted in verse 26.

God had heard Israel's earlier promise to keep the commandments (Exodus 24:7) and commended them. He also expressed his desire that they would do these things, "that it might be well with them and with their children forever" (v. 29). The Lord then sent them to their tents, and Moses stayed and received the rest of God's statutes and judgments.

Deuteronomy 6:1–5

Another invitation was given to Israel to keep and do these things "that it might be well with them." Every good Jew for generations has repeated many times the creed of faith in verse 4 (the *Shema*, as it is called, after the first Hebrew word of the verse, meaning "hear"). The *Shema* constitutes the first words spoken by observant Jews upon arising in the morning and the last words repeated when retiring for the evening. Following the example of the second-century rabbi Akiva, pious Jews want to die with the *Shema* on their lips. Verse 5 is what Jesus himself termed the "first and great commandment" (Matthew 22:36–38; Mark 12:30–32; compare D&C 20:19; 59:5). "First" in this context means, of course, "foremost." From this, we see that love was intended to be at the heart of the Mosaic law. Verse 5 could be the most important concept and commandment in the entire Old Testament. To love God totally is the ultimate commandment, and it lives on today as top priority in our lives; no person or thing should ever take precedence over our devotion to God and his eternal work. And part of the commandment is for fathers and mothers to also dedicate priority time to "teach them diligently unto [their] children" (v. 7).

Deuteronomy 6:6–25

The complete confession of faith (Deuteronomy 6:4–9) was to be perpetuated from generation to generation. It was written on tiny pieces of parchment that were put inside small leather boxes called "frontlets" (Hebrew, *totafot*) or phylacteries, and worn between their eyes, next to their minds, and on their arms, next to their hearts (compare Exodus 13:9, 16). This scripture is also one of the passages placed inside the *mezuza,* a small container with a parchment scroll inside, attached to the door posts of every Jewish structure frequented by observant Jews (see explanatory footnotes, especially 8*b*). The other passage written on the scroll inside the *mezuza* (plural, *mezuzot*) and the phylactery is Deuteronomy 11:13–21.

The people were warned again not to fail to be grateful to God for his blessings, nor were they ever again to "tempt" him (recall Exodus 17:1–7).

Deuteronomy 7:1–11

Again, Israelites were warned not to mix in any way with others, lest they adulterate and lose their spiritual heritage and fail in their mission. They were to destroy all idolatrous peoples and facilities delivered to them by the Lord.

An explanation was given in verses 6–11 of why Israel was chosen, what kind of a God chose them, and that they must keep his commandments.

Deuteronomy 7:12–26

Moses described how God would grant Israelites blessings if they kept their part of the covenant. The destruction of the people they were to replace in the promised land was evaluated in view of the kind of society they were and the potential for multiplication of evils if they influenced the Israelites.

Deuteronomy 8:1–20

Moses reviewed the gracious gifts God had given Israel during their journey from Egypt and warned them not to forget

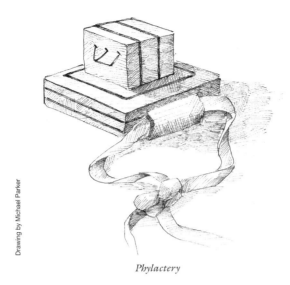

Phylactery

what the Lord had done nor to boast that by their own hands they had freed themselves and established themselves. Verses 2, 5, and 16 give reasons and purposes for the forty years in the wilderness: to humble and prove them and to do them good in the end (see also Hebrews 12:11). Jesus quoted verse 3 in response to the tempter (see Matthew 4:4).

Deuteronomy 9:1–29

The principles involving the removal of one people from a land and the transplanting of others into it are mentioned in verses 4–6. Remember that those to be removed had rejected every commandment of the Lord and were ripe in iniquity (see 1 Nephi 17:32–35).

But lest the Israelites should consider themselves good enough to merit all the blessings they were receiving, Moses reminded them of the many times the Lord had been forgiving in spite of their numerous provocations and of his own prayers to gain mercy for them.

Deuteronomy 10:1–22

After a few more reminders concerning the origin of the two sets of tablets inscribed by the Lord and preserved in the Ark of the Covenant, Moses inserted a brief comment about the travels of Israel and about the calling of the Levites. He then reminded them that he had pleaded for forty days and nights that the Lord would not destroy them. The Lord had granted his plea. (Don't miss the important JST addition in verse 2*b*.)

Israel is told what God requires of man and what manner of God he is. Verses 12–13 would be repeated, in condensed form, by the prophet Micah (6:8) as the duty of upright humans. They are also instructed what they must do for each other, for the needy, and for the stranger. The phrase "God of gods" is an idiom meaning "He is the supreme God."

Deuteronomy 11:1–7

God's people should feel the obligation to keep "his charge, and his statutes, and his judgments, and his commandments"—these are the parts of the Torah. Some of the performances and ordinances would later be discontinued, but the commandments would stand forever (see 2 Nephi 25:30; 4 Nephi 1:12).

Deuteronomy 11:8–17

The land into which God was leading the Israelites was different and more desirable than the land from which they had come. It was a land of mountains and valleys and had a variety of agricultural and mineral products. It would be watered by the rains, but his people had to qualify for God's blessings that the rains might come in their proper seasons. Their promised land was a testing ground for faith and obedience; water would not come from the clouds but from the heavens. The Lord said, "*I* will give you the rain" in its due season (January–March), along with the first, or former, rains (October–November) and the latter rains (April–May). This allowed the Israelites to gather in their corn (grains), wine (grapes), and oil (olives)—the three main crops of the land. According to the Lord's own explanation, if his people turned aside and polluted their inherited land by sin, the Lord, instead of pouring out the vital rains, would pour out his anger and indignation on them by shutting up the heavens. The resulting formula would be no rain = no crop yield = people perish.

Whenever there is an account in the Bible of a famine in Canaan, it means it did not rain. For example, Abraham going down into Egypt because of famine in Canaan (Genesis 12:10); famine while Isaac lived in the Negev and Philistia (Genesis 26:1); Jacob's family going down into Egypt because of famine (Genesis 41:54 to 42:5); Elimelech and family going to Moab because of famine in Judah (Ruth 1:1); the three-year famine in David's time (2 Samuel 21:1); the three-and-a-half-year famine by Elijah's word (1 Kings 17:1); and the seven-year famine in Elisha's day (2 Kings 8:1). Famine generally means no rain.

Israel was helpless in the testing ground called the promised land without the rains. Today, humankind is also helpless in the testing ground called mortality without God's help. They are quite dependent upon God. And just as God warned anciently, now and then he is bound to shut up the heavens so no rain will come. What God said to ancient Israel is true for us today: "I set before you this day a blessing and a curse; a blessing, if ye obey the commandments of the Lord . . . and a curse, if ye will not obey the commandments of the Lord" (Deuteronomy 11:26–28).

Deuteronomy 11:18–32

The earlier verses were bound in "frontlets" (*totafot,* or phylacteries), written upon doorposts (*mezuzas),* and taught in homes (somewhat akin to family councils and times spent together such as in home evenings). All the reminders they could employ to avoid forgetting his commandments would be helpful, because there was a blessing and a cursing set before them, and they must choose. When they entered the land, they were to go to two mountains in the center of the country, Gerizim and Ebal, and shout out the blessings and curses once again—another reminder. They later did so (Joshua 8:33–35).

Deuteronomy 12:1–32

Skim through this chapter of admonishments about worship practices and about foods permitted and forbidden. A Temple in Israel's new land was anticipated, where all should come for certain worship activities (vv. 5 and 11). The human sacrifices required by some other religions were condemned for Israel.

Deuteronomy 13:1–18

Verses 1–3, along with Deuteronomy 18:18–22, teach the concept that prophecies and revelations usually follow established principle and doctrine. If any false prophet arose and tried to lead Israel to worship other gods, they were to remember that such things were tests of their loyalty and that they should not yield (compare D&C 50:2–3). If a false prophet persisted in such attempts, he should be put to death. If loved ones tried to lead anyone into ways of idolatry, they also must be put to death. It was the same warning in different terms that Jesus later gave his followers that a false teacher is more to be feared than a murderer (Matthew 10:28). Infidelity to God was considered most dangerous because it would be the basis of infidelity to all his principles and ways.

Deuteronomy 14:1–21

As he continued his sermon, Moses powerfully declared that because the Israelites were the children of God, they were not to mutilate their bodies or unnaturally change their appearance. They were to be a holy people, chosen to be a peculiar people, a special treasure and possession of the Lord.

On the concept of "peculiar people" see the commentary at Exodus 19:1–6. The clean and unclean meats are reviewed, reminding Israelites of the importance of ceremonial cleanness. For the prohibition of cooking meat in milk (v. 21), recall the commentary at Exodus 23:14–19.

Deuteronomy 14:22–29

The tithe, or tenth, of all increase, was ordinarily contributed "in kind," but if the contributor lived too far from the central place for making the contribution, he could sell the material and carry the money there instead. At the central storehouse he could convert it back into whatever kinds of goods he desired to make the thanksgiving feast that accompanied tithe paying. The goods would be used by the Levites, who produced none of their own, and by the poor (compare D&C 119:3–6).

The word "lusteth" in the phrase "whatsoever thy soul lusteth after" (v. 26) has a bad connotation to us, but it is merely the King James translation of a word that means "to long or yearn for." Also the use of wine and other fermented fluids (here called "strong drink") may surprise latter-day worshipers who are not to use them, but they were permitted in ceremonial meals in ancient Israel; only excessive or improper use was forbidden. Fermented drinks were forbidden to priests in service, however, and to Nazarites and some others, according to Leviticus 10:9–11 and Numbers 6:2–4.

Deuteronomy 15:1–11

Israelites were to forgive their fellow Israelite debtors every sabbatical, or seventh, year, though they were not expected to also release the foreigners who owed them money. If they obeyed God's commandments, they would be blessed with prosperity; they would be able to lend to many peoples and would not need to borrow from anyone.

To the poor among Israel they were to "open the hand wide." Neglecting them and refusing to give would be counted as a sin (compare D&C 56:16).

Deuteronomy 15:12–23

Regulations were given regarding the release of Hebrew servants, with provisions for permanent positions of voluntary servitude for those desiring that status. Those released were to be provided with gifts of animals and produce as a new start.

Mention is made of the sanctification sacrifice of the first-born animals and the ceremonial meal in which their flesh was eaten. The prohibition against consumption of blood is repeated.

Deuteronomy 16:1–22

The three major annual feasts were reviewed (Exodus 23:14–17), along with a reminder of the function of judges and the quality of judgment required. Notice the prominence of the number seven: in keeping the Passover no leaven was to be eaten for seven days; seven weeks after Passover, the Feast of Weeks was to be celebrated (each week was seven days long); and the Feast of Tabernacles was to be kept for seven days. Seven, of course, represented wholeness, completeness, even perfection, and symbolized the covenant itself, as well as sacred oaths made by righteous Israelites. In Hebrew, the consonantal root is the same for "seven" and "oath" or "covenant" (see "The Significance of Certain Numbers in the Scriptures," page 263).

The Lord's specific requirement for the feasts was that three times a year all males appear before the Lord at the Tabernacle and later the Temple. Such is the reason they are called sanctuary festivals. See commentary at Leviticus 23:1–44.

What might the phrase "they shall not appear before the Lord empty" (v. 16) suggest to those who attend Temples today?

The prohibition against planting fertility cult trees near the altars was to prevent the shrines from resembling fertility cult shrines, where Baal, the Canaanite god, and Asherah, the fertility goddess, were worshiped (see Judges 6:25–26). Adopting Canaanite cult practices was an incessant problem for Israelites and became a major cause of Israel's decline and destruction centuries later.

Deuteronomy 17:1–20

Another reminder was given about the quality of sacrificial animals and provisions for the apprehension and trial of alleged idolators. Regarding judges in Israel, discussed in verses 8–13 of this chapter as well as in the previous one, bishops in the LDS Church are designated as judges in Israel (D&C 58:14–17; 64:40). Upon their shoulders rests the heavy responsibility of hearing and judging cases involving Church membership, standing, and worthiness. Anciently, priests of the Aaronic Priesthood performed similar functions.

Verses 14–20 anticipate the time when kings would rule Israel and provide instructions as to how a king should educate himself and keep himself humble, reverent, and obedient. The king must have his own copy of the scriptures and study them every day. It is evident later that neither Saul, David, nor Solomon lived out their lives in accord with the scriptures, and only a very few kings after them did so.

Verses 19–20 put forward five reasons for daily scripture study:

1. To learn to fear the Lord.
2. To be able to keep all the words of the Lord's law and statutes.
3. To keep one humble.
4. To keep one focused on the straight and narrow.
5. To prolong one's days in one's kingdom.

Each of us must discover and rediscover the truths of the scriptures again and again just as ancient Israelite kings were instructed to do.

Deuteronomy 18:1–22

More is given about providing for the living allowances of priests and about spiritualistic practices and other abominations to be avoided.

One of the most important verses in all the standard works is found in this chapter in verse 15. A prophet like unto Moses would be raised up by the Lord. This is Jesus Christ himself. It has been thought to be so important, by prophets and apostles down through the dispensations, that it is found in Acts 3:22–23; 1 Nephi 22:20–21; 3 Nephi 20:23; and Joseph Smith–History 1:40. Very few passages are as well attested. Remember the interesting parallels between the lives and missions of Moses and the Messiah:

1. The life of each was sought during infancy.
2. Both had command over the sea.
3. Both were transfigured.
4. The families of each opposed them on occasion (Numbers 12:1–2; John 7:5).
5. Both were meek (Numbers 12:3; Matthew 11:29).
6. Both provided water for their people (Numbers 20:11; John 4:13–14).
7. Both avoided the glory of the world (Hebrews 11:24, 26; Matthew 4:8–11).

The very important verse 22 tells how to know whether or not a man is truly a prophet and is really speaking in the name of the Lord. Several principles point out a true prophet: the one articulated in this verse; another in Deuteronomy 13:3; the directive that a true prophet will follow established principles and doctrine; and the characteristic outlined in Doctrine and Covenants 50:17–22, that a true prophet will preach by the Spirit and not some other way.

Deuteronomy 19:1–21

The procedure is detailed for guaranteeing the right of trial to one who has unintentionally caused another's death. The procedures and principles involved in the punishment of one who has killed intentionally and with malice are also specified.

Verse 14 discusses the crime of stealing property by

moving a neighbor's landmark. A law such as this was common in many societies.

Precautions were to be taken to have sufficient witnesses and to assure the veracity of the testimony in all cases tried by the courts.

Deuteronomy 20:1–20

Moses again declared that the Lord would give the Israelites help in battle according to their faith. He would fight their battles. However, those males who were "fearful" and those who were newly settled or newly wed could be exempted from military service. In their conquests, any cities that would capitulate and become tributary to Israel could be left intact, but cities that resisted were to be destroyed because of their rebellious nature and potential to corrupt Israel. Obviously, those cities that proclaimed peace and would contribute to the survival and prosperity of Israel's theocracy would happily be spared. In addition, two standards of how to treat resisting enemies are revealed. On the one hand, only males are to be killed (vv. 13–14), but on the other hand, every living thing is to be destroyed (v. 16). The difference is that the first category were inhabitants of cities far away that would not be inhabited by Israel. The second were inhabitants of Israel's inheritance cities, where they would live and practice their religion and needed to remain free of *any* corrupting influences. During times of siege, trees that produced edible fruits were never to be cut down, although other trees could be cut to make implements of war.

Deuteronomy 21:1–23

Rules governing society are set forth. What to do in case the body of a slain person was found and the slayer was unknown is addressed. Permission was given to marry desirable captives, although this seems to be an exception to the rule forbidding marriage with the peoples they were to dispossess. This has been interpreted by the rabbis to pertain to peoples other than Canaanites. Favoritism was not to govern the giving of inheritances.

The discipline and severe punishment of rebellious off-spring was specified. This seemingly harsh and perhaps difficult-to-understand set of rules in verses 18–21 may be explained on the basis of three principles. First, the rules are talking about rebellious sons, not just those who are disobedient out of immaturity or ignorance, but those who consistently refuse correction, are incorrigible, and whose actions significantly affect the community. Second, the situations described here may be seen as a type. These are sons who are a similitude of the great rebel, Lucifer. Most things in the Old Testament are a type and shadow of either Christ or Lucifer, and in this situation we are talking about those whose actions mirror the open rebellion of Satan, whose behavior was the heart of the war in heaven. Third, these verses are talking about rebellious sons who are of older age, those who are old enough to know better, not little boys.

Also discussed in this chapter of tremendous significance is the rule against leaving the body of one executed hanging overnight. Thus, we see in this passage an indirect prophecy of the Crucifixion. History, unlike art, indicates that crucifixion crosses in the Holy Land were often solidly rooted trees, usually olive trees, with branches trimmed off and a crossbar (Latin, *patibulum*) attached. This is especially the case during the Roman period of Judea's history, and this is exactly the image presented to us by the apostles Paul and Peter, who talk about Jesus being hanged on a tree for our sins (Galatians 3:13; Acts 10:39; 1 Peter 2:24). In fact, Paul specifically refers to this passage (Deuteronomy 21:23) when talking about Jesus' atoning sacrifice. Additionally, the Temple scroll, one of the premier documents among the Dead Sea Scrolls, describes crucifixion as being hanged on a tree: "If a man slanders his people and delivers his people to a foreign nation and does evil to his people, you shall hang him on a tree and he shall die" (11QTemple 64:6–13 in Vermes, *Dead Sea Scrolls*, 218).

The rule articulated here in v. 23 was observed by the executioners of Jesus (John 19:31). Rabbinical commentators reasoned that to leave a body hanging was a degradation of the human body and therefore an affront to God in whose image man was made.

Deuteronomy 22:1–30

Miscellaneous rules governed honesty, propriety, kindness, consideration, and purity. Purity was even to be observed in avoiding the mixing of crops, fabrics, or materials. These rules probably reminded the Israelites to keep themselves pure. What do you think of the message of verse 5 as it pertains to today's society?

Betrothed couples were regarded as husband and wife legally. Betrothal was legally and religiously more significant than the subsequent marriage ceremony, after which cohabitation actually began. Betrothal was regarded as finalization of a solemn agreement. It carried the force of a covenant to be honored between God-fearing parties (Genesis 2:24; Ezekiel 16:8; Ephesians 5:21–33). Legal action was required to dissolve a betrothal (Deuteronomy 24:1). Mosaic law recognized the changed status of a man and woman after betrothal by excusing the man from military service until after the wedding ceremony (Deuteronomy 20:7).

Between the time of betrothal and the ceremony that inaugurated cohabitation, a strict code of chastity was enforced (Matthew 1:18, 25). At the time of betrothal the young man took legal possession of the young woman but not physically. Unfaithfulness during the period of betrothal (espousal) could be punished by death (vv. 23–24) but also by private dissolution of the betrothal agreement through a bill of divorcement (Deuteronomy 24:1). The virtue of the betrothed bride was also protected by law against rape by calling for the execution of the rapist (vv. 25–27). All of this helps us to understand the circumstances surrounding the betrothal, or espousal, of Joseph and Mary at the beginning of the New Testament period.

More rules concerning chastity before marriage, during marriage, and in family relationships are presented (compare

D&C 42:80–81). Compare verse 22 with the woman taken in adultery who was flung at Jesus' feet (John 8:3–5).

Deuteronomy 23:1–25

There seems to be some corruption of rules in verses 1–8, because contradictions to many of these can be found elsewhere in the scriptures.

Laws were given on sanitation in military camps, with a good religious reason. Various other rules, many of which were given in Leviticus, are listed again.

Deuteronomy 24:1–22

More laws regarding marriage and divorce are presented. Under the Mosaic code divorce was permitted but regulated (see also commentary on betrothal, at Deuteronomy 22:1–30). The "bill of divorcement" mentioned in verse 1 is referred to in the Sermon on the Mount (Matthew 5:31) and among the Savior's teachings on marriage (Matthew 19:7). A young man recently married may be free from war duty for one year to stay home and "cheer up his wife"! (v. 5). Verse 16 makes it clear that the son is not to suffer for the father's sins (see this also in Ezekiel 18 and in the second Article of Faith).

Deuteronomy 25:1–19

This chapter begins by describing the involvement of judges in civil disputes and punishment for various wrongdoings. The phrase "beaten before his face" could better be rendered "flogged in his [the judge's] presence." Because beatings could be overdone by the executioner, strict standards were employed to prevent abuse. Later on, to ensure the prevention of abuse in punishment, the rabbis made a "fence around the Torah" so that instead of forty lashes, only thirty-nine were administered. Paul made oblique reference to this rabbinic principle when he said that on five occasions he had received "forty stripes save one" (2 Corinthians 11:24).

The "levirate" law (Latin *levir* means "husband's brother") provided that whenever a woman's husband died, his brother became the new husband and would go in unto her and raise up seed to his brother (see Bible Dictionary, "Levirate Marriage"). The story of Ruth is an example of this law in operation (see Ruth 3:12; 4:5–10). Similar laws existed in other ancient cultures.

Deuteronomy 26:1–19

While offering firstfruits and tithes to the Lord, Israelites were to recite before the priest this interesting review of their history (vv. 1–10). This passage constituted an ancient credo or confession of faith. The word "Syrian" (v. 5) is a Greek substitute for the name "Aramean" which refers to Abraham's sojourn in Aram before coming to the promised land.

Verse 15 constitutes a plea that is just as applicable today as it was in ancient Israel. At the end of the second sermon Moses reminded the Israelites of the lofty intentions of God and the plans he had in mind for them. What great blessings they could have received!

Deuteronomy 27:1–26

Chapter 27 begins the report of Moses' third sermon. He indicated that after invading the land a monument was to be made and inscribed on Mount Ebal. A ritual would then be observed with half the people on Mount Ebal and the other half opposite them on Mount Gerizim. Those on Ebal would pronounce the causes whereby people would be cursed, and those on Gerizim would pronounce the blessings for obedience to the law. Dishonesty, perversion of judgment, and unchastity are among the most commonly mentioned evils they tried to combat.

Deuteronomy 28:1–68

A short list of blessings for obedience and a long list of curses for disobedience are recorded (compare D&C 41:1; 130:20–21). What are the implications of the *length* of each list? (blessings make up fourteen verses; curses make up fifty-four verses). Take time to carefully read the following verses containing prophetic commentary on the tragic future of the people of Israel: 20–23 (the heavens overhead being as brass is quite a contrast to a later prophet's windows of heaven being open), 25–26, 33, 36–37, 45–46, 49–52, 62, 64–66. Incidentally, Jehovah is the same God (Jesus) who later cursed Chorazin, Bethsaida, and Capernaum (Matthew 11:21–24).

Deuteronomy 29:1 to 30:20

Moses reviewed the reasons for the law and the consequences of obeying it or of failing to do so. If the Israelites failed and lost the promised land, they still had hope of return through repentance (compare D&C 109:61–67).

The Lord's promise to gather Israel from "the outmost parts of heaven" (30:4) is both powerful and majestic. The idiomatic language employed here is simply intended to represent faraway places on earth, not to suggest that the ten lost tribes are residing on some other planet in space, as some commentators have proposed.

The challenge was again issued to hearken to the instructions for the good way of life and to live it, knowing that to choose one way was to choose "life" and to choose the other way was to choose "death."

Deuteronomy 31:1–30

Knowing that the end of his mortal life was near, Moses again mentioned that though the people were ready to go into the promised land, he would not be able to go with them; however, he encouraged them and their new leader, Joshua. The exhortation to "be strong and of a good courage" was repeated during the actual conquest of the promised land. In our day we have received similar encouragement to bolster our faith and courage to perform whatever deeds the Lord asks of us. Whom the Lord calls he qualifies; and when we're on the Lord's errand, we are entitled to the Lord's help. President Thomas S. Monson has also reminded us that our future is as bright as our faith (*Ensign,* May 2009, 92). Powerful words for these uncertain times.

Again the record mentions that Moses caused all these things to be written and preserved so that on sabbatical years, every seven years, the people could assemble and hear them read. The reading of the law to Israel and teaching it was a main duty of the priests (Deuteronomy 33:10).

Further preparations for Moses' departure were made at the Tabernacle, where Moses and Joshua went to receive God's charge. Moses wrote the words of the law. Verse 29 records what must have been some disheartening feelings for Moses: having envisioned the history of the world, he knew what would befall his people in the immediate future and in the latter days.

Deuteronomy 32:1–52

Moses was a song-writer, too. He had been commanded to compose a song or poem that the people could sing and remember some of the things he had taught them. Chapter 32 is that song to remember, from verse 1 through 44. It includes various topics: praise to God, recognition of Israel's preeminent position, Israel's downfall when materially prosperous, Israel's provocations and punishments, God's power to save and to avenge, and a promise for the future.

Verse 2 inspired the hymn "As the Dew from Heaven Distilling," written by Parley P. Pratt. Verses 8–9 constitute an impressive statement on the nature of Israel's premortal election. Moses is telling us, as well as his own people, that God apportioned this earthly estate among the Father's spirit children with Israel in mind. This earthly apportionment, or placement, was preceded by and based upon a heavenly ordering. The family of Israel was organized in the premortal existence long before this temporal existence. The apostle Paul understood this ordering of people and nations in our premortal existence (Acts 17:26). Thus, Israel was God's chosen people (Deuteronomy 7:6–8) based on premortal actions.

That is why Moses earlier referred to Israel as the firstborn among nations (Exodus 4:22) and Jeremiah would later call Ephraim the firstborn of Israel's tribes (Jeremiah 31:9). Thus, the history and destiny of the house of Israel is obviously of great interest to God the Father and likewise the gathering of Israel in the latter days of his work (3 Nephi 21:26).

Little wonder that Israel is the apple of the Lord's eye, that he led Israel out of the Sinai desert as an eagle broods over her young, that he lifted and built up Israel. But Israel (symbolically called Jeshurun, "the upright one") became spiritually fat and lazy, forsook God, provoked him, and sacrificed to devils.

Note the reference to honey coming out of rock, and oil out of flinty rock (v. 13). In Canaan, bees sometimes built hives in the clefts of rocks (Isaiah 7:18–19); and olive trees, which produced the oil of the land, grow on the rocky hillsides of the Holy Land, especially around Jerusalem. Furthermore, the salvation of the Rock of Israel is the Lord Jesus Christ (1 Corinthians 10:1–4). He "begat" Israel, but they forgot the God who formed them into a nation. This theme continues throughout Moses' magnificent poetic discourse in this chapter.

Moses commended his song and its teachings and warnings to the people. He was shown where he could go to view the promised land from afar.

Deuteronomy 33:1–5

This account of Moses leaving a blessing upon the heads of all of the tribes is also given in Hebrew poetry. The blessing told of the Lord leading the Israelites through the wildernesses of Sinai, Seir, and Paran. Because they were a covenant people, dedicated to him by promises and ordinances, they were called his "saints," or sanctified ones. "King in Jeshurun" means "King in Righteousness" (literally, "Upright One").

Deuteronomy 33:6–25

The blessings are listed for all the tribes except Simeon, who may have been assimilated into Judah. The order of the tribal blessings is generally from south to north, with mention of natural resources and other geographical features.

Moses prayed that the Reubenites might survive in their precarious location.

He asked that Judah be preserved and brought to his place. Much less is said about Judah than was said in Jacob's blessing generations earlier. Levi's blessing is much more extensive, since that tribe had come into prominence due to their priesthood responsibilities. The clause about "thy Thummim and thy Urim" means "Let thy divine revelation [thy Perfection and Light] be of God." Their priesthood affiliation was more vital and close to them than family connections. Their work was to teach, to officiate at the altars, and to bless the people. Moses prayed for their prosperity and protection.

Benjamin would be near the future holy dwelling of the "beloved of the Lord." That, of course, would be at Jerusalem, whose Temple site would lie near Benjamin's southern border.

Joseph was again the tribe that received the most detailed and noteworthy blessings, including a goodly land, riches, power, and glory. Some of the "precious things of the lasting hills" are identified in 1 Nephi 18:25. Verse 16 speaks of "him that dwelt in the bush." We usually define the verb *dwell* as "live," but *shakhan* in Hebrew has other meanings, too (as does *dwell* in English); it also means "to settle, to be situated upon, to abide upon, or to rest upon." Those other meanings are evidently intended also in 1 Nephi 1:6, where a pillar of fire "dwelt upon a rock" before Lehi.

Notice especially the future time of gathering, when Joseph's descendants would be the Lord's instruments to "push . . . together" the other tribes (v. 17), going even to the ends of the earth to find them. Recall Joseph's patriarchal blessing in Genesis 49:22–26; 48:16–20; see also 1 Chronicles 5:1 on Joseph's preeminent position. Concerning Joseph's goodly land, see Ether 13:6–10. Concerning Ephraim's function in the gathering of Israel in the last days "from the ends of the earth," see Doctrine and Covenants 133:30–34 (see also Ogden and Skinner, *Book of Mormon*, 2:138–39). Horns were often symbols of strength and leadership in Hebrew poetry. Joseph's seed through Ephraim and Manasseh was to be far-reaching in time and in eternity.

Zebulun and Issachar were foreseen enjoying their homes and surroundings, and with good reason: their settlements would be in the fertile valley of Jezreel, with good soil and good water, including a river that flowed westward into Israel's only natural harbor.

The large territory allocated to Gad beyond Jordan and one of the first to be settled, was reflected in the rather long blessing on that otherwise unexceptional tribe. Dan's relocation later in the north and east was implied in his blessing.

Naphtali was to inherit the sea (not the "west," as in KJV), meaning the sea of Chinnereth, or Galilee, and some of the rich land around the lake and to the south of it. Asher's territory in the promised land came to be famous for the olive oil produced there. His defenses were predicted to be strong.

The concluding verses combine praise of God and felicitation of Israel.

Deuteronomy 34:1–4

Moses at last saw the promised land from Mount Nebo, in the mountain range also called Pisgah (and Abarim), east of the north end of the Dead Sea. This is the same location where centuries later another great prophet, Elijah, would be taken up into heaven also (2 Kings 2).

Deuteronomy 34:5–6

The later writer of these verses understood that Moses "died" and the Lord buried him, but the Joseph Smith Translation says "the Lord took him unto his fathers" (compare what is said of both Moses and Alma in Alma 45:18–19). Moses was translated. Josephus (in *Antiquities*, bk. 4, chap.

8, para. 48) described Moses' entrance into a cloud and his disappearance, clearly hinting at his translation (see also Bible Dictionary, "Moses").

Deuteronomy 34:7–12

Although he was one hundred twenty years of age, his eyes and strength were unimpaired. The long period of mourning was probably no mere formality in this case. The people must have been sad as they watched their great leader depart for the last time. So Joshua took over, being properly authorized, but neither he nor anyone after him known to the writer of the last verses of Deuteronomy was like Moses in his close relationship with the Lord and in his miraculous powers. Moses was great in the eyes of his people—great not so much because of the power to part the sea, or to sustain hundreds of thousands in the desert, or to start or stop famines, pestilences, and plagues but because of his ability to control himself while possessing and using such awesome powers, or in other words, because of his ability to be Christlike.

Thus ended the mortal labors of one of the greatest of Hebrew prophets. Interestingly, his life may be divided into three forty-year periods:

1. Forty years as *prince,* when he received education and leadership training and discovered his life's mission.
2. Forty years as *pastor* or shepherd, when he learned the work of shepherding, received the priesthood, began raising a family, and met with God.
3. Forty years as *prophet,* when he experienced many trials, overcame personal weaknesses, and performed a noble ministry preparing himself and his people to return to God.

Although the Lord had told Moses he could not enter the promised land because of his disobedience in smiting the rock, there was also another reason that kept him from going into Canaan. The appropriate time had come for a change in leadership: Moses' assignment was completed, and a new, younger, dynamic man of war was needed for conquests. Compare the transition from Joseph Smith to Brigham Young at the time of a modern Israelite exodus in early Church history.

JOSHUA

The book of Joshua is the sequel to the Torah, or Pentateuch, just as the book of Acts in the New Testament is the sequel to the four Gospels. The book of Joshua picks up where Deuteronomy leaves off, with the tribes of Israel camped on the east side of the Jordan River. The narrative opens with the Lord commanding Joshua, Moses' chosen replacement (Deuteronomy 31:1–8), to lead the Israelites across the Jordan on dry ground. It then relates the story of the conquest of the land of Canaan, the land promised by God to Abraham's descendants (Genesis 12:7; 15:13–16, 18; 17:8). The book describes a series of campaigns in the central, southern, and northern regions of the Holy Land, their conquests, division of inheritances to the tribes, and the establishment of refuge cities and Levitical cities. For a sweeping summation of the conquest, read Joshua 21:43–44.

There's an old saying, "It's not enough to leave Egypt; you've got to enter the promised land." The saying has great application to life in general but more literally to our ancient Israelite ancestors. About thirty-eight years earlier some Israelites had met with dismal failure as they tried to invade the country from the south. Now with their dynamic leader, Joshua the Ephraimite, they were set to enter from the east into the heart of the country and divide and conquer.

Holy war is a main theme in the book, describing how God could have truly been Israel's captain and deliverer if Israel would have allowed him to, if he had been honored and obeyed. But, alas, Israel's disobedience and materialism prevented them, and other peoples, from receiving the blessings of the Lord.

Joshua was the son of a man named Nun, pronounced like our English word *noon* (Exodus 33:11). Originally, he was called Hoshea, meaning "salvation," but Moses changed his name to Jehoshua, or Joshua, meaning "The Lord saves" (Numbers 13:8, 16). The Greek form of the name, Iesous, became Jesus in English (Matthew 1:21). It became a popular and well-loved name in Jesus' day, owing to widespread feelings of messianic expectation at the time.

Joshua was Moses' trusted assistant. He was known as "a man in whom is the spirit" (Numbers 27:18). He lived during the period of Israel's Egyptian bondage and was a firsthand witness to God's majesty, miracles, and power on Israel's behalf. He saw the waters of the Red Sea parted and the deliverance of his people. He was among those who saw the Lord on Mount Sinai (Exodus 24:9–10). He was selected from the tribe of Ephraim to be one of the twelve spies, or scouts, sent to reconnoiter the land of promise. He was a military leader, a statesman, a prophet, and a deliverer. He was, above all, a type and foreshadowing of Jesus Christ.

In the Hebrew Bible Joshua is the first book of a subdivision called the Former Prophets, which includes Judges, 1 and 2 Samuel, and 1 and 2 Kings. These are called the historical books in the King James Version, but they were written with prophetic insight. They interpret history from a prophetic perspective, allowing us to understand how God intervened in the history of a people who made covenants with him. They show God's covenant dealings with Israel in actual history. These books report the development and downfall of the nation of Israel, from Moses to the destruction of the kingdom of Judah in 586 B.C.

Some scholars have disputed the idea that Joshua was the author of the book, but we think there are good reasons, both internal and external, to believe that Joshua was indeed the author of the work bearing his name. The Talmud ascribes authorship of the book to Joshua, except for the section reporting his death, which was added by a later editor.

For the next couple of books, you may consult the following entries in the Bible Dictionary for additional information: "Joshua, book of"; "Judges, the"; "Judges, book of"; "High Places"; "Idol"; "Grove"; "Ashtaroth"; "Baal"; "Chemosh"; "Dagon"; and "Molech."

Joshua 1:1–11

As the record opens, Joshua has already been chosen as Moses' successor, according to the pattern described in Numbers 27:18–23. In the first recorded revelation to Joshua as Israel's leader, the Lord instructed him to take Israel into the promised land. There were conditions in order to have success and prosperity.

The boundaries of the promised land were laid out. The dimensions vary from text to text in the Old Testament, but these, in verse 4, represent the farthest extent of the boundaries.

In the face of such a daunting leadership challenge, Joshua was assured the same help and support Moses was given from the Lord. Joshua was told at least four times in this first chapter to be strong and very courageous (vv. 6, 7, 9, 18). He would need both strength and courage. He was commanded to make the "book of the law" the center of his thoughts and actions and was promised "good success" (v. 8). Making the scriptures the center of our lives is still appropriate counsel for all of us in our day, as it has been in other dispensations (see John 5:39; Acts 17:11).

Joshua 1:12–18

Joshua immediately assumed his role and issued commands to the Reubenites, Gadites, and half of Manasseh concerning the responsibilities they were to fulfill before being allowed to settle down in the conquered lands east of the Jordan River. They were to remember that it was the Lord who was giving them the land. Israel's warriors took an oath of allegiance to Joshua. Rebellion (treason) was punishable by death.

Joshua 2:1–24

The story of the spies, or scouts, and Rahab is recounted. Rahab gave testimony of her awareness of the Lord and his will in this matter. In the New Testament, both James and Paul praise Rahab's faith and her good works (Hebrews 11:31; James 2:25). Some commentators think she may be the Rahab mentioned in Matthew 1:5 (the mother of Boaz, the ancestress of David and of Jesus), citing as possible evidence Joshua's comment that she continued living in Israel (6:25).

Josephus, biblical scholar Adam Clarke, and others have suggested softening the identification of Rahab as a "harlot," calling her instead an "innkeeper" or "hostess." The Hebrew word used of Rahab is *zonah,* which in every biblical case means "harlot, adulteress, or prostitute" (see, for example, Judges 11:1; 16:1; Damascus Document IV, line 20, and VII, line 1). Rather than trying to change the reality of Rahab's past, we should allow for the reality of repentance and reformation. This was an individual who found the covenant, committed her life to it, and was blessed. This story is one of the great, compelling reasons to rejoice in the opportunity to change—Heavenly Father's plan of second chances. Verses 8–11 give us Rahab's testimony. Verse 24 is a subtle but sad reminder that Israel could have had their inheritance thirty-eight years earlier.

Joshua 3:1–17

Despite the Israelites' readiness and determination to advance into the land, their eagerness was immediately tempered by some imposing physical obstacles, the first being the Jordan River. The river is characterized by meanders, loops, and bends throughout its course. In elevation it is the lowest river in the world, about a thousand feet below sea level near Jericho, cutting a trough in the middle of the great Rift Valley.

Verse 15 identifies what time of year it was when the

Israelites were going to try crossing it. Following the heavy winter rains in the north and snow on Mount Hermon, springtime is flood season. What a time to try moving hundreds of thousands of people and their baggage across a river! But the Lord would provide. He reassured Joshua that he would "begin to magnify" him "in the sight of all Israel" so they would know that just as the Lord was with Moses, so he would be with his successor (v. 7). This was fulfilled as noted in Joshua 3:17 and 4:14. As it was said of Moses, so it would be with Joshua: both would "be made stronger than many waters" (Moses 1:25). The Israelites walked through wet places on "dry ground" (Exodus 14:16; Joshua 3:17). Thus, Joshua was both a type and reflection of Moses and a type and foreshadowing of Jesus Christ (see "Joshua and Jesus Christ," page 332).

In preparation for the Israelites' crossing the Jordan, the time was set in advance and the waters were stopped on the specified day long enough to allow passage. Describing this phenomenon, the Hebrew Bible says simply: "And the waters flowing down from above stopped; they rose up as a heap very far away at Adam, the city that is beside Zarethan, and those that went down toward the sea of Arabah, the Salt Sea, were completely cut off, and the people passed over right next to Jericho." The place where the miraculous stoppage occurred, about sixteen miles upstream, has an appropriate name: *A dam* (a word play that works only in English, of course).

The river blockage has happened periodically throughout history and can be explained geologically. In the earthquake of 1927, the biggest of the twentieth century, tremors caused the collapse of high clay riverbanks *at the same place,* and the river stopped flowing for over twenty-one hours. "Waste movements, activated by undermining the river erosion banks, or even—although far more rarely—by earthquakes, bring vast amounts of debris down into the riverbed. According to both historical and contemporary eyewitnesses, this activity has even caused temporary cessation of the river's flow for some time" (from *Geography*, 86). This does not, however, explain away the miracle; the miracle is that the Lord caused it to happen right when his people needed it.

The first test of faith would be for the priests bearing the holy Ark, who would have to dip their feet into the Jordan River before the waters would part. Note that the most significant preparation for the conquest was to ensure the preservation of the symbol of Israel's spiritual center—the Ark of the Covenant.

JOSHUA AND JESUS CHRIST

Even a cursory reading of the Old Testament reveals that Joshua, able successor to Moses, was also a similitude of Moses and, hence, a similitude of Jesus Christ. Almost everything said about the ways in which Moses stands as a type and shadow of the Messiah is also true of Joshua. He was a lawgiver, a deliverer (spiritually and militarily), and a prophet. He stood in the presence of the Lord and, just like Moses, was told, "Loose thy shoe from off thy foot; for the place whereon thou standest is holy" (Joshua 5:15; compare Exodus 3:5).

Joshua was also given control of the waters, just as Moses and Jesus were (compare Joshua 3:13–17; Exodus 14:21–31; Mark 4:39–41). Joshua was magnified at the parting of the Jordan River just as Moses had been magnified by the Lord in the eyes of the people when the Red Sea was parted. The Lord promised Joshua, "This day will I begin to magnify thee in the sight of all Israel, that they may know that, as I was with Moses, so I will be with thee" (Joshua 3:7). As Joshua parted the waters of the Jordan and "all the Israelites passed over on dry ground" (Joshua 3:17), the promise began to be fulfilled. "On that day the Lord magnified Joshua in the sight of all Israel; and they feared him, as they feared Moses, all the days of his life" (Joshua 4:14).

But, as Joshua came to realize, the real lesson to be learned was that he stood in the place of the Lord. What Joshua did was actually what the Lord did working through him, "that all the people of the earth might know the hand of the Lord, that it is mighty: that ye might fear the Lord your God for ever" (Joshua 4:24). Thus, Joshua was a similitude of the Lord in the truest sense, for his hand was the Lord's hand, according to the Lord's own decree.

Joshua did what he did through the same means "by which Moses brought the children of Israel through the Red Sea on dry ground" (D&C 8:3). It was accomplished through the Lord's plan and power. Both times Israel passed through water into a new life. Such symbolic association with the concept of baptism in the name of Christ is unmistakable. And what's more, Joshua, who led the people to a newness of life, bore the name by which the Messiah would be known while he sojourned in mortality. The name *Jesus* is the Anglicized Greek form of the Hebrew name *Joshua* (or, more particularly, *Yeshua*). The Hebrew name *Yehoshua* literally means "Jehovah is salvation." Just as Christ is the salvation of all people in an eternal sense, so Joshua, son of Nun, was the salvation of his people in a temporal sense.

Joshua was the earthly commander-in-chief of the Israelite armies during the conquest of the promised land. He represented Jehovah and was a similitude of him—the heavenly battle master of his people throughout history. As Jehovah said to Moses and Joshua, "The Lord your God which goeth before you, he shall fight for you" (Deuteronomy 1:30; compare Joshua 10:14; 23:10).

Joshua's great achievement was his constancy in leading God's people. He was a judge, a mediator, and a beacon to them as they progressed toward an inspired destination. As a similitude of Christ, it may be said with perfect propriety that Joshua led God's people to the promised land as the Messiah leads the way to the eternal land of promise. The concept of being led to a land of promise as a type, or shadow, of the Messiah's mission was powerfully articulated in the Book of Mormon when Alma discussed the spiritual significance of the Liahona with his son Helaman: "And now I say, is there not a type in this thing? For just as surely as this director did bring our fathers, by following its course, to the promised land, shall the words of Christ, if we follow their course, carry us beyond this vale of sorrow into a far better land of promise" (Alma 37:45). Moses, Joshua, and Jesus were like each other in many profound ways. And the former two pointed to the later great One.

Joshua 4:1–24

Typically, a memorial or monument was made so that the children and children's children of future generations might learn of an important event. Those who crossed the Jordan River at that time were to remember it as a testimony that the Lord was with Joshua and that he would be with them in their campaign in Canaan (see Joshua 3:7, 10; 4:23–24). Twelve men were commanded to pick a stone (twelve stones, total) from the middle of the Jordan, where they had crossed on dry ground, and carry them to their new camp on the west side of the river. Joshua used them to construct a monument at Gilgal.

Why use stones? They are plentiful and long-lasting, certainly. But they also represented the "stone of Israel," the Lord who was preparing the way for Israel (Genesis 49:24). "For the Lord your God dried up the waters of Jordan from before you, until ye were passed over, as the Lord your God did to the Red sea, which he dried up from before us, until we were gone over: That all the people of the earth might know the hand of the Lord, that it is mighty: that ye might fear the Lord your God for ever" (vv. 23–24).

Gilgal became Israel's main camp, their bridgehead, during the initial advance into Canaan.

Joshua 5:1–15

Operation Consolidation. When the Israelites entered the promised land, the first thing they did was reconsecrate themselves to the Lord by circumcising all the males who had not been thus initiated during the forty years' sojourn in the wilderness. They then observed the Passover, the celebration of redemption from Egyptian bondage, to solidify their commitment to the Lord. We also learn that the place name,

Gilgal, was given in response to the Lord's statement: "This day have I rolled away the reproach of Egypt from off you" (v. 9). In Hebrew *Gilgal* means "rolling." Verse 12 mentions the cessation of manna and the commencement of normal sustenance. Verses 13–15 give a brief account of a manifestation to Joshua, showing him that the captain of the *Lord's* host was sent to assist in the campaign.

We believe the captain of the Lord's host whom Joshua saw was Jehovah, whose name in mortality was also Joshua. First, there was no attempt to stop Joshua from worshiping (v. 14), even though others have been admonished not to worship when the heavenly messenger has not been the Lord (see Revelation 19:10). Second, Joshua was told to remove his shoes while standing on holy ground. This was the same instruction Jehovah gave to Moses (Exodus 3:5).

Joshua 6:1–19

Chapters 6–9 report Israel's central campaign. To cartographically follow the various sieges of Israel's conquest of Canaan in these next chapters you may consult any good Bible atlas.

Instructions for the extraordinary attack on Jericho were presented. For seven days the siege proceeded. There were restrictions on plunder and booty; some things were to be preserved for holy purposes and other things were to be destroyed—but there was to be no looting.

Throughout ancient times those inhabitants of the Holy Land who controlled the hill country protected themselves from enemy attacks, particularly from the west, the "front door" to their territory. By far the majority of enemy assaults occurred from the west. But the Israelites were coming in the "back door" and had to first gain strategic control over the oasis of Jericho. It was something of a bread basket. Archaeologically, the city exhibits more than twenty occupation levels. It was a crucial site for a new people to control. Since Jericho was undoubtedly a center of idol worship, the

Lord was signaling the overthrow of false religions as well as the conquest of a powerful Canaanite city. The Lord helped again. Fear had caused the thousands living outside the walled city to flee inside it for protection. Marching around the city with trumpets, or *shofars* (rams' horns), signified a declaration of war. The shofar thus became an instrument of warfare. It undoubtedly terrified the indigenous population. The preponderance of the number seven—seven priests, seven trumpets, seven days, seven circumlocutions—emphasized the completeness of the Lord's battle, its connection to the covenant, and the inauguration of a new order and era, much like the seven days of creation. The Ark of the Covenant symbolized the Lord's presence in the action. An earthquake possibly brought the walls down in order for the Israelites to quickly overrun the place. Seismic activity is frequent at that site in the Rift Valley: the epicenter of the strongest earthquake in the land during the twentieth century was near Jericho.

Joshua 6:20–27

As visitors may see today, Jericho was a walled city with a circumference of less than a mile. On the seventh day of the siege, the Israelite army could probably have marched seven times around Jericho in half a day. When the city was opened up and the Israelites stormed in, the promise to Rahab and her family was kept. The account was written or edited some time later, as evidenced by the remark that Rahab "dwelleth in Israel even unto this day" (v. 25).

Joshua had commanded the Israelites that the city and all that was in it was to be devoted to the Lord (KJV reads "accursed . . . to the Lord"; v. 17) and destroyed. Ritual devotion to destruction meant that all things associated with the city were to be "utterly destroyed" (v. 21), including people, livestock, treasures—everything. These things were thought to contaminate pure religion. The Hebrew word from which this practice derives is *herem*. It is related to the word *harem*, denoting sacred or set apart precincts belonging to certain Near

Eastern kings in various historical periods. In ancient Israel the practice was also called "the ban." Things coming under the ban were sometimes regarded as being sacrificed to the Lord.

Moses revealed early that the preconquest, corrupt inhabitants of Canaan were to be destroyed, as well as their spiritually contaminated possessions (Deuteronomy 20:16–18). Peoples and nations who agreed to allow the Israelites to conquer the land and who complied with covenant practices were to be spared. As the Lord said in outlining the laws and constitution of the Israelite nation: "He that sacrificeth unto any god, save unto the Lord only, he shall be utterly destroyed. Thou shalt neither vex a stranger, nor oppress him: for ye were strangers in the land of Egypt" (Exodus 22:20–21).

Joshua 7:1–26

A man named Achan violated the law of the *herem,* or ban, by keeping some material possessions, "the accursed thing," of the people of Jericho (v. 1). His act affected the whole of the Israelite population. This is an example of corporate or group responsibility for the actions of group members. The result was Israel's defeat by the men of Ai, the next city to be conquered during the central campaign.

Israel's warriors had hiked along a northwest passage up into the central hills of Canaan. Scouts were sent to check out the city of Ai, which is "on the east side of Beth-el." They reported that the place looked easy to take, and so a small army was dispatched to subdue it. They were rebuffed. Joshua complained and lamented, but the Lord admonished him, "Get thee up; wherefore liest thou thus upon thy face? Israel hath sinned, and they have also transgressed my covenant" (vv. 10–11). In today's more colorful vernacular God's chastisement might be worded this way: "Get up; quit your bellyaching. The people blew it, so I withheld my help. Now get your act together!"

The sinner who had violated the *herem,* or ban, was

identified, and all the family who were collectively responsible for the transgression (keeping some of the forbidden contraband for themselves) were killed. Purely and simply, Achan had allowed covetousness to overcome him. He treasured the things of the world more than he valued his covenant with God and with Joshua. A beautiful Babylonian robe, two hundred shekels of silver, and a fifty-shekel gold wedge were worth a lot, but certainly not more than Achan's integrity or his life. His punishment sounds harsh, but at the very moment of invading a country, meticulous obedience was requisite.

Joshua 8:1–29

Using the old stratagem of decoy and ambush, Joshua took Ai the next time they attacked (compare Alma 52:21–25; maybe Captain Moroni later learned by reading from the brass plates about Joshua's tactic). The topography of the region perfectly fits the story as described in the Bible. Both of the names Ai and Bethel occur in verse 17; apparently both sites were destroyed by invading Israelites. They are next to each other geographically. In Genesis 12, Ai was spelled "Hai"; because the "H" is the definite article in Hebrew, the name literally means "the ruin"—which is exactly how Joshua left it (v. 28) and the way it remains today.

Joshua 8:30–35

After conquering the first two or three Canaanite towns, the Israelite tribes moved unmolested into the middle of the country to Shechem, to fulfill an assignment that had been given them by Moses. Shechem was where God first appeared to Abraham and was considered a holy place. Now the children of Israel came, to shout out the curses and blessings on Mount Ebal and Mount Gerizim. Reread Deuteronomy 27:4–13, paying particular attention to the altar that the elders of Israel were commanded to build there. Verses 30–35 record the fulfillment of that injunction by Israel's former leader. Archaeologists in recent years claim to have found the remnants of that very altar on Mount Ebal.

Joshua 9:1–27

Israel now controlled the region of Bethel-Ai. This initial foothold in the land may have stirred some nostalgic spiritual memory of their revered ancestors, the patriarchs Abraham and Jacob, who had talked with the great Jehovah at that very place. It was on a hill between Bethel and Ai that Abraham had erected an altar (Genesis 12–13) and where the Lord promised to his descendants the land that they were now conquering. "Know of a surety," the Lord had counseled Abraham, "that thy seed shall be a stranger in a land that is not theirs, and shall serve them; and they shall afflict them four hundred years . . . But in the fourth generation they shall come hither again" (Genesis 15:13, 16).

Next in line of attack were the Gibeonite cities. However, the Gibeonites had heard what Joshua had done to Jericho and Ai, so they planned a clever deception to save themselves from destruction. Their attitude was "if you can't beat them, join them!" With old, worn sacks and wine bottles on their asses, they convinced Israel that they had come from a far country and were anxious to join them in conquering the land. They were anxious to escape destruction and undoubtedly knew of God's warning to Israel about caring for strangers and resident aliens (Exodus 22:20–21). The details of this story accurately fit the region and its agricultural products: at Gibeon archaeologists found eleven wine cellars cut in the rock, with a total capacity of 25,000 gallons!

Verse 14 relates that Israelite leaders made a decision without really checking with the Lord—always a precarious and lamentable thing to do.

Although the Gibeonites (the four cities mentioned in v. 17) were successful in making a league with Joshua to spare their lives, their tactics were exposed. Joshua did keep his promise to spare them but assigned them to menial service.

Joshua 10:1–14

When Jericho and Ai had fallen and Gibeon had made a peace agreement with Israel, you can imagine the feelings of other neighboring city-states. "They feared greatly, because Gibeon was a great city, as one of the royal cities, and because it was greater than Ai, and all the men thereof were mighty" (v. 2). Consider the feelings of Adonizedek, king of Jerusalem—just five miles south of Gibeon—as he watched the deteriorating situation. He would naturally cry for help, and verses 3–5 tell us who responded to his cry. Again, a good Bible atlas will show you the location of those five Canaanite cities; "Amorites" is another term used for the various peoples inhabiting Canaan at the time. The conquest of these Canaanite city-states fits the picture painted by diplomatic correspondence of the Late Bronze Age (1550–1200 B.C.). From the Amarna letters it is apparent that the Holy Land was divided up into smaller regions controlled by fortified cities with hereditary rulers. With the Lord's help, Israel was victorious over the five-city Amorite league.

Verses 10–14 record one of the most famous miracles in the Bible. Daylight was extended, which was said to be done so that Canaanite resistance could be broken in a single day, leaving the enemy no time to recoup and reinforce defenses. Compare the explanation found in verses 12–14 to Helaman 12:13–17. There is no doubt that a miracle occurred; it is only the descriptions of how it occurred that vary.

Joshua 10:15–43

Israelite forces then embarked on a southern campaign, pushing forward to conquer all of the major powers of the southern part of the land. The captains of Israel "put their feet upon the necks of these kings," symbolizing conquest, triumph, and victory, as portrayed in inscriptions of Thutmose III at Karnak and in other ancient cultures (see also 1 Kings 5:3; Psalm 18:37–40; 1 Corinthians 15:25, 27; D&C 35:14; 49:6; 58:22).

Verses 40–42 are a summary statement on regions conquered in the south: the hill country, the south (Hebrew, *Negev*), and the vale (Hebrew, *Shephelah*).

Joshua 11:1–23

Next came Israel's northern campaign. A formidable alliance of city-states was organized in the north of the country to take a united stand against Israel. Hazor, twelve miles north of the Sea of Galilee, "was the head of all those kingdoms" (v. 10). Enemy armies included Canaanites, Amorites, Hittites, Perizzites, Jebusites, and Hivites; only a substantial threat could unite so many diverse cultural and political entities. But Hazor is the only place on record in the north that was utterly decimated and burned to the ground. In the latter part of the twentieth century, Professor Yigael Yadin identified stratum XIII as the final Late Bronze Age city—the largest Bronze Age site in all of Canaan—as the very one destroyed by Joshua. In some places ash layers a meter deep corroborate the biblical claim that Joshua "burnt Hazor with fire" (v. 11). As Mark Twain wrote, "He never left any chance for newspaper controversies about who won the battle" (*Innocents Abroad*, 359). Israelites "houghed" the enemy horses (cut the tendons of their back legs so they could walk but not run, making them of no value in war) and burned their chariots.

The conquest of Hazor was a huge victory. The site was first inhabited 4,500 years ago. Twenty-one occupation levels have been unearthed by archaeologists. They found a stela showing two hands and forearms raised in an attitude of worship to an emblem of a deity found in the holy of holies of a fourteenth-century B.C. temple at Hazor, presumably Canaanite. The burning of the city by the Israelites "was worst in the Canaanite palace. The amount of wood used in its construction and the quantity of olive oil stored there combined to produce a temperature estimated at 2350° F." (Murphy-O'Connor, *Holy Land*, 306–7). No wonder the ash layer was some three feet deep!

The Anakim, who were the men of gigantic stature that frightened Joshua's fellow spies more than forty years before, were also vanquished, except for those in the Philistine cities of Gaza, Gath, and Ashdod in the southern coastal area. More will later be heard of a famous Philistine named Goliath.

In verse 15 we find another fulfillment of Joshua 1:6—the promise that Joshua would be like Moses. "Joshua took the whole land, according to all that the Lord said unto Moses; and Joshua gave it for an inheritance unto Israel according to their divisions by their tribes. And the land rested from war" (v. 23). From that note of finality pronounced following the central, southern, and northern campaigns, you would think that the Israelite conquest of Canaan was conclusive and comprehensive. Two chapters later, however, we find Joshua old and about to die, "and the Lord said unto him, Thou art old and stricken in years, and there remaineth yet very much land to be possessed" (13:1).

The next verses detail the parts of the land that the Israelites had not subdued. In Joshua 21:43–44 we get the impression that the Israelites accomplished a massive, total conquest; in Judges 2:20–22, on the other hand, we are shown a prolonged, extended campaign—a war that would go on for many years—and the reasons for it. In the end, Israelite entrance into the land was not really a conquest but, instead, an incursion, settlement, and assimilation.

God warned his people that if they wanted to stay long upon the land that the Lord had given them, they had to keep his commandments. The tragic refrain of the next several hundred pages of the Bible is that in the end, Canaan triumphed culturally and religiously. At the very point of entering their promised land, the Lord warned his covenant people that if they could not keep Canaan out of Israel, then he would eventually take Israel out of Canaan.

Joshua 12:1–24

These verses preserve a list of all the kings previously defeated by Israel under Moses in trans-Jordan, and another list of the kings conquered by Israel under Joshua in Canaan. A total of thirty-one kings in such a small land (forty to fifty miles wide and one hundred and fifty miles long) emphasizes the fact that it was a disunited group of small city-states.

Joshua 13:1–33

Although the Israelites had conquered many cities, these verses detail the parts of the land that Israelites had not subdued, mainly Philistine territory and regions north and east of Galilee in what today we call Lebanon and Syria.

All the regions with their cities in trans-Jordan as given by Moses to the two and a half tribes of Israel are described—the inheritances of Reuben, Gad, and half of Manasseh.

Joshua 14:1–4

The geographical location of the twelve tribes is explained (including the division of Joseph into two—Ephraim and Manasseh), along with the distribution of Levites throughout all the tribal regions. See Bible Map 3, "The Division of the 12 Tribes."

Joshua 14:5 to 15:63

The story is told of Caleb, the only other survivor besides Joshua of the previous generation and of the scouts sent up to examine the land. In his old age his courage was unwavering and his faith undaunted. He asked for the very city and area (Hebron) that had frightened his fellow spies many years before. President Spencer W. Kimball years ago expressed his admiration for Caleb:

"From Caleb's example we learn very important lessons. Just as Caleb had to struggle and remain true and faithful to gain his inheritance, so we must remember that, while the Lord has promised us a place in his kingdom, we must ever strive constantly and faithfully so as to be worthy to receive the reward.

"Caleb concluded his moving declaration with a request and a challenge with which my heart finds full sympathy. The Anakims, the giants, were still inhabiting the promised land, and they had to be overcome. Said Caleb, now at 85 years, 'Give me this mountain' (Joshua 14:12).

"This is my feeling for the work at this moment. There are great challenges ahead of us, giant opportunities to be met. I welcome that exciting prospect and feel to say to the Lord, humbly, 'Give me this mountain,' give me these challenges" (*Ensign,* Nov. 1979, 79).

The inheritance of the large tribe of Judah is detailed. The people of Judah could not conquer and hold Jerusalem, which was inhabited by Jebusites. Its permanent conquest took place later, in the days of King David. The border between Judah and Benjamin was established at the Hinnom Valley, a little south of Jerusalem's Temple Mount (15:8). The Hinnom Valley was a place where very wicked practices occurred, including child sacrifice (Jeremiah 32:35; 2 Chronicles 28:3; 33:6).

Utahns may be interested to know that in the list of settlements of Judah in chapter 15 was a "Juttah" (Joshua 15:55), whose name is pronounced in Hebrew exactly as we pronounce *Utah*. And there was also "the city of Salt" (Joshua 15:62), like Salt Lake City.

Joshua 16:1 to 17:18

Inheritance of the two tribes descended from the two sons of Joseph is detailed. Note what they failed to do by settling down with some of the Canaanite peoples instead of driving them out (16:10; 17:12–13). This failure was typical throughout the tribes and brought about serious repercussions by intermarrying and causing some Israelites to turn from the Lord.

Joshua 18:1–28

After the large tribes of Judah, Ephraim, and Manasseh had taken their lands as instructed, the remaining seven were apparently reluctant to move out and settle theirs. So at Shiloh, in the center of the lands, at the place where they set up the Tabernacle for a permanent resting place, Joshua assembled the remainder and appointed a committee to survey the remaining land and divide it into seven parts, which they did. Benjamin's territory fell between Judah and Ephraim. The word "coast" is King James English for "border."

Joshua 19:1–51

Again, Bible Map 3 shows the location of tribal inheritances. Verses 1–9 describe Simeon's lot. It was within Judah's assigned territory and was generally south of Judah. The tribe of Simeon was eventually absorbed into Judah. Verses 10–16 describe the inheritance of Zebulun; 17–23, Issachar; 24–31, Asher; and 32–39, Naphtali. The inheritance of Dan (vv. 40–48) was at first located in the middle of the country, but because the first allotment proved too small, they expanded into the northernmost territory. Actually, it was the Philistines in the coastal portion of their original inheritance that made it crowded for Dan.

At the conclusion of the dividing of the land, the people gave their leader an inheritance—a city in the hills of Ephraim—possibly expressing honor and gratitude to Joshua. The division was done by the chief priest, the head of state, and the chiefs of the fathers (the patriarchal leaders) of the twelve tribes.

Joshua 20:1–9

Six cities of refuge were established as prescribed by Moses (in Numbers 35:6–15; Deuteronomy 4:41–43). This provision was intended as a safeguard of justice. These six cities were equidistant from each other on both sides of the Jordan River. Any person accused of murder, or who had accidentally killed someone, could flee to a refuge city and await a fair judgment. This removed the danger of a vendetta from the kinsmen of the slain person, allowing the elders of the refuge city to render an unbiased decision. It is much like a "change of venue" in the United States of America. If found innocent of murder but guilty of unintentional, unpremeditated killing, he was to remain in the refuge city and support his family. If he left the city, he could be slain by a kinsman of his victim. Thus, the guilty party would stay in the city under difficult economic circumstances, like a term of house arrest, until the current high priest died (a kind of statute of limitations). After the death of the high priest, an offender could return home without danger of reprisal. If the accused was found guilty of premeditated murder he was delivered to the victim's next of kin for execution. If he was found totally innocent he could immediately return home. The establishment of cities of refuge shows the Lord's concern for the rights of the innocent against revenge.

Joshua 21:1–45

The locations of forty-eight cities given to the Levites among the tribes are specified for descendants of the three sons of Levi: Kohath, Gershon, and Merari.

As noted before, verses 43–45 give the impression that Israel had accomplished a massive, total conquest and that everything had been done according to instructions. Apparently the tribes were soon sent out to their inheritances, and it was hoped that all was well and that all were at peace. However, we later see that all of the "mopping-up operations" did not go as intended, and the Lord could not fulfill his covenant to help them because they did not fulfill their duty.

Joshua 22:1–34

After Joshua had blessed the tribes located to the east of the Jordan and had sent them to their new homes, they built an "altar"—not for sacrificial offerings but as a "witness" or a memorial—so future generations would remember their relationship with the Lord and with those Israelites west of Jordan. It was to remind them of the true altar of sacrifice at Shiloh where the Tabernacle was. Ironically, the tribes in the west saw it from afar and thought it to be an idolatrous altar. Concerned lest the Lord should punish not only the offenders but all of Israel (as in the affair of Achan at Jericho), they zealously assembled for war against the "rebels." Fortunately the princes and priesthood got together and were able to communicate the intent of it all and avert a war.

Joshua 23:1–16

When Joshua was an old man, he gathered all Israel and their leaders together for his farewell address and counsel. He repeated promises and warnings. A problem was already evident in the failure of the tribes to remove the Canaanites from among them. Though verse 1 states that "the Lord had given rest unto Israel from all their enemies round about," this must be viewed as meaning "temporarily." The thirty-one cities destroyed by the Israelites under Joshua were not the total number the Lord wanted purged from the land of Canaan. Because Israel tended to adopt the values, habits, and culture of those around them, it was crucial that all idolatrous nations in the former land of Canaan be removed. Therefore, in this exhortation, Joshua warned Israel of three dangers to be aware of if the idolatrous and the corrupt were allowed to remain: social interaction, false gods, intermarriage (vv. 7–12).

Is there any application to latter-day Israel? What if we harbor corrupting influences in our midst—in our home? If Israel did nothing to eradicate these dangers, "Know for a certainty that the Lord your God will no more drive out any of these nations from before you; but they shall be snares and traps unto you, and scourges in your sides, and thorns in your eyes, until ye perish from off this good land which the Lord your God hath given you" (v. 13). In fact, if Israel transgressed the covenant and served other gods, said Joshua, "then shall the anger of the Lord be kindled against you, and ye shall perish quickly from off the good land which he hath given unto you" (v. 16). Again a major theme of the Old Testament is reiterated: righteousness and possession of the land are inextricably linked.

Joshua expressed his anticipation of death (v. 14). Similar phrases are used in Job 16:22 and in 2 Nephi 1:14.

Joshua 24:1–28

Joshua gave his farewell address at Shechem, in the center of the land. Like Moses, Joshua reviewed reasons why the Lord's people should remain faithful and grateful to God for his blessings. A high point in his speech is the challenge and testimony voiced in verses 14–15, two of the most important verses in all of scripture. He followed those points by requiring from Israel a covenant and promise of loyalty. In Judges 2:7, 10, we happily learn that the generation of people who made this covenant kept it, although the same cannot be said for their descendants.

It could be assumed from verse 26 that Joshua wrote this book, or caused it to be written, but technically it bears Joshua's name in reference to the covenant that he had just made with his people. In any case, it is evidence that writing was being done in those days.

Once again at the end of his life, Joshua designated an important memorial to be recognized by Israel—a stone. Stones are part of the earth, a living sphere which may someday reveal its own record, its history, and its witness of righteousness, especially when it becomes a great Urim and Thummim (D&C 130:9). The stone also served as a witness and reminder of the Stone of Israel—Christ—as we learned from Jacob's patriarchal blessing given to Joseph (Genesis 49:24) and as recapitulated when Israel first entered the promised land (Joshua 4:8–9). In a sense, then, the book of Joshua comes back full circle to where it began.

Joshua 24:29–33

Joshua's death was noted, along with his great influence on the people of Israel. Then, in fulfillment of an old request, the remains of the great patriarch Joseph were buried in a significant place—the parcel of land Jacob first owned in the promised land, when he purchased it from Shechem's people.

For the request of Joseph, see Genesis 50:25; concerning the purchase of the land, see Genesis 33:19; concerning Jacob's well in the same vicinity, see John 4:5 and, with a slight error, Acts 7:16.

The death of Eleazar, son of Aaron, the chief priest, was also recorded. It is mentioned later that he was succeeded by his son.

Joshua was a man of vision, courage, wisdom, fairness, spiritual power, and energy. His inspiring words have been cited by preachers and teachers throughout the ages (for example, Joshua 1:6–9; 24:15).

JUDGES

The book of Judges might well be entitled The Record of Israel's Heroes or An Account of Israel's Champions. The book of Judges is not about men and women who decided legal issues but rather about military heroes who arose in different parts of the land to deliver their tribes from their enemies during the first centuries Israelites lived in Canaan. Their principal purpose and efforts are described in Judges 2:16— "the Lord raised up judges, which *delivered* [Israel] out of the hand of those that spoiled them" (emphasis added). Thus, the judges were deliverers and may be thought of as symbolically representing the Great Deliverer, the Messiah.

The book of Judges describes invasions of Sidonians, Arameans, Philistines, Amalekites, Ammonites, Moabites, and Midianites; Israel's neighbors were pressing at her borders from all sides. Israel had no central government but was a loose confederation of tribes. The local judges rallied the fighting men of nearby tribes to prevent various enemies from overrunning their lands.

Under Joshua's leadership, the Israelites had conquered a good portion of the promised land. But with the death of Joshua also came the end of national unity. Judges stepped in to fill the leadership void. Apostasy began to grow throughout the loose tribal confederation as the different judges passed away or were ignored. Suffering under oppression and war, the people cried unto the Lord, and other judges were raised up. But once secure, the people again turned to wickedness. And so the cycle went. In the ultimate of ironies, the book of

Judges starts with the Lord delivering the enemies of righteousness to Israel (Judges 1:4). It ends with Israel *as* the enemy of righteousness. As it says, "in *those* days there was no king in Israel: every man did that which was right in his own eyes" (for example, 21:25; emphasis added). Thus, the writer seems to be quite pro-monarchy, which may give an indication of the date of the book's composition in final form.

The book of Judges was probably finished during the period of the united monarchy. Such expressions as "in those days there was no king in Israel" are frequently found (17:6; 18:1; 19:1; 21:25). According to Jewish tradition the prophet Samuel wrote Judges. It seems more likely that Samuel assembled some of the accounts in Judges, and then other prophets and princes associated with the royal court helped to shape and edit the material, creating the final product.

Judges 1:1–15

A review is presented of the campaign by the armies of Judah after the death of Joshua and other prior events. In the affair with Adoni-bezek, the armies of Judah adopted a practice common in virtually all nations of antiquity, which was the torture and mutilation of captives. It was supposed to make others fear to oppose them. Pictures from tombs and temples show Assyrians cutting off the limbs of captives and Egyptian pharaohs counting piles of hands cut off their enemies. It is surprising that Adoni-bezek could moralize about it and consider it just.

Judges 1:16–21

Miscellaneous conquests are recorded. Note the location of the Kenites, the people of Moses' "father-in-law" (properly, his brother-in-law Hobab), who came with Israel (see Numbers 10:29–32; Judges 4:11; 1 Samuel 15:6).

Although Judah was said to have conquered Jerusalem (v. 8), it must have been only parts of the city they conquered and burned, for it is noted in verse 21 that Benjamin could not drive out the Jebusites. As mentioned before, this city did not come into Israelite hands until the time of King David. The Philistine cities said to have been "taken" by Judah must only have been raided, because the Philistines also continued as strong as ever in their five major city-states, including those mentioned here. The Philistines could withstand the attacks because they "had chariots of iron." Later we see that the Philistines also used other iron implements before the Israelites possessed such things, which gave the Philistines an advantage in the wars against the Israelites.

Judges 1:22–36

One exploit of the two tribes of Joseph at Bethel was successful, but neither Ephraim nor Manasseh drove out the Canaanites in the major centers of their inheritances. The results of this failure will be discussed later in this commentary.

The same failure to drive out the Canaanites was found in the other tribal areas and with the same repercussions. Dan's people were not able to come down out of the mountain areas because of the superior forces of Philistines on the plains. Two branches of the great coastal highway ran through Dan's allocated territory. In essence, their assignment was to control international traffic, but they apparently couldn't handle the assignment, so they migrated northward and conquered another part of the land (see Judges 18).

In fact, Israel's failure, in general, to comply with God's commands to drive the Canaanites and Philistines out of the land involves six factors:

1. The Canaanites and Philistines had superior weaponry (see v. 19).
2. Israel disobeyed God by making treaties with the foreign peoples (see 2:1–3).
3. Israel violated the covenant the Lord made with their forefathers (2:20–21).
4. God was continuing to test, prove, and reprove Israel (2:22–23; 3:4).
5. God was schooling Israel as to how to develop

greater strategic understanding of the conquest and a stronger army (3:1–2).

6. Last but not least, Israel ultimately embraced the *profit* motive rather than the *prophet* motive: "And it came to pass, when Israel was strong, that they put the Canaanites to tribute, and did not utterly drive them out" (v. 28).

Judges 2:1–5

An angel apparently delivered a divine remonstrance against Israel's failing to follow directions in the conquest. The Lord had commanded Israel to wipe out the inhabitants of the land and to completely cleanse the land. The warning was, "Don't tolerate it, or you'll gradually adopt it!" God had covenanted to drive out the Canaanites; now he refused. Whose fault was it? Remember that Doctrine and Covenants 82:10 says, "I, the Lord, am bound when ye do what I say; but when ye do not what I say, ye have no promise."

Judges 2:6–10

Those who made the promise to be faithful actually kept it as long as they lived, both before and after the death of Joshua. But the transmission of faith and a sense of responsibility to the next generation was a failure, as the next section shows.

The phrase "gathered unto their fathers" in verse 10 reflects the practice of being buried with one's ancestors in the family grave.

Judges 2:11–23

"And the children of Israel did evil in the sight of the Lord, and served Baalim: and they forsook the Lord God of their fathers." Thus began the downward trend that launched the first of a series of apostasies told throughout the book of Judges.

The phenomenon of going "a whoring after other gods" (v. 17) involves the relationship between God and his people (see also commentary at Leviticus 17:1–16). One of the most sacred covenant relationships is the marriage covenant, and we have frequent mention in the scriptures about God being married to his people (Isaiah 54:5; Jeremiah 3:1–2, 6–8, 14; Ezekiel 16:2–15, 28–33). Prophets adopted this symbolic relationship because no covenant known to humans requires more fidelity, love, commitment, sacrifice, and patience than the marriage covenant. Likewise, nothing can be quite so destructive to the relationship than for either partner to be unfaithful. In our relationship with God, any infidelity, of course, will always be the fault of his partner. The bride or wife is therefore often depicted as the unfaithful one—the harlot. The whole image poignantly portrays the depth of feeling on the part of a jealous and zealous God who has lovingly nurtured and protected his people; it also shows how repulsive it is for him to watch his bride go "a whoring after other gods."

Who are these "other gods" to which the Israelites were exposed? We will pause at this point to define and describe the problem of Baalism.

BAALISM IN CANAAN AND NEIGHBORING LANDS

Our principal sources of written information about the religious beliefs and practices of the Canaanite peoples are the Bible and Ugaritic texts discovered at Ugarit (*Ras Shamra*) in modern Lebanon and Eblaite texts discovered at Ebla (*Tell Mardikh*) in modern Syria. Carefully read the following passages:

Exodus 34:11–17. Warnings are given against adopting the cultic practices of Canaanites; the Israelites were commanded to destroy their altars, images, and groves (or deities).

Judges 2:3, 11–13; 3:7. Canaanite worship practices were a snare to Israel; Jehovah was forsaken, and Israel served Baalim and Ashtaroth/Asheroth (fertility goddesses).

1 Kings 16:30–33. Ahab was the most perverse king of Israel; he and Jezebel built a temple to Baal in Samaria to worship fertility gods.

Jeremiah 19:4–8. Baal worship and child sacrifices occurred in Jerusalem; impending punishments were pronounced upon Jews and Jerusalem.

Following are the names of the main gods and goddesses worshiped by the Canaanites, along with notes about the meaning of their names and their functions:

El: common noun meaning "god"; the supreme god.

Baal: common noun meaning "lord" (compare Babylonian *Bel*); plural Baalim—presiding gods of various localities; Baal was El's son, inferior to El but more present and active. He was sometimes a god of agriculture, sometimes a storm god, but always related to fertility. Baal was also known as "Hadad" in Aram, or Syria. Note the occasional use of the common noun *Baal* in place names and compound personal names: Baal-Hazor, "lord of Hazor"; Baalbek, "lord of the valley"; Baal Hermon, "lord of Hermon"; Baal-zaphon, "lord of the north"; Baal-berith, "lord of the covenant"; Baal-zebub, or New Testament Beelzebub, "lord of the flies."

Asherah: El's wife; a fertility goddess, or sometimes consort of Baal. This name is occasionally mistakenly rendered as "grove" in the King James Bible.

Astarte: alternate names *Ashtoreth, Ashtaroth,* or *Baalah,* meaning "lady"; Baal's wife or consort; the great fertility goddess; compare Babylonian *Ishtar,* the "Queen of Heaven" (see Jeremiah 7:18; 44:17–19, 25), Phrygian *Cybele* and Graeco-Roman *Aphrodite/Venus,* and others).

Anat: Baal's sister or wife.

Mot: name means "death"; god of the underworld; Baal's antagonist.

Yam: the sea god.

Fertility was a dominant motif in Canaanite and Israelite art. Figurines and statuettes, found in great numbers, even in Jerusalem and near the sacred Temple Mount, often featured strongly emphasized sexual features, for example, the nude female figure with deliberately exaggerated sexual parts, frequently with hands raised to enormous, multiple breasts.

Canaanite culture presented elements of remarkable crudity in the offering of human sacrifices and in ritual prostitution.

Mesopotamians and Egyptians both had hundreds of gods representing heavenly bodies (sun, moon, stars, sky), earthly formations (deserts, rivers, air), human traits and experience (motherhood, love, joy, truth, justice, war, writing), and funerary functions (death, cemetery, mummification, resurrection). Earthly animals were typically the physical manifestation of the gods: ram, vulture, cow, jackal, bull, baboon, crocodile, ostrich, serpent, lion, beetle, cobra. Peoples of the Levant (eastern Mediterranean countries), on the other hand, were preoccupied with the rain and the fertile land; therefore, their gods were usually storm gods. Their worship focused on the fertility of the land and of themselves.

Besides temple structures, their sacred places were often open-air sanctuaries situated near trees or water sources, especially on high hills (what the Bible calls "high places," whether natural or man-made). Stones, altars, and pillars were given cultic significance. Officials included sanctuary keepers, priests, prophets, diviners, wailing women, and ritual prostitutes.

It is evident by Israel's prophets' frequent condemnation of the "groves" (the *asheroth,* or fertility goddesses) and the *baalim* that the Israelites adopted some of the local Canaanite religious practices. What the prophets denounced says something specific about the ills of their society. God's true prophets reproved the Ammonites for worshiping Moloch, the Moabites for sacrificing infants to the fire-belching Chemosh, and the Philistines for trusting in their grain or fish god, Dagon, but they also rebuked their own Israelite nation for whoring after the sexual abuses and horrifying human sacrifices of the Canaanites.

We see the counterpart of Satan in Baal's antagonist, Mot, and a parallel to the Godhead in the Canaanites' worship of a father-god and his son. These were corruptions of true worship. Since we also notice considerable corruption of worship that involved goddesses, we may suppose that one of the reasons our Heavenly Father has revealed very little about our Heavenly Mother is perhaps to avoid in modern times further desecration of her sacred role as occurred anciently among Canaanites and later cultures of the Near East.

Judges 3:1–7

It was said by the angel (Judges 2:1–3) that because Israel had not driven out the Canaanites and Amorites but had made treaties, or "leagues," with them and had not destroyed their worship facilities, the Lord would not drive them out. The writer now adds that the Lord left the Canaanite peoples in the land "to prove Israel." This means that since Israel did not pass the test at first, the testing continued. It is, of course, the same with us, either as individuals or nations. The capacity to resist a temptation is usually tantamount to the capacity to remove it. Notice footnote 7*d*. The results of intermarriage between Israelites and heathen peoples are also noted in succinct manner. They served false gods and forgot Jehovah (vv. 6–7).

Judges 3:8–11

In the first example of the cyclical degeneration process, Israel's oppressor for a period of eight years was an Aramean king. His land was called *Aram-Naharaim,* meaning "Aram of the two rivers," that is, between the Habor and the Orontes. *Mesopotamia* means "between the rivers" in Greek and is here used to translate *Naharaim.* The reader gets a false impression because the word *Mesopotamia* is usually used to designate the great plain between the Tigris and the Euphrates Rivers, as it was in Hellenistic times.

The king's name is also interesting. Although he was from Aram, he was derogatorily called by a long name that means "Cushite of double wickedness." What his real name and identity were would be difficult to guess. Othniel of Judah was the deliverer raised up. "Forty years" (v. 11) was commonly used to represent the lifetime or career of one individual.

Judges 3:12–30

Eglon, the obese king of Moab (his name means "the round one") was the next oppressor. He occupied an area near Jericho, "the city of palm trees." The Lord strengthened Eglon, just as He strengthened many of Israel's other enemies against her (Judges 2:14; 3:12; 4:2). Ehud, sent by Israel to deliver the tribute in the eighteenth year of her subjection, delivered also a "secret message" to Eglon, a special dagger Ehud had made for the purpose of killing the king. Other than Ehud's bold deed and his capacity to lead Israel in battle against the Moabites, there is no other detail about his career. The details of Eglon's death are presented in graphic detail (v. 22).

Judges 3:31

Shamgar, identified as the son of Anath, a Canaanite war goddess, was credited with delivering Israel by slaying six hundred Philistines. His weapon, an ox goad, would be as good as the ordinary short stabbing spear; it was a staff about six feet long, tipped with an iron, bronze, or stone point. His name appears again in Deborah's song, Judges 5:6. However, no other details of his "deliverance" were mentioned. Josephus does not mention Shamgar at all.

Shamgar may not originally have been an Israelite. Perhaps his family worshiped Anath, Baal's sister in Canaanite mythology. Perhaps he came from a village named Anath. We do not know.

Judges 4:1–10

Judges 4:1 follows 3:30 as if 3:31 had been a digression.

The oppression this time was from the northern Canaanite city-state of Hazor, whose king was Jabin and whose army chief was Sisera. This was a different Jabin from the one mentioned in Joshua 11, which may mean that "Jabin" was some kind of title at Hazor, perhaps a dynastic royal name.

Deborah, whose name means "honey bee," was a wife, a mother (5:7), and a prophetess to whom Israel went for advice and judgment as she dwelt between Ramah and Bethel in the central hill country of Ephraim (for more on "prophetess," see commentary at Exodus 15:20–27). She called Barak, a man of Naphtali, to lead a war against the Canaanite oppressors, but Barak said he would not go unless Deborah went as well. Deborah responded that she would go, but because of the way he was handling the situation (implying his lack of trust in God), the honor would not be his because the Lord was going to deliver "Sisera into the hands of a woman" (vv. 8–9).

Judges 4:11–24

With Deborah giving the directions and Barak leading the armies, battle was joined against Jabin, king of Hazor, and his commander, Sisera, at Mount Tabor in the eastern Jezreel Valley. True leaders inspire and sometimes shame (Judges 4:9) their followers to nobler action. That is what Deborah did for Barak: "Up; for this is the day in which the Lord hath delivered Sisera into thine hand" (v. 14). The Israelites were victorious. The final coup was administered by another woman, Jael, wife of Heber the Kenite, wielding a hammer and tent peg. As it happens, pitching tents and driving tent pins were women's responsibilities among the nomads.

The ancient laws of hospitality normally meant that one was obligated to protect a guest from harm (see Genesis 19:1–8). Jael, however, chose to remain loyal to her family's previous alliance with Israel.

In his book *The Innocents Abroad,* Mark Twain describes what happened: "Sisera fled away on foot, and when he was nearly exhausted by fatigue and thirst, one Jael, a woman he seems to have been acquainted with, invited him to come into her tent and rest himself. The weary soldier acceded readily enough, and Jael put him to bed. He said he was very thirsty and asked his generous preserver to get him a cup of water. She brought him some milk, and he drank of it gratefully and lay down again, to forget in pleasant dreams his lost battle and his humbled pride. Presently when he was asleep she came softly in with a hammer and drove a hideous tent pin down through his brain! 'For he was fast asleep and weary. So he died.' Such is the touching language of the Bible" (359).

Judges 5:1–31

The Lord chose a good woman to speak for him. It is not surprising that Deborah could have the "gift of prophecy"; it is available today to all who are properly baptized and receive the Holy Ghost. This was powerfully taught to the Lord's ancient American Israelites by the prophet Alma: "And now, he imparteth his word by angels unto men, yea, not only men but women also. Now this is not all; little children do have words given unto them many times, which confound the wise and the learned" (Alma 32:23).

The triumph-song of Deborah (vv. 2–31) was preserved in good Hebrew style and is one of the oldest surviving pieces of Hebrew poetry. To commemorate a national victory with a poetic song was a common practice anciently (see Exodus 15:1–18; Numbers 21:27–30). The lost book of the Wars of the Lord and the book of Jasher may have been collections of songs (see Numbers 21:14; Joshua 10:13). In this more detailed, poetic account of the battle with Sisera, the hand of the Lord was credited with the victory. It is sometimes beautiful (vv. 2–5), sometimes vivid, though the scene is not pretty (vv. 25–27), and sometimes poignant (vv. 28–31). Heavy rains and overflowing banks of the Kishon River in the Jezreel Valley apparently caused Canaanite chariots to bog down in mud and forced Sisera to flee on foot. Aside from some of the details about the death of the enemy, it is chiefly a song of praise to the Lord.

Judges 6:1–10

The Israelites went through the cycle of sin and suffering again. This time when they began to cry to the Lord, he sent a prophet to tell them the causes of their troubles. It seems obvious that one of the reasons for Israel's constant missteps and continual downfalls was that the younger generation was born into relative peace and prosperity. Perhaps they felt there was no need to pay attention to lessons from the past. The inevitable result of disobedience and rebellion is bondage and oppression. This time the tormentors were Midianites, Amalekites, and the *bnei kedem*—children of the east (v. 3).

"They came up with their cattle and their tents, and they came as grasshoppers for multitude; for both they and their camels were without number [at least 120,000 men; see Judges 8:10]: and they entered into the land to destroy it" (v. 5). For seven years they raided Israelite threshing floors and storehouses, until "Israel was greatly impoverished because of the Midianites; and the children of Israel cried unto the Lord."

It's always the same, isn't it? "O how foolish, and how vain, and how evil, and devilish, and how quick to do iniquity, and how slow to do good, are the children of men; yea, how quick to hearken unto the words of the evil one, and to set their hearts upon the vain things of the world!" (Helaman 12:4).

"And thus we see that except the Lord doth chasten his people with many afflictions, yea, except he doth visit them with death and with terror, and with famine and with all manner of pestilence, they will not remember him" (Helaman 12:3).

"In the day of their peace they esteemed lightly my counsel; but, in the day of their trouble, of necessity they feel after me" (D&C 101:8).

The Lord in his mercy will listen when the plea is sincere. Gideon now stepped onto the stage of Israelite history.

Judges 6:11–24

Gideon was called and an angel made the desire and intent of the Lord manifest to him. Observe the reply of Gideon at first: "Oh my Lord [he addresses the angel with the common Hebrew noun *adonai*, which is something like "sir," not *YHWH/Jehovah*], if the Lord be with us, why then is all this befallen us? and where be all his miracles which our fathers told us of? . . . but now the Lord hath forsaken us." He was humble in his estimate of himself.

When Gideon asked for a sign, he seemed to want some evidence that the messenger was a true emissary of the Lord. It is important to use discernment because messengers may sometimes be from the wrong source.

On the issue of discerning whether a messenger is from the Lord or not, see 2 Corinthians 11:13–15; 1 John 4:1–2; Doctrine and Covenants 129. Signs may be given, based upon a person's faith and the will of God: see Doctrine and Covenants 63:10. See the example of Abraham's servant in Genesis 24:14 and of Jonathan in 1 Samuel 14:6–13.

When Gideon made a meal of meat, cakes, and broth, the angel turned it into a miraculous burnt offering. This sign quite overwhelmed Gideon. He exulted in his experience. He had seen the Lord's angel "face to face" (v. 22). Compare Jacob's experience when he saw God "face to face" and received a new name (Genesis 32:24–32). Interestingly, Gideon also received a new name (v. 32), by which he became well-known. The Lord kindly gave him comfort and peace, and Gideon gratefully named the altar he had built as a monument to the Lord *Jehovah-shalom,* which means "Jehovah is peace" (v. 24).

Judges 6:25–40

Gideon started the cleanup of idolatry at home and demonstrated the impotence of idols to oppose his reformation. His first task was to tear down an altar dedicated to Baal that was owned by his father and to build an altar to the Lord in its place. Note the latter was to be built on a rock (v. 26), which of course is symbolic.

Gideon again asked for signs that the Lord would help him when it was time to act against the oppressing Midianite and Amalekite bands. These are quite different from a sign that there is a God or a sign that God has power, which are the common type that the wicked ask for. Gideon asked in faith.

Judges 7:1 to 8:21

Chapter 7 contains one of the best examples in scripture of how the Lord can bring about his purposes, regardless of external circumstances, and teach his children that they must rely on him and not boast in their abilities. Though only tribes from the north (Manasseh, Asher, Zebulun, and Naphtali) joined Gideon's campaign, they were more than enough for the purposes of the Lord. Eventually the 32,000 were reduced to 300 so that the Lord's help would be dramatically apparent to Israel. Various methods were used to reduce the number. "Well of Harod" (Hebrew, *En Harod*) in 7:1 should be translated "spring" not "well."

Against the formidable might of marauders mounted on camels, strategy and the help of the Lord gave the Israelites success where hand-to-hand combat would have been disastrous. The use of camels for military purposes by nomadic desert riders was only beginning to be common in the twelfth to tenth centuries B.C., so of course the first tribes to use them had the advantage.

Some have wondered if the stratagem, or tactic, Gideon used was to put into the hands of all the three hundred men, divided into three companies, the *shofars* ("trumpets"). Since only the leader of each company usually held the light and blew the shofar, the large number of shofars would give the impression of many thousands descending on the enemy armies in the middle of the night and cause great confusion and panic.

President Boyd K. Packer has distilled for us an important lesson from this episode:

"Gideon was chosen to lead the armies of Israel, thousands strong. But of them all, he chose only 300 men.

"Gideon had an interesting way of selecting his recruits. When the men drank water at a stream, most 'bowed down . . . to drink.' Those he passed over. A few scooped up water in their hands and drank, remaining completely alert. They were the ones chosen.

Brigham Young University students reenact Israelite soldiers lapping water at the Spring of Harod in the eastern Jezreel Valley—"every one that lappeth of the water with his tongue, as a dog lappeth" (Judges 7:5).

"We live in a day of 'wars [and] rumors of wars, and earthquakes in divers places.' As prophesied, 'the whole earth [is] in commotion' and 'Satan is abroad in the land.' He seeks to destroy all that is good and righteous. He is Lucifer, who was cast out of the presence of God. Against all of that, we have very positive feelings about what lies ahead.

"Gideon's small force succeeded because, as the record states, 'they stood every man in his place'" (*Ensign*, May 2010, 6).

In our day we must remain alert to the worldly dangers that threaten us. We dominate not by force of numbers but by priesthood authority and power—by the power of God. That is the lesson of the 300 men.

Judges 8:22–35

Gideon showed humility after his military victory and also his understanding of the relationship of the Lord and Israel.

An unfortunate development arose from Gideon's zeal in

making a new ephod (a part of the garment of the chief priest in Israel) out of some of the precious things gathered from the smitten enemy. The people idolized it, and idol worship is condemned as infidelity to God.

The situation at Gideon's death is summarized, along with introducing his seventy or more sons. One of those sons, Abimelech, born of a concubine, was the chief actor and bad character in the next episode.

Judges 9:1–57

In many ways Gideon (Jerubbaal) was the ideal judge, evoking the memory of the prophets Moses and Joshua, while his son was the very antithesis of responsible, faithful leadership. Abimelech was not a judge raised up by God. Notice how he acquired his following and helpers and the manner of spirit which attended his reign. He was, of course, not a king over all Israel; his power and influence were only in and about the city of Shechem and briefly among some of the neighboring towns. This local and temporary usurper is usually not counted as one of the judges and certainly not as one of the kings of Israel. On the contrary, he tried to set himself up as one of the petty kings of the various Canaanite city-states in the region, with Baal's help. Contrast that with his father, Gideon (Jerubbaal), who tried to destroy Baal worship.

Fortified by supporters and money from the temple of Baal-berith ("covenant of Baal"), Abimelech unleashed a horrible slaughter of Gideon's sons. One of those survived the slaughter and tried to awaken the people to their own situation through a parable or allegory.

In Jotham's allegory, the trees represent the leaders of Israel, Gideon being the olive tree and Gideon's sons being the other trees. The bramble is Abimelech, who said to his brothers, "Come and put your trust in my shadow" (v. 15). But because of the bramble's wide-spreading roots, the others choked and perished. Verse 20 contains a grim prediction that Abimelech and the people of Shechem would destroy

themselves. The chapter ends by reporting Abimelech's ig-
nominious death (vv. 53–54) and the fulfillment of Jotham's
curse: "And all the evil of the men of Shechem did God render
upon their heads: and upon them came the curse of Jotham
the son of Jerubbaal" (v. 57).

Judges 10:1–18

Two more judges are briefly summarized. Distressed, the
people needed another leader, but the Lord was out of patience with them. With divine sarcasm, he challenged them
to go to the idols they worshiped and get them to save them
from tribulation (compare the rebuke in D&C 101:7–8).
They saw that it was useless and put away the strange gods,
but still no help came from the Lord this time.

Judges 11:1–40

So the people themselves chose a leader, a former outcast
of a family of Gilead who had shown leadership and was a
mighty man of valor—a man named Jephthah. Notice in verse
11 that he was chosen by common consent: the proposal of
the elders was ratified by the people. He was one of those cited
for faith by the apostle Paul in Hebrews 11:32–35. He had his
good points, but according to the present account he appears
to have made an error when he promised the Lord that he
would sacrifice whatever would come out of his house to meet
him upon his return, if he returned victorious. On the other
hand, there seems to be something wrong with our present
account of Jephthah's vow. Human sacrifices were not part of
the true worship of God and were not allowed in Israel. The
vow of Hannah, recorded in 1 Samuel 1:11, is almost identical
in word and tone to that of Jephthah. Perhaps the intent of
his vow was to "sacrifice" his child to the service of the Lord,
as Hannah did. The Hebrew text of the last line of verse 31
allows for this alternate translation: "and I will offer Him up
an offering or gift." Later in the story, Jephthah's daughter re-
quests time to bewail not her death but her virginity—maybe
she would have to forfeit marriage and children to accomplish

the avowed service, though that kind of sacrifice does not correlate with our knowledge of true religion either. The final verse has other daughters of Israel going up yearly to lament Jephthah's daughter. The Hebrew verb used here means "to rehearse or to talk with," something that certainly couldn't be done if she were dead. All in all, the episode has not come down to us in a pure, intelligible form. Interpretation may have to await clarification in a future day.

Judges 12:1–15

When the Ephraimites complained because Jephthah didn't let them join with him in his campaign, he countered that they had sent him no recruits. There was a brief period of strife as he chastised them for their petulance and presumption.

Three more judges are identified but with no significant details about the twenty-five years they served. The number of sons and daughters is mentioned from time to time, and the fact that they could all be mounted on colts seems to be an ancient symbol of status.

Judges 13:1–25

In the midst of Israel's evil doings and their resulting oppression under the Philistines, whom the Lord had prepared to punish Israel, an angelic herald announced a new judge prepared from before his birth and dedicated to the service of the Lord as a Nazarite. The angel's countenance is described as "very terrible," meaning imposing or truly awe inspiring (v. 6). The details about the appearance and the nature of the angel and the way in which the woman contrived to have her husband also see him are interesting.

Samson was supposed to have become one of Israel's great leaders. His story is a tale of what might have been, a story of a man who might have been great. Samson was born under a Nazarite vow (Hebrew, *nazar*, "to dedicate to God, to separate, to abstain from things"). The restrictions of the vow are laid out in verses 4–5. Samson was set apart from his birth to do the Lord's bidding.

During the early life of Samson the Lord was "moving" him in the camp (v. 25). We are not sure what that means, but it may refer to Samson beginning to show his superhuman strength.

Judges 14:1–20

Samson soon began indulging in whims. He must have been quite a teenager, telling his father, "Get her for me; for she pleaseth me well"! (v. 3). His parents must have been distressed when their foreordained Nazarite son desired to marry someone not of Israel, disregarding the laws of Moses. His proposed marriage, the impossible riddle and betrayal, and the slaughter of thirty men to pay off an immature vow seem unlikely ways to free Israel or bring blessings from God. In fact, Samson's feast mentioned in verse 10, which was customary for bridegrooms, lasted seven days (v. 12; see also Genesis 29:27–28) and usually included drinking wine. It is possible that Samson violated his Nazarite vow.

Judges 15:1–20

The incendiary raid that followed the loss of Samson's Philistine wife and the slaughter of a thousand men with the jawbone thereafter also seem like poor service for a Nazarite to render. This must have been a popular hero story in the apostate days of the rule of the judges, a kind of conceited, self-centered Hebrew Hercules who lacked discipline and vision. Here is also a good lesson in the tragic consequences of failure to honor parents, both mortal parents and eternal Parents.

In verse 1, the "kid" in this case was a goat. In verses 9 through 17 is a play on the words "Lehi" and "jawbone": *lehi* means "jawbone"; "the jaw" in verse 19 is *Lehi* in Hebrew. Verse 20 asserts that Samson judged Israel for twenty years, but we have no record of that service.

Judges 16:1–31

Samson went down to Gaza, one of the five Philistine strongholds and capital cities of their kingdom (Ashdod, Ashkelon, Gaza, Gath, and Ekron), where he spent half a night with a harlot and then slipped out and stole the city gates, gateposts and all.

But alas, the wiles of another woman, Delilah, betrayed the secret of his superhuman strength to the enemy. She won him over with the familiar line, "if you really love me, prove your love . . ." (v. 15) and by pressing him daily with words and coaxing (v. 16).

Potiphar's wife did the very same thing to Joseph, only Joseph refused to succumb (Genesis 39:10). Modern technology presses us daily with words, too. We counteract that by being pressed daily with the Lord's words.

"And she made him sleep upon her knees" (v. 19) until all was lost. Samson's last "service" was to slay more in his death than he slew in life.

The tragedy of Samson can be framed in several simple questions: How many of us have had our births announced by an angel? How much good could he have accomplished for the spiritual quality of Israelite life had he not given in to his own base passions? Where did he go wrong, that he became conceited, self-centered, and undisciplined? Why did he suffer from such lack of spiritual vision, which ultimately resulted in his painful *physical* loss of vision? Samson's problem is summarized in Doctrine and Covenants 3:4: "Although a man may have many revelations, and have power to do many mighty works, yet *if he boasts in his own strength, and sets at naught the counsels of God, and follows after the dictates of his own will and carnal desires,* he must fall and incur the vengeance of a just God upon him" (emphasis added).

Judges 17–21

These chapters constitute something of an epilogue that characterizes the era of the judges: the moral and religious corruption exhibited by individuals, cities, and tribes. This epilogue is made up of two parts, which are unrelated chronologically or to specific judges. First, chapters 17–18 describe a man named Micah, a bribable and thieving individual, who developed a pagan, idolatrous place of worship with a false priesthood and a Levite as spiritual advisor. It also recounts the tribe of Dan abandoning their allotted territory and adopting Micah's corrupt religion. Second, chapters 19–21 describe the sad experience of another Levite and the degenerate town of Gibeah. Brutality and degradation filled the Holy Land through the very people who were supposed to enrich it with the righteous principles of the Abrahamic covenant.

Judges 17:1–13

Here is a sample of Israel's worst days. There is nothing in this whole story that shows Micah and his associates doing what was right. In dedicating an image to the Lord, they seemed to be sinning somewhat out of self-deception; there would be no point in dedicating so much silver as an insult to God and then hoping for his blessing. Micah's installation of a Levite as his spiritual advisor and non-Aaronite priest shows how much the general wickedness of the era had caused a complete dissipation and loss of foundational principles.

Judges 18:1–31

This Danite raid of a town of peaceful Sidonians and a tribe's theft of a man's idol and his priest all illustrate something far less than the proper deeds of "a kingdom of priests, and an holy nation" (Exodus 19:6).

The tribe of Dan made a judicious second choice of a region to settle. Verse 10 suggests that the land where they finally settled was lush, verdant, and productive. There was an abundance of water there. The snowfields on Hermon, prolific springs, rivers, and waterfalls are accurately described as part of the landscape of the region of Laish, or Dan, which lies thirty miles north of the Sea of Galilee (see Bible Map 1).

Judges 19–21

Another episode involving a Levite focuses on his concubine, who was sexually promiscuous. He took her back and set out for Shiloh, where the "house of the Lord" was located (Judges 19:18). During their travels, ironically he refused to stop in Jebus (Jerusalem) because it was filled with non-Israelites. But he did stop for the night at Gibeah, where thoroughly wicked and degenerate Israelite men, replaying a scene reminiscent of Sodom (compare Genesis 19:2–10), sought to abuse the Levite and raped his concubine throughout the night. They are called in the text "sons of Belial" (Judges 19:22), meaning "completely worthless"—a name altogether appropriate for their evil acts of rape and murder of the concubine. In addition, we note that homosexual practices among pagan populations are well known, but for Benjamites (19:16) to have been intent on engaging in this behavior was abominable.

Because the concubine died such a horrible death, the Levite took her body home, dismembered it, and sent twelve pieces to all the other tribes of Israel as a testimony against Gibeah and, perhaps, to awaken Israel to its own state of moral decay. If so, it is ironic that such an act was conducted by one who was himself so selfish, insensitive, and vile. Chapter 20 describes Israel's united war against the city of Gibeah and the tribe of Benjamin. Chapter 21 recounts more bloodshed: The inhabitants of Jabesh-gilead were destroyed for not engaging in war with Benjamin.

The history of Israel has demonstrated many low-water marks spiritually. But the period of the judges is among the lowest. Violence, rape, murder, mob action, homosexual behavior, and the near obliteration of a tribe of Israel complete the picture. Once again we see the explanatory statement made several times by the writer of the record: "In those days there was no king in Israel, but every man did that which was right in his own eyes" (17:6; see also 21:25).

RUTH

The book of Ruth serves as an appendix of sorts to the book of Judges, telling of some nobler events that "came to pass in the days when the judges ruled" (Ruth 1:1). It is a pleasant thing to read about Israelites of that time who were good, faithful, loyal, generous, and devoted to God and others. The book of Ruth presents examples of selfless love and shows to us the converting power of both the covenant and righteous role models. In Ruth there are no kings, royalty, priests, Levites, or named prophets. All characters are ordinary people—far removed from the corridors of power. The German poet Goethe described it as the loveliest complete work on a small scale.

The book of Ruth is the first true "short story" known in literature. It is a heartwarming story with a multitude of contrasting motifs such as "full-empty" and "loss-restoration." After famine and personal loss, abundant harvest and fruitful marriage follow. The story begins at Bethlehem, which means "House of Bread," but alas, there is no bread there. The story ends with the establishment of a messianic ancestry that originated in this ancestress from the east and from whom issued the "Bread of Life." Watch for these contrasts as you read and ponder this excerpt from messianic history. Also look for ways in which the book of Ruth points to the Messiah.

In the Hebrew Bible the book of Ruth is placed in the third division called the Writings, which follows the Law (five books of Moses), and the Prophets. It is one of the five *Megillot* ("scrolls") that are read during a Jewish holiday or fast day. Ruth is read during *Shavuot,* or Feast of Weeks, also known as First Harvest or Pentecost, which occurs fifty days after Passover. The other *Megillot* that are read include the Song of Solomon at Passover; Lamentations during *Tisha B'Av,* the fast commemorating the destructions of Solomon's and Herod's Temples; Esther during Purim; and Ecclesiastes during *Sukkot,* or Feast of Tabernacles.

Ruth 1:1–2

The time, the place, and the people are described. Three of the people have names with significant meanings in the story: *Naomi* means "lovely, pleasant"; *Mahlon* is related to a root word meaning "to be weak, sick"; *Chilion* means "failing, pining." In the story, Naomi's name reflects her character, though she does suffer some bitterness for a time. Perhaps the names of the two sons also give a clue to the reason for their early deaths.

Ruth 1:3–5

The narrative continues with the marriage of two Israelite young men to Moabite young women. Although this is surprising in light of the restrictions so often mentioned about Moabites *not* being admitted into the "congregation of the Lord" (for example, Deuteronomy 23:3; Nehemiah 13:1), the two Israelites received no condemnation by the writer. Moabites were, after all, descendants of Moab, son of Lot and his daughter, and therefore relatives of Abraham.

Ruth 1:6–13

Several possible means of survival existed for widowed women. There was the possibility of another marriage for young widows; there was also the possibility of some security through the land laws of Israel. These laws provided ways to redeem land to its former owners (Leviticus 25:23–28, 35; see especially v. 25). If any "brother" or near kinsman existed, the levirate marriage system could give the young widow a home and a future (review Genesis 38:8; Numbers 27:1–11, especially v. 4; see also Deuteronomy 25:5–6). Note, however, that Naomi was not very optimistic about any solution. She felt that the hand of the Lord was against her, even that he had forsaken her, and so she recommended that her daughters-in-law return to their families.

Ruth 1:14–22

Orpah made her choice, and Ruth made hers. Here indeed was a turning point in human history. What motives for Ruth's choice do you see in her classic statement? (v. 16). What justification is there for supposing she was a convert? (see the last phrases in 1:16 and 2:12). An interesting comparison to this ancient situation is the scene in Nauvoo, Illinois, in the mid-1840s with two other young widows: Emma Hale Smith, widow of Joseph Smith, remained in Nauvoo after the exodus of the Saints, and most of her descendants have continued outside the Church. Mary Fielding Smith, widow of Hyrum Smith, on the other hand, journeyed west with the Saints, and many of her descendants have remained faithful. In fact, her son, Joseph F. Smith, and her grandson Joseph Fielding Smith each became president of the Church.

The greatest lesson in this story is that Ruth chose to follow God, even though it meant leaving her own family and homeland. Many people have sacrificed family and country to follow God. The latter-day pioneers left their homes and farms to gather to Zion. The question this poses to each of us is, "Have I left the world to follow God?" We may not have to cross the plains to follow God, but we may have to cross the family room and turn off the television. We may not have to leave our homes to find Zion, but we may have to leave the practices of the world and create Zion in our homes.

In the phrase "the Lord do so to me, and more also" (v. 17), the word "so" (Hebrew, *koh*) suggests some bodily gesture; the statement may have been accompanied by a gesture similar to drawing the index finger across the throat.

It was a rather gloomy return to Bethlehem and a pitiful prospect facing the two widows. Notice the footnotes 20*b* and 21*a,* which help us understand the significance of names in the story.

Ruth 2:1–16

A young woman could go out as a gleaner at harvest time and gather enough grain for her food for the winter if she was fortunate, but if she were a foreigner and alone, she also risked being molested or driven off. However, Ruth happened to go to the field of Boaz, a kinsman of Elimelech, who was the deceased husband of Naomi. This was indeed a blessing, as Ruth and Naomi later recognized. According to the description given of him in verse 1, Boaz was an honorable man of good standing. Likewise Ruth was described as an honorable woman of good standing (3:11).

Upon making careful inquiries, Boaz found reason to grant Ruth favors and protection and was kind enough to do so (see especially vv. 11 and 12).

Ruth 2:17–23

Naomi expressed her gratitude to Boaz and to the Lord; she realized that the Lord had not forsaken her and Ruth after all. If a marriage were to be arranged, it would be up to Naomi, as the responsible parent, to arrange it. She undertook the opening steps.

A kinsman had the right to purchase, redeem, the land of a deceased relative, marry his widow, and produce offspring—the first of whom would be the heir of the man who had died. Thus a "redeemer" could restore to a widow a degree of security and status she could not of herself attain and even provide for continuation of the seed. Understanding this meaning deepens our appreciation for the prophets' use of the word *redeemer* (Hebrew, *go'el*) to characterize our Savior.

Ruth 3:1–5

By the end of the barley harvest, usually in April, Naomi felt things were progressing well enough to try bringing up marriage. She asked Ruth, "shall I not seek rest for thee, that it may be well with thee?" The word "rest" (Hebrew, *mnukha*) refers to the security and comfort resulting from marriage. She instructed Ruth how to proceed: clean up, put on some perfume and a pretty dress, go to the threshing floor, and lie down at the feet of Boaz. Lying "at the feet" of Boaz would show Ruth to be a humble servant, not a wanton woman; there would have been moral danger in such proceedings were it not for the known character of Ruth and Boaz, in which Naomi implicitly trusted.

Ruth 3:6–9

When Boaz awoke from his sleep by the pile of grain that he and others were guarding, as was the custom during harvest time, he was startled by Ruth's presence. She was direct in her proposal. The word rendered "skirt" also means "wing," and her request was not unlike our idiom "take me under your wing." Gesenius, the famous Hebraist, says it was a proper proposal of marriage, even though the woman was doing the proposing.

Ruth 3:10–18

Notice Boaz's reaction, his attitude, his concern for propriety, his methodical plan for action, and his resolution to do his duty by Ruth—if the one with the prior right to marry her should choose not to do so. Ruth returned home in the morning before it was light enough for anyone to recognize her. Naomi was confident that Boaz would take care of the matter that very day.

Ruth 4:1–10

In ancient Israel, many of life's most important legal decisions were made at the gate of the city with the elders. For example, rebellious sons were taken to the elders outside the city gate (Deuteronomy 21:18–21); when David fought Absalom, his position of power was established by his sitting in front of the city gate (2 Samuel 18:1–5); and the king sat at the city gate and judged his people (2 Samuel 19:8). Legal matters were discussed at the city gate because it was the focal point of the community and because of the perceived strength it projected. So it was that Boaz went to the city gate with the elders to settle the legality of his marriage to Ruth.

The legal proceedings were duly accomplished. Apparently the writer of the story did not even bother to find the name of the kinsman who was at first willing to do the duty of redeeming his dead kinsman's property, but then the kinsman learned that the responsibility of marrying the young widow and raising up a son to the name of the dead was entailed. The first son of such a marriage would be counted the son and heir of the dead husband. Thus, though the "redeemer" paid to get the land back into the possession of the family, it would go to that heir and not increase his own estate.

Again, the Hebrew word *go'el* should be literally and properly translated "redeemer," but here it is rendered merely "kinsman" in the King James English translation. The function of a *go'el* was to make it possible for a widow who had lost home and property to return to her former status and security and to have seed to perpetuate her family. It is easy to see why the later prophets borrowed this word from the social laws of Israel and used it to describe the functions of him who would become the divine Redeemer. Think of what he does to restore us to proper status with God and to give us future security and eternal seed.

Ruth 4:11–22

The prophetic wish of the witnesses that the marriage be as fruitful as that of their forefathers, and as that of the young widow Tamar who bore the fourth great-grandfather of Boaz, turned out to be fulfilled in due time.

So the intrinsic goodness of people involved in the story

and the involvement of the Lord worked together for good in an otherwise bad situation. The Moabitess Ruth, who came into the "congregation of the Lord" and became a part of the most famous line of Judah's genealogy, produced kings of Israel and, ultimately, the Redeemer of the world. Thus we see that good people everywhere are acceptable to the Lord, no matter their original circumstances. Moreover, we see that at least partial functioning of the mission of Israel was possible through the lives of some good Israelites in the evil days of the judges.

If most of the book of Ruth was written near the time of its events, the genealogical appendix contained in verses 18–22 must have been added much later, probably after the days of Samuel and Saul, when David had come into prominence in Israel.

TYPES AND SHADOWS OF THE MESSIAH IN RUTH

Few passages in the Old Testament match the beauty and emotive power of Ruth's profession of faith and commitment. Her virtue and strength of character are an example for the ages. But because Ruth had given up her former religion and her former life in order to unite with Israel, she had no place to turn. She strikingly exemplifies the truth, articulated by the Savior, that choosing to participate in the kingdom of God may separate individuals from their family, friends, and culture: "For I am come to set a man at variance against his father, and the daughter against her mother, and the daughter in law against her mother in law. . . . He that loveth father or mother more than me is not worthy of me: and he that loveth son or daughter more than me is not worthy of me" (Matthew 10:35–37). As Jesus teaches in this passage, he and his gospel require individuals to make choices, sometimes hard choices, and commitments to him over others. Membership in the Lord's family is decided not by blood or birth but by choice and conformity to God's will through the covenant. Accordingly, if anyone sacrifices all in order to follow God, God will not leave any of his covenant family members without help. "But now the Lord saith, . . . them that honour me I will honour" (1 Samuel 2:30). He did not leave Ruth destitute or helpless. He provided a redeemer for her and Naomi and fulfilled a promise of temporal and spiritual redemption. The name of Ruth's and Naomi's redeemer was Boaz, who is a type and similitude of Jesus Christ.

Ruth and Naomi returned to Bethlehem at the time of the harvest. Perhaps under inspiration, Ruth gleaned in the fields of Boaz, who was a "mighty man of wealth" (Ruth 2:1) and a kinsman of Naomi's deceased husband. The ancient law of gleaning was a kind of welfare system. The Lord asked landowners to leave some produce in their fields to allow the needy, the fatherless, the widow, and the stranger the opportunity to harvest enough for their sustenance (Leviticus 19:9–10; 23:22; Deuteronomy 24:19–22). Ruth found favor with Boaz, who wanted to marry her if the nearest kinsman, to whom the right belonged according to the law in Deuteronomy 25:5–10, declined. The kinsman did decline and set the stage for one greater.

Boaz married Ruth and thus became a redeemer and savior of the two widows in a thinly veiled illustration of God's love and redemptive power. Without Boaz, both Naomi and Ruth would have remained on the fringes of society, devoid of meaningful status, security, voice, opportunities, or connectedness to a patriarchal culture that sometimes inadvertently, but wrongly, left widows and orphans powerless and alone. Boaz's gracious and beneficent actions reversed all of that.

"And Boaz said unto the elders, and unto all the people, Ye are witnesses this day, that I have bought all that was Elimelech's, and all that was Chilion's and Mahlon's, of the hand of Naomi.

"Moreover Ruth the Moabitess, the wife of Mahlon, have I *purchased* to be my wife, to *raise up the name of the dead* upon his inheritance. . . .

"So Boaz took Ruth, and she was his wife: and when he went in unto her, the Lord gave her conception, and she bare a son.

"And the women said unto Naomi, Blessed be the Lord,

which hath not left thee this day without a *kinsman,* that his name may be famous in Israel" (Ruth 4:9–14; emphasis added).

The Hebrew word used to describe Boaz in this passage, which the King James Version translates as "kinsman," is *go'el.* This word translates literally as "redeemer." The King James translators may not have completely recognized the deeper significance of the story nor the similitude of Christ inherent in the levirate law of Deuteronomy 25, because they translated *go'el* as "kinsman" or "next of kin." The levirate law (so called from Latin, *levir,* "husband's brother") is itself a typifying of Christ in that it asks that a deceased man's brother or kinsman stand in the place of the deceased to provide for the needs of the widow, to rescue the family from difficulty, and to raise up children in the name of the deceased brother. Thus, the deceased man's brother or kinsman was performing a substitutionary, or proxy, act, a vicarious service that the deceased man could not do for himself. Is this not the essence of the Lord's atonement?

Boaz was a redeemer in that he returned the widow Ruth to her former status as wife. She was no longer a disenfranchised member of society or the family of Israel. She had been purchased with a price. Likewise, all humanity, especially members of the covenant family, have a redeemer who has purchased or "bought [us] with a price," as Paul said, which price is his precious blood (1 Corinthians 6:20; Acts 20:28). The great Redeemer is Jesus Christ. The words of the chief apostle, Peter, also come to mind: "Forasmuch as ye know that ye were not redeemed with corruptible things . . . but with the precious blood of Christ, as of a lamb without blemish and without spot: who verily was foreordained before the foundation of the world, but was manifest in these last times for you" (1 Peter 1:18–20).

Moreover, when Boaz says he purchased Ruth in order that the name of the dead be raised up, do we not think of the resurrection made possible through the act of deliverance accomplished by Jesus Christ? Do we not appreciate the levirate law in a new light?

Ruth's redemption had everlasting consequences for the whole human family. The son of Boaz and Ruth was Obed, who was the father of Jesse, who was the father of David, through whose lineage came the royal Messiah, Jesus of Nazareth.

Truly, Boaz was a similitude of the Messiah, a truth which the story of Ruth may have been deliberately intended to portray. In a place called the House of Bread, at a time when there was no bread, came forth a convert who became the ancestress of the Bread of Life—the great *go'el*, or Redeemer.

FIRST SAMUEL

For the first time since the days of Moses and Joshua, the tribes of Israel became somewhat united, first under the prophet Samuel and then under the first two kings, Saul and David. Samuel was both an inspired judge and a prophet, trying to motivate Israel to begin again to become the "peculiar treasure" and "holy nation" they were called to be. Arguably he was one of Israel's greatest servants. But Samuel's own sons diminished his potential effectiveness, and Saul deteriorated from a man of faith and humble confidence to one imbued with jealousy, violence, and spiritual degeneration that ended in tragedy.

Samuel was born in answer to his mother's prayers (1 Samuel 1:11, 20). His name means "heard of God" (1:20). The Lord used Samuel to establish kingship in Israel. Samuel anointed both Saul and David, Israel's first two monarchs, and helped to educate the people of Israel on how kingship was to operate. He served as the bridge between the periods of the judges and the kings, providing continuity as Israel moved from one system of governance to the other. After Saul was established as king, Samuel seemed to cease acting as a judge, and intensified his work as prophet and chief representative of Jehovah.

It is not certain who was the final writer of the book of Samuel. It was probably compiled from several sources or records and then shaped after the death of King Solomon and the division of once-united Israel into the northern kingdom of Israel and the southern kingdom of Judah (ca. 930 B.C.).

Note the references to "Israel" and "Judah" as separate entities (11:8; 17:52; 18:16; 2 Samuel 5:5; 24:1–9). Originally
1 and 2 Samuel were one composition. It was divided into
two books by the translators of the Septuagint (the Greek version of the Old Testament, referred to as the LXX), and that
division was followed by the translator of the Latin Vulgate,
St. Jerome.

As time and interest allow, you may also want to read two
entries in the Bible Dictionary: "Samuel"; "Samuel, Books of."

1 Samuel 1:1–18

The parents of Samuel are introduced; they lived at
Ramathaim-zophim (or, simply, *Ramah*). Evidently his father
was of the tribe of Levi, though v. 1 calls him an Ephrathite,
perhaps a reference to an area in which he resided (see
1 Chronicles 6:16–28). This is significant in view of Samuel's
later priestly functions. Only certain descendants of Levi
(Aaronites) could serve in the office of priest.

The place of worship at Shiloh was established when the
Tabernacle and the Ark of the Covenant were placed there
(see Joshua 18:1; Judges 18:31). Shiloh was about twenty
miles north of Ramah. Being the site of the portable Temple,
it was imbued with exceptional holiness. Remember, three
times a year all covenant males were to appear before the Lord
at his sanctuary (Exodus 23:14–17; 34:23; Deuteronomy
16:16–17). That custom is reflected in the report of Elkanah's
journey to Shiloh "to sacrifice" (v. 3).

As is evident in earlier Bible stories, childlessness was
looked upon as a curse and motherhood a blessing (recall the
cases of Sarah, Rebekah, and Rachel). Though Elkanah deeply
loved his wife Hannah, "the Lord had shut up her womb"
(v. 5). In the ancient world both barrenness and fertility were
directly attributed to Deity. We are not told explicitly who the
adversary was that sorely provoked Hannah, but it was possibly the other wife, Peninnah, not unlike Hagar who despised
Sarah when she was childless (Genesis 16:4–5). Both Hagar

and Peninnah flaunted their fertility to demean the other wife. Thus, Hannah, the wife of Elkanah who had no children, turned to the Lord for help at Shiloh.

Hannah vowed that if she could be blessed with a son she would dedicate him to the Lord and raise him in purity—under the strictures of the Nazarite vow (see Numbers 6; Judges 13:5; 16:17; and others). Is Hannah's action an example of making and observing covenants by sacrifice, which we must all do? (D&C 97:8; 132:51).

At first, the old priest Eli misjudged her as a "daughter of Belial." Hannah protested to Eli that she was not a daughter of Belial, meaning a "worthless or profane person." "Belial" means worthlessness; therefore, a son or daughter of Belial would be someone of evil affiliation. It is capitalized by the English translators as if it were a name-title for Satan, and it is sometimes so used in later books.

Far from being a daughter of Belial, Hannah was pouring out her desires and longings to the Lord, and Eli blessed her.

1 Samuel 1:19–28

When the blessing was realized and her baby was born, Hannah named him Samuel (Hebrew, *Shmu'el,* "heard of God") because she had supplicated the Lord and the Lord had heard her.

True to her promise and with gratitude for her blessing, she gave Samuel to the care of the priestly family at Shiloh after he was weaned. We see in the next chapter, however, that she kept in contact with him. As a Nazarite, Samuel was everything that Samson was not: a truly righteous boy who grew to become a righteous man.

1 Samuel 2:1–10

Compare Hannah's song of thanksgiving and praise to God with that of Mary's, which is called the *Magnificat* (Latin, "magnify") because of Mary's opening exclamation, "My soul doth *magnify* the Lord" (Luke 1:46; emphasis added). Thus Hannah's psalm may justly be called the Magnificat of the Old

Testament. Also compare Zacharias's psalm of praise called the *Benedictus* (Luke 1:68–79). All three hymns herald the miraculous arrival of a child (Luke 1:46–55).

What is the main thing about God and his ways that seems to have impressed both Mary and Hannah? The usual parallelism and figurative language used here are characteristic of Hebrew poetry. The image of God as a rock connotes firmness, strength, and security. Similar uses of the term are seen in Psalms 27:5; 31:2–3; 62:6; 118:22; and Matthew 21:42. (Compare also Deuteronomy 32:15, 18, 31; 2 Samuel 22:2–3, 32–33; and 1 Corinthians 10:1–4.) Hannah calls him "a God of knowledge"; compare that conception of him with the definition of his glory in Doctrine and Covenants 93:36.

The term "horn," when used figuratively, usually means "power"; notice its use in both the first and the last lines of the poem.

One who was "anointed" of God was a special servant of God, such as a priest, prophet, or king. Properly appointed kings in Israel were always anointed with oil as an ordinance to convey authority. The Hebrew word for anointed, as translated into English, is *messiah;* eventually it was used in the definite form ("the Messiah") as the title for the anticipated divine King to come. The Greek word for the same idea was *Christos,* or in English, Christ. There seems to be a messianic hope already in Hannah's words in verse 10. Hannah's psalm is filled with types and foreshadowings of Jesus Christ.

1 Samuel 2:11–21

The sons of Eli really were "of Belial" (see 1 Samuel 1:1–18). Not only were they discontent with the portion of meat offering specified for the priests to use but they "knew not the Lord" and "abhorred the offering of the Lord" (their immoral and blasphemous acts are identified in vv. 22–25). All of us are commanded to "trifle not with sacred things" (D&C 6:12; 8:10). Such behavior deeply offends the Lord.

Concerning proper priestly portions of the offerings, review Leviticus 2:10; 7:28–34.

Meanwhile, both Samuel and his parents did what was right and enjoyed the grace of the Lord.

1 Samuel 2:22–26

Knowing of his sons' serious violations of the ritual privileges and also of the basic laws of morality (their adultery was likely in imitation of the priests of the fertility cults of Canaan), Eli reproved his sons but did not effectively restrain them (1 Samuel 3:13). As in our day, we have never failed until we have given up. Later we see the results of Eli's failing in his responsibility. What could he have done? (see Alma 39:8–14).

This is a serious challenge for us mortals in our most important role. Parents can teach their children, set proper examples for them, and still see their children use their agency to sin. While parents do make many mistakes in parenting, they are not disqualified from the Lord's service and his blessings because of errant children. It is when the children do wrong because of their parents' poor teaching and poor example that the parents are condemned.

Meanwhile, Samuel grew in favor with the Lord and with men. This immediately recalls Luke 2:52, where we are told that Jesus grew in favor with God and man.

1 Samuel 2:27–36

Eli's house was chastened by a man of God whose name is not recorded. As verse 29 declares, we cannot put our feelings for anyone or anything above the Lord. Jesus taught during his mortal ministry, "He that loveth father or mother more than me is not worthy of me: and he that loveth son or daughter more than me is not worthy of me" (Matthew 10:37). Eli's sin was not that he had rebellious children but that he was indulgent toward them. Why didn't Eli cut off his sons from priesthood duties? If Eli excommunicated them, they would lose their food supply (v. 29). The sacred concept of covenant is noted in verse 30. As we honor the Lord through our sincere attempts at righteous living, he "delights to honor" us (compare verse 30 with D&C 76:5). The "faithful priest" (v. 35) to replace Eli's descendants was Samuel, but thereafter another priestly line would be established: Zadok and his descendants, who came in David's time and served exclusively after Solomon's time.

1 Samuel 3:1–14

This chapter constitutes a powerful and helpful lesson on the process of receiving revelation. Though Samuel became a servant of the Lord by covenant before his birth, this is the first recorded revelation through him. It came in a day when "the word of the Lord was precious." The word "precious," like the Hebrew word it translates, bears the dual sense of rare and valuable. That a spokesman for the Lord had arisen soon became evident to the people (vv. 19–20). It is interesting that at first Samuel didn't recognize the voice calling to him; we all learn line upon line. Note especially how the Lord called several times and how Samuel finally responded, as did Abraham of old, "Here am I" (compare Genesis 22:1). Ultimately, Samuel's response must be our response if we desire to receive more revelation, more opportunities, more blessings from the Lord: "Speak . . . for thy servant heareth" (v. 9).

Because Eli was an enabler of his sons' misbehavior—"he restrained them not" (v. 13)—he was condemned by the Lord. President Joseph F. Smith warned all parents about the kind of error made by Eli: "God forbid that there should be any of us so unwisely indulgent, so thoughtless and so shallow in our affection for our children that we dare not check them in a wayward course, in wrong-doing and in their foolish love for the things of the world more than for the things of righteousness, for fear of offending them" (*Gospel Doctrine*, 286).

1 Samuel 3:15 to 4:1

Poor old Eli, well-meaning but weak according to the accounts given of his attitudes and his actions, humbly submitted to the will of the Lord, apparently feeling that his rejection was justified.

Samuel's reputation grew as his revelations proved true, and the word of the Lord was no longer rare in Israel. However, as we continue to learn more about Samuel, we see that he too struggled in raising his sons.

1 Samuel 4:1–22

All through this period of time the Philistines were making incursions from their coastal territory in attempts to penetrate the hill country to the east. Now we find Israelites and Philistines squaring off near Aphek, located east of the coastal town of Joppa (see Bible Map 10), a city shown by twentieth-century archaeological excavations to be of great importance for many centuries before and after this time period. The governor of Canaan under Pharaoh Ramses II owned a palace at Aphek, and Herod the Great later built a fortress and city there. Cuneiform (wedge-shaped writing) tablets and ostraca have been discovered with Sumerian, Akkadian, Canaanite, Hittite, Egyptian, and Hebrew inscriptions on them. The geographical importance of Aphek not just to Israel but to the entire Near East lies in its position along the international highway. The city is situated at the springs that immediately become the Yarkon River, which flowed out toward the Mediterranean. The Yarkon was usually obstructed at its mouth, and the backed up waters created swamps that were impassable throughout history until the modern day. All traffic, local and international, was therefore channeled into the mile-wide corridor between the springs and the hills. Geographical factors had thus given strategic value to the site of Aphek, and the Philistines wanted that strategic advantage.

Apparently it was with superstitious hope rather than real faith in God that the sons of Eli committed the final sacrilege of taking the holy Ark into battle. While the Israelite armies were reassured by it, the Philistines were stimulated to greater effort by fear and took the Ark. It had no legitimate place in the war. The story of its return to Israel follows later.

The Philistines may have penetrated into the heart of the Israelite hill country and destroyed Shiloh; at least it ceased to be a sanctuary at that time. In King Saul's day there was a shrine at Nob, on or near the Mount of Olives, that was staffed by a remnant of the house of Eli. All of them but one were massacred there (see 1 Samuel 21–22). The destruction of Shiloh was remembered by later writers (Psalm 78:60–63; Jeremiah 7:12, 14; 26:6).

The pathetic story of the birth and naming of Eli's grandson Ichabod is mentioned. Ichabod's mother, wife of the infamous Phinehas, one of Eli's corrupt sons, seems to have been a righteous woman, aware of things proper and improper with regard to the Ark.

1 Samuel 5:1 to 7:2

The Philistines placed the Ark in the temple of their god, Dagon, at Ashdod on the Mediterranean coast. A statue of this false god kept falling on its face, and some plagues broke out in their communities: The "hand of the Lord was against the city with a very great destruction; and he smote the men of the city, both small and great, and they had emerods in their secret parts" (1 Samuel 5:9). The Hebrew lexicon indicates that "emerods" (Hebrew, *ophalim*) really does mean hemorrhoids (blisters or tumors of the anus). There was apparently another plague, perhaps bubonic, associated with the emerods, since the destruction was so great. The Ark of the Covenant was in Philistine territory for seven months. The Philistines were finally inclined to return it to its rightful owners, and they decided to placate Israel with a trespass offering of golden images of emerods and mice (possible carriers of the plague).

The last verse of chapter 6 tells us that the men of Bethshemesh requested that the inhabitants of Kirjath-jearim come and take the Ark to their town. The Ark stayed in that place for twenty years (see 7:1–2), until David later carried it up to Jerusalem for its placement in the Temple his son would build.

Concerning the men of Beth-shemesh who were smitten for sacrilege (6:19), the Hebrew account says, "And he smote among the people seventy men, fifty thousand. . . ." That is not a proper Hebrew expression for the number 50,070. That figure is unreasonable, anyway; there wouldn't have been that many persons in the whole town. The "fifty thousand men" appears to be an added phrase, or gloss, and is possibly a scribal error. The Septuagint and Josephus both say "seventy men."

1 Samuel 7:3–17

Samuel brought about a reform and a rededication of all Israel unequalled since the days of Joshua. He gathered them in a great revival convocation at Mizpeh, a short distance north of his hometown of Ramah, to fast and make resolutions.

The Philistines wanted to crush any stirrings of Israelite nationalism or independence, so they invaded. However, under the inspired leadership of Samuel and with the help of the Lord, the Philistines were repulsed and subdued so that they did not harass Israel during the rest of Samuel's administration. After he was replaced by a king, however, Philistine depredations resumed.

Don't miss the brief record of Samuel's other services to his country told in verses 15–17. There will be others to note later in the account.

1 Samuel 8:1–5

As Samuel's benevolent rule wore on, no worthy successor was found. His sons were apparently not as bad as the sons of Eli, but yet as judges they could be corrupted by bribes. In any case, the elders, who were still the patriarchal leaders and representatives of the tribes of Israel, came together and asked for a king. One of the principal motivations behind it is indicated in the phrase "like all the nations." Because of incessant attacks from neighboring nations on all sides and the corrupt leadership of Samuel's sons, the elders of Israel saw it politically expedient to unify the tribes by having one man ruling over them and facing enemy armies with a united front.

In the spirit of a "peculiar" and a "holy" people, the Lord had wanted his covenant people to regard him as their King, assuring them, upon their faithfulness to him, that he would fight their battles. Nevertheless, he had foreseen the coming situation when Israel would desire a king "like as all the nations" (Deuteronomy 17:14). He counseled them about what to look for in the man who would lead them. The chosen leader was to be warned not to multiply silver and gold, or horses, or wives, any of which would turn his heart away. He was supposed to make a copy of the scriptures and study from them every day, and he must not lift up his heart above his brethren nor disregard the commandments (Deuteronomy 17:15–20).

1 Samuel 8:6–22

Samuel feared for Israel's freedom under a king, who could easily become an autocrat or tyrant. But in spite of his plain warnings of this danger, and his concept of the theocratic republic they should have retained, they insisted on a king, and the Lord instructed Samuel to grant them their request even if it was to their detriment (compare Mosiah 29:33–38). He comforted Samuel by telling him that Israel's rejection of wise counsel was a rejection not of him but of the Lord.

Note how the Lord's warning to his people, conveyed by Samuel, is composed of several sections each beginning with "he will take" (vv. 11–17). The king's unfair demands would inevitably be followed by the united protest of Israel, "ye shall cry out" (v. 18). It is almost impossible to find a king who would not be wholly self-centered, whose materialistic demands would not far exceed that which Israel was to consecrate to their Heavenly King. That is why the Book of Mormon emphasizes so strongly the idea that if it were possible to have just men occupy the throne, men who put

God first, it would be expedient to have kings (Mosiah 23:8; 29:13, 16). But that is not possible. Three sad stories of kingship follow in the books of Samuel and Kings—of Saul, David, and Solomon.

This speech of Samuel's against the institution of monarchy in Israel (vv. 10–20) was used by George Washington in rejecting the proposal that he become a king of the American colonies that had been freed from England through the Revolutionary War.

1 Samuel 9:1 to 10:16

Saul of the tribe of Benjamin (*Shaul ben Kish*) is introduced. He was called by prophecy, anointed to become king, and endowed with the Spirit of God which made a new man of him. The change was so dramatic that he was able to prophesy and thus surprise those who knew him before. Certainly, each of us is changed and made a new creature when the Lord's Spirit comes upon us. But we wonder also if this isn't the biblical writer hinting at Saul's true nature, what he was really like when he ignored the Spirit and refused to allow it to work with him.

Compare the parenthetical note in 1 Samuel 9:9 about the terms "prophet" and "seer" to Mosiah 8:15–17. Most Bible dictionaries and commentaries indicate that the change simply indicated an evolution of the prophetic function, but the passage in Mosiah shows that in their usage the term "seer" designated a greater breadth of activities than that of "prophet" only.

The Lord and Samuel were still determined to draw a distinction between the King and the king. The Lord was still to be considered their King, and Saul was to be anointed "captain over the people of Israel" (9:16; 10:1).

1 Samuel 10:17–27

Again Samuel gathered Israel at Mizpeh in a sort of coronation assembly. Saul's physical prowess was impressive and important, as was his humble spirit, shown by the fact that he was "hiding" when the time for coronation came. That spirit is also shown in the story in the next chapter of Samuel. It is interesting that many have humility when they first start out.

Samuel instructed the people about the nature of the kingdom as it was to be constituted and wrote his instructions "in a book" (v. 25). Though not a formal constitution as we understand the concept, it must have served as such. Recall also the prophetic instructions to Israelite kings in Deuteronomy 17:14–20. They were to rule by divine authority but not by divine right, as later conceived in other kingdoms. The confirming, sustaining voice of the people was an important factor as seen both here and later in the installation of kings Saul, David, Solomon, and Rehoboam.

1 Samuel 11:1–15

Saul met his first challenge with decisiveness and dispatch and achieved success, saving the transjordanian Israelites at Jabesh-Gilead. The Ammonite leader's condition had been to "thrust out all your right eyes" (v. 2). This would allow those Israelites to continue as good farmers, but they would be poor warriors because they would have no depth perception with only one eye.

Incidentally, in verse 8 we already see a subtle division between the northern tribes and the southern tribe of Judah. Eventually that rift would become permanent as two separate nations were formed.

Further qualities of Saul are in evidence: magnanimity toward his people and gratitude toward God. Unfortunately, the first signs of deterioration from this initial state appear all too soon in the stories that follow.

1 Samuel 12:1–25

Samuel's farewell address to Israel is here recorded. He reviewed their action in adopting a monarchy and was in effect given a vote of thanks for his leadership. The people even repented and confessed that having God as their King was best (vv. 12, 19). He reassured them, however, that if they would serve the Lord with all their heart, he would not forsake them. If they did wickedly and failed to serve the Lord, they had no guarantee.

The positive facets of Israel's behavior during Samuel's administration can best be seen by comparing this period to their spiritual condition described at the end of the book of Judges. However, they do not seem to have approached fulfilling their potential.

1 Samuel 13:1

The chronology is uncertain because the Hebrew text lacks information, including how old Saul was when he began to reign. Since he was a young man when he was first anointed to become king and later had a mature son serving as one of his leaders, some years must have elapsed between the time of his anointing and the time of his coronation or public inauguration. In the next generation the same thing happens to David: he is anointed as a boy but actually becomes king later, at age thirty; compare Jesus, the "son [descendant] of David," beginning his ministry at age thirty (see commentary at Luke 3:23–38 in Ogden and Skinner, *Four Gospels*).

1 Samuel 13:2–18

After two years of relative peace, Saul and Jonathan organized to restrain the ever-encroaching Philistines. Saul selected three thousand men and stationed them in the heart of his country at Michmash, Bethel, and Gibeah. Michmash is between Bethel and Gibeah in the tribal land of Benjamin (see Bible Map 4). The Philistines also had a garrison of soldiers right in the middle of the country at nearby Geba, which says something about their military objectives and strength at the time and the shakiness of the fledgling Israelite state. The establishment of an Israelite kingdom was seen by the Philistines as open defiance of their own attempted rule of the land. They wanted to do just as the Israelites had done—divide and conquer. If they could drive a wedge between the tribes of Joseph and the tribe of Judah (that is, take the central Benjamin plateau), they could dominate the hill country and severely reduce or destroy Israelite authority. They understood, just as Joshua did, the strategic importance of controlling the central hill country.

Jonathan led one contingent of his father's army against the Philistine garrison at Geba, which resulted in the Philistines sending up a punitive force (an innumerable host) to overthrow the Israelites. The men of Israel were terrified and hid themselves in the hills, in caves, in pits, and some even fled to Transjordan (vv. 6–7).

Saul was in Gilgal waiting for Samuel to arrive and offer sacrifices to the Lord. Saul grew impatient at Samuel's tardiness and decided to perform the offering himself. Now unfolds a serious flaw in Saul's leadership. Saul had begun his role as king as a model of humility; however, the increased attention given him helped him gain an exaggerated opinion of himself and his own importance. The problem with power is that once a person has it, he feels he must concentrate all his efforts on keeping it, or so it is widely believed. Worldly authority has a tendency to adopt an attitude that ecclesiastical authority is subordinate. This was the pitfall Saul fell into when he usurped priesthood authority in administering offerings in Samuel's absence. This act of priestcraft, combined with other acts of disobedience, caused the kingdom to be removed from him by the Lord. Saul forgot the real source of Israel's strength and who his real Master was.

Does this happen to some of us sometimes? Joseph Smith described rather pointedly: "We have learned by sad experience that it is the nature and disposition of almost all men, as soon as they get a little authority, as they suppose, they will immediately begin to exercise unrighteous dominion. Hence many are called, but few are chosen" (D&C 121:39–40).

Samuel told Saul he had acted foolishly and that he would soon be replaced on the throne (notice that verse 14 foreshadows David, a man after the Lord's own heart). Saul's replacement on the throne, however, had nothing to do with the worthiness of Jonathan, who would have been his natural successor, other things permitting. Whatever Saul's motivations, conditions continued to grow worse for him. The Philistines divided their forces into three groups of "spoilers" to destroy crops, cattle, homes, and harass the civilian population (vv. 17–18). These troops went out in three directions from the main Philistine camp at Michmash.

1 Samuel 13:19–23

The military disadvantages Israel suffered included the lack of metal armaments. It was even necessary for them to get metal farm implements from Philistine foundries and to have them sharpened by Philistine smiths. Though in times of peace the Philistines were willing to engage in peaceful trade with Israelites, they did not wish to teach them the arts and crafts involved in metalwork. Thus, while Saul and Jonathan had a sword or a spear, most of the others had only stone and wooden weapons.

1 Samuel 14:1–23

Hard pressed, Israel was in hopeless straits until Jonathan courageously decided that the Lord would help those who try rather than those who merely sit and wait. Jonathan, who like David in his early life greatly trusted in the Lord, called his armor bearer to accompany him in a surprise raid on the Philistine outpost on the opposite side of the canyon separating them from the Philistines. From his own camp at Geba, now held by Israel, the two bold Israelites set out to cross the deep canyon. Through his profound faith in God, Jonathan's private raid resulted in a rout of the Philistines.

1 Samuel 14:24–52

Saul, meanwhile, also desiring help from the Lord, proclaimed a fast and waited without acting. When he inquired of the Lord after Jonathan's raid as to whether he should follow up and break the Philistine power, he received no answer and concluded that this was because the Lord was angry with

Israel. Learning that Jonathan had in the heat of the battle broken the fast without knowing of the proclamation, he insisted that Jonathan be punished; that the Lord had helped Jonathan win a victory seems to have made no impression on Saul. How different he was from his former self when he once refused to kill any of the offenders after the Lord had wrought salvation in Israel in the affair at Jabesh-Gilead. However, the will of the people was stronger than the will of the king, and Jonathan's life was spared.

With the panic and disarray caused by Jonathan's surprise attack, the Philistines began a hasty retreat down the Beth-horon Pass, with Saul's forces, including some of the trembling Israelite soldiers now coming out of their hiding places, following hard on Philistine heels down into the Aijalon Valley.

"So Saul took the kingdom over Israel, and fought against all his enemies on every side, against Moab, and against the children of Ammon, and against Edom, and against the kings of Zobah [Syrians], and against the Philistines: and whithersoever he turned himself, he vexed them" (v. 47). See Bible Map 4 for the approximate limits of the kingdom of Saul.

1 Samuel 15:1–31

A Chinese proverb says that a man wrapped up in himself makes a mighty small package. As we have already seen with the incident of unauthorized sacrifice at Gilgal, when Saul was under pressure, he couldn't maintain personal discipline. He was always trying to excuse himself, blame others, or cover up; he was not honest with himself. Again, at the commandment to annihilate the Amalekite peoples in the Negev region, Saul's tragic flaw became apparent. Instead of utterly destroying as he was instructed, he thought it best to spare some of the animals and even the king. Samuel listened to Saul's feeble excuses and then made it clear to him that the Lord had rejected him as Israel's king. "To obey is better than sacrifice"—the Lord wants exact obedience.

Verse 22 is one of the greatest lessons of the Old Testament. Saul himself recognized the root cause of his disobedience: "I feared the people, and obeyed their voice" (v. 24). Pride overtook him and contributed to his downfall. Do we worry, at times, more about what others think of us than what God thinks of us? Though Saul admitted he had sinned, the Lord did not seem to wipe the slate clean; he didn't forgive the king. That is because there was no true repentance. Saul admitted his misbehavior for the sake of appearances: "I have sinned: yet honour me now, I pray thee, *before the elders of my people*" (v. 30; emphasis added).

1 Samuel 15:32–33

This is a strange scene. Apparently the word translated "delicately" has suffered an interchange (metathesis) of letters in Hebrew and should have been a different word meaning "bound" or "in bonds." Samuel's wielding the sword himself to "hew in pieces" the enemy "before the Lord," as most victors did in giving thanks to their gods, is a surprising picture. Perhaps the writer described this execution of a king who had killed many Israelites in terms of the context of the times. "Before the Lord" does not mean that the deed was done as a sacrifice to the Lord of the life of the vanquished king, because human sacrifice was never required by the Lord.

1 Samuel 15:34–35

The consequences are tragic to all involved here. The use of the phrase "the Lord repented" was clarified previously in connection with Genesis 6:6. Recall that the Hebrew word is *nikham,* meaning basically "to sigh"; hence, it expressed the idea "to grieve" or "to regret." Verse 29 of this chapter teaches that the Lord is not a man; therefore he does not lie nor does he need to repent. A common problem in translating Hebrew is that it is a "picturesque" language, and when it is translated into the more specific languages such as Greek or English, the context has to suggest the specific connotations. Only an inspired translator could be sure that he faithfully rendered the intended meaning of the original author. The Joseph Smith Translation of the last line of verse 35 is "and the Lord rent the kingdom from Saul whom he had made king over Israel."

1 Samuel 16:1–13

Samuel's regret over this tragic deterioration of the relationship between the monarch and the Lord may have left him without hope until the Lord instructed him to provide a successor to Saul. The feelings ran deeper than one might suppose from superficial evidences; Samuel knew that Saul was possessive of his status as king and sensitive to the fact that Samuel had said that the Lord had rejected him and already chosen a successor "after his [the Lord's] own heart" (13:14) who was "better than" Saul (15:28). Therefore, the anointing of a new king was to be kept secret.

Samuel was instructed to go to the little town of Bethlehem and seek out a man named Jesse, a man destined to become the ancestor of all subsequent Judahite kings and the Messiah. This journey represented a turning point in the Israelite kingdom. Now, instead of a Benjamin-based monarchy, there would be a Judah-based monarchy.

Seven of Jesse's sons were paraded before Samuel, but none of them was to be anointed the next king. This episode provides the context for one of the most important verses in all of scripture about how the Lord evaluates us: "Look not on his countenance, or on the height of his stature," the Lord advised his prophet, "for the Lord seeth not as man seeth; for man looketh on the outward appearance [Hebrew, "on the eyes"], but the Lord looketh on the heart" (v. 7). David, the youngest, was brought in from the shepherds' fields and anointed. David was later called in to Saul's court to soothe the king's troubled spirit with music.

Right at the beginning of his story, the historian gives us an interesting character sketch of David: he was "cunning in playing, and a mighty valiant man, and a man of war, and prudent in matters, and a comely person, and the Lord [was] with him" (v. 18). The "Spirit of the Lord" came upon David, as it had upon Saul after his anointing (10:16).

1 Samuel 16:14–23

By contrast, the Spirit of the Lord left Saul, and an evil spirit came upon him. None of the usual explanations of the curious phrase "evil spirit from the Lord" seems satisfactory. In the amended text by Joseph Smith, however, it reads "an evil spirit *which was not of* the Lord." Ironically, it was because of this bad spirit, or depression, that David came to serve Saul as a well-recommended musician who could soothe Saul's troubled soul. David also became the armor bearer of Saul and was loved and trusted by him at first.

1 Samuel 17:1–58

The war story of David and Goliath is one of the best-known stories in the Old Testament. The arrangement whereby the fate of the two armies could be determined by the outcome of a single battle between two champions was common anciently in many lands. David was stimulated to action by the tolerance, or the fear, shown by the Israelites for the blasphemous challenger, Goliath. David's confidence that something could be done was based upon his experiences as a young man in meeting predatory animals and in being blessed by the Lord to overcome them. Other men, his brothers, and King Saul were all affected by David's confidence. That Saul showed confidence in David and the Lord is not surprising; he had been a very religious man and still was, in his better moments.

David rejected Saul's armor because he had not "proved" it. The word used here and translated "proved" is the word used in Exodus 17:2 when the people "proved," or "tempted," the Lord; it means "tested" or "tried." David used what he had "proved": his sling and stones and his faith in the Lord.

The concept of the covenant relationship between Israel and the Lord is again mentioned, as it often was in the books of Moses. David believed that if Israel did what was required, God would do his part to save Israel, for his own sake as well as for Israel's sake (vv. 45, 47).

It is helpful to look at the story in its geographical and political context. The Israelites and Philistines were again at war. Philistine penetration into the hill country north of Gibeah had been checked, but now they threatened to push into Israelite territory again, this time from the west, through the lowlands (Hebrew, *Shephelah*). Their objective was to control the lowlands, establishing a base for an assault into the hills. The first three verses give us considerable detail about the relative positions of the armed forces. The two armies faced each other across the Elah Valley. This valley and the valleys of Aijalon, Sorek, Guvrin, and Lachish—important valleys in the Shephelah, the buffer zone and battleground between Judah and her enemies—all run west to east from the coast to the hill country (see Bible Map 10). The Philistines were encamped between Shochoh and Azekah, on the south side of the valley. The place called Ephes-dammim, meaning literally "no blood" or "end of blood," is unknown. Verse 3 says, "the Philistines stood on a mountain on the one side, and Israel stood on a mountain on the other side: and there was a valley between them."

Goliath was a giant from the Philistine town of Gath, a few miles to the west. According to the measurements given here, he was over nine feet tall, though the Septuagint puts Goliath's height at four cubits and a span, which is something like 6 feet 9 inches. He taunted and harassed Saul and his armies for a month and a half. Finally Jesse asked his youngest son, David, to hike down to the battlefront, twenty miles away, with food for his three oldest brothers, who were soldiers in Saul's army. Apparently soldiers were supplied by family members.

You know the rest of the story. David, sling in hand, selected five smooth stones from the brook in the valley of Elah, one stone for performance and perhaps four for confidence.

The brook runs along close to the northern side of the valley, near where the Israelites were camped. David took his ammunition, crossed the brook, and went out to confront the giant bully who had been defying the armies of the living God. With trust in God and confidence in the anointing and blessing he had received from Samuel, David went out and slew Goliath.

To verify and be impressed with the Bible's reliability and accuracy in connection with this famous story, we should mention something about the typical response from "desk scholars," who have never been on location.

Some individuals try to explain away prophecy and miracles by ascribing to biblical stories demeaning terms such as legend, myth, fairy tale, etc. For example, Auerbach, in his book *Mimesis,* labels this early episode in David's life as "purely legendary and traditional. . . . In the stories of David the historical report predominates. Here too, much that is legendary still remains, as for example the story of David and Goliath. . . . Now the difference between legend and history is in most cases easily perceived by a reasonably experienced reader. It is a difficult matter, requiring careful historical and philological training, to distinguish the true from the synthetic or the biased in a historical presentation; but it is easy to separate the historical from the legendary in general. Their structure is different. Even where the legendary does not immediately *betray itself by elements of the miraculous,* by the repetition of well-known standard motives, typical patterns and themes, through *neglect of clear details of time and place,* and the like, it is generally quickly recognizable by its composition. It runs far too smoothly. . . . Legend arranges its material in a simple and straightforward way; it *detaches it from its contemporary historical context*" (18–19; emphasis added).

Auerbach is pointedly wrong in his characterization of this David and Goliath episode. It is not presented with "neglect of clear details of time and place" and definitely does not detach itself from "its contemporary historical context." There is considerable and specific detail regarding time and place, and the context was the Philistines' constantly trying to penetrate and overrun the hill country. It was incumbent upon someone—on this occasion, David—to stop them. The story fits. The Bible knows what it's talking about.

Another impressive lesson about this historic encounter is often overlooked. In Israel there was also a giant to face Goliath—the king himself. He is said to have been a head taller than all the men of Israel. It was Saul who should have gone against Goliath to deliver Israel, but by that time he had lost the Spirit and had no courage. So a young man named David went forth. And the rest is history.

Ultimately, the story of David and Goliath demonstrates a number of "thus we see" principles.

- Israel was not to fear her enemies but to trust in God (Exodus 14:13–14; Numbers 14:9; Joshua 10:8; 2 Chronicles 20:17). Thus we see (v. 11) that Saul's and Israel's great fear illustrated a loss of faith in the covenant promises of Jehovah (Exodus 23:22; Deuteronomy 3:22; 20:1–4).
- Though David was young and accused of pride by those older, he spoke with boldness and faith (vv. 26–28). Thus we see that age does not guarantee wisdom or courage.
- The report of David's rallying cry helps us to see that there is a time to stand up and be counted (v. 29).
- David recognized the Lord's hand in his life (v. 37), teaching us that we may likewise see His hand in our lives.
- David would not go out to battle with armor he had not "proved," or tested (v. 39). Thus we see that we should not trust in things that we have not proven, and certainly not the things of the world.
- Though "David prevailed over the Philistine with a sling" (v. 50), David knew it was the Lord who

had delivered Goliath into his hands (v. 46). Thus we see that if we try our best to live righteously, be humble, and go forth with faith in God, we can accomplish great and amazing things.

- Finally, we see that the power of youth must never be underestimated (v. 42).

All of us have Goliaths in our lives, as President Spencer W. Kimball once said. But with the Lord's help we can conquer them (see Kimball, *Ensign,* Nov. 1974, 79–83; see also Thomas S. Monson, *Ensign,* Jan. 1987, 2–5).

1 Samuel 18:1–4

Here we have the beginning of the famous covenant of loving brotherhood and friendship between David and Jonathan, who would ordinarily have been rivals. We are reminded of Joseph Smith's statement that friendship is a grand fundamental principle of Mormonism, designed to revolutionize and civilize the world, cause wars and contentions to cease, and allow men to become friends and brothers (*Teachings of the Prophet Joseph Smith,* 316). Even when David's anointing to become king later was made known, no rivalry resulted, though Jonathan was next in line for the throne through his father, Saul. It appears that Jonathan was already making a gesture of transferring any claim he had upon kingship over to David by giving him certain garments and accoutrements (v. 4; compare 23:17). The motto of both Jonathan and David seems to have been "service, not status." This chapter provides a profound contrast between father and son, Saul and Jonathan.

1 Samuel 18:5–30

Saul placed David over his armies, and great praise was heaped upon David because of his military prowess. Saul became insanely jealous of him, and David's life was in jeopardy for some time. He became a fugitive from Saul's rage. Three different verses note that during this time David "behaved himself wisely" (vv. 5, 14–15).

Saul devised a plan to bring about David's death, but David seemed quite unsuspecting. Indeed, he only protested his unworthiness to be the king's son-in-law—the possibility of which had been offered in the plan. Later he accepted another daughter of Saul, taking Saul's intended trap as a worthy challenge and killing twice the number of enemy soldiers that had been required. Thereupon the Philistine lords fled, and David's reputation improved even more. The frankness of verse 29 is chilling: "Saul became David's enemy continually."

1 Samuel 19:1–24

The story of Saul and David would make an extraordinary Shakespearean tragedy. It has all the elements of nobility, power, jealousy, romance, murderous ambitions, chase scenes, sorcery, suicide, all woven into a believable plot.

When Saul took open measures to kill David, Jonathan dissuaded him, and David was temporarily restored to favor. The great irony associated with Jonathan's question, "Wilt thou sin against innocent blood" (v. 5), is that though David's innocent blood was saved, he himself later shed Uriah's innocent blood (2 Samuel 11:14–15). Notice what brought the evil spirit upon Saul again (vv. 8–9). Here the Joseph Smith Translation declares that the evil spirit was not of God (as in 16:14–16; 18:10). David's wife was devoted to him in spite of the enmity of her father, Saul. Unfortunately, however, her risking herself to save David brought about a spiteful action by Saul, who married her off to another man after David had escaped.

The following list gives places where David stopped and also events that occurred while he fled from Saul:

1. He was at Ramah with Samuel (chapter 19).
2. He was at Gibeah with Jonathan (chapter 20).
3. He was at Nob with priests (chapter 21).
4. Saul ordered a massacre of the priests at Nob (chapter 22).
5. David rescued Keilah from the Philistines, and Saul

pursued him. David went to Ziph with Jonathan.
He then went to Maon (chapter 23).

6. En Gedi is where David had a chance to kill Saul. A
place called "the hold" is mentioned. The Hebrew
text says they "went up into the metsuda," which is
likely what today we call Masada (chapter 24).

7. David went to the village of Carmel, and the episodes with Nabal and Abigail unfolded there (chapter 25).

8. David went to Ziph, and Saul pursued him (chapter
26).

9. David went to Ziklag, among the Philistines (chapter 27).

David next took refuge at Samuel's home in Ramah,
where strange spiritual phenomena saved him for a time from
Saul's emissaries and even from Saul himself. A religious exercise of singing or chanting praises to God was called "prophesying"; see 1 Samuel 10:1–16.

1 Samuel 20:1–42

David and Jonathan made a lasting covenant of mutual
benevolence. Jonathan offered to do anything David required,
so they planned signals to indicate danger for David. Their
covenant was made in full knowledge that David was the heir-
apparent to the kingship, which Jonathan approved in spite
of his father's outrage. Mutual trust and personal regard, not
sentiment or politics, were at the foundation of their covenant.
Jonathan was a truly great soul who understood the nature of
true friendship. He knew that friendship involved loyalty and
seeking the welfare of the other. Jonathan was charitable and
involved the Lord in his friendship with David (vv. 8–17).

1 Samuel 21:1–9

David went to Nob to get help from Ahimelech, the
priest. The shrine at Nob, where a considerable number of the
priestly line of Eli was established, seems to have been a sort
of substitute for the former facilities at Shiloh, although the

only accoutrements at Nob were the priestly ephod and the table of shewbread. Jesus later used the example of David's emergency consumption of the hallowed bread to ridicule the Pharisees' condemnation of his disciples picking and eating grain on the Sabbath day (Matthew 12:1–4).

Goliath's sword, obtained by David from the shrine, must have been kept there as a memento of his triumph in the name of the Lord earlier in his life. The priest at Nob did not suspect that David was a refugee from the king.

1 Samuel 21:10–15

It may seem strange that David could take refuge with the Philistine enemy at Gath, but since Saul was the enemy of both Achish and David, Achish hoped to use David against Saul. When the precarious relationship became really suspect, David had to contrive a way to be deemed harmless so he could flee.

1 Samuel 22:1–5

From his "hold," or "stronghold," in the hill country between Judah and the Philistine-dominated coastal plain, David sent his parents to find sanctuary and safety from Saul in Moab. The grace of the king of Moab in receiving them is surprising. Whether the fact that David's great-grandmother Ruth had come from there had any influence on the king is not known. More likely, the Moabite king, like Achish of Gath, was willing to take a chance on befriending David due to his prowess and his potential as Israel's future leader, as well as to his enmity toward Saul.

David was gaining a following as he attempted to flee from Saul's irrational enmity. There was also prophetic guidance available to him through a prophet named Gad.

1 Samuel 22:6–23

The Edomite mercenary who gained Saul's favor by betraying the fact that David had received refuge at Nob is typical intrigue. Saul bitterly resented that his Israelite people and even his own son were more loyal to David than to him. In unreasoning rage, Saul caused the Edomite to slay the whole house of priests, because his Israelite footmen refused to lift the sword against priests. Someone must have joined in the massacre of the village of Nob because surely the Edomite could not have killed everyone by himself. It seems that Saul was so emotionally unbalanced that he sought to kill any who showed any kindness to David.

Assuming the blame for inciting Saul's wrath against Abiathar's house, David apparently tried to compensate for Abiathar's loss as best he could.

1 Samuel 23:1–18

David was close to the Lord and used divine guidance in all major decisions and actions. One example is his decision to help the village of Keilah, a town in the territory of Judah, and later his decision to flee from there lest he be given over into Saul's hands.

How and when it was made known to Saul and Jonathan that David would be the next king has not been told, but here it is seen that it was indeed known. The gallantry of Jonathan is again impressive. As verses 16–18 also make clear, Jonathan not only put David's interests before his own, just as he put the Lord's interests first, but strengthened his friend by helping him to find strength in the Lord.

1 Samuel 23:19–29

Apparently there were people even in David's home tribe of Judah who would have still showed loyalty to the king by betraying David's whereabouts to Saul. The example here is the community of Ziph, a village southeast of Hebron. However, another Philistine raid diverted Saul's attention for a time, and David and his band of men retreated eastward to one of the canyons flowing into the Dead Sea.

1 Samuel 24:1–22

The famous episode of David's refusal to slay Saul at En-Gedi shows his integrity and ethical principles in resisting that opportunity and in resisting also the encouragement of his men to slay the king. Saul's repentance upon learning of David's respect for "the anointed of the Lord" was probably sincere, even though it did not last.

1 Samuel 25:1–44

After a long life of dedication to the Lord, the great prophet Samuel died and was buried in his hometown of Ramah. Friction arose between David and a rich man named Nabal, from whom he had requested supplies for his men. David had done no harm and had actually given protection to owners of property and flocks, so he might expect some compensation by way of supplies. But Nabal refused David's request.

Except for the wisdom and finesse of Abigail, wife of Nabal (a man whose name means "foolish" in Hebrew), there could have been some violence. She interceded on David's behalf. Her praise of David and her plea are quite poetic. David's response, "I have accepted thy person" (v. 35), meant "I accept you and your message."

The description of Nabal's death may suggest that he suffered a stroke. David lost no time in rewarding Abigail with a proposal of marriage soon after Nabal died, and Abigail did not hesitate to accept David's offer. The marriage must have improved David's financial assets.

1 Samuel 26:1–25

The beginning of this chapter contains several parallels to 23:19–29 in movements and locations mentioned, although there are more details in this account. David once again spared Saul's life. One gem is David's reasoning that only the Lord could justly remove a man whom the Lord had appointed. David's dramatic plea to Saul was again well expressed. Saul accepted this appeal temporarily.

1 Samuel 27:1–12

This is another episode in which David took refuge with the Philistine king, Achish, of Gath (recall 21:10–15). This time David seems to have felt secure for a long time with him.

David's integrity was not such that it prevented his deceiving his Philistine host concerning his activities while under the scourge of being a fugitive from Saul. Remember that the Bible does not merely tell the exemplary activities of its characters; it tells frankly their faults as well as their virtues and sometimes leaves the reader to judge as to which is which. That being said, however, the Near Eastern mind-set sometimes did not think in terms of acting *deceptively* but rather of acting *cleverly*—in this case cleverly enough to avoid Saul's constant harassment.

1 Samuel 28:1–2

When David was placed in the awkward position of being aligned alongside Achish to go to battle against his fellow Israelites, he managed to respond in such a way that Achish made him "keeper of head," apparently his personal bodyguard.

1 Samuel 28:3–25

Here is the pathetic story of King Saul as he prepared for his last battle. He could get no guidance from legitimate avenues of communication with the Lord, including the use of the Urim and Thummim, so he turned to diviners, whose activities were violations of the law of Moses and who had been banished by Saul himself in better times (see Exodus 22:18; Deuteronomy 18:10). The phrase "familiar spirit" (v. 7) in Hebrew means literally "skin-bottle," or necromancer (see commentary at Leviticus 20:1–27). Webster's 1828 dictionary defines necromancy as "the art of revealing future events by means of a pretended communication with the dead." So a true revelation from God was not and could not be received through the spiritualist medium. It seems more likely that the medium and her "spirit" communicants deceived Saul into thinking the dead Samuel had responded to his plea.

President Charles W. Penrose of the First Presidency more than a century ago wrote: "It is beyond rational belief that such persons could at any period . . . invoke the spirits of departed servants or handmaidens of the Lord. They are not at the beck and call of witches, wizards, diviners, or necromancers. Pitiable indeed would be the condition of spirits in paradise if they were under any such control" (*Improvement Era,* May 1898, 498).

The gloomy prediction was devastating to Saul. The medium's description of "gods ascending out of the earth" suggests that she had a vision of a whole concourse of spirits in this momentous séance. On the other hand, the Prophet Joseph Smith changed the phrase from "gods ascending out of the earth" to "*the words of Samuel* ascending out of the earth." Verse 11 was also changed from "Bring me up Samuel" to "Bring me up *the words of* Samuel" (JST), as in our present verse 20. If the forces of evil wished to bring about Saul's final destruction, things were well calculated to accomplish it. The apparition reminded Saul of his rejection and his hopeless situation.

A pathetic contrast to his former self, the fear-racked and emaciated Saul accepted food under some compulsion from the compassionate witch-woman and then went his way in the night to his doom.

1 Samuel 29:1–11

Though David had won the confidence of Achish, other princes of the Philistine confederacy were skeptical of his loyalty to their cause, and he was fortunately not permitted to go into battle against Saul and Israel.

1 Samuel 30:1–31

While David was away, Amalekites invaded the Negev Desert and took his town of Ziklag (see Bible Map 4 for a possible location), burned it, and carried away captive the wives and children of David and his men. David and six hundred men pursued the Amalekites southward, most of them crossing the Brook Besor (see Bible Map 10). They found an Amalekite's Egyptian servant lying half dead, not having eaten nor drunk anything for three days, and revived him with food and drink. David learned from the Egyptian slave that the Amalekites had raided all parts of the Negev. Each time the word "south" occurs in the story, the Hebrew word is *Negev*, sometimes erroneously spelled "Negeb."

Upon pursuing and routing the Amalekite raiding parties, David recovered his wives and all his property and carried great quantities of spoils back to Ziklag. While distributing spoils to his men, he was wise enough to save some and send them to his friends and the elders of Judah.

Some of David's soldiers had been too exhausted to accomplish the long forced march, and David established the generous principle that "they also served who sat and waited," keeping watch over the camp while the others fought.

1 Samuel 31:1–6 (1 Chronicles 10:1–6)

Now we return to the battle between the Israelites and Philistines on the slopes of Mount Gilboa, twenty-five miles south-southwest of the Sea of Galilee. The Philistines had penetrated as far north and east as the eastern end of the Jezreel Valley, their deepest incursion into Israelite territory in history, and they were winning the battle against Israel. Hard-pressed, seriously wounded, and with an armor bearer who, like David, refused to raise his hand against the Lord's anointed, Saul became one of the Bible's few cases of suicide. The loyal armor bearer even followed him in death, as did Saul's three sons. Saul's concern over the Philistines' possible "abuse" of him was justified. It was not uncommon for foreign armies to mutilate the corpse of a high-ranking enemy. A slightly different account of Saul's death is found in 2 Samuel 1:1–10.

1 Samuel 31:7–13 (1 Chronicles 10:7–14)

The Philistines discovered the bodies of Saul and his sons among the dead and hanged them on the city wall of Beth-shan (see Bible Map 10). The dead king's armor was placed in the temple of Ashtaroth. This temple, built by Ramses II of Egypt in the thirteenth century B.C., was apparently used continuously by various conquerors of Beth-shan into this Philistine period, just past 1000 B.C. The city, including the ruins of this temple, was excavated by the University of Pennsylvania from 1921 to 1930, and more was excavated later in the twentieth century.

We should note the death of Jonathan, who among all the characters of this and the two succeeding generations, was one of the best and least sinful people appearing in this period of the biblical record. He is certainly one of the least heralded characters in the Bible. He was true to David while still trying to honor his father. He seems to have been above jealousy and was not threatened by David's future kingship. During this historic period, Jonathan seems to have been one of the few truly noble and great ones.

In grateful memory of Saul's service to them in the beginning of his reign, the people of Jabesh-Gilead heroically retrieved the bodies, burnt them, gave their bones a proper burial, and observed a proper period of mourning. The men of Jabesh-Gilead had not forgotten how Saul had come to their defense when threatened by Ammonites (1 Samuel 11).

So ends the first book of Samuel. Obviously it was not all written by Samuel, for his death was recounted before the end of the first book and the second book of Samuel follows. Perhaps the books covering an era influenced by him were given his name, much as the plates of Nephi continued to be written upon long after Nephi's death.

PSALMS

Our English word *psalms* derives from the Greek *psalmoi,* meaning "sacred songs sung to musical accompaniment," and is a translation of the Hebrew plural noun *tehillim,* usually rendered "songs of praise" (Abbott-Smith, *Greek Lexicon,* 487). The book of Psalms, also called the Psalter, was ancient Israel's hymnbook. Specific Hebrew designations of various individual psalms found in their opening ascriptions further suggest ways they were to be used in Israelite worship. Some bear the designation *shir* (vocally performed song, or ode), while others (fifty-seven in the Masoretic text) are called *mismor* (melody, sacred song accompanied with an instrument). Still others are left simply as *tehillah* (singular of *tehillim*). According to Jewish tradition, the psalms were sung in front of the Tabernacle and, later on, upon the steps of the Jerusalem Temple. All the singers, or chanters, were Levites; while the priests, or *kohanim,* from the Levitical family of Aaron, accompanied the songs with instruments.

The book of Psalms is a collection of different sets of hymns compiled over the centuries. In its final form, the Hebrew version of the Psalms, from which the King James Version of the Bible ultimately derives, contained 150 psalms. Psalms is the longest book in the Old Testament (our LDS edition is ninety-seven pages; the longest prophetic book, Isaiah, is eighty pages). Other psalms were not included in the final edition of the Masoretic Text, the traditional Hebrew text, and thus were not considered for inclusion in the King James Bible. Scholars see five "books" of psalms within our

414

present book of Psalms, our Psalter, perhaps intended anciently to imitate the Pentateuch, or five books of Moses.

Above all else, from first to last, the psalms are poetry. Therefore, before examining selections of these ancient song-poems, or lyric hymns, which are some of the world's great literature, a few notes about Hebrew poetry in general are in order (see Bible Dictionary, "Psalms"). All biblical books contain some poetic imagery and figurative language that stimulate sensory experiences in our imagination. Poetry is a unique, extraordinary use of language. It is more concentrated or compressed than prose and more artistic. Poetry conveys meaning with figurative expressions and concrete images. Consider, for example, these well-known images: "the apple of the eye" (Psalm 17:8), "angels' food" (78:25), "at their wits' end" (107:27), and "fruit of the womb" (127:3).

Certain terms used in the Psalms and throughout the Old Testament need a little explanation. For example, the word *shew*, as we have already seen, is the King James English spelling of the modern word *show*, and it should be pronounced "show." Compare *sew*, which is also pronounced in modern English with a long "o." The verb *fear* often means in scripture not so much to tremble at something frightening but to "reverence," "respect," or "honor." The biblical term *terrible* has quite a different meaning from its modern meaning; for example, verses 3 and 5 in Psalm 66 read: "Say unto God, How terrible art thou in thy works!" and "Come and see the works of God: he is terrible in his doing toward the children of men." Rather than meaning "horrible," "dreadful," or "frightful," *terrible,* in some Old Testament passages, means "wonderful" or "awesome."

It is evident, then, that some English words have changed meaning over the centuries. The footnotes in the LDS edition of the Bible will in many cases help identify alternative usages.

The Psalms contain praises, prayers, laments, blessings,

vows, and exultations. They include much thanksgiving, honoring the mortal king and the eternal King, and acknowledging wisdom, prophecy, and the judgments of God. Quite a few were written by King David.

One of the most prominent features of Hebrew poetry, as already noted in Genesis 4:17–24 and Exodus 15:1–19, is the pattern, or form, called parallelism. Most Hebrew poetry is written in this verse form, involving the repetition of words or thoughts in parallel or successive lines, with the two or more parts somehow balancing each other in order to give additional emphasis to the original thought. The various forms of parallelism are synonymous (same or similar), antithetic (opposite), synthetic (completing or complimentary), and climactic (building to a climax).

Following are examples of synonymous parallelism, the most common form:

The heavens declare the glory of God;
and the firmament sheweth his handywork.
(Psalm 19:1)

The Lord is my light and my salvation; whom shall I fear?
the Lord is the strength of my life; of whom shall I be
afraid? (Psalm 27:1)

I will praise thee, O Lord, among the people:
I will sing unto thee among the nations.
(Psalm 57:9)

God is greatly to be feared in the assembly of the saints,
and to be had in reverence of all them that are about him.
(Psalm 89:7)

Following are examples of antithetic parallelism, which expresses a contrasting or opposite thought:

Weeping may endure for a night,
but joy cometh in the morning.
(Psalm 30:5)

For evildoers shall be cut off:
but those that wait upon the Lord,
they shall inherit the earth.
(Psalm 37:9)

The words of his mouth were smoother than butter,
but war was in his heart:
his words were softer than oil,
yet were they drawn swords.
(Psalm 55:21)

Following are examples of synthetic parallelism, which expands on, completes, or supplements the original thought:

I cried unto the Lord with my voice,
and he heard me out of his holy hill.
(Psalm 3:4)

The law of the Lord is perfect, converting the soul:
the testimony of the Lord is sure, making wise the
    simple.
The statutes of the Lord are right, rejoicing the heart:
the commandment of the Lord is pure, enlightening
    the eyes.
The fear of the Lord is clean, enduring for ever:
the judgments of the Lord are true and righteous
    altogether
(Psalm 19:7–9)

An incomparable example of climactic parallelism comes from verse 31 of Isaiah 40, one of the most beautiful chapters in the Bible:

They that wait upon the Lord shall renew their strength;
they shall mount up with wings as eagles;
they shall run, and not be weary;
and they shall walk, and not faint.

Various themes are found throughout the Psalms: praise for God's greatness, gratitude for the wonders of Creation, exhortations to righteous living, the desire to come into God's presence, petitions for redress of wrongs committed by the wicked against the righteous, gratitude for God's watch-care over Israel, acknowledgment and awe of God's power, and so forth. The most important focus is on the Messiah.

MESSIANIC PSALMS

Just like hymns today, many psalms express messianic sentiments, some even prophesying of the Savior's life and ministry and foreshadowing specific events during his life. Of this Jesus himself stated: "All things must be fulfilled, which were written in the law of Moses, and in the prophets, and *in the psalms,* concerning me" (Luke 24:44; emphasis added). Consider, for example, the following psalmic prophecies and their fulfillment:

Psalm	Prophecy	Fulfillment
2:7	"Thou art my Son; this day have I begotten thee."	Hebrews 1:5; Acts 13:33. No other being is the Son of God, only Jesus Christ, as early apostles testified.
16:10	"Thou wilt not . . . suffer thine Holy One to see corruption."	Acts 2:31–32; 13:34–45. The Savior's flesh did not see corruption; he was raised up in the Resurrection.
22:1	"My God, my God, why hast thou forsaken me?"	Matthew 27:46. Jesus asked the Father why he had forsaken him.

Psalm	Prophecy	Fulfillment
22:7–8	"All they that see me laugh me to scorn: . . . they shake the head, saying, He trusted on the Lord . . . : let him deliver him, seeing he delighted in him."	Matthew 27:39–43. Jesus was mocked.
22:16	"They pierced my hands and my feet."	Mark 15:25. Jesus was crucified.
22:18	"They part my garments among them, and cast lots upon my vesture."	Matthew 27:35. The soldiers cast lots for Christ's clothes.
31:5	"Into thine hand I commit my spirit."	Luke 23:46. Jesus commended his spirit to the Father and died.
34:20	"He keepeth all his bones: not one of them is broken."	John 19:33–36. None of Jesus' bones was broken.
41:9; 55:12–14	"Yea, mine own familiar friend in whom I trusted, which did eat of my bread, hath lifted up his heel against me."	John 13:18, 21. Jesus was betrayed by a friend.
69:8	"I am become a stranger unto my brethren, and an alien unto my mother's children."	John 1:11; 7:5. Jesus was not received by his own people.
69:20	"Reproach hath broken my heart; and I am full of heaviness: and I looked for some to take pity, but there was none; and for comforters, but I found none."	Mark 14:32–41. Jesus suffered alone in Gethsemane.
69:21	"In my thirst they gave me vinegar to drink."	John 19:28–30. Jesus was given vinegar for his thirst.
91:11–12	"For he shall give his angels charge over thee, to keep thee in all thy ways. They shall bear thee up in their hands, lest thou dash thy foot against a stone."	Matthew 4:6; Luke 4:10. Satan quoted this passage to Jesus when tempting him.

Psalm	Prophecy	Fulfillment
107:23–30	"They that go down to the sea in ships . . . ; these see the works of the Lord, and his wonders in the deep. . . . Then they cry unto the Lord in their trouble, and he bringeth them out of their distresses. He maketh the storm a calm, so that the waves thereof are still."	Matthew 8:23–27. Jesus calmed the winds and the waves when the apostles were greatly distressed.
110:4	"Thou art a priest for ever after the order of Melchizedek.	Hebrews 5:8–10. Jesus was the great high priest.
118:22	"The stone which the builders refused is become the head stone of the corner."	Matthew 21:42; Ephesians 2:20. Jesus was the stone who was rejected but who became the chief cornerstone.
118:26	"Blessed be he that cometh in the name of the Lord."	Matthew 21:9. Jesus was heralded as the messianic King at his triumphal entry into Jerusalem with these very words.

THE PRESENCE OF GOD

Another significant theme in Psalms of great interest to Latter-day Saints is the expressed belief that one who was pure and worthy could come into the presence of God in the Temple and, in fact, be rewarded by a face-to-face meeting with God in his holy House (see Barker, *Temple Themes*, 135–49). "Seeking the face/presence of the Lord had been at the heart of the temple [beliefs and practices]," and the Psalter reflected this core message (Barker, *Great High Priest*, 6).

This should not surprise us; after all, we know that a profound connection exists between the Temple and many psalms, as scholars both in and out of the LDS community have noted. "Many of the Psalms . . . though also sung at home or in the synagogue, . . . were originally designed or later adapted for use in (or in connection with) the Temple"

(Welch, *Sermon on the Mount,* 43). More to the point, another scholar has stated flatly that "the Psalms were the hymns of the Temple" (Barker, *Gate of Heaven,* 45). Thus, we should expect to find some discussion of one of the Temple's central purposes—bringing worshipers into God's presence—in certain ancient hymns of Israel that were composed in or for the Temple. Psalm 55:14 contains a sentence that epitomizes the glory and beauty of earnestly seeking God in the Temple experience: "We took sweet counsel together, and walked unto the house of God in company." The Spanish translation of that verse, dating from half a century before the King James Version, is even better: *Juntos comunicábamos dulcemente los secretos y andábamos en amistad en la casa de Dios* ("Together we sweetly communicated the secrets, and we walked in friendship in the House of God"). Psalms that exhibit this profound theme of Temple worship include 11, 15, 17, 21, 24, 27, and 63 (see commentary on these psalms below).

MUSICAL FEATURES IN THE PSALMS

Hebrew notations are in alphabetical order. Many meanings are uncertain, but following are some possibilities.

- Aijeleth Shahar (22): Name of psalm's melody
- Alamoth (46): Female voices or high musical instruments
- Al-taschith (57–59, 75): "Do not destroy"—a song title or melody
- Asaph (50, 73–83): One of the Tabernacle/Temple choir directors
- Gittith (8, 81, 84): Musical instrument from Gath or a vintage song
- Hallelujah (many): Literally, "Praise ye Jehovah" or "Praise ye the Lord"
- Higgaion (9): Interlude
- Jeduthun (39, 62): One of the Tabernacle/Temple choir directors

- Jonath-ele-mrechokim (56): "The dove of them that are distant"—a song title
- Mahalath (53): Name of a melody, or an instrument
- Mahalath Leannoth (88): "Sickness to Afflict"—a melody
- Maschil (many): A didactic poem, or a musical instrument
- Michtam (16, 56–59): A style of poem or musical title
- Muth-labben (9): A melody or tune for the psalm
- Neginah (61): A stringed instrument
- Neginoth (4, 54–55, 67, 76): Stringed instruments
- Nehiloth (5): Flutes or wind instruments
- Selah (in 71 psalms): Possibly indicates advancement, crescendo, or an interlude
- Sheminith (6, 12): An octave
- Shiggaion (7): Song, ode of praise
- Shoshannim (45, 69, 80): Direction to sing to a certain tune
- Shushan-eduth (60): "Lily of Testimony," the name of a melody

Great musical works have been created over the centuries based on passages from the Psalms. Johannes Brahm's *German Requiem* (Opus 45) uses parts of Psalms 39 and 84. Felix Mendelssohn set to music words from Psalms 16, 55, and 108 in "Cast Thy Burden upon the Lord" (*Hymns,* no. 110). George Frideric Handel's *Messiah* adapts texts from Psalms 19, 22, 24, and 68.

Psalms 25, 34, 37, 111, 112, 119, and 145 are *alphabetical* acrostics; that is, each of the verses begins with the next letter of the Hebrew alphabet, something that is lost, of course, when translated from their Hebrew original into another language. In the case of Psalm 119, there are twenty-two groups of eight verses, each group beginning with the next letter of the alphabet. In Psalm 119 the Hebrew letters for the twenty-two groups are printed in our LDS Bibles. The ninth group ("TETH") is a near-perfect acrostic even in English (change verse 67 to begin with "Till" and verse 71 to begin with "Tis" and all verses commence with the "T"

sound of that Hebrew letter; see additional explanation of acrostics at The Lamentations of Jeremiah in volume 2 of this commentary.

One of the favorite devices among ancient Semitic writers was to compare something in the human experience with something in nature. The prophets, and even Jesus, compared humans to grass, plants, olive trees, fig trees, vines, sheep, goats, fish, wolves, vipers, and more. God himself is often cast in the role of the stone or rock, the branch, the sower or husbandman, the true vine, the sheep, the shepherd, the lamb, and so forth. All of these images have a two-part meaning: there is a literal comparison (surface meaning) and a higher or didactic comparison (underlying meaning); the latter requires serious reflection and meditation to understand the full intent and meaning. Poetry is not meant to be literal, as illustrated by the expression "poetic license." Someone has suggested that poetry is saying one thing but meaning another. Note, for example, the following striking examples of figurative language from the later prophetic book of Hosea, a series of rich images poetically describing an apostate northern kingdom of Israel, represented by its leading tribe, Ephraim: "Ephraim is a cake not turned" (7:8); "Ephraim is also like a silly dove without heart" (7:11); "Ephraim feedeth on the wind, and followeth after the east wind [symbolic of destruction]: he daily increaseth lies and desolation" (12:1); "therefore will I be unto Ephraim as a moth" (5:12); "I will be unto Ephraim as a lion" (5:14); "Ephraim is smitten, their root is dried up, they shall bear no fruit" (9:16); "therefore I will be unto them as a lion: as a leopard by the way will I observe them: I will meet them as a bear that is bereaved of her whelps" (13:7–8).

SELECTED PSALMS

See whether you can visualize in the following psalms of David the situations out of which they arose. Bear in mind that not all of the psalms subtitled "A Psalm of David" were necessarily written by King David; authorship of many of the psalms is still uncertain and tentative. In Hebrew, the subtitles ascribe seventy-three of our present one hundred and fifty psalms to David. Read the following psalms *aloud*.

Psalm 1

In Psalm 1, the righteous are contrasted with the ungodly. Notice that this psalm begins with a Beatitude: "Blessed is the man . . ." It is an ancient form of instruction that Jesus also used (Matthew 5:3–11; 3 Nephi 12:1–11). The word "Beatitude" (Latin, *beatus*) means "to be fortunate, blessed, or happy" (see "Psalms and the Beatitudes," page 435.)

Psalm 2

The Messiah-King is prophetically anticipated in Psalm 2.

Psalm 3

Found in Psalm 3 is a prayer of thanks and of supplication in time of trouble, possibly referring to Absalom's rebellion. In verse 4 we find the musical direction "Selah," possibly meaning crescendo, or increase in volume. It is used seventy-one times in Psalms.

Psalm 4

Psalm 4 is a vehement prayer against ungodly enemies. Herein is contained one of the most common admonitions in Psalms and in all of scripture: "Put your trust in the Lord" (v. 5; see also 5:11; 9:10; 18:2; 56:11; 62:8; 118:8–9).

Psalm 6

Psalm 6 is a prayer provoked by a stinging conscience.

Psalm 7

David's confidence in the Lord and his enemies' condemnation are depicted in Psalm 7.

Psalm 8

Psalm 8 contains a philosophical look at God and his creations, especially man, supporting the exclamation: "How Great Thou Art!" Note especially verse 5: "Thou hast made him a little lower than the angels." In Hebrew the phrase actually reads: "Thou didst make him lack little of God," which explains the topic in the Topical Guide, "Man, Potential to Become like Heavenly Father."

Psalm 11

Psalm 11 is a Temple psalm. David exults that "the Lord is in his holy temple" (v. 4) and that "his countenance doth behold the upright" (v. 7). Other psalms give the assurance that when the Lord's countenance shines on someone, great blessings come (4:6; 31:16; 67:1–2; 80:3, 7, 19; 119:135). Note the author's use of parallelism in verse 4 to describe God's *two* dwelling places, his earthly Temple which is a mirror of his heavenly home: "The Lord is in his holy temple; the Lord is on his heavenly throne" (translation ours).

Psalm 14

Compare the Joseph Smith Translation revision (vv. 1–7) with the King James Version.

Psalm 15

Psalm 15 is also a Temple psalm. The term "holy hill" is a reference to the Temple, much the same way as the Temple is called the mountain of the Lord's house (see, for example, Isaiah 2:1–2). Some Jewish scholars maintain that this psalm reduces the 613 commandments found in the Torah to ten foundational principles. Others see in this psalm something of an ancient recommend, or declaration of worthiness, to enter the Temple, consisting of ten parts:

"1. walks with integrity,
"2. works righteousness,
"3. speaks truth,
"4. despises reprobates,

"5. and has sworn to do no evil;

"6. has not slandered ('trip on his tongue'),

"7. has done no evil to his neighbor,

"8. has not lifted up a reproach against his relative,

"9. has not charged interest for his money [see Bible Dictionary, "Usury"],

"10. and has not taken a bribe against the innocent" (Parry, "'Who Shall Ascend,'" 732–33).

Some biblical scholars have suggested that at times during the existence of Solomon's Temple, a priest or priests stood at the Temple gate(s) and ensured the worthiness of worshipers, and hence the sanctity of the Temple, by posing questions to those seeking entrance. Hans-Joachim Kraus suggested a similar, though reverse, scenario. The worshipers stood outside the gates of the temple and asked, "Who is worthy to enter the temple?" Then, "from the inside a priestly speaker answers them with the declaration of the conditions of entrance" (Kraus, *Psalms 1–59*, 227). These conditions are found in Psalms 15 and 24.

Psalm 17

In Psalm 17, the psalmist pleads with the Lord to hear him, for He is righteous; and it is because of His righteousness that the psalmist has faith that he will achieve his ultimate goal: to see God's face and be satisfied in His presence. This is accomplished in the Temple.

Psalm 18

Psalm 18 expresses gratitude for deliverance from many forms of distress.

Psalm 19

Psalm 19 rejoices in the glory of God that is seen in God's creations and in his teachings.

Psalm 21

Psalm 21 is a Temple psalm of praise and rejoicing. The Lord granted the king (the psalmist) the desire of his heart and will meet him with rich blessings. He has placed a crown of pure gold upon his head (v. 3), given him length of days forever and ever (v. 4), and made him exceedingly glad with His countenance.

Psalm 22

Psalm 22 is an outcry of anguish. The first line was spoken by Jesus on the cross; other parts of the psalm seem also to have anticipated his suffering (see chart, pages 421–422.)

Psalm 23

The best known of all the psalms, Psalm 23, is a vivid and succinct definition of the providence of God. Compare it to modern, lengthy, and often abstract theological and dictionary definitions. Ancient Hebrew writers knew how to economize words, to describe the sheep-shepherd relationship in a few powerful, dignified words rich with meaning. Although we authors have both sung the words of Psalm 23 accompanied by soul-stirring music (and one of us has even sung the words of the psalm in the Salt Lake Tabernacle with full choir, organ, and orchestration), they have never understood and *felt* the meaning of the words better than in their original setting—the shepherds' fields around Bethlehem, where David exclaimed, "The Lord is *my* shepherd" (emphasis added). It is not absolutely essential, of course, to be on the site where revelations are given and where inspiration is received to be able to understand the divine messages. Knowing something about the physical setting, however, does help us to better understand the meaning. That is why our leaders and teachers encourage us to learn all we can about the background of the scriptures, including their historical, geographical, linguistic, and cultural settings.

The following details of the rest of Psalm 23 will bear out this truth. "He maketh me to lie down in *green* pastures" (emphasis added). During the heavy winter rains, from January to March, a lovely green carpet of grass covers the whole country—even desolate desert areas—and then the hot, dry winds come in from the desert and burn up the green pasturelands, leaving the land bare and dry the rest of the year. Anyone visiting the land through much of the year would understand the delightsome image of "green pastures."

"He leadeth me beside the still waters." Water is life in that part of the world. Far more important than oil or any other commodity is the precious water that comes from the heavens (see commentary at Deuteronomy 11:8–17). No image from the land stirs greater gratitude and favor than the image of living water.

"He leadeth me in the paths of righteousness." These are the paths that we, the sheep of the good Shepherd, must walk, following his course—the paths of Righteousness (another of his name-titles).

"Yea, though I walk through the valley of the shadow of death." When the sun begins to set in the west, long shadows stretch across the hill country of Judah, producing dark valleys. Most people in that land today call them *wadis,* the Arabic term for what Americans call ravines, or gullies, and what Hispanics call arroyos, that is, channels that have water in them only seasonally. Such darkened valleys can raise fears of evil predators, such as the lion and the bear that David encountered while herding sheep in those fields around Bethlehem (1 Samuel 17:34–36).

"I will fear no evil: for thou art with me; thy rod and thy staff they comfort me." The rod represents the Lord's care, and the staff, his defense. Trusting Him, there is comfort indeed, and no need of fear.

The next images reinforce the Lord's provision of comfort: preparing a table, anointing our head with oil, and causing our cup to run over.

"Surely goodness and mercy shall follow me all the days of my life: and I will dwell in the house of the Lord for ever." The

Lord's securest sheepfold for us is his "house," his Temple. There, goodness and mercy constantly accompany us.

Psalm 24

The questions in Psalm 24 could have served as Temple recommend interview questions in ancient times: "Who shall ascend into the hill of the Lord? or who shall stand in his holy place?" Answers to those questions are provided. Purity is the fundamental requirement for entrance into the Temple. It has been suggested that Psalm 24 contains the "laws of the sanctuary," the "special rules and special demands as to the qualifications of those to be admitted" into the Temple (Mowinckel, *Psalms in Israel's Worship,* 1:177). Psalm 24 is one of the so-called Psalms of Ascent or Procession, sung by the Levites and priests while devotees went up to the Temple to worship and participate in sacrifices offered there.

Biblical commentator Franz Delitzsch referred to this psalm as "preparation for the reception of the Lord who is about to come [into his Temple]" (*Psalms,* 1:332). Accordingly, in his view, the psalm was to be sung antiphonally, by a "chorus of the festive procession," commencing with verses 1 and 2 and starting out below the "hill of Zion." Separate voices responded to the chorus with the critical questions and answers found in verses 3–4. The chorus, in turn, replied with verses 5 and 6 as the procession moved up the hill. Then, upon arriving at the gate of the Temple, the chorus sang verses 7–10 (Delitzsch, *Psalms,* 1:332–33).

Though in the King James Version, Psalm 24:3 uses the words "hill of the Lord," the Hebrew literally translates as "who shall go up to the *mountain* of Jehovah," a reference to the Lord's mountain house as seen in Isaiah 2:2. And the phrase "who shall stand in his holy place" refers directly to the Temple because a section of the Jerusalem Temple was explicitly called the Holy Place.

The version of Psalm 24 preserved in our King James Bible appears to have something missing in verse 6, near the name "Jacob." From the context provided in the rest of the verses, it is not Jacob's face that is sought but the Lord's. The Septuagint (LXX) is much more explicit (especially v. 6) in pointing out that the ultimate intent of going up to the Temple was to "seek the face of the God of Jacob." And that opportunity rested on specific requirements of worthiness:

"3 Who shall go up to the mountain of the Lord, and who shall stand in his holy place?

"4 He that is innocent in his hands and pure in his heart; who has not lifted up his soul to vanity, nor sworn deceitfully to his neighbour.

"5 He shall receive a blessing from the Lord, and mercy from God his Saviour.

"6 This is the generation of them that seek him, that seek the face of the God of Jacob. . . .

"10 Who is this king of glory? The Lord of hosts, he is this king of glory (LXX Psalm 23:3–6, 10)" (Brenton, *Septuagint,* 711).

Jesus Christ used the doctrinal foundation of Psalm 24 to make the same promise to the pure in heart: they will see God (Matthew 5:8; D&C 93:1).

Psalm 27

Psalm 27 is another Temple psalm. David's desire to trust in the Lord and rely on His divine guidance centered in the Temple. Like others before him, he desired to be in the Temple to seek the face of the Lord, the rock of salvation:

"One thing have I desired of the Lord, that will I seek after; that I may dwell in the house of the Lord all the days of my life, to behold the beauty of the Lord, and to enquire [or contemplate] in his temple.

"For in the time of trouble he shall hide me in his pavilion: in the secret of his tabernacle shall he hide me; he shall set me up upon a rock. . . .

"When thou saidst, Seek ye my face; my heart said unto thee, Thy face, Lord, will I seek" (vv. 4–5, 8).

Psalm 37

Psalm 37 provides the scriptural foundation for two of the Beatitudes in Jesus' Sermon on the Mount. Verse 11 is quoted almost verbatim by the Savior: "The meek shall inherit the earth" (Matthew 5:5). And verses 21–22 form the basis of Matthew 5:7: "Blessed are the merciful: for they shall obtain mercy." Ultimately, the psalmist indicates that the merciful are drawn to the house of the Merciful One, the Temple: "But as for me, I will come into thy house in the multitude of thy mercy: and in thy fear [reverence] will I worship toward thy holy temple" (5:7).

Psalm 42

Verse 2 of Psalm 42, in combination with Psalms 63:1–2 and 107:9, undergirds the beatitude in Matthew 5:6: "Blessed are they which do hunger and thirst after righteousness: for they shall be filled." The term "righteousness" here may be understood as "the Righteous One."

Psalm 46

Verse 10 of Psalm 46 extols the virtue of inspired contemplation.

Psalm 51

David's poignant plea for forgiveness after his sin with Bathsheba is expressed in Psalm 51. Out of the agony of his repentance comes marvelous doctrinal truth. The intent behind the offering of sacrifices is taught—to witness to God a broken heart and contrite spirit (v. 17), characteristics the Savior himself exhibited as he worked out the infinite and eternal Atonement.

Psalm 63

Again in Psalm 63 a powerful Temple psalm reflects the purpose for entering the House of the Lord—to seek God (note vv. 1–4).

Psalm 76

Psalm 76 speaks of the Lord dwelling in his Temple in Zion, which is Jerusalem.

Psalm 90

The messianic Psalm 90 tells of David as an anointed one.

Psalm 104

Psalm 104 tells of the beauty of God's creations. As with others, we recommend reading this psalm *aloud*, in a quiet place with time for reflection.

Psalms 113–18

Psalms 113–18 form the Great Hallel (Hebrew, *hallel,* "to praise," as 113:1 indicates). The Great Hallel or parts of it were sung during the Seder, or Passover, meal in ancient times because sections are intensely messianic. This constituted the "hymn" sung by Jesus and his apostles as part of their last Passover service together, before they went forth to Gethsemane (Mark 14:26). Note especially 118:21–25.

Psalm 122

Psalms 120–34 are called Songs of Degrees, or Songs of Ascent; they may have been sung while ascending the Temple steps to the Holy Place. There are fifteen of them, the same as the number of steps leading to the inner court. Psalm 122 expresses heartfelt praise and gratitude for the House of the Lord and for the Holy City of Jerusalem.

Psalms 125–28

Psalms 125–28 are more of the short Songs of Ascent. Notice certain verses about Jerusalem, about the Lord's House, and about wives and children. See also commentary about Israelites' poignant feelings about Jerusalem in Psalm 137 at 2 Kings 25:27–30.

Read certain other gems in the Psalms: 14:1; 30:5; 46:1–3, 10; 80:8–15, the history of Israel in a brief allegory; 84:10; 90:3–6 on the transitory nature of man; 119:105.

After reading the Psalms, there should be no question why the book of Psalms is the Old Testament book most quoted in the New Testament (at least 116 times) and why Jesus referred to the Psalms more than any other Old Testament book. Jesus singled out the book of Psalms because it testified of him and his eternal gospel, the single most important purpose any book could have.

PSALMS AND THE BEATITUDES

After Jesus sat down on a certain hill in Galilee to deliver what is probably his most famous sermon, the Sermon on the Mount, he began to lay out a series of formulaic pronouncements called the Beatitudes, because of the first words of each statement, "Blessed are . . ." In Latin the opening word is *beatus,* from which our English word *beatitude* derives. It means "to be fortunate, to be blessed, to be happy." The literary form of each of the Beatitudes is based on an ancient Hebrew form of speech, *'ashre* (pronounced *ahsh-ray*), a well-known literary construction in the Hebrew Bible as well as in intertestamental literature. In the Masoretic Text (the traditional text of the Old Testament) alone, "the term *ashre* occurs 44 times, . . . and 30 verses begin with it" (Lachs, *Rabbinic Commentary,* 70).

Significantly, most uses of *'ashre* are found in Psalms (twenty-six times). The very first psalm begins with *'ashre*— *'Ashre ha'ish 'asher lo' halakh . . . ,* "Blessed is the man that walketh not in the counsel of the ungodly" (Psalm 1:1). Other examples include "Blessed are all they that put their trust in him [the Lord]" (Psalm 2:12); "Blessed is he whose transgression is forgiven, whose sin is covered. Blessed is the man unto whom the Lord imputeth not iniquity, and in whose spirit there is no guile" (Psalm 32:1–2); "Blessed is that man that maketh the Lord his trust, and respecteth not the proud" (Psalm 40:4); "Blessed is he that considereth the poor" (Psalm 41:1); "Blessed are they that dwell in thy house" (Psalm 84:4); "Blessed are they that keep judgment, and he that doeth righteousness at all times" (Psalm 106:3); "Blessed are the undefiled in the way, who walk in the law of the Lord. Blessed are they that keep his testimonies, and that seek him with the whole heart" (Psalm 119:1–2); "Blessed is every one that feareth the Lord; that walketh in his ways" (Psalm 128:1).

Thus we see that the Beatitudes are based on an original form of Hebrew speech found more often than not in the Psalms. This might be expected given that many of the Psalms are closely related to the holy environment of the Temple and express the ultimate in praise, worship, blessing, happiness, and holiness, while the Beatitudes are a list of characteristics, attributes, and blessings possessed by those who are themselves praiseworthy, holy, or striving for holiness and who are or will be citizens of the kingdom of heaven.

You may want to expand your study of the Psalms with examples of psalmic material in other books of scripture.

Read 1 Peter 2:9–10 and see why we should praise our God for calling us out of darkness into his marvelous light.

Read 2 Nephi 4:15–35 and discover possibly the most personal glimpse into the heart of a prophet in all of scripture as Nephi agonizes over his weaknesses and groans over his sins and yet recognizes that he can trust in God to lovingly rescue him in his struggle to overcome mortal imperfections. The influence of the biblical Psalms is clearly evident in Nephi's deeply moving sentiments.

Read 2 Nephi 9:8–20 and notice that the first sentence in verses 8, 10, 13, 17, 19, and 20 is an exclamation of and exultation in God's wisdom, mercy, grace, goodness, justice, and holiness. Jacob, Nephi's brother, who was also intimately acquainted with the scriptures that came out of Jerusalem, including the biblical Psalms, gives us devotional literature in its finest form. "O" is an expression of awe. He is exclaiming "How great thou art!"

And finally, read Doctrine and Covenants 128:19–23 and celebrate with the Prophet Joseph Smith the sublime doctrines and preeminent events of the latter-day Restoration.

Exclamation points are plentiful in these verses, along with heavenly metaphors and poetic personification, as the Prophet and all the creations praise the Eternal King for bringing about on planet Earth the most glorious cause in the universe. Praise ye the Lord—*Hallelujah!*

SECOND SAMUEL

As we have said, 1 and 2 Samuel were originally one book. Thus, 2 Samuel continues the story of David's rise to the throne, his anointing, early kingship and consolidation of power, conquest of Jerusalem, successes and failures, adultery with Bathsheba and murder of Uriah, other family tragedies, and preparations for the future construction of the Temple at Jerusalem.

Near the end of 2 Samuel we are presented with some of David's last words, including a song, or psalm, also preserved in the Psalter, that praises God for his deliverance of the great king and expresses hope that he and his house are right with the Lord and that future kings will issue from his line (see 2 Samuel 22–23). Of course the great tragedy of David's story is that he can never ascend to the heights that will be enjoyed by exalted persons, even though he was, originally, a man after the Lord's own heart. In this regard, 2 Samuel is not only powerful history but a great cautionary tale for the ages. There is much to appreciate about 2 Samuel in its relevance for our time.

In your study of the final historical books in the first half of the Old Testament, you may want to read the following entries in the Bible Dictionary: "David," "Jerusalem," "Ark of the Covenant," and "Uzzah."

2 Samuel 1:1–16

The report of Saul's death came to David at his refuge in Ziklag. The Amalekite mercenary soldier who brought the report told a different tale from that recorded in 1 Samuel 31.

It is possible that he hoped for favors from David for killing King Saul and for taking David the news. Obviously he did not know David's attitude concerning the "Lord's anointed." He was punished instead of being rewarded.

2 Samuel 1:17–27

Verse 18 is puzzling because the Hebrew merely records: "And he said to teach the sons of Judah [the] bow; behold it is written in the book of the upright [*Jasher* means "upright"]." Many reconstructions and interpretations have been suggested, but obviously something is missing. It is quite possible that the "bow" was the literal title of the lament, which is recorded in verses 19 through 27.

David's lament over Saul and Jonathan is a good example of his poetic expressions so well-known from the book of Psalms. The eulogy honors Saul for his good characteristics and ignores his faults. However, we should not assume that the compliments are invented. It is quite possible that during the peaceful years of Saul's life, of which we have no record, he was able to bring about the prosperity to Israel suggested by the wording of verse 24.

Also, Jonathan's loyalty to his father and his fidelity to David are well reflected in verses 23 and 26; the tragedy of his being slain at the height of his potential career is suggested in verses 25 and 26. It is interesting, given all the trouble that Saul made for David, that David could say without sarcasm, "Saul and Jonathan were lovely and pleasant in their lives" (v. 23). This statement testifies of David's greatness of soul. Note in that same verse that something else David said about them was later said about Joseph and Hyrum Smith: "In their death they were not divided" (compare D&C 135:3).

The concluding verse powerfully declares the futility of war.

2 Samuel 2:1–7

David supplicated the Lord to know how to take over the kingdom and, according to the reply received, went to

Hebron of Judah which was sacred, being regarded as the home of Abraham from patriarchal times. Just how the men of Judah were assembled and David anointed king over their tribe is not told here.

The addition of information about the kind deed of the men of Jabesh who buried Saul and Jonathan belongs to the next paragraph.

In contrast to his reaction to the Amalekite who brought him news of Saul's death, David responded with appreciation for those who had given decent burial to the bodies of Saul and Jonathan.

2 Samuel 2:8–11

Abner, the head of Saul's armies, championed Saul's surviving son as king over Israel, temporarily separating the northern tribes from Judah, until David won them over seven years later (2 Samuel 5:1–5). Permanent division came eighty years after that, at the end of Solomon's reign (1 Kings 12).

2 Samuel 2:12–32

The two military leaders of the forces of Saul and David took some initiative to determine which king should reign over all Israel. The vicious "play" to show dominance was indecisive. Given the type of dueling employed, it is not surprising that all combatants were killed on both sides. The duel of Abner with Asahel, brother of Joab, was also tragic; though Abner finally engaged and slew Asahel unwillingly, Joab never forgave him, and vengeance was the result. All of that nearly frustrated David's efforts to unite the tribes of Israel.

The pool of Gibeon mentioned in verse 13, along with associated water tunnels, was uncovered at the site of that city in the 1950s by archaeologists from the University of Pennsylvania.

2 Samuel 3:1–21 (1 Chronicles 3:1–4)

The long strife between the houses of Saul and David is tersely stated. David had only two wives when he went to Hebron and was made king there. However, several are named as mothers of his first six sons. This was probably mentioned to give evidence of the house of David waxing "stronger and stronger" in contrast to Saul's house, which "waxed weaker and weaker" (v. 1).

Though David had gained steadily in power, it was by an unexpected move toward an alliance that he began to achieve union of all the tribes in his kingdom. Ishbosheth's accusation of Abner, his friend and military champion, was tantamount to accusing him of seeking to be Saul's heir. So incensed was Abner that he committed himself to making David king over all Israel. Abner's power and influence in Israel could have made the transition easy from Saul's rule to David's.

The earlier forced separation of Michal from David was unfortunate, but a reunion under the conditions noted here would only bring further sorrows.

2 Samuel 3:22–39

Joab's vengeance upon Abner did not promote justice or peace and probably would have thrown the two Israelite factions into open warfare again if David had not been able to convince the northern people of his innocence in Abner's assassination. The first line of his lament (v. 33) could mean "has a just man and warrior thus been deceived and put to death?" His lament, followed by a little fasting and mourning, impressed the people of northern Israel.

Ironically, David's political fortunes were enhanced, not impaired, by Joab's rash interference, even though David took no action against him. Something about David "pleased all the people" (v. 36). We see these hints that David truly was a charismatic person.

2 Samuel 4:1–12

Obviously Abner was the power behind the kingship of Saul's son. When Abner was dead, nothing was left to hold that kingdom together.

Verse 4 introduces us to the little lame prince, son of

Jonathan. Further developments in his story are recorded in chapter 9.

When two misguided brothers assassinated the son of Saul who was a potential heir to the throne of his father, they received the just reward of their deed from David. Recall and compare the case of the Amalekite who claimed to have dispatched Saul (2 Samuel 1:1–16).

2 Samuel 5:1–5 (1 Chronicles 11:1–3)

This chapter records watershed events that affected David's political life as well as Israel's fortunes as an increasingly important nation in the Near East.

The principal factors that made David king over all Israel were genealogical, practical, and divine. In the words of the united voice of all the tribes, he was an Israelite, he was the leader of Israel's army, and the Lord spoke to him. He became king through a covenant ("league"), done according to the usual Hebrew custom of cutting a sacrificed animal in pieces and eating it together. David's reign would last forty years altogether, making him seventy when he died. His first capital was at Hebron, where he ruled seven years over the tribe of Judah, which later came to be known as the kingdom of Judah. He would rule over united Israel for almost thirty-three years in Jerusalem after he conquered it. The twelve tribes would later split into two kingdoms after the death of David's son and successor, King Solomon: the kingdom of Judah and the kingdom of Israel.

2 Samuel 5:6–10 (1 Chronicles 11:4–9)

David was brilliant and likely inspired to choose Jerusalem as his capital—a city between the northern and southern factions of Israel but belonging to neither, as it was still held by the Canaanite people called Jebusites. There was great wisdom in securing a central and neutral location belonging neither to the north nor to the south, much as the capital of the United States was situated in the District of Columbia, which is not part of any state and cannot be claimed by any individual state.

The manner of conquering the city has been discussed at great length because of the problematic Hebrew word rendered "gutter" in English. This word most likely designates a water channel or shaft, as it is similarly used in Mishnaic Hebrew. A shaft running perpendicular to a water conduit would have given people inside the city walls access to water in time of siege, but it could also have made it possible for invaders to enter the city secretly and open the gates from within. Joab is said to have accomplished such an entry (1 Chronicles 11:6).

Jerusalem was small, merely twelve acres in total area, with perhaps two thousand to three thousand inhabitants. But it was a natural fortress because of its location on a rise surrounded on three sides by deep valleys. It was even called "the fort" (v. 9). So the Jebusites were extremely confident that their walls could be easily defended. Thus, there is some sarcasm in the Jebusites saying that David would have to overcome their lame and blind, as if such would have been sufficient to defend the city. David thereafter scathingly referred to all the Jebusite defenders as "the lame and the blind" (v. 8). In rabbinic tradition the "lame and the blind" were not men but Jebusite idols placed on the walls of the city.

Here is the first biblical mention of "Zion" (v. 7). This was the fortress of Jerusalem on the lower part of the hill south of Mount Moriah. The meaning of the word "Zion" in Hebrew has been much discussed but not yet satisfactorily defined. Earlier uses of the word, however, may be seen in Moses 7:18–69. It was used as the name of Enoch's city of the "pure in heart" (D&C 97:21). The name may also have been attached anciently to Melchizedek's city of Salem (later called Jerusalem; JST Genesis 9:21–25; 14:25–40; Alma 13:17–19). The name has gone on to gain many earthly uses and some heavenly connotations.

The Millo, around which David built inside the city walls, is usually identified as the stone-terraced retaining structure on the slope of the hill, uncovered by Israeli archaeologists in the 1980s.

2 Samuel 5:11–16 (1 Chronicles 14:1–7)

A long and mutually beneficial commercial relationship between Israel and the Phoenician cities of Tyre and Sidon was begun. Israel received building materials and the services of skilled craftsmen, and the Phoenicians received food from the agricultural produce of Israel. The peaceful relationship between these two neighbors was rare and noteworthy in that era.

David further practiced the prerogatives of the rulers of the time and took many wives and concubines (see D&C 132:38–39). Among his children were sons with the names Nathan and Solomon. Luke 3:31 traces Jesus' genealogy through this Nathan, who is not the prophet of the same name who lived in David's time; Matthew 1:6 traces Jesus' lineage through Solomon and the line of royal succession.

2 Samuel 5:17–25 (1 Chronicles 14:8–17)

For many years the Philistines had been pleased with the apparent friction and rivalry which existed between the northern tribes and the tribe of Judah. The situation improved during the period of judges, and Saul's Benjamin-based monarchy had somewhat moderated that divisiveness. However, during David's fugitive years, the Philistines sought every opportunity to drive the wedge between the north and the south of Israel, even trying to use the rivalry between Saul and David for their own political advantage.

The Philistines must have appreciated the disunity and instability of the separate states that existed while Ishbosheth reigned for a couple of years from Transjordan and David reigned from Hebron. However, now that David had been crowned king over all Israel and had declared the former Jebusite center as his new administrative capital, the Philistines lost no time in mobilizing their military forces to stop him.

The unity created under a leader as dynamic as David could prove the undoing of Philistine dominion.

The Philistine army advanced towards Jerusalem via the Valley of Rephaim, but with the guidance of the Lord, David countered them once by frontal assault and once by surprising them from the rear. David eventually controlled the Philistines to a greater extent than Saul had done and kept them at bay, as they were in the days of Samuel's leadership.

2 Samuel 6:1–11 (1 Chronicles 13:1–14)

David gathered the leaders of Israel and revived interest in the Ark of the Covenant, which had not been used as a sacred object in worship services since its loss to the Philistines in the days of Eli and its return to the area of Kiriath-Jearim, here called Baale of Judah. After it was returned to the Israelites, the Ark had remained in the house of Abinadab, who had dedicated his son Eleazar to care for it.

The Ark was escorted up to Jerusalem with great pageantry, music, and dancing. However, Uzzah, one of the sons of Abinadab sent to drive the cart that carried it, died when he reached out to steady it when the oxen stumbled. David was displeased and frightened and left it at another house for three months until it was evident that the blessing of the Lord and not his curses would accompany it. A modern idiom that has arisen out of the incident, in which a person seeking to "right" the Church without having authority is said to be "steadying the ark" (D&C 85:8).

2 Samuel 6:12–23 (1 Chronicles 15:1–16:3)

When the house that received the Ark was blessed, David took courage and arranged for descendants of Aaron and other Levites to properly take it into Jerusalem. A tent was erected to protect it as in the days of the Tabernacle in the wilderness.

David's spectacle in dancing with all his might, apparently immodest or at least irreverent, as the Ark came into Jerusalem, was degrading in the eyes of Michal, his restored wife. Their marriage relationship took one more turn for the worse. He seems to have been quite insensitive to Michal and proud and arrogant when declaring, "I will yet be more vile than thus, and will be base in my own sight." Then he twisted the blade by saying, "And of the maidservants which thou has spoken of, of them I shall be had in honour" (v. 22). Can we imagine any righteous, humble follower of Christ acting and speaking that way to his wife? Do we seem to be witnessing a change in David's character?

2 Samuel 7:1–29 (1 Chronicles 17:1–27)

When David's conscience stirred him to build a house for the Ark, Nathan the prophet at first gave his personal approval (v. 5). Later, revelation from the Lord sent him back to David with different orders (v. 12). Not only was David to be otherwise occupied in his lifetime but, it was pointed out, his occupation with warfare and bloodshed made him an inappropriate choice to build a Temple of the Lord (see 1 Kings 5:3; 1 Chronicles 22:8). Nevertheless, he was promised blessings and perpetuation of his "house," meaning his descendants, one of whom would build a proper Temple. With the sacred Ark now in the capital city and the plans laid for a future Temple, David set Jerusalem on the way to its eternal status as a spiritual center, a holy city.

David submitted to the will of the Lord humbly and gratefully and uttered a psalmlike prayer unto the Lord.

2 Samuel 8:1–18 (1 Chronicles 18:1–17)

David was at the height of power. He expanded the kingdom to the extent envisioned by Moses and as promised to Abraham (Genesis 15:18; Numbers 34:1–12; Deuteronomy 1:7). For the first time in Israelite history, we now have what we could call an Israelite empire. All of the old neighboring enemies were subdued: Syria (Aram), Ammon, Moab, Edom, Philistia, and Amalek. With this brief summary of battlefronts, we can only try to imagine the political, economic, and social repercussions of these many wars on Israelite society at the time.

David's chief aides included military leaders, scribes, record keepers, and priests. One of the leading priests was Zadok, descendant of Ithamar, son of Aaron; another was Ahimelech, son of David's old friend Abiathar, also a descendant of Ithamar. Zadokite priests of the Aaronic Priesthood continued to be dominant after David and Solomon's time down through the time of Christ.

2 Samuel 9:1–13

There was a noble gesture on the part of David in befriending the young, crippled son of his friend Jonathan. He sought to do kindnesses to "any that were left of the house of Saul." Again, we see the largeness of David's soul in restoring to Mephibosheth all the land of Saul. This was also a shrewd political move. The two are not incompatible.

2 Samuel 10:1–19 (1 Chronicles 19:1–19)

When David attempted a magnanimous gesture toward a suppressed neighbor, Ammon, the Ammonites did not accept it as such but assumed his messengers to be spies and cut off half their beards and clothes. Such an insult brought on full-scale war, in which the Syrians of three nearby cities were also enlisted, and later all those between the Jordan and the upper Euphrates, all of whom were made to serve Israel.

2 Samuel 11:1–27

Things were getting too easy for David; he had the leisure to stay at home while Joab and his men were out fighting Ammonites and Syrians (1 Chronicles 20:1). One evening as he was attempting to cool off, he looked down from his palatial rooftop at his neighbor's wife. Leisure and lust led to adultery and then to murder, which sins had eternal repercussions as well as tragic earthly results. It is one of the shocking and serious warnings of the Old Testament that a man may be ever so good and great and still have weaknesses that can lead

445

to deeds that entirely overshadow and defeat his better nature and reduce his eternal potential. It is often the case that a man's greatest tests come at times of his greatest successes. It seems to be the case in most situations of sin that the offender considers himself to be above some commandment, to be an exception to a rule.

"At the time when kings go forth to battle" in verse 1 refers to summer months. During winter months few wars were fought in the eastern Mediterranean region because chariots and men became bogged down in mud. While his army was fighting fifty miles away at Rabbah, the capital of the Ammonites (modern-day Amman, Jordan), David had an immoral relationship with Bathsheba. Perhaps if David had been out fighting "at the time when kings go forth to battle" and hadn't had a palace *looking down* on the city, the whole affair might not have occurred. Read verses 2–4 carefully. At what point did David sin? President Spencer W. Kimball once warned: "The time to protect against the calamity is when the thought begins to shape itself. Destroy the seed and the plant will never grow" (*Miracle of Forgiveness,* 114).

Elder Dallin H. Oaks of the Quorum of the Twelve Apostles spoke of King David's grievous sin, saying in essence that though David was a spiritual giant in Israel, he allowed himself to look upon something he should not have viewed. In that way, he, a prophet-king, fell from his exaltation. Elder Oaks went on to compare David's situation with the modern-day circumstance of seeing pornography and then allowing oneself to continue to view it. It is a powerful application of an ancient scriptural episode to a modern circumstance (*David and Bathsheba: To Look Upon,* at lds.org).

Uriah is called "the Hittite," but with a good Hebrew name like Uriah (*ur* means light, and *Yah* is the Lord, Jehovah; together they mean "the Lord is my Light"), it appears that he had converted to belief in the true God of Israel and was an honorable man. The purpose of the parenthetical comment "for she was purified from her uncleanness" is to certify that Bathsheba, being ceremonially pure, was definitely not pregnant by Uriah (v. 4). The penalty prescribed by the law of Moses for infidelity was death (Leviticus 20:10; Deuteronomy 22:22), and yet, ironically, it was guiltless Uriah who was sentenced to death by the guilty one (v. 15).

2 Samuel 12:1–14

President David O. McKay taught that "no one can transgress the laws of chastity and find peace" (*Gospel Ideals*, 473). All too frequently, it is only when a sinner learns that his sin is known that he begins to repent. The Lord explicitly sent his prophet to David for a day of reckoning. The figure of Nathan boldly accusing the king to his face by an allegorical parallel is impressive. Nathan's allegory was skillfully drawn, and his climactic *Attah ha ish!* ("Thou art the man") must have crashed in upon the conscience of David like the harbingers of doomsday. From latter-day revelation we learn that Nathan was the Lord's prophet, holding the sealing keys of the priesthood (D&C 132:39).

One can hardly imagine a more sobering, arresting condemnation than the one proclaimed by the Lord through Nathan. He reminded David of all the things the Lord had done for him, including the giving of many wives, and then declared, as though he were himself the Lord, "And if that had been too little, I would moreover have given unto thee such and such things. Wherefore hast thou despised the commandment of the Lord, to do evil in his sight?" (vv. 8–9). Where much is given, much is required. David was not some immature teenager lacking judgment in the heat of the moment. He was the Lord's prophet-king! He was guilty of premeditated adultery and murder. The Lord pronounced an immediate grave consequence: he would raise up evil against the king out of his own family. In verse 12 the Lord also taught a profound lesson about David's attempt at keeping his wickedness a secret. His private immorality would have public consequences, which is an important principle to keep in mind in our day.

David's sins would be responsible for ongoing hostility among his posterity; terrible family and national problems were promised by the prophet. Notice the Hebrew and Joseph Smith Translation notes on 13*b*.

His repentant feelings were no doubt sincere, but he could not repent enough to restore the life of Uriah nor the virtue of Uriah's wife. Though he later hoped and prayed that his soul would not be left forever in hell (the spirit prison), the eternal destiny of doers of such sins does not look good (see Hebrews 6:4–6; Revelation 22:14–15; D&C 132:27, 39).

The tragedy and severity of the eternal consequences of David's sins are magnified by statements from the Prophet Joseph Smith. On one occasion he quoted Acts 3:19–20 and commented:

"The time of redemption here had reference to the time when Christ should come [a second time]; then, and not till then, would their sins be blotted out. Why? Because they were murderers, and no murderer hath eternal life. Even David must wait for those times of refreshing, before he can come forth and his sins be blotted out. For Peter, speaking of him says, 'David hath not yet ascended into heaven, for his sepulchre is with us to this day.' His remains were then in the tomb. Now, we read that many bodies of the Saints arose at Christ's resurrection, probably all the Saints, but it seems that David did not. Why? Because he had been a murderer" (*History of the Church,* 4:359).

On another occasion the Prophet stated: "A murderer, for instance, one that sheds innocent blood, cannot have forgiveness [immediately]. David sought repentance at the hand of God carefully with tears, for the murder of Uriah; but he could only get it through hell: he got a promise that his soul should not be left in hell.

"Although David was a king, he never did obtain the spirit and power of Elijah and the fullness of the Priesthood; and the Priesthood that he received, and the throne and kingdom of

David is to be taken from him and given to another" (*History of the Church*, 6:253).

The matter seems clear. David's soul would not be left in hell. But, by his act of sending Uriah to his death in order to cover up his own adultery, David, a great prophet and king, forfeited the opportunity for exaltation, which is to receive the fulness of the priesthood. His eternal kingdom will be given to another. How utterly tragic.

2 Samuel 12:15–25

The child born of David and Bathsheba's illicit union did not live, but there is no reason to look upon that as punishment of the child for the sins of the parents. Removal from this earth by the hand of the Lord must come at one time or another to everyone and can be a blessing to an individual, brought about for his best interest at whatever time the Lord deems it best. The parents did suffer remorse over it. After David knew that the baby was dead, he ceased mourning, however, and philosophically and hopefully explained, "I shall go to him, but he shall not return to me" (v. 23). David's hope to "go to him" in death was not realistic because David could not hope to go to the kingdom of glory to which innocent children are heirs.

It appears that David promised Bathsheba that her next son would be his heir, for later actions were taken according to that assumption (see v. 24; 1 Kings 1:17; 1 Chronicles 22:9). The Messiah, the Savior of the world, would later come through that lineage.

2 Samuel 12:26–31 (1 Chronicles 20:1–3)

Joab completed the conquest of Ammon and sent for David to lead the forces into the capital city lest Joab be accredited as the conquering king. Whatever else the faults of Joab were, he was always loyal to and promoted the interests of his king, and the king rewarded him. Punishment for Joab's sins came later (1 Kings 2:5–6, 28–34).

2 Samuel 13:1–19

Evils soon began to rise in David's house as Nathan had prophesied (12:11). David apparently had lost the Spirit and was unable to recognize the danger of the situation. Absalom had a beautiful sister, and his brother Amnon (David's son by a different wife) fell in love with her. He was so infatuated with her that he became sick and devised a way of getting her into his room alone so he could rape her. The story of Amnon's lust and incest committed according to the suggestions of a "subtle" friend is an indelicate one, but it deserves careful study. Tamar was admirably patient and wise. Caught unwittingly in Amnon's trap, she pointed out rationally why for his sake and hers an immoral deed should not be done. Also, notice how quickly and typically his desire changed to revulsion because what he really felt was lust, not love. (Compare the story of Joseph and Potiphar's wife in Genesis 39:7–18.)

Tamar's "garment of divers colours" uses the same phrase that was used of Joseph's coat (Genesis 37:3). It refers to a tunic, or outer garment, reaching to the palms of the hands and the soles of the feet, apparently signifying modesty and chastity, "for with such robes were the king's daughters that were virgins apparelled" (v. 18).

2 Samuel 13:20–39

In a way paralleling David's own sequence of sins, Amnon's immorality led to homicide by another son seeking vengeance. Absalom hated Amnon because of what he had done to his sister, and he planned for two whole years just how he could kill him. Finally he arranged for all the king's sons to attend a sheepshearers' party at Baal-hazor fifteen miles north-northeast of Jerusalem and on that occasion had Amnon slain. According to Leviticus 20:10–17, such punishment should have been officially administered, not undertaken as private vengeance.

Absalom then fled to Geshur while his father, David,

longed to see him. With Absalom a fugitive, David had now, in a sense, lost two sons.

2 Samuel 14:1–20

It appears that the loyal but otherwise unscrupulous Joab sought to play a kindly role, for once, in his attempt to reconcile David and Absalom. It is plausible that he foresaw the potential of Absalom to win the hearts of the people and usurp the throne; but if that were so, he probably would simply have had Absalom assassinated. Perhaps he was honestly trying to bring happiness back to the king when he saw that after three years the king was still yearning for his son Absalom.

The approach of persuading the king that it was more serious to terminate the family line than to allow a murderer (Absalom) to go unpunished was ingenious, and the "wise woman" played her role well. There is a foreshadowing of divine atonement in her citing that God himself "doth devise means, that his banished be not expelled from him" (v. 14).

2 Samuel 14:21–33

Even though the persuasion was effective in getting Absalom back from his foreign refuge, David's petulance prevented reconciliation, and for two crucial years Absalom remained ostracized, not being admitted to the king's presence. Finally David did summon Absalom and the two were reconciled, but the restored relationship did not last. The bitterness engendered in Absalom may have spawned the plots of revolt by the handsome and popular prince.

2 Samuel 15:1–37

By showing magnanimous consideration, empathy, compassion, and an eagerness to serve everybody, Absalom easily "stole the hearts of the men of Israel" and prepared for the day when he could proclaim himself king. With a bit of feigned piety and with shameless deceitfulness, he was able to set the stage for a *coup d'etat,* setting up his own coronation in Hebron, his birthplace and his father's former capital. As

Absalom's following gained strength, a messenger came and told David that the "hearts of the men of Israel" were with Absalom (v. 13).

But David still had some powerful and loyal friends. Among them were the priests Zadok and Abiathar; the faithful foreigner, Ittai the Gittite; the wise counselor Hushai; and the old soldier Joab. All of these men played crucial roles in preventing the overthrow of David's government. David, preferring to avoid bloodshed, fled with his head covered, barefoot, and weeping, up over the Mount of Olives and through the wilderness to the transjordanian political center of Mahanaim.

It was possibly sometime during this period that Absalom "reared up for himself a pillar, which is in the king's dale" (18:18). A monument that stands today in the Kidron Valley is called by tradition Absalom's Pillar, but it actually dates to a much later (Hellenistic) period. Absalom's pillar would have been erected further south where the "king's dale" or "king's garden" was located.

2 Samuel 16:1–14

As David was fleeing Absalom, one Ziba, the servant of Mephibosheth, met him with many provisions. Apparently Ziba intended to ingratiate himself with the king and gain the lands and property of his master, Saul. Ziba administered them on behalf of the lame prince Mephibosheth, son of Jonathan. Ziba's ruse was that Mephibosheth was trying to become king. The sequel, with Mephibosheth's denial and reinstatement, will be seen in 19:24.

David made his way to Bahurim and there chose to endure the curses of Shimei of the house of Saul; that dishonor was negligible compared to the dishonor of his own son taking his kingship and seeking his life. If he suffered his afflictions patiently, perhaps the Lord would have mercy upon him and requite him later. Perhaps the Lord himself had commanded Shimei to curse him, and since Abishai and Joab were men of violence, David countered as usual with more moderate action. Later, it will be seen that David was not as magnanimous as he seemed, however.

2 Samuel 16:15–17:29

Here the scene switches to Absalom's activity in Jerusalem. In the contest of the counselors, Ahithophel, who was actually loyal to Absalom's interests, did not make as favorable an impression on Absalom as did Hushai, who was only feigning loyalty to his cause. Doubtless, had Ahithophel's advice been followed, David would have been successfully deposed and probably killed.

Hushai informed David that his counsel had been accepted, and David was spared, while unfortunate Ahithophel, though he had been right in giving advice, was deemed wrong and took his own life.

David was able to live not only by the help of Hushai's stratagem but also by the generosity of some of his loyal subjects in trans-Jordan who made vital contributions.

2 Samuel 18:1–33

David was a good organizer. While still in exile from his own kingdom, he formed the men who were with him into an army and sent them forth in three units commanded by Joab, Abishai (Joab's brother) and Ittai the Gittite. They requested that David not lead them and he agreed. They marched into the field to meet and defeat the army of Israel. However, one request tendered by David with regard to Absalom went unheeded—in spite of all, he wanted his son's life saved.

Absalom and his rebel troops pursued David's men across the Jordan and engaged them in battle in the land of Gilead, in "the wood of Ephraim" (17:24, 26; 18:6). Absalom got tangled up in an oak tree by his hair and was killed there by Joab (2 Samuel 14:26 tells us that Absalom's hair was so thick that he used to cut it every year's end when it became too heavy for him; it weighed two hundred shekels, estimated at being between two and four pounds!).

It is hardly surprising that Joab again took matters into

his own hands. This was his usual role in protecting the king, whether the king wanted it or not. This deed of violence was better motivated on this occasion than in some of Joab's other radical acts, but the administration of justice was not properly in his hands.

It appears that Ahimaaz, the priestly son of Zadok, wished to cushion the blow of the bad news that Absalom was dead but to no avail. Tragedy had been in the making for a long time in the lives of David and Absalom, and the climax had to come in one way or another. David returned to Jerusalem mourning over the personal, familial, and national catastrophes that had befallen him.

2 Samuel 19:1–15

Absalom's death evoked great weeping and mourning from David, so much so that the nation's victory was turned into mourning. David bore his tragedy so bitterly that they who had defended and saved him were shamed by their success, and Joab saw that David would be utterly forsaken if he did not change his demeanor.

The king was persuaded to appear at the gate to give his thanks to the people, and the people decided to restore him to the throne. The priests were asked to seek the approval of the elders of Judah, since all Israel was asking for his return. Perhaps in hope of reconciling the factions, Amasa, the rebel general, was appointed in Joab's stead, apparently because Joab had killed the king's son, and the men of Judah consented.

2 Samuel 19:16–40

One of the first to see danger in this turn of events was Shimei, the man of Saul's family who had cursed David. He sought to be the first of "all of the house of Joseph" to welcome the king back ("Joseph" and "Ephraim" were names often used for the northern tribes collectively). He sought forgiveness and it was granted, notwithstanding Abishai's suggestion that he be executed. It may have been out of political expediency rather than the principles of magnanimity that David pardoned him for the time being.

Next to meet David was Mephibosheth, whose physical appearance seems to symbolize contrition and repentance. The latter explained how his servant Ziba had betrayed him and slandered him to King David.

Whether Mephibosheth or his servant Ziba was blameworthy is left unspecified. David allowed both of them to continue as before. The aged and affluent Barzillai was duly thanked for his sustenance while David was in refuge, and arrangements were made later through his servant for rewarding his house (see the sequel in 1 Kings 2:7).

2 Samuel 19:41–20:3

When Judah consented to bring the king back, their leaders went out to get him without notifying the northern Israelites. The northern Israelites were angry at being ignored in the official action so they turned to another rebel, Sheba, a Benjamite, who led a movement for secession, which was a harbinger of things to come.

According to the law, a father's wife or concubine was not to be taken by a son (Deuteronomy 22:30; 2 Samuel 15:16; 16:20–22); therefore, the women whom Absalom had abused lived "in widowhood" the rest of their lives.

2 Samuel 20:4–26

When Amasa was slow in taking action against Sheba and the northern tribes, Joab's brother Abishai was sent. When Amasa appeared in Joab's garment, perhaps showing his status, Joab took occasion to assassinate him and resume command of David's forces. The people were momentarily stunned but soon followed Joab again. Again a "wise woman" played a saving role: by her intercession, the city where Sheba had fled delivered his head to Joab, and a siege was averted.

2 Samuel 21:1–14

Constituting something of an appendix to the rest of the book, 2 Samuel 21–25 recounts additional episodes associated with David's reign but not necessarily in chronological order. One of these episodes was a three-year famine, brought on by Saul's slaughter of Gibeonites. To make amends and assuage the Lord's anger, according to the text as we have it, David acceded to the wishes of the Gibeonites by handing over to them seven male, direct-line descendants of Saul, who were put to death by the Gibeonites.

If this terrible episode is at all accurate, it must have occurred in the days of David's spiritual deterioration. The law would not have permitted sons to be put to death for the guilt of a father or a forefather (Deuteronomy 24:16; Numbers 35:33). It cannot have been a revelation from the Lord that either required or approved this deed done "to avenge the Gibeonites," some of whom Saul had slain in spite of the former promise of Joshua that they might live in Israel.

It is a pathetic picture to envision the innocent mother of innocent sons guarding their bodies from the birds and beasts, and it is repulsive to read, as well as hard to believe, that after all this was done "God was entreated for the land." This is either apostate theology, comparable to that of the Canaanite-Baal religions, or the present text has been corrupted.

The name *Michal* must be a mistake for *Merab*, for it was Merab who married Adriel (v. 8; 1 Samuel 18:19). If it is indeed Michal, David's wife and Saul's daughter, who is meant, this is a very bitter ending to their relationship as man and wife.

2 Samuel 21:15–22:51 (1 Chronicles 20:4–8; Psalm 18:1–50)

Other accounts of heroes and battles are also part of a corrupt text appended to the history at this point but apparently not in their chronological place.

Chapter 22 presents one of David's earlier psalms, praising

and thanking the Lord for his preservation from all enemies and exulting in the might of the Lord and in his control of all things of earth, sky, seas, and winds. Another copy of it occurs in Psalm 18, with some alterations.

2 Samuel 23:1–39 (1 Chronicles 11:10–47)

Yet another part of the appended materials is the poem in verses 1–7, presented as "the last words of David." Verse 2 states David's claim to inspiration. In David's better days, he wrote many prophetic things in psalms. The Gospels, particularly Matthew, witness of this. As to the role of the "Spirit of the Lord," or the Holy Ghost, in inspiring the writers of ancient scripture, note what Peter said in 2 Peter 1:21.

More anecdotes of the deeds of David's mighty men (Hebrew, *gibborim,* meaning "heroes," "great ones") are appended. Three of these "great heroes" are mentioned in verses 13–17. They fulfilled the king's wish for a drink of water from the well at the gate of his old home in Bethlehem by going through enemy lines to bring it. He offered it to the Lord as a libation poured upon the ground, for the water obtained at such a price was too precious to drink.

2 Samuel 24:1–25 (1 Chronicles 21:1–22:1)

This chapter tells of some of David's other actions in his degenerate days. Again, the text seems corrupted in certain places. The Lord is represented as having been angry with Israel and, therefore, having concocted a plot to get David to do something disapproved of so that He would have an excuse to administer punishment. The other account of this episode, in 1 Chronicles 21, changes the statement to read that *Satan* moved David to take the offensive census. David acknowledged his sin (his "heart smote him"; v. 10), and he asked forgiveness. The plague is said to have ended when the Lord "repented" (footnote 16*a*) and felt it was enough without smiting Jerusalem. Though perhaps written according to the understanding of the people, the text does imply important lessons. First, the Lord does feel sorrow when his people, his children, go astray; he desires to give us the minimum amount of punishment allowable under the law if we return and seek him. Second, implied in this story about the pestilence in the land is the connection between the righteousness of the people and the productivity, health, and fertility of the lands of inheritance the Lord gives to his people. The Hebrew verb used in the phrase "the Lord was *intreated* for the land" means "to pray" or "to supplicate." The sentence could otherwise have been rendered "they made supplication to the Lord for the land's sake."

Gad, the prophet and seer of David's last years, commanded David to build an altar on the threshing floor purchased from Araunah the Jebusite. A threshing floor is a large open area where a flat bedrock base allows for grain to be threshed and winnowed without getting dirt in it. This area, the bedrock top of Mount Moriah, later became part of Solomon's Temple (see 2 Chronicles 3:1). In fact, the spot was holy, and it became the place where the great altar of the Temple would be erected. That Araunah owned this area tells us that Jebusites were still left in the city of Jerusalem and that righteous alien residents of the promised land were accepted of God (compare Exodus 22:21; 23:9).

Significantly, the altar on the rock mass used previously by Araunah the Jebusite as a threshing floor set the precedent for the use of that holy spot for centuries of sacrifices foreshadowing the great and eternal Sacrifice. Verse 24 contains an important lesson: there must be no sacrifice to the Lord without its appropriate *cost*.

SOURCES

Abbott-Smith, G. *A Manual Greek Lexicon of the New Testament*. Edinburgh: T&T Clark, 1954.

Anderson, Lavina Fielding. "Church Publishes First LDS Edition of the Bible." *Ensign*, Oct. 1979, 8–18.

Auerbach, Erich. *Mimesis: The Representation of Reality in Western Literature*. Translated by Willard R. Trask. Princeton: Princeton University Press, 1974.

Baker, Carlos. "The Place of the Bible in American Fiction." *Theology Today* 17 (Apr. 1960): 53–76.

Barker, Margaret. *The Gate of Heaven: The History and Symbolism of the Temple in Jerusalem*. London: SPCK, 1991.

———. *The Great High Priest: The Temple Roots of Christian Liturgy*. London: T&T Clark, 2003.

———. *Temple Themes in Christian Worship*. London: T&T Clark, 2007.

Benson, Ezra Taft, Gordon B. Hinckley, and Thomas S. Monson. "First Presidency Statement on the King James Version of the Bible." *Ensign*, Aug. 1992, 80.

Brenton, Lancelot C. L. *The Septuagint with Apocrypha: Greek and English*. Peabody, Mass.: Hendrickson, 1995.

Brinkerhoff, Val. *The Day Star: Reading Sacred Architecture*. 3d ed. Sandy, Utah: Digital Legend Press, 2012.

Brown, Francis, S. R. Driver, and Charles A. Briggs. *Hebrew and English Lexicon of the Old Testament*. Oxford: Clarendon Press, 1975.

Budge, Wallis. *The Gods of the Egyptians*. Vol. 2. London: Kegan Paul, 2004.

Bullinger, E. W. *Number in Scripture: Its Supernatural Design and Spiritual Significance*. Grand Rapids, Mich.: Kregel, 1967.

Buttrick, George A. *Interpreter's Dictionary of the Bible.* Vol. 4. Nashville, Tenn.: Abingdon Press, 1962.

Cerny, Jaroslav. *Ancient Egyptian Religion.* Westport, Conn.: Greenwood Press, 1952.

Cowley, Matthias F. *Wilford Woodruff, Fourth President of The Church of Jesus Christ of Latter-day Saints: History of His Life and Labors.* Salt Lake City: Bookcraft, 1965.

Delitzsch, F. *Biblical Commentary on the Psalms.* Vol. 1. Translated by Francis Bolton. Grand Rapids, Mich.: Eerdmans, 1949.

Encyclopedia of Mormonism. Edited by Daniel H. Ludlow et al. 4 vols. New York: Macmillan, 1992.

Faust, James E. "Obedience: The Path to Freedom." *Ensign*, May 1999, 45–47.

First Presidency [Gordon B. Hinckley, Thomas S. Monson, and James E. Faust]. "The Family: A Proclamation to the World." *Ensign,* Nov. 1995, 102.

Galbraith, David B., D. Kelly Ogden, and Andrew C. Skinner. *Jerusalem, the Eternal City.* Salt Lake City: Deseret Book, 1996.

Geography: Selections from Encyclopedia Judaica. Israel Pocket Library. Jerusalem: Keter, 1973.

Gordon, Cyrus H. "Where Is Abraham's Ur?" *Biblical Archaeology Review*, June 1977, 20–21, 52.

Hafen, Bruce C., and Marie K. Hafen. "Crossing Thresholds and Becoming Equal Partners." *Ensign,* Aug. 2007, 24–29.

Harrison, R. K. *Introduction to the Old Testament.* Grand Rapids, Mich.: Eerdmans, 1969.

Herford, R. Travers. *Pirke Aboth—The Ethics of the Talmud: Sayings of the Fathers.* New York: Schocken Books, 1962.

Hertz, J. H. *The Pentateuch and Haftorahs.* 2d ed. London: Soncino Press, 1967.

Hoskisson, Paul Y. "Research and Perspectives: Where Was the Ur of Abraham?" *Ensign*, July 1991, 62–63.

Hymns of The Church of Jesus Christ of Latter-day Saints. Salt Lake City: The Church of Jesus Christ of Latter-day Saints, 1985.

Isbouts, Jean-Pierre. *The Biblical World: An Illustrated Atlas.* Washington, D.C.: National Geographic, 2007.

Jackson, Kent P. "All Things Point to Christ." In *1 Kings to Malachi.* Studies in Scripture, vol. 4, 1–3. Salt Lake City: Deseret Book, 1993.

Josephus, Flavius. *Antiquities of the Jews*. In *Josephus: Complete Works*. Translated by William Whiston. Grand Rapids, Mich.: Kregel, 1960.

———. *Wars of the Jews*. In *Josephus: Complete Works*. Translated by William Whiston. Grand Rapids, Mich.: Kregel, 1960.

Journal of Discourses. 26 vols. London: Latter-day Saints' Book Depot, 1854–86.

Keil, C. F., and F. Delitzsch. *Biblical Commentary on the Old Testament*. Grand Rapids, Mich.: Eerdmans, 1949.

Kimball, Spencer W. "The Blessings and Responsibilities of Womanhood." *Ensign*, Mar. 1976, 70–73.

———. Conference Report, Oct. 1943, 15–17.

———. "The Davids and the Goliaths." *Ensign*, Nov. 1974, 79–83.

———. "The Example of Abraham." *Ensign*, June 1975, 3–7.

———. *Faith Precedes the Miracle*. Salt Lake City: Deseret Book, 1972.

———. "The False Gods We Worship." *Ensign*, June 1976, 3–6.

———. "Give Me This Mountain." *Ensign*, Nov. 1979, 78–79.

———. "God Will Not Be Mocked." *Ensign*, Nov. 1974, 4–9.

———. *Humility*. Brigham Young University Speeches of the Year, Jan. 16, 1963.

———. *Integrity*. Brigham Young University Speeches of the Year, Feb. 25, 1964.

———. *The Miracle of Forgiveness*. Salt Lake City: Deseret Book, 1969.

Kraus, Hans-Joachim. *Psalms 1–59: A Commentary*. Translated by Hilton C. Oswald. Minneapolis, Minn.: Augsburg Publishing House, 1988.

Lachs, Samuel Tobias. *A Rabbinic Commentary on the New Testament: The Gospels of Matthew, Mark, and Luke*. Hoboken, N.J.: KTAV, 1987.

Lectures on Faith. Salt Lake City: Deseret Book, 1985.

Lee, Harold B. "Understanding Who We Are Brings Self-Respect." *Ensign*, Jan. 1974, 2–6.

Ludlow, Daniel H. *A Companion to Your Study of the Book of Mormon*. Salt Lake City: Deseret Book, 1976.

Marshall, George C. Quoted in Jack Uldrich, *Soldier, Statesman,*

Peacemaker—Leadership Lessons from George C. Marshall. New York: Amacom, 2005.

Maxwell, Neal A. "Meekness—A Dimension of True Discipleship." *Ensign,* Mar. 1983, 70–74.

———. *Notwithstanding My Weakness.* Salt Lake City: Deseret Book, 1981.

———. "Put Your Shoulder to the Wheel." *Ensign,* May 1998, 37–39.

McConkie, Bruce R. *Doctrinal New Testament Commentary.* 3 vols. Salt Lake City: Bookcraft, 1965–73.

———. "Joseph Smith—The Mighty Prophet of the Restoration." *Ensign,* May 1976, 94–97.

———. *The Millennial Messiah: The Second Coming of the Son of Man.* Salt Lake City: Deseret Book, 1982.

———. *Mormon Doctrine.* 2d ed. Salt Lake City: Bookcraft, 1966.

———. *The Promised Messiah.* Salt Lake City: Deseret Book, 1978.

———. "The Promises Made to the Fathers." In *Genesis to 2 Samuel.* Studies in Scripture, edited by Kent P. Jackson and Robert L. Millet, vol. 3, 47–62. Salt Lake City: Deseret Book, 2003.

———. *A New Witness for the Articles of Faith.* Salt Lake City: Deseret Book, 1985.

———. "The Story of a Prophet's Madness." *New Era,* Apr. 1972, 4–7.

McKay, David O. *Gospel Ideals.* Salt Lake City: Improvement Era, 1953.

———. Quoted in James E. Faust, "Obedience: The Path to Freedom." *Ensign,* May 1999, 46.

McKay, Llewelyn R., comp. *Home Memories of President David O. McKay.* Salt Lake City: Deseret Book, 1956.

Millard, Alan R. "Where Was Abraham's Ur—The Case for the Babylonian City." *Biblical Archaeology Review* (May/June 2001): 52–53, 57.

Monson, Thomas S. "Come, Learn of Me." *Ensign,* Dec. 1985, 48–46.

———. "Meeting Your Goliath." *Ensign,* Jan. 1987, 2–5.

———. "Stand in Holy Places." *Ensign,* Nov. 2011, 82–86.

———. "True to the Faith." *Ensign,* May 2006, 18–21.

Mowinckel, Sigmund. *The Psalms in Israel's Worship.* 2 vols. Translated by D. R. Ap-Thomas. Nashville, Tenn.: Abingdon, 1979.

Murphy-O'Connor, Jerome. *The Holy Land: An Oxford Archaeological Guide.* 5th ed. Oxford: Oxford University Press, 2008.

Nibley, Hugh. *Lehi in the Desert and The World of the Jaredites.* Salt Lake City: Bookcraft, 1952.

NIV Archaeological Study Bible. Grand Rapids, Mich.: Zondervan, 2005.

Nyman, Monte S., and Charles D. Tate Jr. *Second Nephi: The Doctrinal Structure.* The Book of Mormon series. Provo, Utah: Brigham Young University, Religious Studies Center, 1989.

Oaks, Dallin H. "The Great Plan of Happiness." *Ensign,* Nov. 1993, 72–75.

———. *David and Bathsheba: To Look Upon* [video]. Available at lds.org.

Ogden, D. Kelly, and Andrew C. Skinner. *Acts through Revelation.* Verse by Verse series. Salt Lake City: Deseret Book, 1998.

———. *The Book of Mormon.* 2 vols. Verse by Verse series. Salt Lake City: Deseret Book, 2011.

———. *The Four Gospels.* Verse by Verse series. Salt Lake City: Deseret Book, 2006.

Ogden, D. Kelly, and Jeffrey R. Chadwick. *The Holy Land: A Geographical, Historical, and Archaeological Guide to the Land of the Bible.* Jerusalem: Jerusalem Center for Near Eastern Studies, 1990.

Old Testament Student Manual, Genesis–2 Samuel. Prepared by the Church Educational System. Salt Lake City: The Church of Jesus Christ of Latter-day Saints, 1980.

Origen de Principiis. Translated by Frederick Crombie. Vol. 4 of *Ante-Nicene Fathers.* Grand Rapids, Mich.: Eerdmans, 1885.

Packer, Boyd K. "Atonement, Agency, Accountability." *Ensign,* May 1988, 69–72.

———. "On Zion's Hill." *Ensign,* Nov. 2005, 70–73.

———. "The Power of the Priesthood." *Ensign,* May 2010, 6–10.

———. "Scriptures." *Ensign,* Nov. 1982, 51–53.

Parry, Donald W. "'Who Shall Ascend into the Mountain of the Lord?': Three Biblical Temple Entrance Hymns." In *Revelation, Reason, and Faith: Essays in Honor of Truman G. Madsen.* Edited by Donald W. Parry, Daniel C. Peterson, and Stephen D. Ricks. Provo, UT: FARMS, 2002.

Perry, L. Tom. "Obedience to Law Is Liberty." *Ensign,* May 2013, 86–88.

Peacock, George M. *Unlocking the Numbers: An LDS Perspective on Scriptural Use of Numbers.* Springville, Utah: CFI, 2005.

Pearson, Glenn L. "The Book of Mormon As a Witness of the Old Testament." *Ensign,* June 1986, 14–18.

Penrose, Charles W. "The Witch of Endor." *Improvement Era,* May 1898, 495–500.

Petersen, Mark E. *Moses—Man of Miracles.* Salt Lake City: Deseret Book, 1977.

———. *Noah and the Flood.* Salt Lake City: Deseret Book, 1982.

Pickthall, Marmaduke. *The Meaning of the Glorious Koran.* New York: Dorset Press.

Polano, H. *The Talmud—Selections.* New York: Frederick Warne & Co., 1973.

Pope, Alexander. *An Essay on Man.* Quoted in Thomas S. Monson, "True to the Faith," *Ensign,* May 2006, 18.

Romney, Marion G. "The Message of the Old Testament." In *A Symposium on the Old Testament,* 1–7. Prepared by the Church Educational System. Salt Lake City: The Church of Jesus Christ of Latter-day Saints, 1979.

———. "Records of Great Worth." *Ensign,* Sept. 1980, 2–7.

———. "Temples—The Gates to Heaven." *Ensign,* Mar. 1971, 12–16.

Scott, Richard G. "The Power of Scripture." *Ensign,* Nov. 2011, 6–8.

Selman, M. J. "Ur." In *Major Cities of the Biblical World.* Edited by R. K. Harrison. Nashville, Tenn.: T. Nelson Publishers, 1985.

Skinner, Andrew C. *Gethsemane.* Salt Lake City: Deseret Book, 2002.

———. "The Influence of the Hebrew Scriptures on the Founders and Founding of the American Republic." In *Lectures on Religion and the Founding of the American Republic,* edited by John W. Welch, 39–48. Provo, Utah: BYU Press, 2003.

———. "Serpent Symbols and Salvation in the Ancient Near East and the Book of Mormon." *Journal of Book of Mormon Studies* 10, no. 2 (2001): 42–55.

Smith, Hyrum M., and Janne M. Sjodahl. *Doctrine and Covenants Commentary.* Salt Lake City: Deseret Book, 1978.

Smith, Joseph. *History of The Church of Jesus Christ of Latter-day Saints*. Edited by B. H. Roberts. 2d ed., rev. 7 vols. Salt Lake City: The Church of Jesus Christ of Latter-day Saints, 1932–51.

———. *Joseph Smith* [manual]. Teachings of Presidents of the Church series. Salt Lake City: The Church of Jesus Christ of Latter-day Saints, 2007.

———. *Teachings of the Prophet Joseph Smith*. Selected by Joseph Fielding Smith. Salt Lake City: Deseret Book, 1977.

———. *The Words of Joseph Smith*. Compiled and edited by Andrew F. Ehat and Lyndon W. Cook. Provo, Utah: Grandin, 1991.

Smith, Joseph F. *Gospel Doctrine*. Salt Lake City: Deseret Book, 1968.

———, John R. Winder, and Anthon H. Lund. "The Origin of Man." *Improvement Era*, Nov. 1909, 75–81.

———, John R. Winder, and Anthon H. Lund. In *Messages of the First Presidency of The Church of Jesus Christ of Latter-day Saints*. Edited by James R. Clark. 6 vols. Salt Lake City: Bookcraft, 1965–75.

Smith, Joseph Fielding. *Answers to Gospel Questions*. 5 vols. Salt Lake City: Deseret Book, 1957–66.

———. Conference Report, Oct. 1943, 15–17.

———. Conference Report, Oct. 1967, 121–22.

———. *Doctrines of Salvation*. Compiled by Bruce R. McConkie. 3 vols. Salt Lake City: Bookcraft, 1954–56.

———. "Fall—Atonement—Resurrection—Sacrament." In *Charge to Religious Educators*. 2d ed. Prepared by the Church Educational System. Salt Lake City: The Church of Jesus Christ of Latter-day Saints, 2004.

———. *The Restoration of All Things*. Salt Lake City: Deseret Book, 1964.

———. *Seek Ye Earnestly*. Salt Lake City: Deseret Book, 1970.

The Soncino Chumash. Edited by A. Cohen. Hindhead, Surrey: Soncino Press, 1947.

Speiser, E. A. *Genesis*. Anchor Bible series, vol. 1. New York: Doubleday, 1964.

Sperry, Sidney B. "Abraham's Three Visitors." *Improvement Era*, Aug. 1931, 583, 585.

Talmage, James E. *A Study of the Articles of Faith*. Salt Lake City: The Church of Jesus Christ of Latter-day Saints, 1924.

———. *Jesus the Christ*. Salt Lake City: The Church of Jesus Christ of Latter-day Saints, 1915.

Tuttle, A. Theodore. "Altar, Tent, Well." *Ensign*, Jan. 1973, 66–67.

Twain, Mark. *The Innocents Abroad.* 1869. Reprint, New York: Penguin Books, 1966.

Vermes, Geza. *The Complete Dead Sea Scrolls in English.* Revised ed. London: Penguin Books, 2004.

Vorhaus, Renee. "I Have a Question: Since God is all-powerful, couldn't he have freed the Israelites from Egyptian bondage without sending all those plagues?" *Ensign*, Sept. 1980, 64–65.

Webster, Noah. *An American Dictionary of the English Language.* 1828. Reprint, San Francisco: Foundation for American Christian Education, 1980.

Welch, John W. *The Sermon on the Mount in the Light of the Temple.* Farnham, Surrey: Ashgate, 2009.

Widtsoe, John A. *Evidences and Reconciliations.* Collector's Edition. Salt Lake City: Bookcraft, 1987.

Wilbur, William H. *The Making of George Washington.* Caldwell, Idaho: Caxton Printers, 1973.

Woodruff, Wilford, George Q. Cannon, and Joseph F. Smith. *Millennial Star* 52, no. 3 (Jan. 20, 1890): 33–35.

Young, Brigham. *Discourses of Brigham Young.* Compiled by John A. Widtsoe. Salt Lake City: Deseret Book, 1966.

INDEX

Aaron: calling of, 186, 187, 189;
  supports Moses, 204; Aaronic
  Priesthood leadership and, 229,
  281; golden calf and, 233–34;
  prepared for priesthood service,
  248–49; sons of, 249, 269;
  entry of, into Holy of Holies,
  252; speaks against Moses, 276;
  death of, 287
Aaronic Priesthood, 223, 229,
  269, 281
Abel, 57–58, 61
Abiathar, 408, 452
Abigail, 409
Abimelech: Abraham and, 107–9;
  Isaac and, 127
Abimelech (son of Gideon), 365,
  365–66
Abishai, 453, 455
Abner, 438, 439
Abominations, 254–55
Abraham: calling and journey of,
  87–91; honor and significance
  of, 88–89; Sarah's relationship
  with, 91–92; settles in promised
  land, 92–93; saves Lot, 93–94;
  posterity of, 96–97; Hagar
  and, 97–98; son promised to,
  102–3; God's trust in, 103–4;
  Abimelech and, 107–9; and
  birth of Isaac, 108; commanded
  to sacrifice Isaac, 109–10; and
  significance of Moriah, 111–
  12; and journey to Moriah,
  112–13; and binding of Isaac,
  113–14; as type of God,
115–16; trials and, 116–17;
  and burial of Sarah, 117–18;
  seeks wife for Isaac, 118–21;
  family of, through Keturah,
  121–22; death of, 122; similarities between Isaac and, 123–24;
  faithfulness of, 126–27; obedience of, 285–86; erects altar
  between Bethel and Ai, 339. *See
  also* Abrahamic covenant
Abraham (book), 170
Abrahamic covenant: established
  with Adam, Enoch, and Noah,
  75–76; terms of, 100–101;
  circumcision as sign of, 101–2;
  perpetuation of, through Isaac,
  122
Abram. *See* Abraham
Absalom, 377, 424, 450–54
Achan, 337–38
Achish, 407, 410
Acrostics, psalms as, 422–23
Adam: role of, in Creation, 27;
  creation of, 32–35; in premortal existence, 35–36; Eve as
  help meet for, 38–40; clothing
  of, 52–53; children of, 56–57,
  61–62; Seth in image of, 64;
  blood of, 254; obedience of,
  284–85. *See also* Fall of Adam
Adamic language, 28, 38
Adoni-bezek, 351
Adonizedek, 340
Adultery: commandment against,
  214, 216; as abomination,

ordinance, 197–98; and significance of number eight, 264
Cities of refuge, 296–97, 345–46
City gate, 376–77
Civil disputes, punishments in, 318
Climactic parallelism, 417–18
Clothing: of Adam and Eve, 52–53; as sign of covenant, 229, 230; for sacred times of worship, 252; fringes on, 279. *See also* Garment(s)
Coat of many colors, 144–45, 450
Colonial America, 7, 258–59
Commandment(s): to study Old Testament, 7–8; work as, 51–52; against eating blood, 78, 79, 248, 253–54; against lust, 214, 254; as unchanging, 217; regarding purity, 270–71; obedience to, 284–86, 304, 308. *See also* Ten Commandments
Concubine, of Levite, 371
Continents, division of, 84–85
Corn, 151
Covenant(s): with house of Israel, 19; renewal of, 80; salvation through, 133; as Exodus subtheme, 174. *See also* Abrahamic covenant
Coveting, commandment against, 215
Cows, 195
Creation: method of, 21–22; Holy Ghost and, 22–23; stages of, 24–26; of humankind, 26–29, 32–36; unknown aspects of, 29–30; rest following, 30–31
Crucifixion: Enoch's vision of, 66; indirect prophecy regarding, 316
Cult practices, 312–13
Culture, influence of Old Testament on, 6–7
Cush, 82

Dagon, 356, 389
Dan, tribe of: inheritance of, 162–63, 345; blessings for, 324;

military campaigns of, 352; settlement of, 370
Darkened valleys, 428
Darkness, as plague, 196
David: Moriah and, 110, 458; as king, 399–400, 437–38, 440, 444–45; defeats Goliath, 400–404; Jonathan's friendship with, 404, 406; as Saul's enemy, 404–9; marriage of, 409; spares Saul's life, 409; pursues Amalekite raiding party, 411–12; psalms of, 423–25, 456–57; repentance of, 431; lament of, over Saul, 436–37; increasing power of, 438–39; lament of, over Abner, 439; conquers Jerusalem, 440–41; children of, 442; unity under, 442–43; brings Ark to Jerusalem, 443–44; Bathsheba and, 445–49; Absalom and, 451–54; mourning of, 454–55; punishment of, 457–58
Day: length of, 24, 31; extended during attack on Canaan, 340
Day of Atonement, 252–53, 258
Death: as consequence of Fall, 47–48, 55–56; redemption from spiritual, 282
Deborah, 202, 358–59, 360
Debts, forgiving, 311
Defiance, 279. *See also* Rebellion
Delilah, 369
Delitzsch, Franz, 429
Desert, 145
Deuteronomy, 298–300
Discernment, of messengers, 362
Divination, 410–11
Divine potential, 425
Divorce, laws regarding, 318
Dove, 186
Dreams: of Joseph, 144; Joseph interprets, 150, 151–52
Drinks: intoxicating, 250; fermented, 311. *See also* Wine

Earth: orbital relationship of, to other astronomical bodies,

195; pillar of, 200, 274, 323; symbolism of, 246; strange, 250–51

Firstborn: death of, 196; consecration of, 200

"First flesh upon the earth," 33–34

First Presidency: on King James Version, 10; on children of God, 28; on Adam as first flesh, 34; on capital punishment, 78–79

First words and phrases, books named after, 19

Flaming sword, guarding Eden and tree of life, 53–54

Flies, 194

Flood(s): conditions preceding, 68–74; description of, 75–77; events following, 78–79; promise regarding, 79–80, 86; impact of, on earth, 84–85

Food: sources of, 29; Joseph stores, 152; laws regarding, 221, 250–51, 310

Former Prophets, 328

Forty, 265–66

Friendship: as fundamental principle of Mormonism, 404; of David and Jonathan, 406

Fringes, 279

Frog, 194

Frontlets, 200, 306, *307*

Gabriel, 68, 81–82. *See also* Noah

Gad (prophet), 458

Gad, tribe of, 295, 324

Garden of Eden: location of, 35–36; trees in, 37; Adam and Eve expelled from, 53

Garment(s): of diverse colors, 144–45, 450; as sign of covenant, 229, 230; making of, 241; for sacred times of worship, 252; fringes on, 279. *See also* Clothing

Gate, city, 376–77

Gathering of Israel: promise of, 320; tribe of Joseph's role in, 323

Gazetteer, 13

Generations, use of term in Genesis, 63–64, 73

Geneseos, 19

Genesis (book), 19–20

Gerizim, 319, 338

Gershom, 205

Gershon, descendants of, 269

Gesenius, 376

"Giants," 70

Gibeah, 370, 371

Gibeon: Israelite attack on, 339; pool of, 438; Saul's attack on, 456

Gideon, 361–65

Gift-giving, 154–55

Gilgal, 334–35, 395, 397

Gleaning, law of, 379

Gnats, stinging, 194

Goat hair, 226

God: body of, 27; language of, 28; rests following Creation, 30–31; name of, 40–41; mercy of, 71, 72, 104; repentance of, 72–73, 235, 292, 398; trust of, for good men, 103–4; glory of, 106–7; Abraham as type of, 115–16; tempting, 204; presence of, 208, 237, 420–21, 426; commandment to worship, 209–10, 217, 253; honoring name of, 211–12; as unchanging, 217; Israelites retreat from, 217–18; Israelite elders see, 222–23; fearing, 255; love for, 305; dependence on, 309, 363; infidelity to, 310; relationship between covenant people and, 353–54, 400–401; potential to become like, 425; providence of, 427–29; trust in, 428

"God of gods," 308

Go'el, 377, 380

Golden calf, 233–34

"Golden rule," 220, 255–56

Goliath, 400–404; sword of, 407

Gomorrah, 103–6

Gopher, 75
Gospel: described in Old Testament, 3; commandment to declare, 7–8; early knowledge of, 61–63
Grain, 246
Grant, Jedediah M., 117
Grasshoppers, 195
Great Hallel, 432
"Great whales," 26
Greed, 275–76, 289–91
"Green pastures," 427–28
Guilt offering, 246, 248

Hagar, 97–98, 108, 383–84
Hail, 195
Ham, 80–81, 82–84
Hamitic peoples, 82–84
Hannah, 366, 383–85
Haran, 87
Hardened heart, 187–88
"Hate," 135–36
Hathor, 195
Hatred, 255
Hazor, 341, 358–59
Heart, hardened, 187–88
Heaven, as sky, 25
Heavenly Mother, 356–57
Hebrew, Old Testament records written in, 1
"Hebrew, the," 94
Hebrew Bible, divisions of, 15
Hebrew poetry, 202, 415–18, 423
Hebrews, 84
Hebrew servants, release of, 312
Heifer, red, law of, 281–82
Heqet, 194
Herem, 219, 287, 336–38
Hinckley, Gordon B., 10
Hinnom Valley, 344
Hittites, 118, 129
Hobab, 274
Holy Ghost: role of, in Creation, 22–23; in Old Testament times, 233; and gift of prophecy, 360; and inspiration of writers of ancient scripture, 457
Holy of Holies, 227, 241, 252, 253

Home, importance of, 212
Homosexuality, 371
Honey, from rock, 322
Horeb, 183, 300, 303. *See also* Sinai
Horites, 143
Hormah, 287
Horns: on altars, 227, 247; Moses and, 239; symbolism of, 324, 385
Humankind: creation of, 26–28, 32–36, 38–40; responsibilities and powers given to, 28–29; premortal organization of, 56–57
Human sacrifice, 310
Humility, 276, 306–7
Hur, 204
Hushai, 452, 453
Hyksos, 152, 155, 158, 175–76

Ichabod, 389
Idolatry: commandment against, 210–11, 217, 253; of Israelites, 233–35, 293, 303, 353–57, 366; punishment for, 256; in Jericho, 335–36; Israel warned against, 347–48; Gideon works against, 362
Ignorance, 279
Immorality: acceptance of, 105; consequences of, 254–55. *See also* Adultery
Incense, 232
Integrity, 295
Intermarriage, 68–70, 357
Intoxicating drinks, 250
Iron implements, of Philistines, 352, 396
Isaac: significance of, 89; birth of, 108; sacrifice of, 109–10; Moriah and, 111–13; binding of, 113–14; as type and foreshadowing of Jesus Christ, 114–16; wife for, 118–21; similarities between Abraham and, 123–24; challenges of, 125; travels to Gerar, 126–27; character of, 127–29; and birthright

Joshua: name of, 205; as scout, 277; as successor to Moses, 294, 325; encouragement for, 320; life of, 328; as author of book of Joshua, 328–29; as leader, 329–30; as type of Moses and Jesus Christ, 331, 332–34; spares Gibeonites, 339; and conquest of Canaan, 342; inheritance of, 345; death of, 347–49, 350
Jotham, allegory of, 365–66
Jubilee year, 258–59
Judah (son of Jacob): and sale of Joseph, 145, 146; Tamar and, 147–48; takes leadership of family, 154; change in, 155–56; blessing given to, 162
Judah, tribe of: blessings for, 323; inheritance of, 344; tribe of Simeon and, 345; military campaigns of, 351–52; division between northern and southern, 393
Judas, 146, 166–67
Judges: in Israel, 313; in civil disputes, 318
Judges (book), 350–51
Juttah, 344

Kadesh-barnea, 276–77
Kenites, 351
Keturah, 121–22
Khu-Sebek, 169
Kimball, Spencer W.: on creation of LDS edition of KJV, 11; on origins of humankind, 28; on creation of Eve, 39; on role of husbands, 51; on marrying outside of Church, 70; on Abraham, 104; calling of, 187; on transfiguration, 208; on profanity, 211; on humility of Moses, 283; on righteousness, 301; on Caleb, 343–44; on controlling thoughts, 446
King James Version: reasons for studying, 9–10; study helps

in LDS edition of, 10–13; sequence of books in, 16–17
King(s): instructions for, 313; Israelites want, 390–92
Kohath, descendants of, 269–70
Korah, 280
Kosher dietary restrictions, 221, 250–51, 310–11
Kraus, Hans-Joachim, 426

Laban, 130, 135, 137–39
Lamech (descendant of Cain), 61
Lamech (son of Methuselah), 67
Land: creation of, 25; link between righteousness and, 254–55, 259, 297, 458; rest for, 259
Language: influence of Old Testament on, 6; Adamic, 28, 38; used in book of remembrance, 63, 64; tower of Babel and, 85–86
Latin Vulgate Bible, 239
Laver, 232–33
Leah, 135–36, 138
Lee, Harold B., 56–57
Legend, David and Goliath story as, 402–3
Lehi, 5–6
Leprosy, 251–52
Levi, 141–42, 145, 161
Levirate law, 318–19, 373–74, 380
Levites: excluded from census, 267; as priests and replacements for firstborn males, 269; population of, 270; responsibilities of, 270; cleansing of, 273; cities of, 346
Leviticus, 243–44
Liahona, 333–34
Life spans, 81
Light: Creation and, 23; for Noah's ark, 75; radiating from heavenly beings, 239
Light of Christ, 23
Linen, 226
Locusts, 195
Lot: settles in promised land,

92–94; and destruction of
Sodom, 104, 105–6; daughters
of, 107
Ludlow, Daniel H., 170
Lund, Anthon H., 28, 34
Lust: commandment against, 214,
254; meaning of term, 311; of
David, 445; of Amnon, 450
Lying, 214–15

Machpelah, cave of, 117–18, 159,
165
Magnificat, 384
Mahlon, 373
Man. *See* Humankind
Manasseh: meaning of name, 153;
blessing of, 159–60; inheritance
of, 163
Manasseh, tribe of: inheritance of,
344; and driving out Canaanites,
352–53
Mandrakes, 136
Manna, 182, 203–4, 274
Maps, in LDS edition of KJV, 13
Mark of Cain, 60
Marriage: unity in, 39; of Adam
and Eve, 39–40; Joseph Smith
on, 136–37; of captives, 315;
betrothal and, 317; laws regarding, 318; levirate law and,
318–19, 373–74, 380; idolatry
and, 353–54; of Ruth, 375–77,
379. *See also* Intermarriage
Marshall, George C., 280–81
Mary, Hannah and, 384–85
Maxwell, Neal A., 52, 149, 276
McConkie, Bruce R.: on Old
Testament as testament of Jesus
Christ, 2–3; on plan of salvation in Old Testament, 3; on
Creation, 27; on consequences
of Fall, 47–48; on separation of
continents, 85; on sacrament,
94; on Jesus Christ and Moses,
177–78; on priesthood, 207;
on obedience of Abraham, 285;
on Balaam of Pethor, 289–91
McKay, David O., 103, 447

Meal offering, 245, 246
Meekness, 276
Melchizedek: Lot and, 93;
Abraham and, 94–95; paral-
lels between Jesus Christ and,
94–95; Temple and, 111
Memorial: to crossing Jordan River,
334; designated by Joshua, 348
Menorah, 224–25, *227,* 229, 258,
273
Mephibosheth, 439–40, 445, 452,
455
Merab, 456
Merari, descendants of, 269
Mercy: of God, 71, 72, 104; for
sin in ignorance, 279
Mercy seat, 224
Merneptah, Victory Stele of, 172,
173
Messengers, discernment of, 362
Messianic psalms, 418–20
Metalwork, of Philistines, 352, 396
Methuselah, 67, 68
Mezuza, 306
Micah, 370
Michael, 35–36. *See also* Adam
Michal, 443–44, 456
Michmash, 394
Midianites, 147, 295, 361
Midwives, 176–77
Millennium: all things to be re-
vealed during, 21; as Sabbath,
31; earth during, 85; Jesus
Christ to reign during, 263
"Millo," 441–42
Min, 195
Miracles: as reward of faith, 185;
shown to Pharaoh, 191–97; as
manifestations of higher laws,
201; of extended daylight, 340;
scholarly opinion on, 402
Miriam, 202, 276, 282
Missionary work: Abraham and,
90–91; Nazarite vow and, 271;
obedience in, 284
Mizraim, 83
Moabites, 289–92, 373, 407
Molech, 256

Christ, 67–68; conditions during time of, 68–74; during Flood, 75–77; following Flood, 78–79; sons of, 80–81, 82; life span of, 81–82; obedience of, 285

Nob, 406–8

North America, as land of inheritance, 163

Numbers (book), 261–62

Numbers, significance of, 262–66, 294–95, 312

Oaks, Dallin H., 46, 446

Oaths, 118, 295

Obedience: Joseph Smith on, 91; blessings of, 203, 241, 319–20, 327–28, 353; exact and strict, 283–86, 397–98; reason for, 304; to law of *herem*, 337–38

Oil, symbolism of, 246. *See also* Olive oil

Old Testament: language of, 1; reasons for studying, 1–10; arrangement of books in, 14, 16–17; reliability and historicity of, 17–18

Olive oil, 229, 249

Opposition, need for, 37–38, 49

Ordinances, instructions concerning, 231

Ordination, principles and patterns for, 294

Origen, 125

Oshea, 277

Osiris, 195, 196

Packer, Boyd K.: on LDS edition of KJV, 11; on Topical Guide, 12; on Jesus' submissiveness, 167; on Gideon, 363–64

Parallelism: synonymous, 51, 61; in Hebrew poetry, 202, 416–18

Parents: sins of, 60, 211, 318, 456; commandment to honor, 212; fearing, 255; responsibility of, to teach children, 386, 387

Passover: bread and wine in, 94; as

protection from tenth plague, 196–98; symbolism of, 198–99; celebration of, 220–21; overview of, 257–58; law and ordinance of, 273; importance of, 274; number seven in, 312; in promised land, 334–35; Great Hallel sung during, 432

Peace offering, 245, 246–47

"Peculiar treasure," Israel as, 206–7

Peleg, 84

Peninnah, 383–84

Penrose, Charles W., 411

Pentecost. *See* Feast of Weeks

Perfection: of Noah, 73; of Abraham, 98; concept of, in scriptures, 99; through suffering, 116; of early patriarchs, 130–31

Perry, L. Tom, 215–17

Pesakh. See Passover

Petersen, Mark E., 76

Pharaoh (Exodus): orders infanticide, 176–77; seeks to slay Moses, 180; freedom asked of, 189; plagues and, 191–97; pursues Israelites, 200–201

Pharaoh (Genesis): Joseph works for, 151–53; brings Joseph's family to Egypt, 157; Jacob's audience with, 158

Phelps, W. W., 138–39

Philistines: Judah's conquest of, 352; conflicts of, with Israelites, 388–89, 394–97, 401, 412; invasion of, 390; David's control over, 442–43

Phinehas, 293

Phoenicians, 441, 442

Phut, 83

Phylacteries, 200, 306, *307*

Pillar of cloud, pillar of fire, 200, 274, 323

Plagues: preceding Exodus, 191–97; suffered by Philistines, 389; under reign of David, 457–58

Plan of salvation: described in Old Testament, 3; Creation and,